An ArtevinoStudio Project

Original title: *Vini e Terre di Borgogna*

Written by Camillo Favaro and Giampaolo Gravina

Translated and edited by Burton Anderson
in collaboration with Joanie Bonfiglio

Editorial coordination and graphic project by Antonella Frate

Photographs by Maurizio Gjivovich

Administration: Elisabetta Bottala and Fabrizio Gallino

Maps and charts extracted from *Les Vins de Bourgogne* and *The Wines of Burgundy*
(Collection Pierre Poupon, www.collection-pierrepoupon.com)
with the authorization of the authors Sylvain Pitiot and Jean-Charles Servant.

General maps kindly provided by
Bureau Interprofessionnel des Vins de Bourgogne

www.artevinostudio.it / www.fil-rouge.it

CAMILLO FAVARO | GIAMPAOLO GRAVINA

Preface by BURTON ANDERSON

WINES AND VINEYARDS OF BURGUNDY

CHABLIS | CÔTE D'OR | CÔTE CHALONNAISE | MÂCONNAIS

Photographs by MAURIZIO GJIVOVICH

CONTENTS

PREFACE

by Burton Anderson

When Camillo Favaro and Giampaolo Gravina asked me to transcribe into English a book they'd written in Italian about the wines of Burgundy, I felt more than a little perplexed. Having spent the better part of a lifetime trying to get a handle on the wines and winemakers of Italy, I'd let the rest of the world's wines pass me by—though not without regrets. The greatest of those regrets was, without a doubt, not having come to know Burgundy.

Nonetheless, with due regrets, I told them it's too late for me, adding something on the order of: how could an aging apostle of *vino*, whose knowledge of the Côte d'Or and environs is tantamount to a dribble in a spit bucket, convey an Italian take on the wonderland of wine to the privileged cliques of English-speaking Burgundy buffs? Those might not have been my exact words, but I trust you get the gist.

Well, they wouldn't budge, countering with something on the order of: after Italy, think of this as an opportunity to learn about the great wines of France. Learn? Me? In other words, they seemed to expect me to maneuver my way through the labyrinth of *grand crus* and *premier crus*, of *châteaux* and *clos*, of *vignerons* and *négociants*, *climats* and *terroirs* and the Jurassic underworld of Bajocian and Bathonian and Kimmeridgian formations and explain it all to folks who could look it up in a jiffy on the net. Anyhow, who reads books anymore?

Well, they sent me a copy of *Vini e Terre di Borgogna* and I scanned through it and was impressed. The more I browsed, the more I realized that my Italian friends had put together a volume that deftly bridged the yawning gap between the encyclopedic approach and still another adaptation of "Burgundy for Dummies." It seemed loaded with vital information that only hardheaded writers who dig and persist and taste and query and contemplate could come up with. So, in a weak moment, I agreed to take on the task. And task it was surely going to be. But, I figured, if nothing else, maybe I could scrape together my earnings to get my hands on a few precious bottles from Vosne-Romanée or Chassagne-Montrachet to covet in reverent sips in the twilight years.

As it turned out, the task wasn't quite as arduous as I'd feared. In fact at times it was almost enjoyable in a vicarious sort of way as I silently stalked Giampaolo and Camillo through Chablis and the Côte de Nuits and Côte de Beaune and Côte Chalonnaise and Maconnais and off on forays to the fringe areas away from the vaunted *crus* to spend a little time with some down to earth *vignerons*. As it turned out, some of the less ballyhooed versions of "the world's most astonishing wines" could be considered almost affordable. As I translated away, I took a liking to the way Camillo and Giampaolo approached the hallowed halls of winedom, the utopian slopes they'd come to know intimately that had always been teasingly beyond my grasp and my means. They'd obviously read up on things, but their real secret was that they'd spent an inordinate amount of time hanging out around Beaune and environs. Their insider knowledge of the places is as astonishing as their love of the wines, and their admiration for the people who make them. What won me over is their no-frills approach to it all, profoundly knowledgeable but never pedantic, their candid assessments of the wines and the vintages, the lack of inhibition in questioning the worth of a legend and their heartfelt enthusiasm in exalting a little know gem from a heretofore unheralded winemaker. Their pitch to *vignerons* to wangle a visit to their cellars, as described in the Introduction, is priceless. You can read it there, but one line stood out: "We won't bother you, we'll speak softly without gesticulating—we aren't your typical Italians…"

Camillo and Giampaolo don't seem to be your typical wine writers either, in Italian or any other language. And I do know a thing or two about that. They tell it straight with evaluations that are cool and calculated, based on the technical knowledge of a full-fledged winemaker and the professorial assessments of a full-fledged professor—of philosophy no less. Their praise is as measured and meditated as their criticisms and, bless their souls, they don't taunt and baffle wine freaks with pontifical point ratings.

In short, this really is one of those books you ought to have with you if you're planning a trip to Burgundy. Or even if you're visiting vicariously like me.

INTRODUCTION

The world is strange. It's always been inclined that way, but on the afternoon of Friday, September 7, 2012, for us it was even more strange than usual. We were in Beaune, in the Athenaeum bookshop, obligatory stop on all of our visits to Burgundy, but this time not to buy a book on wine, but as objects. That is, we weren't there to merely wander around the shelves, following a time-tested ritual guaranteed to deplete credit cards by acquiring the latest edition of the most useless of treatises on the wines of Burgundy. No, this time we were *inside* that book. We had written it. And now we were obliged to present it. But who did we expect to show up? The heat was African, the harvest imminent... We looked up and found ourselves facing fifty people, almost all *vignerons*, unequivocally Burgundians.

The world is strange. In the previous ten months we had stalked them, those *vignerons*, trying every trick to weaken their resistance and finally get the coveted appointment for a visit to the cellars. Just an hour of your time, a brief chat with no microphones and a few quick tastings. What do you say? We won't bother you, we'll speak softly without gesticulating—we aren't your typical Italians… Certainly, but of course: what remains in the glass we'll pour back in the barrel, goes without saying… In fact, if need be, we could bring a glass with us from home. And now here they are, seated before us, the book in their hands, eager to listen. Maybe they just came to be polite, or they were pressured by the book seller—you know the type. Why deny it?

And yet, we had a different impression. As though we'd established a stronger reciprocal bond: we listen to their wines, they listen to our words. Consider it a métier of sorts, being condemned to listen, which seems almost inscribed in the DNA of wine, a prerogative of its cultural nature.

Wine is strange. Bastion of civilization and inspiration of human endeavor since the days of monks and abbeys, wine may be the medium that best fuses, in a single dimension, physical and corporeal elements with the most spiritual of man's vocations. Wine needs books, writings capable of describing both the sensory landscapes and the cultural horizons of our backgrounds; of words sewn like zippers between the material and the imaginary, of images like windows half-shuttered between dreams and essentialities. Is that not why we keep returning to Burgundy? Is it not really to explore the margins, to fathom the non-soluble residue of perceptions suspended between the insufferable hyperbole over the price of a bottle and the irrepressible desire to savor its magic?

Burgundy is strange. The vineyard comes first, as you hear around. It's an expression used frequently to indicate the compelling need to subordinate the taste of wine to the nature of the vineyard, to restrict expressiveness to the climatic quality of the vintage, to the geological identity of the place, to the artisanal talent of the winemaker. But elsewhere they just talk about it, here it's a reality. Such beliefs become law with hierarchies of values and systems of merit. The trouble is that the more one adheres to sets of rules, the more obvious it becomes that, rather than legitimizing doctrinal attitudes and constrictions, they stimulate a critical spirit, a state of interpretive restlessness. Burgundy is strange and complicated. The more it impels you to accept its regulations, the more it challenges you to dismantle them with all their variations and exceptions that disrupt and destabilize the rules, revealing how in many cases the wording of the official version already contains the germ of its revocation.

Burgundy is strange. It seems a quintessentially stable land, with its archipelago of vineyards maintained with immutable severity over the centuries. But, instead, it's a region in profound upheaval, animated by changes, contradictions, ferment more vibrantly alive than ever before. Generations of *vignerons* change, and those we know today seem less inclined to compromise, more sensitive to the ideals of a living land, of sustainable viticulture, of respectful enology. The approach has changed, enduring certainties are no longer unassailable, the rewards to be won are no longer taken for granted but must be proved in the field. In other words, the name of a great vineyard on the label is not enough to guarantee a great wine, just as a little-known *terroir*, in the hands of a winemaker endowed with authentic talent, can provide more than enough of a base for the creation of a wine to be placed on a pedestal. Tastes change. And the preference for flavors that are reassuringly composed—a tendency that, to tell the truth, has never found fertile ground here—has ceded to a more vital need for spontaneity, contrast, tension, in other words, for expressive transparency. The landscape changes, shifting toward the margins, toward the less noble *terroirs*. And it's gone so far as to enlarge the panorama, to reorganize the critical perspective, so as not to lose sight of the progress of those talents who work on the perimeters of the Grand Crus. That explains this new edition, which is more inclusive in its range of selections, aimed at relating the most significant movements on the peripheries, from *Artisans Vignerons de la Bourgogne du Sud* to the *bioterroiristes* of Chablis and Epineuil. Without neglecting the Hautes Côtes...

Burgundy is strange. A quick glance takes in an idyllic, glossy image, free of clouds or shadows: cult labels coveted everywhere on the planet, droves of wine tourists paying homage to the Grand Crus of the Côte d'Or, as if they were Hollywood sets. Same old script. But in fact the proverbial glass is only half full, for a peek around the corner of this Burgundian Eden can reveal chinks and cracks in the image. If it's true that the demand for wine in the prestigious *appellations* still surpasses the actual supply, the same does not apply to areas cut off from the media hype. And if it's true that price lists are constantly on the rise, it's equally true that the latest harvests have recorded a drastic decline in production, as has rarely occurred in the past.

Nature is strange. The 2015 harvest, bountiful in terms of quantity and highly promising in terms of quality, was welcomed with a unanimously liberating sigh of relief. But the smiles turned to tears on the two nights at the end of April 2016, which recorded the most dramatic spring freeze of the last forty years. The damage to the vineyards was huge, as was the blow to the morale of *vignerons*. The same vineyards, already hard hit by frost, were struck in the summer by an attack of peronospora of an intensity unequalled in human memory. As a result of the destruction, the 2016 vintage was scarce as never before; many wineries found themselves with less than half the production of a normal vintage year.

The market is strange. The economic repercussions of these various cataclysms will presumably generate new aftershocks in coming years, the impact of which is not yet fully foreseeable. However, we have collected testimony from *vignerons* who found themselves having to cover huge annual leases and fees in places where the vineyards suffered most from the weather, with no discounts from proprietors (who have shown a discomforting lack of solidarity) and facing the sad reality that the bottles they place on the market will cover only a small part of their costs. That's why some small family *domaines* have been sold to large groups or, in any case, dismembered in favor of companies with more solid financial structures. But, worse, recently there have been notices of sales at record prices, beyond any market logic (if there is any logic to the market). Also some *domaines* that illuminated the history of this land (Bonneau du Martray, Domaine des Lambray, Clos de Tart) have been bought by global financial empires for completely surreal and senseless figures. Thus they've set the scene for further increases in the registers of property income, as well as in inheritance taxes, calculated inappropriately on the average worth of the properties.

Even friendship is strange. It's nourished by affection, esteem and empathy, of course, but also by improbable links, bilateral but fully compatible. So a fellow who writes about wine and another who makes wine for a living can find themselves together trying to sort through the tangle of questions behind the bizarre conviction that in Burgundy there is still a lot to learn. Learning to drink, for one, since knowing how to drink assumes the explorative value of a job, of an education, rather than depending on a set of technical skills to be assimilated and knowledge to be transmitted. Learning to communicate as well, it goes without saying, because a tongue that tastes without a tongue that speaks (and a hand that writes) simply doesn't function. At the end of our endeavors we feel an irrepressible need for sharing, a desire to express our foremost and most grateful thoughts to the wonderful working group that literally shared in the development and realization of this book.

Books are strange, they don't consist of writing alone. This one was realized with the passionate and competent contribution of a close-knit, brilliant and combative staff: people for whom talent and sensitivity, humanity and technique are sides of the same coin, components of an exacting system. Not only did they provide their professionalism, but they reinvented the work with us day after day *au fur et à mesure*. Our thanks go to all of them. We wish you a *bon voyage* and a good read.

Giampaolo Gravina and Camillo Favaro

THE STORY OF WINE IN BURGUNDY

THROUGH HISTORY

THE ORIGINS

Scholars by now generally agree that the vine arrived in Burgundy from Italy. Although data available at this time bring various hypotheses into play, the evidence seems quite clear that it was the Gauls, invaders of Italy in the fourth and fifth centuries BC, who brought home the vine shoots. From there vineyard cultivation spread through Gaul during the long period of Roman domination as wine came to compete with the typical barley beer loved by the Celts. Beginning around 50 AD, a true culture of wine was established in the territories of today's Burgundy. Wine flourished to the point that, in 92 AD, the Emperor Domitian issued an edict ordering the removal of half of the vineyards of Gaul to limit competition with the winemakers of the Italian peninsula. Only two centuries later did the Emperor Probus grant the local population permission to plant vines and make wines freely.
The oldest written document providing a detailed account of the culture of the vine in the Côte d'Or was dated 312 AD. It was a panegyric dedicated to Emperor Constantine written by Eumene, a professor of eloquence who presided over the University of Autun, where the Gallo-Roman élite was educated at a time when Beaune and Dijon were still rather modest towns.

With the fall of the Roman Empire, in 476, during a long period of wars among barbarian populations, the Burgundi tribe (of Nordic origin) settled in the region between the valleys of the Rhone and Saône. At the end of the fifth century, under the reign of Gondebaud, the Burgundi established a set of written laws with frequent references to viticulture, testifying to continuing work in the vineyards during a turbulent period of civilization, and paving the way for the advent of the Merovingian dynasty and the kingdom of the Franks.

THE WINE OF THE ABBEYS

The centuries that followed marked the era of the wine of abbeys and monks. Those vineyard plots that today are the most precious resource of Burgundian wine were established thanks to the work of various religious orders. In 640, Duke Amalgaire endowed the Abbey of Bèze with some vineyards in Gevrey, already known for their value. Later walled in, they became Clos de Bèze, the first *clos* of the Côte d'Or. In the same period, much further north, near Auxerre, the Clos de la Chaînette was founded. In 775, King Charlemagne donated his vineyard of Aloxe (which became Corton-Charlemagne) to the collegiate church of Saint-Andoche, which retained the property for a millennium until the French revolution. In 838, the Parisian abbey of Saint-Germain des Prés recorded owning vineyards around the future Clos de Vougeot. The monks of Saint-Vivant settled in Vosne and Flagey in 113. The Bernardine nuns of the Abbey of Tart settled in Morey in 1141 and established the Clos de Tart. In the heart of the village of Chablis, also in the first half of the twelfth century, the Cistercian nuns of Pontigny worked the first vineyards near their residence called Le Petit Pontigny (the current Grand Cru Vaudésir). In 1232, the Duchess of Burgundy Alix de Vergy donated some of her best lands to the nuns of the Priory of Saint Vivant de Vergy: the most renowned vineyard is the current Romanée-Saint-Vivant.
There were hundreds of these religious communities in Burgundy alone, where vineyards complemented the spiritual message and, by producing wealth, allowed monasteries and priories to flourish. The Abbey of Cluny (909), which remained the largest church of all Christianity until the construction of St. Peter's in Rome, prospered at a time of expansion and vitality, while developing the viticulture of the Mâconnais. Later, with the decline of the hegemony of Cluny, the Abbey of Citeaux (1098) succeeded in making the Cote d'Or the thriving epicenter of Burgundy wine production.
The great monastic orders saw their capital increase, rarely sharing it, thus be-

coming vast landed entities. These abbeys controlled the land, the product and the distribution as they began to build wine's image. A new approach to vineyard management was established: the Cistercian style, rigorous and proficient. The monks made use of paid workers for heavy labor while reserving for themselves the noble endeavors the required skill and knowledge by directing operations in vineyards and cellars. They lived their lives in rigidly closed communities and based their savoir faire on long empirical practices handed down from generation to generation. Such skills as vineyard management, viticultural research, assessing the value of *terroirs*, winemaking methods and the art of *élevage,* all owe much to the monastic way of life, ideally suited to perfecting the techniques behind a product that requires time and patience.

As Jean-François Bazin acutely observes (the authors owe much to his *Histoire du Vin de Bourgogne*): "The nature and quality of wine here more than elsewhere derived from the single plot of land and the Côte d'Or soon became a mosaic of small plots where each parcel of vines, each *climat* claimed its identity, laying the foundations for future *appellations*." Between the thirteenth and fourteenth centuries, references to viticultural toponymy multiplied in written documents. For instance, in 1276, Campus Bertin is mentioned, soon to become Chambertin. In a similar way, the name Montrachet evolved from Mont Rachaz (1252), Mont Rachat (1380) and Montrachat (1473). It wasn't until 1826 that a land registry map for the first time identified the vineyard names in integral form, though it's obvious that the roots of the Burgundian *lieux-dits* reach well into the depths of medieval history.

THE WINE OF THE DUKES

In the following decades the vicissitudes of viticulture intertwined with those of the Valois Dukes of Burgundy, who proclaimed themselves "lords of the best wines of Christendom" and cultivated the habit of presenting wine as a business gift, thus stimulating its prestige and gaining favor by acquiring it from the nobles and bourgeois of the time. That was the case of Duke Philip II the Bold, who, in 1375, to negotiate peace with the English, brought them barrels containing "*vin de pinot vermeil*." That was the first written reference to the Pinot vine, which had been known for centuries as *noirien*, and already described in the first century AD by the Roman Columella. To make room for Pinot, known as an aristocratic wine of low yields, the same Duke Philip, with a famous ordinance of 1395, imposed the uprooting of Gamay vines, hitherto extremely widespread precisely because it was very productive, resistant to diseases and was the source of popular and easy-to-drink wines. That was a sign of the coexistence of two markets: that of a wine linked to local and current consumption, and that of the Pinot destined for connoisseurs and foreigners, a luxury product reserved for the more affluent classes. The daily and popular destination of the former threatened the prestige (and prices!) of the latter, to the point that rulers of the time strongly opposed this dual role of Burgundy's vineyards. The result has been the gradual disappearance of Gamay in Burgundy, confined almost exclusively to the Beaujolais region, where a factor in its decline is the recent encroachment of its territory by the urban sprawl of Lyon.

BEFORE AND AFTER THE REVOLUTION

The splendor of the Renaissance was followed by a period of relative eclipse for the wines of Burgundy, coinciding with an era of wars and adversity for France as a whole. Markets for Burgundy were challenged by growing competition from the wines of Champagne and Malaga, which persisted between the sixteenth and seventeenth centuries. And yet, in seventeenth-century society there emerged a growing awareness of the notion of taste, which, freed from purely doctrinaire bounds, became the object of discussions and disputes, and ended up being applied, in a figurative sense, also in areas beyond the original context of food flavors. For example, to define the attitudes of well-bred persons, adept at the art of conversation and conducting themselves as models of etiquette and decorum, while cultivating an appreciation of artistic beauty.

But not until the eighteenth century, with the illuministic impulse to cultivate knowledge of the senses, did scholars begin to contemplate the reasons for the excellence of Burgundy wine. To that end, the abbot Claude Arnoux, in 1728, published in London his *Dissertation sur la situation de la Bourgogne, sur les vins qu'elle produit*, etc . That was the first book dedicated entirely to the wines of Burgundy, with advice on how to acquire and best preserve them, descriptions of *terroirs* and *climats*, accompanied by pioneering maps. Arnoux was not content to just describe, but sought explanations. The book speaks of terrains and subsoils, of climate and vineyard expositions, revealing that in some ways wines were sold at the time with the names of their *terroirs*, thus anticipating future *appellations*. At that time, a new professional figure appeared on the scene: the *négociant-éléveur*, a sort of merchant-refiner who buys wine at the property, follows its refinement and aging and then sells it. Some of the early *maisons de négoce*

were established in Beaune: Champy in 1720, Bouchard in 1731, Verry-Chanson in 1750, and gradually others. A royal decree of 1776 established the free circulation of wines throughout the kingdom of France, a stimulus that activated and modernized the trade among specialists who began shipping wine across borders, oriented toward the Belgian and English markets, but above all to the German.
The Revolution of 1789 marked a drastic change of course, a watershed that profoundly altered the politics of power and the economic balance of the Burgundy of wine. Among the consequences was a sweeping redistribution of property through the sale of national assets; those of the clergy were confiscated by the state and sold at auction between 1790 and 1793. It marked the advent of a new business bourgeoisie, often unscrupulous in speculations as it assumed control of the Grand Crus. For the *vignerons*, the revolution caused a thorough upheaval but without appreciable advantages. Only a minor part of them managed to buy some small vineyard plots, though invariably modest in terms of quality. In most cases they were destined to remain sharecroppers, with the difference being that their wages came not from the monks but from the *nouveau riche*.

WINE IN THE NINETEENTH CENTURY

In Burgundy, vineyards and wines had long conformed to a hierarchy based on *climat* and *terroir*. But only in the nineteenth century did this inspired principle acquire its own cogency as it was transformed from a widespread tendency into a binding standard, progressively creating the need for the emergence of a classification of vineyards and a ranking by merit. The steps that mark the advent of this *classement*, fundamental to the institution of a system of *appellations*, are characterized by the recovery of the ancient notion of *cuvée* regenerated from a new perspective: that the grapes entering a determined *cuve* (vat) belong only to a single *climat*. This advanced the idea of establishing a guarantee of origin in the early pioneering attempts to introduce a classification of vineyards.
The authors A. Jullien (1816), J-A. Cavoleau (1827) and D. Morelot (1831) wrote works that framed the *crus* repertoire in a hierarchical perspective. But, above all, a book by Jules Lavalle, *Histoire et statistique de la vigne et des grands vins de la Côte d'Or* (1855), led to the evaluation of the attributes of each *climat*, community by community, organized by classes of merit: from the finest *hors ligne*, to the *tête de cuvée*, to the three successive ranks of *cuvées*. Shortly thereafter, the Comité d'Agriculture de Beaune (1861) created maps inspired by and largely assimilating the system.

As widely noted, the major classifications of Bordeaux wines were realized in that same period (1855). But Burgundy must be considered from a different perspective, since it defines identity on the basis of *terroir*, not of property (Bordeaux), or of trademark (Champagne) or of vine variety (Alsace). The *climat* stood as protagonist often further identified in those same years by the practice of joining the name of the best known vineyard to the name of the village. So Gevrey became Gevrey-Chambertin (1847), followed by the others: Aloxe-Corton (1862), Vosne-Romanée (1866), Chambolle-Musigny (1878), Chassagne-Montrachet and Puligny-Montrachet (1879)), Nuits-Saint-Georges (1892).

The last part of the century brought the epidemic of phylloxera, a catastrophe known in Burgundy as *le mal noir* (the black evil). The progression was inexorable: 50 hectares destroyed in 1884, 300 in 1885, 500 in 1887, 4,000 in 1888. Half of the vineyards were soon contaminated with an urgent need to graft the vines onto American rootstock. Although phylloxera was without doubt the most dramatic disaster in the history of wine, there were some positive repercussions. If before vineyards were planted everywhere with avaricious densities of over 20,000 plants per hectare, there was now a tendency to redimension viticulture by planting in the best *terroirs* at lower densities to facilitate access to the vines with horse-drawn plows and implements to perform rational maintenance and treatments.

In some way, the disaster became the pretext for greater attention to quality in winemaking and the transition to the new century coincided with years of profound change. Growers and winemakers communicated more closely with the scientific community, favoring innovations in production techniques. The *Ecole pratique d'agriculture et de viticulture* (1884), the future Lycée viticole, was opened in Beaune. Dijon founded an Institute of Oenology, which later became the University Institute of Vines and Wines named after Jules Guyot, who, in the mid-nineteenth century, at the research center of the Château of Savigny-lès-Beaune, had laid the foundations for a new system of vine training, known as Guyot. The first Manual of Viticulture was published in 1896 as the practices of growing grapes and making wine were substantially revolutionized.

THE TWENTIETH CENTURY AND THE NEW MILLENNIUM

The First World War radically changed the ownership structure of Burgundy's vineyards. Since the 1920s, many noble and bourgeois proprietors left the land, resulting in an impressive increase in ownership among small and medium-scale producers (by now well over 3,000). At the same time the need for greater control and a more binding guarantee of origin became pressing, to secure and protect the production system from fraud and illegal expediencies. After an agonizing series of trials and sentences condemning abusive references to some of the most important vineyards on labels (Montrachet, Echézeaux), a decision was finally reached in a law (of July 30, 1935) which instituted the appellations of origin system and a commission to control them (see the chapter on the appellations system, Page 115).

In the meantime significant advances were recorded in the mechanization of labor. If the use of the horse was seen in the early twentieth century as a sign of progress and evolution, within decades it had become the image of backwardness, with the advent of five-wheel hoes (1920) drawn by futuristic straddle tractors (1932). In the wineries, machinery and equipment such as presses and containers evolved visibly under the impulse of new technologies. Following World War II, the use of chemistry in viticulture became widespread, marked by a growing tendency to increase productivity through the use of chemicals, notably in the form of herbicides and insecticides.

The second half of the twentieth century is recent history, so trends initiated then are often reflected in current realities. For example, in Burgundy, on the productive and commercial side, there have been the rise and the subsequent decline of cooperative wineries; the practice of direct sales at the property; the complicated branching and fragmentation of *domaines familiales*; the concentration and constant growth in business volume among the *négociants* (see the chapter *Maison* or *Domaine?*, Page 29); the exponential rise in commercial value of the vineyards. In the 1960s, after decades of semi-abandonment due to the catastrophes of phylloxera and two world wars, the concept of high quality viticulture returned to the Hautes Côtes. On the consumer side, the diffusion of wine and food criticism and the affirmation of wine as a media phenomenon have added a new sense of value to tasting as a key factor in the culture of the territory. It is precisely this respect for the territory that inspired us to compile this brief, and far from complete, historical survey.

A theme that has always been central to the wine of Burgundy, which has structured its territorial identity from time immemorial, is respect for the earth and environmental sustainability, ever more vital both for those who produce and those who consume. The consolidation of organic and biodynamic viticulture, increasingly widespread throughout Burgundy, is a response not only to nutritional and health needs or ideas of taste following whims of fashion or moods of the market, but above all to a more integral view of the relationship between man and nature.

Other factors, no less decisive, have contributed to recent radical changes in the equilibrium of Burgundy's economic structure. A certain media overexposure and the rampant growth of commercial interest in the wines have driven an equally exaggerated increase in land value. Suffice it to say that the cost of a vineyard classified as Premier Cru in an *appellation* of established reputation often abundantly exceeds one million euro per hectare, as illustrated by the hype surrounding recent acquisitions (Bonneau du Martray, Clos de Tart, Domaine des Lambrays). Inevitably, the increasing financial influence linked to attracting foreign capital ends up facilitating speculative dynamics rather than providing an effective boost for agricultural investments. That is, agricultural investments of broader and more consistent scope, which need strengthening on many fronts to meet the challenges of climate change, the threat of new pests and blights, and the pressing need for greater guarantees of transparency demanded by consumers everywhere.
In that regard, the recent registration of 1,247 different *climats* of the Côte d'Or in the Unesco World Heritage List (July 2015) marks an achievement of undoubted prestige. But the protection of a territory of such vital importance to the history and culture of wine will require still more work.

MAISON OR DOMAINE?

Looking back over the main stages of the history of the wines of Burgundy, we have already discussed the founding of the first *maisons de négoce* in the eighteenth century, as well as their proliferation and consolidation in the following century. After passing into the hands of the *négociants*, the sale of wines remained largely under their control until fairly recent times. And even today, data in hand, most of the turnover in wine in Burgundy passes through commercial houses. But here an explanation seems in order about a complex relationship that the foreign reader might not find easy to comprehend. The relationship between *maisons* and *domaines* might be considered a sort of *liaison dangereuse* between two radically different and historically alternative wine entities, whose interests, however, are deeply intertwined and in many ways complementary.

Until the beginning of the twentieth century, in fact, the respective interests of production and trade in the wines of Burgundy followed parallel paths that never coincided. On the one side were the *vignerons*, committed to growing grapes in conditions of relative poverty, with the primary need to ensure selling the crop; on the other were the *négociants*, buyers of grapes or wines, who alone in the production chain were equipped for bottling and commerce. To propitiate the meeting of *négociants* and *viticulteurs* over matters of supply and demand, there emerged the historical figure of the *courtier*, the mediator, who knew the circumstances of both those who had grapes or wine to sell and those who intended to buy, and determined the allocations.

Not until the twentieth century did certain growers quit selling cultivated and harvested grapes to *négociants* and begin producing and selling wines from their own *domaines*. There were a few isolated precursors (Rousseau, Liger-Belair, D'Angerville, Ramonet) favored between the two wars by the new *Revue du Vin de France*, whose critical acclaim helped build their commercial success. But only after World War II—and in a more systematic way since the 1970s—did the *domaine* phenomenon acquire real significance as the example set by those pioneering *vignerons* was followed by an ever-increasing number of small family estates, which left the orbit of the *négociants* to bottle the wine *à la propriété* and seek commercial outlets in an independent way. The phenomenon reached vast proportions, causing a veritable hemorrhage of wine from the *maisons de négoce*, and creating in a few decades a new productive pattern in Burgundy while transforming the family *domaine* into a potent status symbol.

Burgundy's reputation as the region of small producers par excellence was therefore acquired relatively recently, bringing with it new implications. While the *vignerons* have made artisanal *savoir faire* a guarantee of the true expression of territorial character in wines, the *négociants* have changed their methods and strategies to meet the challenge of high-quality competition. Burgundy, with 30,000 hectares of vineyards, accounts for only 3% of the total area under vine in France, while the nearly 300 Burgundy *maisons* account for more than 10% of the national trade in wine with business volume constantly increasing. At the same time, the *maisons* have increased vineyard holdings so that all the main *négociants* now own *domaines*, having extended and consolidated possession of vineyard parcels while, in some cases, gaining control of entire estates, with significant shares also in the most prestigious *climats*.

The transformation of the *négoce* also involves ways of intervening on the market. In most cases, the buyer wants to guarantee maximum control, so the increasingly widespread practice is to make a contract to buy grapes well in advance of the harvest. Such agreements often stipulate how vineyards should be worked, while setting the final price according to the maximum yields permitted by the regulations of different *appellations*, thus encouraging growers to focus on quality rather than quantity.

The custom is that growers harvest on the dates set by the *négociants*, who usually collect the crop at the vineyard. But increasingly buyers exercise their option to organize and train their own harvest teams. Less common, although not completely abandoned, is the practice of selling the crop in the form of freshly pressed must (for whites) or wine in barrels after completion of alcoholic fermentation (for reds).

Observing the overall scenario, a reciprocal influence can be noted. If the work of the *négociants* is often positively stimulated by the high quality standards guaranteed by the best *domaines*, the *vignerons* don't always resist the temptation to do a little business on their own. Today it is not so infrequent that a *domaine*, even of modest size, includes some *négociant* activity in its production. There can be different motives for this. One is that there are certain financial advantages that allow a grower to identify as a *négociant* to buy his own grapes along with those of others and market all the wines under a single brand name. Another is the opportunity to reach a critical mass more in line with the size of the investment. Last but not least is a need to satisfy a demand for wine that often exceeds supply, especially in recent years with ever more frequent extremes of weather, such as spring frosts or summer hailstorms. Proof can be found in recent harvests, 2016 above all, when more than a few *domaines*, in the face of a decimated crop, took the opportunity to buy batches of grapes to be vinified and marketed with their own brand. The chance to improvise the role of *négoce* in an emergency served as a sort of safeguard to limit economic damage and avoid the necessity of ceding shares of vineyards.

The lines between the activity of the *négociants* and that of the *domaines* are nuanced, so labels may cause a certain ambiguity or confusion. But at the same time old prejudices have fallen. The role of *négoce* turns out to be a potential resource for *vignerons* and other small-scale growers who lack the means to buy vineyards and try their hand at making and marketing their own wine. Thus the *maisons de négoce* have assumed new dimensions, sometimes inspired by the almost sartorial notion of a *négoce haute couture* with no shortage of ambition, but more often burdened by the enological protocols that have long conditioned the *modus operandi* of the *négociants*. In any case, winemaking has become more sensitive to that model of craftsmanship based on the culture of *terroir* to which finest wines of Burgundy are so firmly anchored.

A LAND OF VINEYARDS

CLIMATS

The notion of *climat*, so difficult to translate into other languages, designates the specific and original identity of a certain vineyard parcel, known for centuries by the same name. Above all, it is a historical-cultural identity of a plot of land where the vineyard has always been present, without interruption, epitomizing the legacy of an ancient civilization; thus handing down a production tradition on which the economy of the Burgundian community has been founded and consolidated. Accordingly, a historic viticultural site that has been transmitted over the centuries almost unchanged in its borders, and whose activity is today more alive than ever. The interweaving of history, culture and nature becomes complex here as the identity of the *climat* also draws a relative value from the geology of the soil, the exposure and the microclimate that affect that particular vineyard. It seems that one of the most plausible and credible etymological hypotheses of the term *climat*, whose first citations were already affirmed toward the end of the sixteenth century (1584), leads back to the notion of "inclination" of the land (in Latin, the word "clima" also has to do with the concept of inclination). Considered as a whole, a *climat* is a unitary nucleus in which it is difficult, if not impossible, to separate the *genius loci* from human genius, which instead have been integrated and completed in the course of a long lasting historical process.

Each *climat* therefore claims its own history, its place in the hierarchy of *crus*, its distinctive character in the wines that derive from it. To confirm the extraordinary singularity of this veritable mosaic of vine parcels, the 1,247 different *climats* of the Côte d'Or were officially declared a UNESCO World Heritage Site in July 2015.

GEOLOGY

The geological conformation of Burgundy dates back to the Upper and Middle Jurassic periods of the Mesozoic era. At that time, between 150 and 170 million years ago, the region was covered by the sea, in a semi-tropical climate that scholars compare to the current Florida (James Wilson, *Terroir*). With the progressive emergence of the land, the calcareous rock support was stratified through a process of sedimentation and compression that lasted millions of years, forming the terrains on which today the Chablis, Côte d'Or Côte Chalonnaise and Mâconnais vineyards stand. However synthetic and brief it may seem, this reconstruction already contains the most significant reasons for the extraordinary diversification of the Burgundian *climats*. It should be emphasized that the vineyards are planted today on what was once a seabed, and like every seabed it changed every fifty meters or so: here a muddy bend, there a bank of sea lilies, further ahead the stones and fossils of an oyster bed, still further on, a bit of gravel, and so on, according to a principle of permanent variability. Variability further scrambled by the slow wrinkling and folding of the different sedimentary layers, to the point of shaping a subsoil that has been imaginatively likened to a roller coaster system (Charles Frankel, *Terre de Vignes*).

In the scale of geological eras, each macro-period corresponds to a connection between different eras or phases, to which diverse stratigraphic stages are linked, each with a peculiar physiognomy and its own characteristics (though usually different strata coexist under a single *climat*).

Our reconnaissance starts from the northernmost department of Burgundy, the Yonne, named for the river that flows through it. The white wine zone of Chablis is the region's viticultural area of most recent geological formation: the substratum dates to the **Kimmeridgian** stage of the Upper Jurassic period. The name derives from the village of Kimmeridge, in the English county of Dorset, linked to the first appearance of a peculiar species of ammonite. Unlike the Côte d'Or, where irregularities are common, the geology of Chablis is more uniform and easily divisible into sectors. In Chablis the southernmost slope is characterized by chalky calcareous marl atop a thick layer of Tonnerre limestone (often used in construction). In the northern quadrant soils often contain an extraordinary abundance of small oyster fossils called *Exogyra virgula* (notably in the *climat* of Les Clos) as well as other lamellar shells mixed with gray marl and calcareous debris.

In the Côte d'Or the rock strata of greatest interest date back mainly to a period between 155 and 170 million years ago. The **Bajocian** layer takes its name from the town of Bayeux, in Normandy, and is characterized by a calcareous rock called encrinite containing crinoids (*calcaire à entroques*) the fossils of sea lilies calcified in mud. This substratum is found in some prestigious *climats* of the Côte de Nuits, including parts of Chambertin in Gevrey and parts of Clos de Tart in Morey. The so-called *Ostrea acuminata* is also an important type of rock in the Bajocian: it refers to an amalgam of calcareous clays, or marl, incorporating fossils of oyster shells from the Jurassic. Traces are found in the soils of Marsannay (Champs Perdrix) and Gevrey (Clos de Bèze), as well as in Vosne (Romanée-Saint-Vivant) and in Nuits (Les Vignes Rondes).

The English spa town of Bath gives its name to the so-called **Bathonian** stage of the Middle Jurassic, a layer made up of exceptionally hard calcareous formations that force vines to struggle in sinking their roots. An example is the marble stone of Comblanchien found in vineyards of Prémeaux and Chassagne. Differences in consistency and permeability are noted in the so-called white ooliths, egg-shaped spheres that incorporate formations of calcium carbonate found, for example, in the soil substratum of the Clos du Roi, a prestigious *climat* of Corton, and of the Grand Cru Musigny of Chambolle.

Still another English locality, the hamlet of Kelleways Bridge near Chippenham in Wiltshire County, lends its Latinized name to the **Callovian** layer, which incorporates in its compact calcareous rocks hard fossils of a vast population of oysters and other bivalve mollusks. This formation underlies vineyards in the Côte de Nuits (Aux Reignots at Vosne) and in the Côte de Beaune (Clos des Epeneaux at Pommard).

Another original feature of the geology and landscape of the Côte d'Or is observable in the so-called *combes*. These are narrow canyon-shaped gorges, crossed by streams flowing from the Hautes Côtes, which have dragged downstream over the millennia alluvial material in the form of stones, pebbles and assorted debris. This material has been stratified in certain *climats* of the *combes* in what are called "dejection cones," which confer peculiar traits to the soils. Near the combes microclimates change significantly due to the flow of air currents through the gorges, as well as to different rates of soil drainage and more pronounced day-night thermal excursions.

The vineyards of the Côte de Nuits are planted on the slopes of a calcareous ridge exposed to the east with an extremely complex soil composition. This is evident in the stratification of different types of rock in the section of the Côte running from east to west in relation to the vineyards of Vosne-Romanée. In the flat area the subsoil is composed mainly of alluvial material (sand and gravel) in vineyards of relatively modest qualitative value. Moving up the slopes the rock formations diversify to extremes with calcareous layers of the Bajocian, marl of *Ostrea acuminata*, the hard rock of Prémeaux rich in silicon and oolitic stones (granules of calcium carbonate).

The Côte de Beaune shares with the Côte de Nuits the same period of geological formation: the rocks of the subsoil are for the most part composed of the Callovian marl, oolitic limestone and Bajocian marl. The vineyards of this area, unlike the Côte de Nuits, are moderately oriented to the southeast. In the lower and flat parts of the terrain the soils are also constituted here by silt and alluvial deposits. Gradually moving up the slope we find a Callovian calcareous strip with ample clay. The subsoil of the Grand Cru Montrachet consists of a hard bioclastic base (calcareous formations of organic material, such as shell fossils) crossed by a reddish strip of marl with a high iron oxide content. The upper part of the slope consists of a substratum of thin and stony soils Comblanchien marble (the same as at Chambolle-Musigny).

As the Italian author Armando Castagno points out, there is also another aspect that distinguishes the Côtes de Nuits and the Côtes de Beaune from a purely geological point of view. In the Côte de Nuits the oldest rocky stratifications are close to the surface in the middle part but deep down at the northern and southern extremes, following a model of a convex curvature called *Anticlinale de Gevrey*. The Côte de Beaune has an entirely different curvature, that is to say concave, following a model called *Sinclinale de Volnay*, which means that the oldest geological stratifications are close to the surface at the extremes (at Corton and Santenay) and submerged in the middle.

The Côte Chalonnaise, a natural geographical continuation of the Côte d'Or, has a geological origin that has been traced back to an era between the Bathonian and the **Oxfordian** stages of the Upper Jurassic. Soil composition varies between formations of hard calcareous stone (similar to that of different areas of the Hautes Côtes and of Saint Romain) and softer marl. Exceptions are the Mercurey area with calcareous marl deposits well suited to Pinot Noir and the small *appellation* of Bouzeron where Oxfordian calcareous formations are ideal for white *Aligotè* grapes alone in a terrain that shows unexpected similarities to that of Corton-Charlemagne, on the Pernand side. To the south, near the border of the Côte Chalonnaise, in the small *appellation* of Montagny the geological eras of the substrata change progressively from Middle Jurassic to Lower Jurassic.

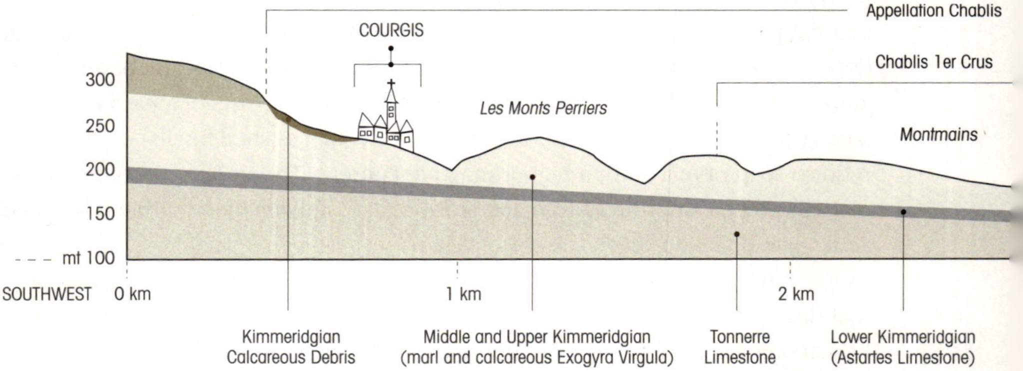

The border between the Côte Chalonnaise and the Mâconnais is marked by the valley of the river Saône, which widens in a lively succession of valleys and hills that reach as much as 500 meters in height, creating a more varied and irregular landscape than that left to the north. This discontinuity is also found in the subsoils of the Mâconnais, where different types stand out: calcareous and calcareous marl (particularly in the areas of Pouilly and Saint-Véran), hard marls of the Lias group and the Upper Oxfordian (Viré-Clessé) and markedly siliceous soils on granite beds of volcanic origin further south, towards Beaujolais.

CHABLIS

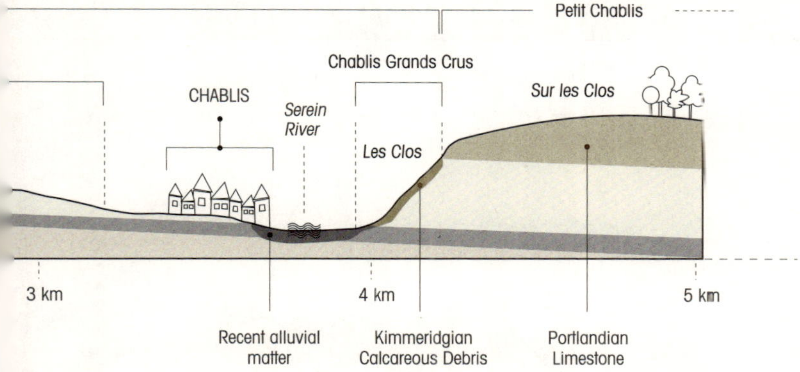

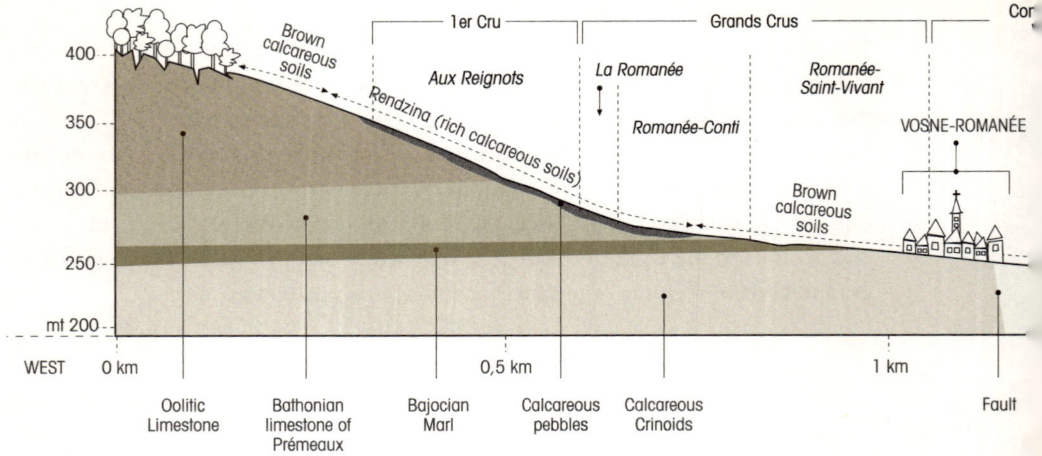
1er Cru
Grands Crus
Brown calcareous soils
Aux Reignots
La Romanée
Romanée-Saint-Vivant
Rendzina (rich calcareous soils)
Romanée-Conti
VOSNE-ROMANÉE
Brown calcareous soils
400
350
300
250
mt 200
WEST
0 km
0,5 km
1 km
Oolitic Limestone
Bathonian limestone of Prémeaux
Bajocian Marl
Calcareous pebbles
Calcareous Crinoids
Fault

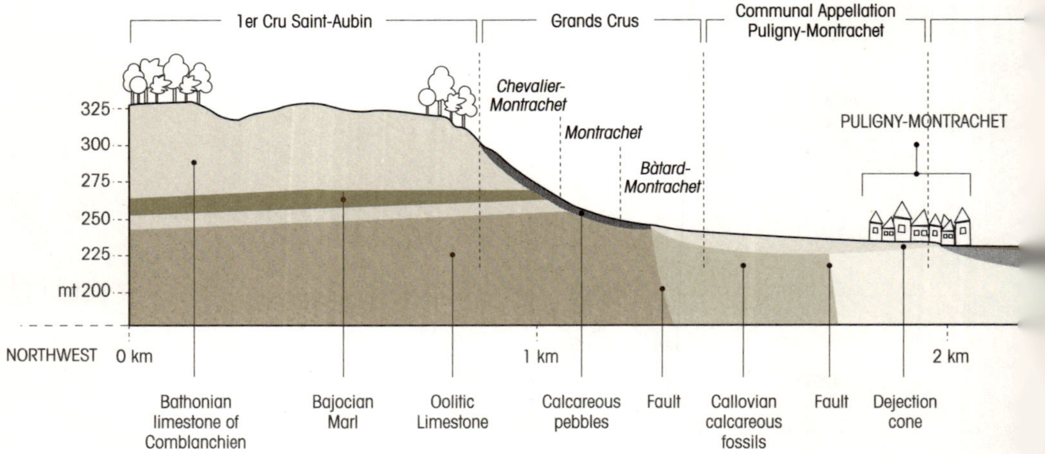
1er Cru Saint-Aubin
Grands Crus
Communal Appellation Puligny-Montrachet
Chevalier-Montrachet
Montrachet
Bàtard-Montrachet
PULIGNY-MONTRACHET
325
300
275
250
225
mt 200
NORTHWEST
0 km
1 km
2 km
Bathonian limestone of Comblanchien
Bajocian Marl
Oolitic Limestone
Calcareous pebbles
Fault
Callovian calcareous fossils
Fault
Dejection cone

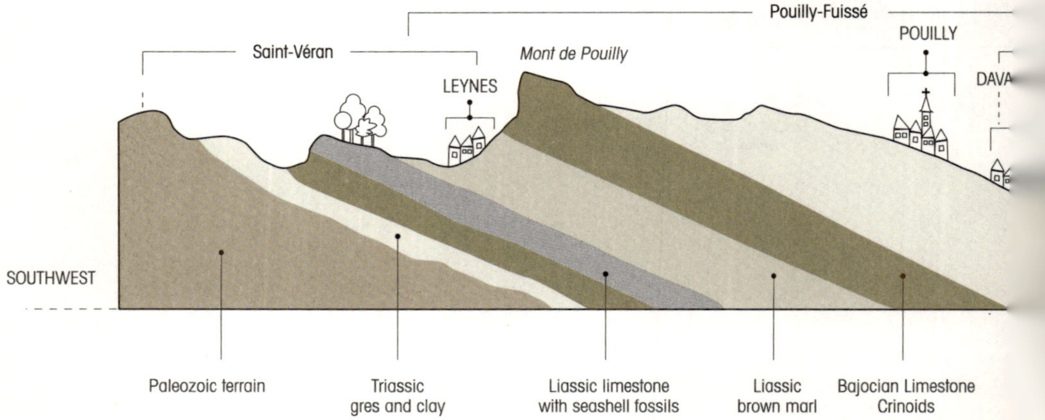
Pouilly-Fuissé
Saint-Véran
Mont de Pouilly
LEYNES
POUILLY
SOUTHWEST
Paleozoic terrain
Triassic gres and clay
Liassic limestone with seashell fossils
Liassic brown marl
Bajocian Limestone Crinoids

CÔTE DE NUITS

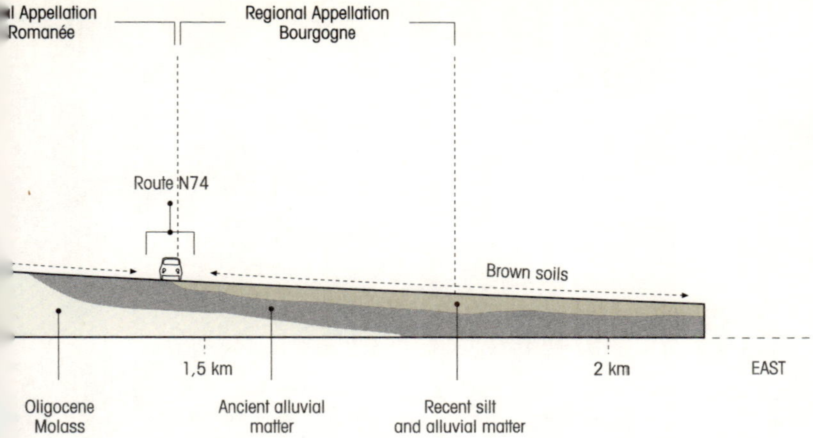

CÔTE DE BEAUNE

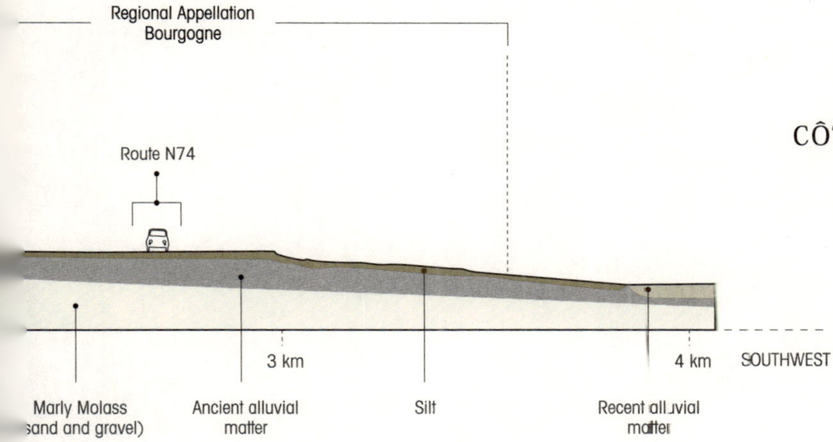

MÂCONNAIS

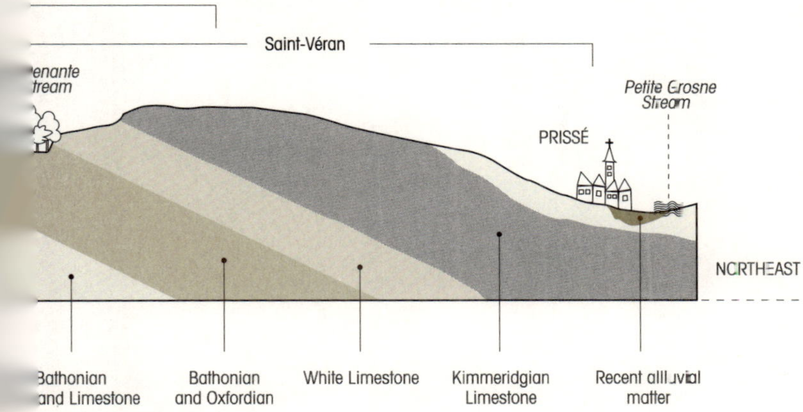

THE GRAPES

PINOT NOIR

Pinot Noir has been the most important grape variety in the production of the red wines of Burgundy for almost a millennium. It is generally asserted that this leadership was confirmed during the fourteenth century, at the end of which (1395) an ordinance of Duke Philip the Bold imposed the uprooting of Gamay vines (see page 23). Rapidly replacing vines such as the *noirien* (now extinct) and Gamay, Pinot Noir has reigned for centuries in Burgundy as a sovereign, from the outskirts of Dijon to Givry and beyond.

Cultivation is by no means limited to Burgundy alone, or to France alone (where it has long been prominent in Champagne and certain other regions), but has spread almost everywhere, from the United States to New Zealand, from Germany to Australia, from South Africa to Switzerland and Italy, occupying a total area of nearly 100,000 hectares of vineyards.

The physical features of wine from Pinot Noir have undergone alterations over the centuries, starting with color. It seems that in the late Middle Ages the red wines from Pinot Noir were normally rich in color, heavy and demanding in flavor, which explains why the custom spread of diluting them with water, at around 20%, a practice that remained in vogue long after.

In the seventeenth century, during a period of lower than average temperatures, wines tended to be by nature paler in color, as vermilion tones made way for more subdued hues, such as the classic "eye of the partridge." By the eighteenth century attitudes and tastes became more decisive and the fashion for wines of greater color took hold, progressively eliminating the dubious practice of using white grapes in blends.

Pinot Noir is noted for delicate and precarious balances in wines from grapes of dark violet hue grown in small, compact bunches that render abundant juice of pale color. A key factor behind its eccentricities is the particularly thin skins that explain the fragility of a variety that is exceptionally sensitive to seasonal changes in weather. Pinot Noir "feels" the vintage intensely, manifesting a definite intolerance toward excessively cool and northerly exposures (and latitudes) in wines that tend to be thin and acidic, often flawed by vegetal odors and green flavors. From hot seasons with early harvests, wines often show signs of being overripe and rustic. In damp and cool years, vines are highly susceptible to attacks of mold and acid rot.

Not only. Pinot Noir is also subject to a phenomenon, fairly common in Burgundy, known as *millerandage*, in which grape bunches develop berries that differ in size and maturity due to irregular flowering caused by cool and damp weather in late spring. This lowers yields drastically, but can result in wines of extra dimensions, rich in tannins and color with excellent aromatic attributes as noted in certain *millerandage* vintage years (notably 2010, 1995, 1988). Some *domaines* even carry out separate harvests for the affected bunches, destined for special *cuvées*, such as the Clos des Corvées of Prieuré-Roch or the Pouilly-Vinzelles Les Quarts Cuvée Millerandée of La Soufrandière.

When raised in its ideal habitat (Burgundy) by its ablest interpreters, Pinot Noir is the prototype of enchanting reds: "the world's most astonishing wine," as Armando Castagno proclaims. Luminous in color, brilliant in tone, magically fragrant, easy to drink, it inherently combines such distinctive qualities as finesse and energy, freshness and grace, delicacy and persistence. The high tenor of terpenes favors an irresistible aromatic vitality, but the main attribute of Pinot Noir wines is their uncompromising expression of the character of their *terroirs* of origin. Transmitting the standard Pinot Noir varietal notes into the wine is not a prerogative. Indeed, the term *pinoter* refers to low quality wines marked by such varietal character. The priority is to put in the foreground the place of origin, to express the qualities of finesse that exalt the incomparable character of the different *terroirs*.

CHARDONNAY

Although cited in texts as "*chardenet ou pinot blanc*" since the eighteenth century, it was only in the second half of the nineteenth century that Chardonnay established its lead role in Burgundy as the dominant and almost exclusive variety in the panorama of white wine.
Recognizable in the vineyard for its leaves without lobes, Chardonnay is a precocious variety with compact bunches and consistent grape skins and remarkable potential of structure and energy. It comes as no surprise that, in tastings, Burgundian producers prefer to offer their white wines from Chardonnay grapes after the reds from Pinot Noir. "*Blanc sur rouge, rien ne bouge,*" as a local adage has it.
It would be a mistake to think of Chardonnay in the popular image of recent decades as a white wine characterized by intensely fruity and vanilla-like aspects as conceived in the so-called New World. Instead it is precisely a scarcely aromatic character due to its extraordinary assimilation of the multiple climatic and geological variations of Burgundy's *terroirs* that sets Chardonnay apart, reinforced by important stylistic differences in winemaking and use of barrels for fermentation and refinement during *élevage*. Almost invariably the Chardonnay of Burgundy is fermented and refined *en fûts*, that is to say in oak barrels, mainly in 228-liters *pièces*, though in recent times the use of so-called *demi-muids* of 400 to 700 liter capacity has increased. In any case, it is the capacity to assimilate variations in climate and terrain that accounts for an extremely diversified and nuanced range of expressions. From Chardonnay grapes Burgundy can provide whites of pronounced minerality, rich in acidity and infused with iodized austerity, as in the best of Chablis. Or it can offer wines that are full and fleshy with buttery aromas and ripe fruit components, enveloping and creamy on the palate, yet warm and alcoholic, as often found in the Mâconnais (where the small village of Chardonnay claims the primogeniture of the name). Longevity remains the most fascinating feature of the finest whites of the Côte de Beaune, where Chardonnay has found its habitat of choice, notably in the *climats* of the hills of Corton and those between Meursault and Chassagne, where the star of Montrachet shines brightly.

ALIGOTÉ

An ancient vine, resistant to diseases and vigorously productive, Aligoté comes in small clusters. In Burgundy there are two biotypes: Aligoté Vert, with greenish

skins, is the most common in wines of marked acidity; Aligoté Doré is appreciated for wines of quality that are better balanced and smoother. In the region of Burgundy, where Aligoté covers more than 1,200 hectares, corresponding to about 7% of the total area under vine, it is present almost everywhere where conditions aren't favorable for Pinot Noir and Chardonnay. The small *appellation* of Bouzeron, in the Côte Chalonnaise, dedicates some fifty hectares entirely to Aligoté.
Aligoté whites, which often serve as base wines in a producer's range, are noted for strong personality that relies more on salinity and acidity than nuanced traits. They are the main base of *Kir*, Burgundy's popular aperitif, blended with cassis cream. An encouraging trend in parts of the Côte d'Or is reflected in whites from Aligoté that combine sharp character with surprising complexity, as in those labeled Coche-Dury and d'Auvenay (though the list is longer). Complexity is exalted in the Morey-Saint-Denis 1er Cru Clos de Mont Luisants of the Ponsot family, coming from a *climat* recently reconverted to its original role of producing exclusively Aligoté.

GAMAY

No discussion of Gamay in Burgundy can ignore the ordinance of Duke Philip II the Bold, in 1395, imposing the uprooting of Gamay vines which were described as "awful and disloyal" and the wines as "terribly stinky." Rather ungenerous descriptions of a vine that in Beaujolais, on soils with acidic pH in the southernmost outcrop of Burgundy's vineyards, has proved to be the source of widely appreciated wines, some of which rate the dignity of *crus*.
Compact in cluster, precocious in vegetation, Gamay makes wines with attributes of color and polyphenols more appreciable than those of Pinot Noir, if much more limited in expressivity and longevity. To the north of Beaujolais, in Burgundy proper, Gamay occupies little space today. It is found in the Coteaux Bourguignons *appellation* and in certain denominations of the Mâconnais, where it makes reds focused on fruit, mostly immediate and unpretentious. On the other hand, we'd like to propose a toast to the reds of the Bourgogne Passetoutgrains *appellation*, where Gamay may figure at up to 70% in blends with Pinot Noir. Fluidly smooth and zestily fruity, wines from certain producers (Lafarge, Rouget) provide delicious pleasure while showing the most convivial, sympathetic and egalitarian facets of Gamay, which—with due respect for dukes—seems anything but disloyal.

CLIMATE

Climate trends, as already emphasized, are a key element in the complex equation of the *terroir*. Sun and rain, light and humidity, wind and hail, frosts and thermal excursions alternate like the tiles of a mosaic that assumes a different design every year, making each vintage unique and unrepeatable. Among the most fascinating challenges in the work of the *vigneron*, in Burgundy as elsewhere, is the need to fathom and interpret climate trends and either profit from or "tame" them as far as possible to avoid the consequences of bad weather. The challenge is especially aggravating in Burgundy, and above all in the Chablis zone, due to complex climatic factors created by exposure to both Mediterranean and continental influences and the capricious whims of weather that are often more difficult to deal with than elsewhere. Wind is a major determinant of the variability of the Burgundian climate. When it blows from the southwest it is warm and humid, often laden with rain, which with the influx of hotter winds from the south in the summer months risks turning to hail, dreaded by *vignerons*. Northerly winds, on the other hand, can play an important role close to the harvest, especially after rainy summers, when fresh ventilation can be an excellent antidote to vine mold and rot. Northwest winds are often accompanied by rain, which is why winemakers generally prefer winds from the northeast, more pungent and cold, but marked by clear weather with intense luminosity that favors sharp acidity without compromising the sugar content of grapes.

An important testimony to the decisive role of light came from Henri Jayer, legendary *vigneron* of Vosne-Romanée, who died in 2006 and was rightly considered a tutelary god of modern *terroir* viticulture (see Page 246). According to Jayer, a fundamental factor in the quality of a vintage is the number of hours of sunshine in the thirty days before the harvest. In his estimation, vintages that recorded from 160 to 180 hours of sunshine were average, those that benefited from 180 to 200 hours were generally good, but only those with more than 200 hours of sunshine were considered exceptional. He confirmed that luminosity is no less important than heat in influencing the quality of a vintage.
Excessive heat can often be a problem, especially for a vine as sensitive as Pinot Noir, whose thin skins quickly dry out, resulting in aggressive tannins and compromising aromatic finesse. That was the case with difficult vintages, such as 1976, 1983 and 2003, as well as the harvest of 2017.
The average rainfall in Burgundy's vineyards is about 700 mm a year spread over 150/160 days. Heavy rains, especially at harvest time, can be a problem, though hail has proved to be more of a menace. Hail caused major damage in 1983 and 2004 and, recently in the Côte de Beaune, in 2012, 2013 and 2014. When it occurs in the summer months, it damages not only the grapes, but also the leaves and the shoots, with serious inhibiting effects on the process of photosynthesis.
Frosts also take a toll on the vineyards in winter and spring, though for different reasons. Winter frosts sometimes kill off vines that have already been pruned or which are planted in vineyards with humid soils and are most exposed to severe weather. For example, in mid-December of 2009, when temperatures dropped by more than 30 degrees (from +15° to -20°) in the course of a single night, or in the winter of 1985, when temperatures of -30°C were reached. Spring frosts almost always take major tolls on crops, especially when vines have sprouted early, as recorded on April 27, 2016 and April 19, 2017, with temperatures of -4°C at dawn and hundreds of hectares of vineyards devastated by frost in a few hours.

THE VINTAGES

The ranking of vintages is a particularly tricky matter, even for the most savvy and assiduous connoisseurs of the wines of the Burgundy. Climatic conditions during the year are the prime consideration in determining the worth of a vintage, yet the savoir faire of each individual *vigneron* can play an equally decisive role, especially in the so-called minor years. Aubert de Villaine, charismatic patron of the Domaine de la Romanée-Conti, reminds us: "In a difficult year, the *terroir* speaks louder than the *millésime*. The wines of minor vintages are the true wines of amateurs... It is true that nothing is more seductive than a great wine from an exceptional vintage, but there is nothing more admirable than a great wine from a minor vintage."

This assertion becomes all the more valid when arbitrary attitudes spread among wine drinkers, building resistance to minor vintages and boosting enthusiasm for vintages acclaimed by the critics. It's hard to avoid certain *clichés*, especially when the purchase of an old vintage involves a considerable economic sacrifice (as happens with a certain frequency in Burgundy).

Yet, among attentive consumers, it would seem opportune to cultivate a more open and unbiased interest in the wines of this "land of exceptions," which often contradict the critical consensus about a vintage, bucking the trend with bottles of unexpected excellence.

With these considerations in mind, we put together a review of vintages among the wines of Burgundy intended to analyze the relative strengths and weaknesses of each harvest without attempting to rank them with points or symbols indicating degrees of merit. Our evaluations were influenced by writers, such as Jacky Rigaux (*Millésimes en Bourgogne 1846-2006*) and Armando Castagno (*Borgogna, le vigne della Côte d'Or*), whose works are much more systematic and detailed than ours—we recommend them to readers in search of in-depth knowledge. We have endeavored to describe the significant features of recent vintages with solid information rather than hasty judgments. Our profiles of the last 25 vintages include references to confirmed critical analyses mixed with our notes on direct tasting experiences, resulting in evaluations that are not always necessarily in line with the officially accepted versions. By omitting any reference to the first half of the twentieth century, we have limited ourselves to a stringent selection of only memorable vintages from the post-war period to the end of the 1980s.

2016-1991

2016 Decimated but promising

The year began with mild weather; average temperatures over the winter of 2015/2016 made it the least rigid on record since 1900. The cold arrived late in the season, on the nights of April 26 and 27, in the most devastating spring frost since 1981 and a memorable blow to Burgundy's *vignerons*. Crop losses reached peaks of 80% in places, though none of the region's vineyards was spared, from Mâcon to Chablis. Summer brought more problems with attacks of peronospora so severe that many producers regularly committed to organic cultivation had to abandon the certification and resort to conventional treatments to deal with the malady. Then, in mid-July, a radical change occurred with the arrival of a high-pressure system bringing warmer temperatures and constant ventilation, a delayed blessing for the hard-hit vineyards. Thanks to a sunny September, the few grapes left on the vines ripened completely for the harvest that began on September 20. Although the crop was ridiculously reduced, among the scarcest of the last half century, the vintage was not to be neglected. Early tastings revealed wines of svelte grace, brimming with the fresh flavors of unexpectedly pure fruit. We would not be surprised to see some of the reds of 2016 arrive at the levels of the best vintages described in this chapter.

2015 Concentrated but not heavy

The relatively warm and damp winter was followed by a normal spring, despite early flowering, which, however, is in line with trends of the last two decades years. The summer was very hot with high temperatures from the end of June through most of July, peaking at around 40°C. Limited fluctuations in day-night temperatures, rare at these latitudes, meant that many nights the thermometer did not drop below 30°C. To see the glass as half full, the heat made vineyard treatments and pest control easier. The first half of August was marked by some light rain and normal temperatures until the harvest, which began in early September with only one report of hail damage (at Chablis, on August 31). Unlike in the previous torrid year of 2003, ripening of grapes was fairly even, without arrested vegetation or problems of "cooked" grapes, permitting many *domaines* to vinify the bunches with the stems, either entirely or in great measure, even where the practice is not usual. The media hype heralding the release of this vintage, billed as exceptional even before the harvest, conditioned us to approach it with more than a little caution. But our fear of overblown and monotonous wines, as was the case in 2009, gradually faded during our tasting trips, especially in recent months. Tastings that have underlined the quality of the reds, ripe and ready, concentrated and velvety, but able to integrate the density of the material with qualities of plasticity and sweet savory balance. The whites, as is inevitable in generous vintages like this, lose in terms of momentum and freshness what they gain in terms of sweetness and weight, thereby reflecting the variability of *terroirs* as well as the sensitivity of *vignerons*. But here too there is no shortage of pleasant surprises.

2014 Classic

The vintage was marked by significant climatic inconsistencies, which can be considered in distinct time frames. The first applies to a warm early spring, a natural continuation of an equally mild winter, as budding began in the first days of April. In the following weeks, above average temperatures and almost no rainfall culminated in the violent storms of early summer and the disastrous hail of June 28 that struck the Côte de Beaune for the third year in a row. Summer brought a drastic change of course, with continuous rains and temperatures well below average through July and August, especially in August, when the dreaded *drosophila suzukii*, a new and insidious parasite that infests grapes during the ripening stage, arrived in Burgundy. A sunny and warm September helped limit the damage, thanks to the always welcome north winds. The harvest in the Côte de Beaune started on September 12, followed days later in the Côte de Nuits.

Though interrupted by thunderstorms, the harvest continued with little difficulty to conclude around September 26. With all due caution considering the vicissitudes of weather, we'd like to underline the success of a vintage that produced red wines that are fresh, fragrant, exemplifying seductive elegance in a classic mold. As for white wines, if possible, the level is even higher: tense and streamlined in the best interpretations of leading *terroirs*, they are rich in energy and aromatic complexity, destined to stand tall for decades.

2013 Late and cool

An irregular vintage to be evaluated on a case-by-case basis, practically vineyard by vineyard. The vegetative cycle got off to a late start due to a cold winter and spring rainfall that was well above the seasonal average. Flowering began on June 20, more than a month later than in 2007 and 2011. Summer weather provided a bit of everything, with intense heat often interspersed with violent storms and hail, which on July 23 devastated the vineyards of the entire Côte de Beaune. The harvest began at the end of September and continued in the Côte de Nuits until mid-October. To liken the 2013 vintage to other high profile late harvests (1978, 1964, 1961) may be stretching a bit, though it is not uncommon to come across fascinating wines, especially among the reds. Particularly striking are the subtle but pure aromatic tones, the citrus-like acidic freshness and the fragrant juiciness of the fruit.

2012 Between highs and lows

The fluctuating climatic phenomena of the year brought about equally irregular results, which Armando Castagno described as "the most diverse among whites and reds of the last 20 years at least." Weather reports read like battlefield bulletins: a wave of frost in February, almost summery temperatures in March, cold and rain in April and May, nice weather in June but with an irregular flowering, summer storms in various parts of the region, but most violent in the Côte de Beaune (hailstorms at Meursault and Puligny). The *vignerons*, forced to defend their vineyards from attacks of peronospora and oidium, had no respite until the harvest began on September 19. Yields were low, but grapes were generally healthy with thick skins, factors that saved the vintage, especially for red wines, which tend to be round, smooth and soothing. White wines were less successful on the whole, often lacking in vibrancy and freshness.

2011 Incomplete

The vegetative cycle got off to an early start, due to hot, dry weather in April with flowering well ahead of normal. But July brought an abrupt turnaround, with below-average temperatures and humidity that favored the formation of mold, without, however, slowing the precocious process of ripening. The harvest, begun at the end of August, was among the earliest in history. The resulting red wines generally lack appeal, short on charm and limited in aging potential. White wines, if flavorful, lack zesty acidity yet show a certain warmth and energy though little complexity.

2010 A Favorite

Anticipated by one of the most severe frosts of recent decades (the night of December 19, 2009, the temperature dropped in a few hours to -18°C), the vintage season continued to undergo setbacks: the difficult flowering and subsequent onset of *millerandage* (in which grapes of differing size and ripeness develop in sparse bunches) affected a harvest that was 30% lower than average in volume. Still, despite an unusually cool and damp August, *millerandage* favored full ripening of grapes, which arrived in the cellars with good concentrations of color, acidity and sugars, as well as an ideal skin to pulp ratio. Prolonged malolactic fermentations, especially among reds, translated into wines of crisply fruity freshness and juiciness while allowing the distinctive character of the different *climats* to emerge in a clear and legible way. Many *vignerons* consider 2010 their *millésime du coeur*, among their favorites of a lifetime, for wines of great personality, brimming with nuances and vitality of flavor. We agree.

2009 Sunny and abundant

A hot year, which began with rains that proved invaluable, allowing vineyards to store reserves of water needed to endure an unusually dry summer, especially in July and August. Aubert de Villaine often expounds on the subject of hydro-equilibrium, which "permits the foliar apparatus to play its full role as a *sugar factory*, allowing grapes to reach exceptional maturity." Heat, concentration and alcoholic richness are the special traits of the vintage, which produced highly colored and powerful reds, greeted by critics (especially in the Anglophone sphere) with an enthusiasm that sometimes seems excessive. Certainly the wines show fleshy fruit with soft and sweet tannins and remarkable qualities of fullness and intensity. But wines with these basic assets sometimes seem short in terms of freshness and complexity. Many *vignerons* see a promising future for the wines of 2009, though we've come across a number that have peaked early, entering a lethargic state that could linger. Still, if forgotten in the cellar, in coming years they may perhaps hold pleasant surprises in terms of elegance and flavor.

2008 Uneven but surprising

Marked by a particularly negative summer, with a cold and rainy August and widespread problems of peronospora, oidium and assorted rot (especially in the Côte d'Or). Only in mid-September did sunny weather return in a stable way, reactivating photosynthesis and rewarding those patient *vignerons* who knowingly delayed the harvest until the beginning of October. In 2008, producer intuition played a decisive role in the success of the wines, which in the leading examples (more frequent among whites than reds) convince for freshness and floral notes, in line with the classic style.

2007 Better for whites

Vineyards already verdant in mid-April with very early flowering mark a vintage that started in a similar way to 2003. Then the season changed course and veered toward a summer of humid heat, affected by frequent rains (especially in July) that complicated work in the vineyards as outbreaks of oidium occurred in places. The harvest began in the first days of September and turned out to be uneven in terms of quality. *Vignerons* strived to express the special traits of the different *climats*, using various approaches to capture the character of individual vineyards in what has been called a *millésime de terroir*. Among the whites, marked acidity made them seem a bit rigid at first, but many are showing surprising freshness and aromatic distinction. The reds also show aromatic attributes, though they tend to be a bit lean and fleeting.

2006 Very good at Chambolle-Musigny

Despite a cold winter, with half a meter of snow at the end of February, a very rainy March and rather unstable weather in early spring, the vineyards benefited from a start of flowering in almost summer conditions. From May to July it was decidedly hot, then August was cool and rainy. The harvest started in mid-September in the Côte de Beaune and about a week later in the Côte de Nuits. The best reds show a delicate style and silky texture, a certain sensuality that convinced Jacky Rigaux to classify the vintage as uniquely great. We are by instinct more cautious. If the virtues of expressiveness and territorial identity are by no means lacking in the reds of Chambolle-Musigny, the overall picture appears more divergent, with problems of botrytis and overripe grapes evident here and there.

2005 Uniformly excellent

The vegetative cycle progressed in an exemplary way: temperatures always in the norm, opportune rainfall and essential thermal excursions leading up to the harvest, which started on September 12 in the Côte de Beaune and September 17 in the Côte de Nuits. The condition of the grapes approached perfection, with thick skins and well-leached seeds. In emphasizing the complexity of wines, Jacky Rigaux has repeatedly praised their consistency: "the texture is of great class, with beautiful *souplesse* and notable viscosity." Thirteen years later, we'd found that the alcoholic vigor in whites tends to upset structural equilibrium subduing a bit of polish in flavor. Reds continue an upward course among wines that opened slowly to epicurean maturity from a vintage in which differences in *climats*, and the hand of the winemaker, are less evident than the overall character of the vintage. As Armando Castagno points out: "everything is very good, and all quite similar."

2004 Controversial

The start of the season was very regular, promising a classic vintage, at least until late July. But in August expectations were shattered, as violent thunderstorms swept the region, accompanied by devastating hail in the Côte de Beaune (especially on August 27). Attacks of oidium, mold and rot were not long in coming, necessitating vineyard treatments, canopy pruning and leaf thinning to let sunshine do its part (in the first ten days of September grapes gained over two degrees in potential alcohol). The harvest began around September 20, resulting in wines that are often marked by vegetal flavors. On average, whites are better than reds, but finding wines of satisfactory quality is a challenge.

2003 Torrid

The summer of 2003 will be remembered in Europe, without a shadow of doubt, as one of the hottest and driest of recent times. In Burgundy the season broke all records in terms of precociousness, aridity, luminosity and temperature, recording in August some ten straight days with highs around 40°C. In such extreme conditions, with a serious water deficit (about 40% less rain than an average vintage), only shrewd vineyard management and smart choices of harvest times could guarantee appreciable results. The harvest began in the Côte d'Or on August 19, consecrating the radical nature of the vintage, with rather low yields and irregular quality.

though with more favorable results in wines from older vines and from *vignerons* who chose to wait. From the vantage point of his 80 years, Henri Jayer counseled calm and patience, pointing out that physiological maturity could never have been reached before the beginning of September. As Jacky Rigaux reminds us, he was right this time too. The whites, often acidified, are generally high in alcohol and not very impressive. Better the reds: although atypical and early maturing, in some cases they show surprising tenacity.

2002 Splendid in the Côte de Nuits

Summer climate trends, decidedly capricious in other parts of Europe, spared Burgundy, where unstable weather arrived in September but without trauma. A couple of weeks of north winds swept away humidity from isolated thunderstorms, avoiding attacks of *pourriture grise* in the vineyards. The harvest, starting on September 16, was sunny with fermentations that guaranteed slow and balanced refinement of wines, favoring aromatic complexity (especially to the north of Corton, in the Côte de Nuits, where they often show spicy verve and purity of fruit) and considerable aging potential. While Italians were licking their wounds over a rainy harvest, Burgundians were "licking their mustaches" over what they'd already proclaimed the vintage of the century.

2001 Autumnal

After a wet winter, a cold spring culminated in the frost of April 14. Climate trends remained cooler than seasonal averages until mid-July, when intense heat brought with it thunderstorms and hail (on August 2 and 3) particularly harmful in Pommard and Volnay. Cool, sunny weather helped avoid mold, but alcohol levels remained low as the harvest began with some hesitation on September 17 (most *vignerons* waited a few more days). Vosne and Gevrey reached peaks of excellence, but quality was mixed south of Beaune in a vintage that does not shine due to a lack of tannic finesse in wines that often show an austere and "autumnal" profile.

2000 Alternating currents

The season was marked by a mild winter and a warm, dry spring, resulting in very early and rapid flowering. But summer progressed under alternating currents: a splendid June followed by a stormy July followed by a warm and sunny August followed by a stormy September with floods in the Côte de Beaune on September 12. Quality was generally superior in the Côte de Nuits, more diluted south of Beaune in wines of a gentle, almost "loving" nature, seductively ready to drink.

1999 Reassuring

Often classified among exceptional years, the vintage combined quality and quantity even more convincingly than in 1996. The winter was mild with a bit of rain and some frost in January. A hot spring accelerated the vegetative exuberance leading up to an abundant harvest, which began in mid-September. In the best cases, reds are colored and fleshy, rounded with "dark fruit" vitally intact. Certain Grand Crus show tannins of rare finesse to the delight of collectors, the most expert of whom insist that many of them are worth a still longer wait.

1998 Whites to avoid

The vintage is remembered for a particularly dry trend, with temperatures in May reaching up to 30°C, though the real problems came in August with peaks of 40°C, causing evident "cooking" of the grapes during ripening (especially Chardonnay). Rains in early September caused mold, but the harvest, which began on September 17, was fortunately distinguished by warm and windy weather. The results prompted Jacky Rigaux to describe it as a "*millésime de vigneron*" while pointing to important differences between one *domaine* and another. Armando Castagno was less diplomatic, likening the whites to "punch drunk boxers" while tending to save only the reds of the best Grand Crus.

1997 Precociously mature

After an irregular flowering, frequent summer thunderstorms lowered temperatures until late July, slowing vegetation. Then in mid-August heat gained the upper hand, with peaks of up to 36°C, as grapes ripened in an uneven pattern throughout the Côte d'Or. The harvest, which began around September 10, rewarded those who were able to wait. Between September 12 and 18 alcohol levels gained a full degree. The quality of wines reflects the irregularity of the vintage in reds of rather dull character with low acidity (big Italian red wines such as Barolo and Brunello 1997 often suffered from similar problems).

1996 Wait (and hope)

Greeted at the beginning as an exceptional year, 1996 combines quality and quantity. A regular flowering and a dry summer (just a few thunderstorms in late August) allowed the grapes to arrive at harvest in excellent condition, thanks also to the benefits of constant north winds in September, which helped maintain high levels of malic acid. In short, an abundant harvest that compelled everyone to make choices

Among the whites there is no shortage of peaks of excellence, though among reds, to be honest, maybe we expected something more. They tended to close early and remain in many cases still marked by sharp acidity and hard edges slow to smoothen.

1995 Scarse but vital

A year of unstable weather and irregular and difficult flowering has been linked above all to the phenomenon of *millerandage*. Instability continued through the summer, drastically cutting yields but not causing mold leading up to the harvest. Wines emerged tannic and svelte with excellent aromatic qualities, as often happens in the vintages marked by millerandage (1947, 1969, 1978, 1988, 2010). If lacking the structure and three-dimensional assets of exceptional vintages, wines show fine balance between *souplesse* and aromatic complexity, a vitality that explains their appeal to those seeking high quality at less than great vintage prices, also among the whites.

1994 Mediocre

The early spring was interrupted by a freeze on the night of April 14-15, which partly spared the Côte d'Or but caused serious damage in Chablis. What spoiled the vintage, however, was the incessant rain between late August and early September. Despite painstaking selection during the harvest (the so-called *tables de tri* sorting counters were not yet widespread), the vintage retains a fragile image, with wines lacking complexity.

1993 Richly colored and lively

The season was marked by extreme changes in weather. Early May was very rainy, late May and the entire month of June very hot, though spotted with thunderstorms, culminating on July 1 with a particularly harmful hailstorm in the area of Nuits-Saint-Georges. The humid heat of early July continued in August with a crescendo of temperatures that eventually brought ripening to a halt. A short spell of rain at the beginning of September revived the vineyards and saved the harvest, which began in mid month, with high levels of quality. Especially among reds, which are richly colored and tannic due to exceptionally thick grape skins. In the best of cases, the aromatic vitality is still lively and the fruit intact.

1992 First-class whites

Winter and spring were marked by well above average temperatures. Then came a rainy July followed by a hot August that averted problems with mold. The harvest began on September 12 under a radiant sun. The best examples among the reds might be described as enjoyable *vins de plaisir*, though low acidity and a lack of balance between grape skins and pulp restrained the extractions necessary for the decisive flavors that only a few wines showed. On the other hand, everyone agreed about the excellent quality of whites that have maintained their impressive class for over twenty years. With a little luck you might still uncork some gem of harmony and elegance.

1991 Underrated

A light frost in late April and cool, dry weather in May were followed by a largely sunny summer, marred by a hailstorm on August 22 which caused serious damage in several parts of the Côte de Nuits, halving the crop at Chambolle and Morey. The harvest began on September 28 in optimal conditions, but, in the opinion of Jacky Rigaux too many *domaines* vinified pushing for heavy extraction to build body in the reds. In the best cases, however, the wines combined freshness and complexity with a taut tannic set of a certain severity. Taken as a whole, the vintage was decidedly underrated.

1990-1947: THE BEST VINTAGES

1990 Velvety, long-lived reds

A mild winter and early spring were followed by a very hot, dry July. Rains arrived in the last days of August to accelerate ripening in the stable conditions that remained through the harvest, which began on September 20. Wines were naturally high in alcohol, but in balance with sustained acidity. Still, many *vignerons* have confessed a regret for not having imposed lower yields. Though whites could not always equal the considerable complexity of 1989, the Côte de Beaune produced fascinating reds that are highly sought after today: certain Volnays of extraordinary *souplesse*, or certain powerful and expressive Pommards. Almost all the Grand Crus are quoted at astronomical prices.

1989 Seductive

The frosts of late April involved most of Burgundy, while sparing the Côte d'Or. Then a sunny summer led up to the harvest around mid-September when quantity and quality went hand in hand. Healthy and abundant grapes produced wines of fascinating aromatic amplitude, centered on ripe and creamy fruit, in reds of sensual but brilliant softness.

1978 Extraordinary reds

The season got off to a late start in terms of flowering in an unstable spring and a cool summer with little sunshine through June and July until mid-August. The harvest was redeemed by a simply perfect September with ten hours of sunshine a day and winds from the north to ensure healthy grapes. Yields were very low (around 20 hl of wine per hectare) in a decidedly late harvest, starting around October 5. Henri Jayer confessed a particular weakness for 1978, according to Jacky Rigaux, who writes that his Cros Parantoux still reveals "an unfathomable complexity."

1969 Solid

A late harvest, marked by a capricious spring and dry summer, which caused problems in many vineyards. The rains arrived close to the harvest (started on October 7) and marked a positive turning point beyond all expectations. Thanks to firm and dense tannins, the best reds will soon reach a half century with a surprising integrity of longevity.

1961 Austere and vigorous

A mild spring, with precocious vegetation, was followed by a cool and variable season, causing problems of flowering and frequent attacks of *millerandage*. This natural limitation of yields put the vines in an ideal condition to face a particularly dry summer, with a slightly delayed harvest (starting September 25). The resulting wines, though austere in flavors and aromas, were vigorous and long-lived, especially in the Côte de Beaune.

1959 Legendary

Conditions were almost ideal: early flowering followed by a summer among the sunniest of the last 60 years in which sparse bunches ripened through a dry July and August, hastened by sporadic rain before the harvest began in mid-September.

The vintage combined quantity with quality—as in other years ending in 9: 1989, 1999, 2009. The best wines are celebrated for their intensity and energy; as Armando Castagno writes: "the trademark of the *millésime* is the amazing gustatory impact of its loftiest examples."

1947 Intense and mature

Climatic conditions were optimal throughout the vegetative cycle, up to the harvest starting in mid-September, with temperatures decidedly above the norm, as in 1959. In certain cases, wines are still in excellent condition, ripe, balanced and surprisingly persistent.

Dominique Lafon | Domaine des Comtes Lafon | Meursault

Vincent Dauvissat | Domaine René et Vincent Dauvissat | Chablis

Christophe Perrot-Minot | Domaine Perrot-Minot | Morey-Saint-Denis

Thierry Pillot | Domaine Paul Pillot | Chassagne-Montrachet

Sylvie Esmonin | Domaine Sylvie Esmonin | Gevrey-Chambertin

Anne Morey | Domaine Pierre Morey | Meursault

Jacques Devauges | Clos de Tart | Morey-Saint-Denis

JEAN-CHARLES DE LA MORINIÈRE | DOMAINE BONNEAU DU MARTRAY | PERNAND-VERGELESSES

Yves Confuron | Domaine Confuron-Cotetidot | Vosne-Romanée

Thomas Bouley | Domaine Jean-Marc et Thomas Bouley | Volnay

Roger Saumaize | Domaine Saumaize-Michelin | Vergisson

Eric de Suremain | Château de Monthélie | Monthélie

Alexandre Bernier | Domaine de la Romanée-Conti | Vosne-Romanée

Montagny les Buxy

VOSNE-ROMANE

Saint-Vincent Tournante 2017 | Mercurey

Lalou-Bize Leroy | Domaine Leroy | Vosne-Romanée

David Duband | Domaine David Duband | Chevannes

Benjamin Leroux | Domaine Benjamin Leroux | Beaune

CHAMBERTIN
CLOS DE BEZE

CLOS
DE
TART
Clos de Tar
GRAND CRU

Juliette e Caroline Chenu | Domaine Louis Chenu Père & Filles | Savigny-les-Beaune

THIERRY VIOLOT-GUILLEMARD | DOMAINE THIERRY VIOLOT-GUILLEMARD | POMMARD

Cyprien Arlaud | Domaine Arlaud | Morey-Saint-Denis

Chantal Remy | Domaine Chantal Remy | Morey-Saint-Denis

Jean-Baptiste Bouzereau | Domaine Michel Bouzereau & Fils | Meursault

Laurent Ponsot | Domaine Ponsot | Morey-Saint-Denis

Thierry Matrot | Thierry et Pascale Matrot | Meursault

Frédéric Mugnier | Domaine Jacques-Frédéric Mugnier | Chambolle-Musigny

THE CLASSIFICATIONS: APPELLATIONS, DOMAINES AND WINES

THE CLASSIFICATION OF WINES AND THE SYSTEM OF APPELLATIONS

The qualitative differentiation between Burgundy's vineyards, already well known to the monks in the late Middle Ages, gained prominence during the eighteenth century with the developing activity of wine merchants and the growing interest of the haute bourgeoisie in purchasing vineyard parcels. In the nineteenth century the tendency was translated into the first attempts at classification, conducted by Denis Morelot, in his *Statistique de la Vigne dans le Département de la Côte d'Or* (Dijon, 1831), and by Jules Lavalle, in his pioneering work of 1855, *Histoire et Statistique de la Vigne et des Grands Vins de la Côte d'Or*. The work of these precursors, who elaborated on the notion of *Tête de Cuvée* as the forerunner of the modern concept of Grand Cru, inspired the first official classification attempt, published in 1861, by the *Comité de l'Agriculture de l'Arrondissement de Beaune*. That classification, though patchy and incomplete, rated the vineyards in three categories with different colored codes (pink for first class, yellow for second and green for third). Not until the first decades of the twentieth century was a register of geographic boundaries instituted, paving the way for the introduction of the laws of *Appellation d'Origine Contrôlée* (1935). The aim of controlling and protecting wine production from fraud and illegal shortcuts was right on target. By 1939, due to the introduction of more stringent and binding rules, only 3 million hectoliters of wine were declared as AOC, compared to the 15 million hectoliters of five years earlier.

The classification system is today manifested in the structure of a pyramid of four distinct levels. The lowest is the *appellation régionale* of Bourgogne, which is not in fact a single *appellation* but a fragmented range of as many as 23 different regional denominations, covering more than half of the wines produced in Burgundy. The generic regional name sometimes adds the name of the vine variety, as in the case of Bourgogne Pinot Noir, Bourgogne Chardonnay, Bourgogne Aligoté. These are the base wines, the entry labels in the winery lists, realized under codes that allow higher yields per hectare and less binding production regulations for grapes that often come from lesser vineyards and/or younger vines. It would be useless to look for much finesse or complexity in such wines, but they do often provide enjoyable bottles at competitive prices. Speaking of enjoyment, Bourgogne Passetoutgrain is distinguished in the regional context. A wine rooted in the country tradition, the result of an uncustomary assemblage of Pinot Noir (minimum one third) and Gamay (maximum two thirds), the name suggests "pass all the grapes" which in Pinot country seems a concession to Gamay.

Two regional denominations, Hautes Côtes de Nuits and Hautes Côtes de Beaune, which come from a large hilly area to the west of the Côte d'Or, clearly deserve special consideration, so we decided to devote a section to them (see Page 269).

In 2017, the new *appellation* of Bourgogne Côte d'Or was launched to apply only to wines, both white and red, produced in the 40 communities between Dijon and Maranges. As a regional *appellation*, it allows higher grape yields per hectare than for wines classified above it on the pyramid.

The next level up is the Villages *appellation*, which applies to wines from vineyards within specific communities regulated by more restrictive rules of production. Burgundy's 44 Villages *appellations* produce more than a third of the region's wine. The level of quality is obviously more consistent and closely controlled since every communal *appellation* has a local identity. Some labels refer to a *lieu-dit*, or the name of a specific vineyard plot that has been historically recognized and categorized on land-registry maps. To be clear, this further geographical specification doesn't certify higher quality, but only indicates with greater precision the location of the single vineyard of origin. Therefore, in the large range of Villages *appellations* some wines may come from a single vineyard and others from an assemblage of grapes from different *lieux-dits* of the same community. Here are a couple of examples: in the only Gevrey-Chambertin Villages produced by Claude Dugat, the grapes of fifteen different parcels in community's territory converge; on the other hand, Jean-Marc Roulot harvested, vinified and bottled separately his five different Villages of Meursault, with five different labels referring to their respective *lieux-dits* (Tessons, Tillets, Meix-Chavaux, Vireuils and Luchets).

In such a large field of wines, there is room for some of mediocre quality and others of exemplary local character, with appropriate variations in terms of price. For example, it is by no means rare to buy excellent bottles of Villages wine for around 20 euro at the cellars, where, for a bottle of the Vosne Romanée Clos Goillotte of Prieuré-Roch, as for the Meursault La Sève du Clos of Arnaud Ente, the price is much higher (provided you can find them) often arriving at the level of a good, if not great, Grand Cru. An original extension of the Villages category is found in Chablis, where, in 1944, the AOC Petit-Chablis was created as a singular hybridization between the regional and communal levels of denominations, not all that difficult to understand (see Page 124).
The top two levels of the pyramid apply to *appellations* for *climats* of superior quality: Premier Cru and Grand Cru. Premier Cru signifies added value in terms of the quality of a wine by going beyond the communal reference to single out individual *climats*. The list of Premier Crus in Burgundy takes in 640 *climats*, in terrains extending from Chablis to Montagny (but soon to include Fuissé), that account for 10% of the wine produced in Burgundy. Labels usually indicate the name of the community followed by the name of the *climat* classified as Premier Cru (for example, Chablis Premier Cru Montmains, Pommard Premier Cru Les Pézerolles). In some cases, though, Premier Cru will name the community but not the vineyard, indicating that the wine came from grapes grown in two or more *climats* classified as Premier Cru.
The Premier Cru classification was not designated in the *appellations* legislation of 1935, but was instituted during the war (in 1942) when a specially established commission identified a first selection. This followed an agreement with the German occupiers, who agreed to not requisition vineyards with the status of Cru. This background helps to explain a certain disparity in the validity of the sites. If some Premier Crus have nothing to envy of a theoretically nobler neighboring Grand Cru, others have never produced wines worthy of special recognition. This disparity is also reflected in prices, with no shortage of examples. If the Chambolle-Musigny Premier Cru Les Amoureuses can be worth as much as or more than a Grand Cru, the Chambolle-Musigny Premier Cru Les Plantes often shows the simplicity of a Villages. Other highly esteemed Premier Crus include Vaulorent at Chablis, Clos Saint-Jacques at Gevrey, Les Saint-Georges at Nuits, Les Rugiens at Pommard, Les Perrières at Meursault. All seem to have the special attributes worthy of recognition as Grand Cru. And it is not to be excluded that this could happen in the next few years.
Grand Cru is the summit of Burgundy's classification system: 33 distinct *appellations*, representing only 1.4% of total regional production, for wines that carry the

name of the *climat* of origin on the label. Each is a denomination in its own right, regulated by its own production code, distinguished by the singular character of its *terroir*. The resulting wines are almost always more complex and long-lived than others of the same community, sometimes even among the most fascinating of all wines. A complex fusion of factors linked to tradition, the market and local policies lies at the base of the selections, which, on the one hand, guarantee visibility and prestige to all the wines of Burgundy, but, on the other, are the subject of endless discussions and doubts. And that's as it should be. When praise becomes so hyperbolic and prices so demanding—if not indeed prohibitive—it seems legitimate to demand greater consistency at all levels of production. Still, it would be naïve to expect fundamental consistency in the variegated repertoire of Grand Cru in light of such considerations as the following. Vineyards may be enormous or minuscule, ranging from the 160 hectares of Corton to scarcely a hectare of Romanée. Official registries reached by unanimous consent may be pervaded by last-minute additions raising reservations and doubts. Some properties have been monopolized for centuries by a single lineage of owners, others are broken up into dozens of micro-parcels. Such disparities and asymmetries somehow enhance the fascination of the Burgundy of wine, highly structured as it is yet subject to conflicting interpretations, strictly regulated as it is by a hierarchical pyramid structure that the most savvy of critics, as well as the most naïve of wine buffs, can redesign every vintage with their personal classifications.

HOW TO EVALUATE OUR SELECTIONS
ADVICE FOR READERS AND NAVIGATORS

The following sections comprise a selection of 200 *domaines* and nearly 800 wines of Burgundy, a *tour de force* that begins at Chablis, the northernmost zone, and winds up in the Mâconnais, more than 200 kilometers to the south. How did we proceed? What criteria did we follow? It's not easy to sum it all up in a few words. For a start we reassessed the selections made in the previous edition of this book, published in Italian in 2012. That fortuitous edition exhausted its modest print run of three thousand copies in less than two years, thanks to a fascination with Burgundy among Italians that shows no sign of abating. We promoted the book through a stimulating tour of Italy that took in some fifty meetings and tastings in various places as far south as Scicli in Sicily. These gatherings gave us a chance to meet our readers and consider their impressions, their comments, criticisms and suggestions that have proved essential in inspiring this new edition. A new edition not limited to Italian this time, but translated into English for readers in countries where the fascination with Burgundy seems every bit as keen as it is in Italy. Being well aware of the numerous books on Burgundy published in English, our aim is not so much to compete as to complement with observations, judgments and insights that provide different, but we hope equally valid, points of view.
We arrived at the 2016 session of the *Grands Jours de Bourgogne*, Burgundy's annual rendezvous for wine professionals, charged with new ideas to apply to a more extensive and complete second edition no longer focused on the Côte d'Or alone.

During that whirlwind week of tastings, this volume began to take shape, though its completion turned out to be more complicated than expected, taking almost two years. As often happens, we wanted to "save both the goat and the cabbage," as we say in Italian: to preserve and enhance the intuitive inspiration of the first book while enlarging the framework of the second to take in the region as a whole. Once again, we were supported by the *Bureau Interprofessionnel des Vins de Bourgogne* (BIVB), which provided its headquarters, in the *École des vins de Bourgogne* in Beaune, to hold precious comparative tastings. The evidence gathered there turned into a challenge: so many new tasting samples to check out through visits to numerous *domaines* still outside our radar to better understand their projects and their styles.

Then came the most demanding phase, or perhaps most regimented is the better term: six weeks in Burgundy, split into three intervals between the end of November 2016 and the beginning of spring 2017. Weeks crammed with visits to wineries and comparative tastings (about three thousand), interviews with the *vignerons*, during which the contours of the new work became better defined and the selections more focused.

That's how we came to select the 200 wineries that follow, as well as the nearly 800 wines that we venture here to describe, interpret, recommend. Not all with the same emphasis, of course. Some wines are more expressive and others more reticent, some more emotive and others more cerebral, some vibrantly local (many) and others attractive mainly for their packaging (not many). Similar comparisons can be applied to the *vignerons*: some more scientific and others more sanguine, some worldly and others ascetic, the evergreen and the emerging, the sacred monsters and the outsiders. Without establishing any specific criteria of merit, let alone resorting to the shortcut of point ratings, we've aspired through our writing to address the (irrepressible) need for evaluating differences and indicating similarities. Above all, we've tried to capture the specific expressiveness of the wines as they relate to the different *climats* of origin, a bond that in some cases is solid and precise and in others rather weak and unconvincing. In an attempt to give shape to a book, even more than a guide, we decided to provide only the indispensable information of each *domaine* (name, address, contacts) thus avoiding accumulations of symbols, asterisks or ad hoc notes. We also decided to avoid the rigid scheme of devoting one page to each winery and instead evaluated on a case by case basis the space to be allocated to each *domaine*. These evaluations were based more on our perception of the quality of wines tasted than on the historical prestige of the cellars, or the established reputations of the *vignerons*. We have placed our faith in those cellars where the expressiveness of the wines particularly

impressed us, thereby forming our own critical perspective, not without some risks, often straying from the established paths of the wine trade press.
The elaboration of this book coincided with extensive tastings of wines from the felicitous vintage of 2015. The bountiful reserves of this sunny and precocious harvest provided us with a major share of wines selected. Still, due to the timing of our tastings as well as to producers' wishes, we also reviewed numerous wines from 2014, a vintage enshrined as a Burgundian "classic" of which we've become very fond. During a couple of Burgundy blitzes in the summer of 2017, we had the opportunity to taste and admire wines of 2016, a harvest decimated in quantity due to extremely bizarre weather, but on whose quality we are solidly inclined to place bets.

With these extensive prerequisites behind us, it seems opportune to offer some advice to readers and potential navigators on how to confront the main body of the text.
The course through Burgundy's *appellations* follows a north-south direction with stops along the way at 13 enclaves to consider the *domaines* and wines of areas grouped following a criterion of territorial continuity and not of similarities between the wines. For example, the first of the 13 enclaves covers Chablis alone; the second groups Marsannay, Fixin and Gevrey-Chambertin; the next Morey-Saint-Denis and Chambolle-Musigny; and so on to a final destination of the entire Mâconnais. Each grouping is introduced by a summary of the salient features of the vineyard landscape of each *appellation* and a page reference to the incomparable color maps of Sylvain Pitiot and Jean-Charles Servant. Then we get to the essence of our quest with notes on each *domaine*, its proprietors and its wines. In each block of texts we have included those *domaines* that have cellars in the area as the company headquarters. As will be seen, certain companies in certain areas also own the bulk of the vineyard parcels, as reflected in their lines of wines. Under each *domaine*, the sequence of wines reviewed normally follows an order starting with the simplest of Bourgogne *appellations* and gradually moving up to eventual Grand Crus, as experienced during our visits. Unfortunately, there is no guarantee that wines will be available for purchase at the cellars. Indeed, the more the *domaine* is noted for quality the less the chance that its wines will be available. Since this is a critical issue, and often the cause of frustrated experiences, we repeat our advice to always call ahead to book a visit, perhaps stating your expectations and crossing your fingers. Bon voyage!

1

CHABLIS

CHABLIS

map *page* 500

Chablis and its territory comprise the most important wine district of northern Burgundy. The nucleus of vineyards covers more than 5,300 hectares, entirely dedicated to Chardonnay for one of the most admired and imitated of the world's white wines. This part of Burgundy is close to the northern limit of vine cultivation, so terrain is of primary importance: the geography and, even more, the geology of the place, essential not only to the expression of the wine's authenticity, but also to understanding the classification system that regulates production.

The landscape of Chablis is defined by a system of sinuous valleys situated on both sides of the Serein river. Here vineyards are planted on terrains with rather uniform and regular geological stratifications: the distinctive element is gray Kimmeridgian marl, found in varying formations which account for the peculiar calcareous aspects of the different soils. In the southern part, for example, there is a strong presence of Tonnerre chalky limestone. In the northern quadrant gray marls alternate with calcareous shoals rich in fossils of small oysters known as *Exogyra virgula*, as well as other seashells (*calcare à astartes*). Climbing slightly in altitude, to plateaus ranging between 150 and 230 meters of altitude, the geological substratum changes sharply, revealing more recent formations dating back to the so-called Portlandian period. There the calcareous quota increases in soils that are more burnished and hard, compact and uniform, meaning that wines from there tend to be rather simple and monotonous by nature

On these Portlandian soils are planted the vineyards of the Petit Chablis *appellation*: about a thousand hectares of Chardonnay destined for light and fruity wines of refreshing simplicity, accounting for almost 20% of the total production of Chablis. These wines play an important role in bringing consumers closer to the *chablisien* typology, proving that wines of Chablis can be accessible in terms of both flavor and price. It's worth noting that the Petit Chablis *appellation* was launched toward the end of World War II (1944) to boost the disastrous financial situation of local winemakers. In the best cases, Petit Chablis can offer the quality of Village-level wines at *appellation* Bourgogne prices, although the contrary is quite often true.

A major share of the *vignoble chablisien* is occupied by vineyards for wines of the next level up on the pyramid: the generic *appellation* Chablis, equivalent to the Villages designation used elsewhere in Burgundy. (Chablis Premier Cru and Grand Cru are the two higher levels). Produced in all of the zone's communities, in extremely diverse locations and exposures, Chablis AOC occupies two thirds of the vineyard area, for an extension of about 3,500 hectares. The landscape is too vast and varied to be able to discern effective distinctions. The enlargement of the surface area, in 1978, has favored the production of wines that reflect even less the special features of the various *climats*, while Chablis has become, in a sense, the victim of its own commercial success. Success which has certainly aided the local economy, ensuring more widespread prosperity, but which has also triggered the dynamics of industrial production in the massive use of chemicals in vineyards, the mechanization of harvesting, the preponderance of stainless steel tanks, as well as the adoption of expeditious winemaking techniques designed to speed up production in response to ever-increasing demand. Unfortunately, all of these factors have standardized the quality of Chablis AOC at more common and predictable levels, while inevitably blurring the wine's image.

To find credible guarantees of craftsmanship and *terroir*, we need to move up a level to Chablis Premier Cru, an *appellation* comprised of almost 800 hectares of vineyards, equal to about 15% of the total area under vine in Chablis. These vineyards are divided into 17 *climats*, each of which is split into a total of 79 *lieux-dits*. The Premier Cru vineyards of Chablis are situated along both sides of the river Serein. Along the left bank wines are noted for finesse and elegance, as in the whites of Vaillons, as well as the mineral complexity of Montmains, especially notable in the *lieu-dit* Les Fôrets. Along the right bank of the Serein, wines often emerge with more energetic and fruity character, with outstanding exceptions in the elegant wines of Monteé de Tonnerre, as well as in the best expressions of Fourchaume, Vaulorent and Mont de Milieu.

In the end, though, the most authentic versions of Chablis come from the 100 hectares of vineyards classified as Grand Cru. The Grand Cru *appellation* is singular, though it covers seven different *climats* all located on the right bank of the river, northeast of the town. Five of these *climats* were ratified in the 1935 classification (Blanchot, Les Clos, Grenouilles, Valmur and Vaudésir), while Bougros and Les Preuses were added in 1938. It's hard to capture the most interesting elements of the wines in so little space, since they show such distinct individuality. To simplify a bit, Chablis Grand Cru ranges from the solid magnitude of Les Clos, from which the most powerful and long-lasting bottles often come, to the subtle aromatic finesse of Valmur. Between the two extremes, a series of whites is maturing at a marathon pace, some requiring decades to truly express themselves. They hold their initial acidity, which adds tension and vibrancy to a virtuous marriage of fruit and flavors. And with time they acquire volume, in a range of styles that goes from the most soothing grace to the most restless and exhaustive spirit.

Jean-Claude BESSIN

CHABLIS
18, Rue de Chitry - Tel. +33 (0) 3 86 424677
dnejcbessin@gmail.com

12.3 hectares

To a career as an architect, Jean-Claude Bessin preferred the perhaps slightly less geometric calling of *vigneron* and, judging by the results, he seems to have made the right choice. His adventure in the land of Chablis began in 1992, when he decided to take over the twelve hectares of vines owned by his father-in-law, who until then had sold the grapes to a cooperative winery in the area. The value of the vineyards, positioned in some of the best *climats* of the *appellation* (Montmains, La Forêt, Fourchaume and Valmur), along with Jean-Claude's pragmatic rigor have helped to make this risk more calculated. Since then this winery has been quietly producing some of the most convincing and reliable wines of Chablis, reinforced by an artisanal approach that manages to contain the wines' youthful exuberance to then revive it after several years of refinement in bottle as more tense and vital than ever.

Chablis Vieilles Vignes 2015

Four hectares of old vines planted in 1950 and 1974 for the by no means clandestine distribution of about twenty-five thousand bottles. Enjoyment heightened by dynamic flavors.

Chablis 1er Cru La Forêt 2015

Clay soils of iridescent chromatic shadings and stones that drain the terrain give life to a white of bracing saline tones, enlivened by uncompromising nerve.

Chablis 1er Cru La Fourchaume 2015

The fleshy, creamy density of the vintage is invigorated by the flavor tension deriving from Kimmeridgian marl soils to create a captivating dynamic balance.

Chablis Grand Cru Valmur 2015

A Grand Cru distinguished by aromatic qualities and finesse, it strikes the palate in a discreetly easy way to then erupts with fragrant nuances while flaunting surprisingly persistent flavors.

Jean-Marc BROCARD

PRÉHY

3, Route de Chablis - Tel. +33 (0) 3 86 414900
info@brocard.fr | www.brocard.fr

200 hectares

Starting with no vineyards in 1973, Jean-Marc Brocard settled in the village of Préhy, southwest of Chablis and, after marrying the daughter of a *vigneron* from Saint-Bris, began an impressive expansion of his estate. Today he manages an expanse of vineyards covering about 200 hectares total, including his own as well as leased plots and acquisitions from growers. Brocard produces about a million bottles, covering the entire range of northern Burgundy's *appellations*, channeled into a large reserve of connected brands (Domaine Sainte Claire, de la Boissonneuse, des Chenevières, de la Conciergerie and Ronsien) while exporting to more than fifty countries. Yet a visit to the winery will give you reason to reconsider a whole series of clichés and prejudices, including any preconceived notions about the connection between (large) quantity and (poor) quality. Here, instead, there is an effortless harmony between the two, resulting in wines worthy of notice. Since Jean-Marc's retirement his son Julien and his son-in-law Frédéric Gueguen have assumed control. The winegrowing has steadily moved to organic methods, with sixty hectares of certified organic vineyards and forty hectares certified as biodynamic. A ladybug on the label indicates wines produced in this way—wines that never cease to amaze us with their precision and freshness.

Chablis Vieilles Vignes de Sainte-Claire 2015

The company's calling card label comes from seventy-year-old vines and offers a fleshy and sunny white wine, bright and enjoyable

Chablis Premier Cru Vau de Vey 2015

Leaving Chablis in the direction of Auxerre, this *climat* is perched on a steep slope to the left, with full eastern exposure. Here Brocard obtains a surprisingly delicate Chablis, enlivened by a refreshing saline punch.

CHÂTEAU de BÉRU

BÉRU
32, Grande Rue - Tel. +33 (0) 3 86 759043
contact@chateaudeberu.com | www.chateaudeberu.com

15 hectares

After a successful career in the world of finance in Paris, in 2006, Athénaïs de Béru returned to the village that gave its name to her family, a few kilometers east of Chablis. She began gradually to recover vineyards that her father had entrusted in *fermage* for over twenty years, the grapes having been sold in large part to local cooperatives. To reinvent herself as a winemaker, she commuted to Beaune for studies, earning a patent as a professional enologist (BPREA). But her most valuable experience came in the field, with precious advice from friends, such as the *vignerons* Thomas Pico and Alice and Olivier De Moor, as she quickly converted her fifteen hectares of vines to organic cultivation, then, from 2010, to biodynamic. Brilliant and determined, Athénaïs seeks balance but avoids half-measures. She returned to working the land and harvesting only by hand, bringing grapes to the cellars with minimal, but essential precautions, limiting the use of sulfites to racking and bottling, and extending maturation to over twelve months. For this she has been experimenting with recently installed amphorae. The rewards arrived quickly in wines that have nothing to do with the diluted and anonymous whites from high-yield vineyards, but which, on the contrary, are full, engaging and dynamic expressions focused on creamy and delicious fruit. The range is completed by a side activity as a small *négociant* with wines under her "Athénaïs" label, among them a few light and fanciful reds, with the unique stamp of her personality.

Bourgogne Epineuil 2015

The aromatic range of this wine reveals brightly expressive delicacy in a smooth but sumptuous red that highlights the light and inspired hand of Athénaïs even from purchased grapes.

Chablis Clos Béru Monopole 2015

The nucleus of vineyards surrounding the castle is a *clos* of five hectares that benefits from the cool temperatures at around 300 meters of altitude, as well as southern exposure giving vines abundant sunlight. The result is a white wine of enveloping texture, in which the sweetness of the fruit coexists with a trace of chalky minerality that innervates the finish with a lively saline twist.

Chablis Côte aux Prêtres 2015

The sharp flavor tension that animated the 2014 vintage (among the finest ever) returns to the fore even from a more abundant and sunny harvest, lending dynamism to a white that thrives on juicy and appetizing contrasts.

Chablis 1er Cru Vaucoupin 2015

The Béru area has no vineyards classified as Premier Cru, the nearest at that level being in the community of Chichée, a few kilometers to the west toward Chablis. Those vineyards are on the right bank of the Serein, but the wines show traits usually associated with those of the left bank, with crisp acidity and pervading minerality. In Vaucoupin over the last ten years Athénaïs has recovered a small plot of a third of a hectare, situated on a very steep slope and exposed to the east, for a white wine marked by floral, wisteria-like aromatics and remarkable finesse, rich in depth of flavor.

COLINOT

IRANCY

1, Rue des Chariats - Tel. +33 (0) 3 86 423325
vin@irancy-colinot.fr | www.irancy-colinot.fr

13 hectares

In the nebula of little known vineyard areas in the surroundings of Chablis, it is not easy to find cellars that relate the story of their home grounds while offering wines of distinct personality. This *domaine* is a conspicuous exception, with thirteen hectares of vineyards destined for the production of red wines of surprisingly expressive vitality. The company, founded by Jean-Pierre Colinot, a bizarre and comical character who refers to himself as a "volatile viscount," is today run by his daughter Stéphanie, a winemaker with no lack of ideas—or talent—of her own. They enjoy the advantage of having preserved in the vineyards a certain quota of César (present in almost all the blends, never exceeding 10%). This red grape, which lends color to wines, is considered indigenous in the Yonne area, though it is also found in Corsica, where it is known as Niellucciu (*niellu* in Corsican means black). The beauty of the Irancy area, as well as its distinctive wines (and their favorable quality/price ratio) seem to first-rate reasons for a potential detour from the route to Chablis.

Irancy 2015

This is a *cuvée* of very old vines (80 years) with crisp and slightly rustic flavors reminiscent of black-skinned berries, enlivened by a finish of unexpected mint-like freshness.

Irancy Palotte 2015

This vineyard, bordering on the town of Cravant, is exposed to the south. This vintage reveals a certain fullness and a tight tannic grip, though we preferred the 2014 version, which was juicier and played with delicate floral nuances.

Irancy Les Maselots 2015

This emerged in tastings as the most refined and graceful red of the *domaine*: the tannins, although certainly present, are measured and carefully extracted leading to a finish that provides a tasty contrast.

Jean COLLET et fils

CHABLIS

15, Avenue de la liberté - Tel. +33 (0) 3 86 421193
collet.chablis@wanadoo.fr | www.domaine-collet.fr

37 hectares

The quest to profitably combine quantity and quality in wine production is a challenge that involves (and often defeats) a considerable number of winemakers. When you come across one who has beaten the challenge at Chablis, where quantity often gains the upper hand, it seems only natural to acknowledge the success. The Collet family has been registered for wine activities at Chablis since the time of the French Revolution. In 1952, Jean Collet, backed by fifteen hectares of vineyard, began to bottle his entire production. In 1979, he was succeeded by his son Gilles, at a winery that has arrived at almost forty hectares of vineyards for a production that in favorable years reaches 250,000 bottles. Since 2009, with the arrival of young Romain, organic experiments have been started on some parcels and ten hectares have been converted to bio. The wines manage to express the character of the different *climats* while respecting market demands in bottles noted for reliability—and attractive value.

Chablis Les Truffières 2014

This parcel of just over a hectare in the community of Villy was the first to be designated as organic and the only one already certified. Vinification in stainless steel for a wine that is more taut than broad, more vibrant than fruity.

Chablis 1er Cru Montmains 2014

From the left bank of the river Serein comes a wine with scents of white flowers, saline and incisive on the palate, which could bring pleasant surprises after a few years of bottle.

Chablis 1er Cru Montée de Tonnerre 2014

Regularly the most convincing wine of the Collet range, and in this vintage it is right on the mark: citric and saline notes frame well-structured and persistent textures of flavor.

La CROIX MONTJOIE

THAROISEAU
50, Grande Rue - Tel. +33 (0) 3 86 324094
contact@lacroixmontjoie.com | www.lacroixmontjoie.com

11 hectares

If you plan a trip to Burgundy not just to visit wineries and taste wines, but also to discover the beauty of its rural landscape, it would be a shame not to include a visit to the village of Vézelay. It is a small, well-preserved hamlet, which from the top of its hill dominates the valley of the Yonne. The village has witnessed subtle restorations but remains remarkably original, and well off the beaten path. At the heart of the habitat stands the Romanesque basilica of Sainte Marie Madeleine, recognized as a UNESCO world heritage site. In the valley to the east, in a still-intact agricultural setting about three kilometers from Vézelay, the Croix Montjoie *domaine* was established in old farm maintained with respect for every detail. The estate has eleven hectares of vineyards and breathtaking views of the basilica with a sweeping background of the slopes of the Morvan. In 2009, the owners, Sophie Woillez and her husband Matthieu, both agronomists just over forty, moved to Vézelay for a new life adventure. Their range of white wines essentially consists of three labels selected on the basis of different ripening stages of the grapes and of different ages of the vines, rather than on the differences between *climats*.

Bourgogne Vézelay "Impatiente" 2015
Fresh and lively, vitalized by the exchange between fruity pulp and fresh tartness—a carefree white, perfect as an aperitif.

Bourgogne Vézelay "Elégante" 2015
This thirty year-old vineyard and its calcareous soils favor a wine of superior articulation. A quarter of the vinification is completed in *fúts*, which do not diminish its iodized vitality and saline finish.

Bourgogne Vézelay "Voluptueuse" 2015
This wine is made from individually selected parcels, entirely vinified and aged in wood; the oak has yet to be integrated, but the finish shows fair aging potential.

Vincent DAUVISSAT

CHABLIS

8, Rue Emile Zola - Tel. +33 (0) 3 86 421158
dauvissat.vincent@wanadoo.fr

14.5 hectares

After succeeding his father René in 1989, Vincent Dauvissat has been running the family *domaine* for almost thirty years, representing the third generation of *vignerons*. His grandfather Robert started bottling his own wines in 1931 and the reputation of the winery was further enhanced over time, but thanks to Vincent the name Dauvissat has been associated for more than twenty years with the excellence of Chablis, producing some of the most esteemed whites of France. A shy and pragmatic man, Vincent from the start assumed an artisanal approach based on tradition in his quest for high quality grapes through careful manual work and minimal vineyard treatments. Since 2002, the *domaine* has used biodynamic formulations without declaring certification in line with the understated philosophy of the house: severe pruning of vines (which average over fifty years old), and drastically restricting yields, which rarely exceed fifty hectoliters per hectare. In the cellars classical traditions reign supreme: fermentations in used barrels, no *bâtonnage*, decantation and tartrate precipitation due to natural cold, no new barrels for the *élevages*. Thus an enviable endowment of almost fifteen hectares of vines, including two Grand Crus and three Premier Crus, renders wines of rare transparency and expressive purity, but always vibrant and sincere, never lacking tension, and capable of aging very well while expressing with nonchalance extreme precision and stylistic self-awareness.

Petit Chablis 2015

This parcel is almost always the last to be harvested, since it is positioned rather high, above the Grand Cru Les Clos, with which it shares a full southern exposure. The aromatics and articulation are much superior to the *appellation*'s standards.

Chablis 2015

Vital and deep, yet easy to approach, this bottling integrates sweetness of fruit into an amalgam of engaging harmony, light years away from certain lean and austere versions of Chablis.

Chablis 1er Cru Séchet 2015

Coming from well-drained calcareous soils and vinified mainly in 132-liter *feuillettes*, this is a wine of essential quietude. Yet its delicate discretion does not preclude verticality and length on the palate.

Chablis 1er Cru Vaillons 2015

This vast *climat* on the left bank of the Serein is home to the most ample and fleshy wines of the *appellation*. Here too, the palate is enveloping, more broad than tense, but not without energy, with a background of floral aromatics (verbena, resin) and a burst of lime and citrus to stoke the contrast.

Chablis 1er Cru La Forest 2015

This may be Dauvissat's most famous bottling: La Forest is a rich and complete wine, with an elegant bouquet that recalls hawthorn and candied lemon. Flavors are animated by an articulated complexity, able to harmonize a wide and elegant fruit-driven palate with incisive minerality on the finish.

Chablis Grand Cru Les Preuses 2015

The portion of Les Preuses that belongs to the *domaine* is ensconced in the natural amphitheater of Vaudesir, characterized by steep slopes and a sunny exposure to the south. Vincent has crafted a 2015 of almost overflowing aromatic intensity, yet still restrained and not at all open on the palate: true to its Grand Cru status, one can easily imagine a promising long-range evolution.

Chablis Grand Cru Les Clos 2015

In the most extensive and esteemed Grand Cru of Chablis, Dauvissat has a large plot of over one and a half hectares, source of a severe, compact wine, with impressive persistence on the palate. In this embryonic phase, it is not easy to read, being so disinclined toward conventional pleasure. But if you manage to read between the lines you'll find traces of purity among the folds of intensity that proudly proclaim this wine's bright future.

Gérard DUPLESSIS

CHABLIS

5, Quai de Reugny - Tel. +33 (0) 3 86 421035
cavesduplessis@wanadoo.fr | www.chablis-duplessis.com

8 hectares

Lilian Duplessis, who took over the *domaine* from his father Gérard, represents the fifth generation of a family dedicated to viticulture in the Chablis countryside. In the eight hectares of vineyards, divided into twenty different parcels, he has reinforced the winery's commitment to sustainable viticulture with the conversion to organic farming in 2009. In the cellars fermentations are always conducted in stainless steel, without selected yeasts. The Premier Cru and Grand Cru are refined by *élevage en fûts* for a duration that Lilian evaluates on a case-by-case basis. This often results in release on the market later than the average for the *appellation*. The style of the house confirms the sincere and classic minerality on which the excellent reputation of these wines has always relied.

Chablis 2015

Obtained from three portions of a vineyard opposite the Premier Cru Vaillons, this is a white of simple frankness that goes especially well with food.

Chablis 1er Cru Montée de Tonnerre 2015

The gray clays of the soils of these five different parcels enhance the almost chalky mineral stamp that gives the wine its superior driving force.

Chablis Grand Cru Le Clos 2015

Covering just over a third of a hectare, the most important Duplessis vineyard is in the heart of the *climat* of Le Clos, bordering parcels belonging to Raveneau on one side and Dauvissat on the other, in one of the best positions of the entire Grand Cru. From these vines, Lilian creates a rich and raring rendition of a wine that we'd comfortably rate at the very top of the *appellation*.

GOISOT

SAINT BRIS LE VINEUX

30, Rue Bienvenu Martin - Tel. +33 (0) 3 86 533515
www.goisot.fr

26.62 hectares

Jean-Hugues Goisot, his wife Ghislaine and son Guilhem run a vast *domaine* located in the gentle hillsides of Saint-Bris, southeast of Auxerre, in an area rarely visited even by the most erudite of Burgundy lovers. This gives us an excellent opportunity to re-evaluate the wines of *appellations* that are generally marginalized in standard tastings, perhaps because too often wineries in these areas are plagued by excessive yields, even in latitudes where full ripening is never guaranteed. This *domaine* extends over a wide area of twenty-seven hectares of vineyards, of which more than two-thirds are dedicated to white varieties—Chardonnay, Aligoté and Sauvignon—and farmed by certified biodynamic methods. The wide-ranging quality of Goisot's wines is all the more impressive if we consider that these are small denominations, generally little known, and which rarely reach a similar level of expression, maturity, or flexibility, anywhere else.

Bourgogne Côtes d'Auxerre La Ronce 2015

With aeration, the slight aromatic reduction disperses in a generous and tasty wine, poised between fragrant aromatics and pleasant rusticity, with an almost piquant finish.

Saint-Bris Corps de Garde 2015

Made from the Fié Gris variety (better known as Sauvignon Gris), this white wine is focused on the harmonious expression of fruit (citrus, nectarine) and offers a creamy and enveloping palate of long persistence.

Saint-Bris Exogyra Virgula 2015

The aromatic spectrum of this wine is bright and original, light years away from the varietal stereotypes of most raw and aggressive Sauvignon Blancs, marked instead by notes of yellow flowers, resinous propolis and mountain herbs. In the mouth it shifts to a higher gear, with a flash of surprising energy and an incisive lengthening of flavor.

Dominique GRUHIER

EPINEUIL

Rue du Clos de Quincy - Tel. +33 (0) 3 86 553251
vin@bourgognevin.com | www.bourgognevin.com

29 hectares

Less than half an hour's drive from Chablis, Epineuil is the base of Dominique Gruhier's *domaine*, established in the granary of the medieval Abbaye du Petit-Quincy in the late 1980s. He got off to a rocky start, due to a series of unexpected and unfortunate events and the errors of inexperience. "At the time of my first bottling, when the effects of global warming weren't as evident as in recent seasons, the wines had alcoholic gradations that struggled to reach 11°. They were often undrinkable," admits Dominique. In the meantime, a geological era seems to have passed and today the wide range of labels consists of highly recommendable wines. "Saline and chalky, juicy and vivacious," as Becky Wasserman has defined them, highlighting their freshness and sensuality. Success is certainly a result of some on-target advice (from both Benoît Pagot and Philippe Pacalet) but even more a reward of the dedication of Dominique, who recently completed the Ecocert organic certification.

Bourgogne Epineuil 2015

From ten hectares of Pinot Noir vines planted in Kimmeridgian soils, Dominique produces more than 60,000 bottles. In addition to the favorable price, we particularly admired his ability to put the chalky minerality of the soils at the service of lively tart fruit.

Bourgogne Epineuil L'Âme des Dannots 2015

Obtained from grapes that are about 80% destemmed, this wine reveals spherical fruity consistency (raspberry) contrasted by a savory slipstream that lengthens the palate. The transparency, the lightness, the fresh smoothness of the best Pinot Noir of Champagne are recalled here with a supplement of juiciness.

Alice et Olivier de MOOR

COURGIS
4 et 17, Rue Jacques Ferrand - Tel. +33 (0) 3 86 414794
aodemoor@aliceadsl.fr | www.aetodemoor.fr

9.7 hectares

Beyond the numbers—22 harvests, 10 hectares of vines split into 10 different parcels, 3 grape varieties, including Aligoté—Olivier reminds us not to forget that "there are also two children and a cat." Joking aside, this is an important elucidation, since quality of life (both familial and professional) was the original motive for the work of Alice and Olivier de Moor as winemakers. Quality of life also applied to their vineyards, of course, which represented the first real test when they started making wine in the mid-nineties, when the emphasis was still on "winemaking." That is, at a time when many "winemakers" shared the stubbornly myopic conviction that good wines could come from soils rendered sterile by chemical weeding, from grapes harvested by machine and then "adjusted" in the cellars. Turning this approach upside down, De Moor soon became a key point of reference in Chablis for "natural" and organic wine enthusiasts (the *domaine* was certified as organic in 2008). From their perspective, this philosophy coincides with more demanding work in the vineyards, greater selectivity in yields and higher risks in winemaking, without sulfites, stabilization, filtration or shortcuts of any kind. The result is expressed in their original and refreshing whites, tenacious and tasty, showing a fascinating spontaneity, found also in their *négociant* label, Le Vendangeur Masqué.

Bourgogne Aligoté "Plantation 1902" 2015

This wine comes from half a hectare of vines near the town of Saint-Bris, bearing on the label the original date of planting in a pre-phylloxera era. Striking for its savory vitality and the spontaneous freshness of the finish.

Chablis "L'humeur du temps" 2015

The one hectare plot in Courgis delivers a wine and a manifesto of the de Moor approach: a sort of hymn to the unstable humor of the seasons, overflowing with energy and flavor.

Christian MOREAU Père et fils

CHABLIS

26, Avenue d'Oberwesel - Tel. +33 (0) 3 86 428634
contact@domainechristianmoreau.com | www.domainechristianmoreau.com

11.5 hectares

Founded two centuries ago by an enterprising barrel-making ancestor, the Moreau family winery remained linked to *négociant* and mediation activities until the mid-seventies. Then, over a period of almost thirty years, the J. Moreau brand passed into the hands of large industrial groups (Hiram Walker, Boisset) before the ownership of the vineyards was reclaimed in 2002, with the creation of the new *domaine*. Fabien Moreau, in succeeding his father Christian, took charge of the vineyards of almost twelve hectares, including more than two-thirds concentrated in the ample spreads of the Premier Cru Vaillon and the Grand Cru Les Clos. In the vineyards he has put the focus on manual harvesting, while in the cellars he has stopped using selected yeasts and moderated the use of oak after fermentation, which is done mainly in stainless steel.

Chablis 1er Cru Vaillon Cuvée Guy Moreau 2015

Dedicated to Fabien's grandfather, who planted the parcel of nearly a hectare in 1933, this *cuvée* expresses the usual elegance of the Premier Cru Vaillon, integrated in this version by a complement of breadth and maturity of fruit.

Chablis Grand Cru Les Clos 2015

The three different parcels of vines in Moreau's large holdings of Les Clos are harvested and vinified separately. Bracing vigor and interior density are the main assets of a wine enhanced by notable extractive weight.

Chablis Grand Cru Les Clos Clos des Hospices 2015

This vineyard, which was acquired from the Hospices de Beaune in 1904, consists of almost half a hectare on south-facing slopes of dense white clays. The grapes have always been used for a distinctive bottling of a wine with a classic profile, enriched with notes reminiscent of candied orange peel, and a long aromatic persistence.

PATTES LOUP

COURGIS

2, Grande Rue Nicolas - Tel. +33 (0) 3 86 414638
thomas.pico@pattes-loup.com | www.pattes-loup.com

15 hectares

Thomas Pico, a third generation *vigneron*, started his career in 2004 at his father's Domaine de Bois d'Yver. The following year, after recovering eight hectares owned by his grandfather, he launched his personal project, renamed Pattes Loup. Extremely sensitive to environmental issues, Thomas oriented his viticulture toward full organic farming from the beginning; Pattes Loup was certified by Ecocert in 2009. Although today most of the grapes of Chablis are harvested by machine, Thomas picks his fifteen hectares of vines exclusively by hand. This same sensibility, aimed at enhancing the full expressive potential of the wines, also guides his choices in the cellar: sulfites employed at the barest minimum, no selected yeasts, *bâtonnage* only if essential, and no filtration. In short, enology at a minimum, but such precision, translated into wines of muscular elasticity, bursting with spontaneous energy and flowing into long, vibrant finishes. These wines have been drawing widespread attention, ruffling the feathers of the long established hierarchy of Chablis. Some of the most important wine critics, both French and American, have dared to challenge the habitual stars of Chablis by proclaiming Thomas Pico as the new reference point for the *appellation*. Yet Thomas appears to be immune to media flattery while focusing, as usual, on his work. This is especially true in recent years, which have been studded with all sorts of climatic disasters and penalized by drastic reductions in yields—first by hail in September 2015 and then by the devastating frosts of late April in both 2016 and 2017. Bottles of Pattes Loup, already much sought after, have therefore become ever more rare and hard to find. Tracking down these "wolf paws" requires a bit of dedication, but worth the effort more than ever.

Chablis 2014

An assemblage of vineyard parcels in the Courgis area with an average of forty years of age. Vinified in stainless steel tanks and ovoid cement containers, this Chablis is a clear, sharp, well defined white wine.

Chablis 1er Cru Côte de Jouan 2014

This little known *climat* in the community of Courgis lies at an altitude of almost three hundred meters with full southeastern exposure. In contrast to the usual fresh and acidic 2014s, this is a more open and richly vinous wine which retains that precisely saline and dexterous tartness that distinguishes the entire Pattes Loup range.

Chablis 1er Cru Beauregard 2014

This vineyard was promoted to Premier Cru status in 1978, but after forty years there are still *vignerons* who question its re-classification. In response, Thomas has unleashed a version of Beauregard overflowing with energy and verticality, which should keep everyone quiet.

Chablis 1er Cru Butteaux 2014

White soils with high clay content give depth and volume to the fleshiest wine in the range, yet this weight doesn't hinder the wine's momentum as it finishes with a beautiful sapid minerality.

Chablis 1er Cru Montmains 2014

Beneath a still closed and unyielding façade, this wine barely hints at its inner energy—a true thoroughbred ready to burst through the gate with a bit of time.

PINSON Frères

CHABLIS

5, Quai Voltaire - Tel. +33 (0) 3 86 421026
www.domaine-pinson.com

14 hectares

Directed by brothers Laurent and Christophe, Domaine Pinson boasts a family tradition in viticulture dating back over three and a half centuries. The winery's fourteen hectares of vineyards are all dedicated to Chardonnay, with important plantings within the Premier Crus and a large (two and a half hectare) plot in the Grand Cru Les Clos. The focus of their work remains faithful to a traditional style, although in recent years, since the young Charlène (Laurent's daughter) joined the company, the wines seem to have gained something in terms of definition. Though rather severe in their youth and slow to come out of their shells, they show good potential for evolution and a peculiar iodized trait that makes them precious company at the dinner table.

Chablis 2015

Chablis from three hectares of younger vineyards, planted in the early 2000s, two in the left bank area, near Montmain, and the other at the foot of Mont de Milieu. Energetic and pulpy, this wine is a classic example of the *appellation* in an almost didactic way.

Chablis 1er Cru Mont de Milieu 2015

Modulated by an elegant amalgam of iodized notes and hints of candied citrus fruit enhanced by a pleasantly spicy finish, this wine, from a rather large parcel of more than four hectares, is sure to please fans of the svelte and streamlined style of Chablis.

Chablis 1er Cru Montmain 2015

From a hectare of vines planted in a single block more than forty years ago, this is a Premier Cru of savory and almost salty character, capable of combining creaminess and flexibility with no loss of tension on the finish.

François RAVENEAU

CHABLIS

9, Rue de Chichee - Tel. +33 (0) 3 86 421746

9.5 hectares

Starting from a modest endowment of three hectares of vineyards in 1948, François Raveneau gradually built the reputation of his *domaine* to stand among the very best in the field of bona fide Chablis. The property has grown moderately, but still doesn't exceed ten hectares under the management of his sons Bernard and Jean-Marie, who have been in charge for more than twenty years.
In retracing their ascent, it's worth remembering that when the technology of mechanized grape harvesters and stainless steel tanks spread through the vineyards and cellars of Chablis, the Raveneau brothers alone (along with Dauvissat) remained faithful to manual harvesting and to selected *élevages* of wines in wooden barrels, including *feuillettes*. That is why their most successful wines of the nineties, today in splendid condition with impressive potential for further evolution, dominate the rest of local production by a wide margin, with very few comparisons. They are whites whose historic style is linked to a deliberate production strategy. The minerality of the soils is emphasized in the wines thanks to drastically low yields, harvesting at perfect ripeness, and skillful *élevage*. The result is aromatic character that may be rather reserved at first, but with time turns toward those unmistakable notes of anise and honey, and a full, round and creamy palate. A few years of bottle age are needed to expand the myriad of pervasively rich flavors. The depth and consistency of these wines continues to guarantee the *domaine* a large measure of international success, despite the increasingly fierce competition.
The entire production is sold well in advance to loyal customers worldwide. So it would be an exercise in futility to arrive at the *domaine* expecting to purchase even a few bottles of the scarce 50,000 produced. Better instead to seek them out on wine lists in the very best of restaurants worldwide.

Chablis 2015

Still rather reticent in its aromatics, but tonic in flavor and svelte in *silhouette*, with a refreshing finish.

Chablis 1er Cru Montée de Tonnerre 2015

This wine is produced from the *domaine*'s largest parcel, spread over three hectares, and together with Premier Cru Butteaux—another *cuvée* of scope—is the only wine Raveneau ferments in part in casks instead of the usual stainless steel. In this still embryonic phase, there are notable hints of thyme and a mounting acceleration of flavors that will only grow in tension and fluency.

Chablis Grand Cru Les Clos 2015

Raveneau's parcel is located in the center of the *climat*, source of a wine that manages to combine the delicate minerality of Blanchots with the power and weight of Valmur, while exceeding both of them in its broad and promising range of potential evolution.

2

FROM MARSANNAY TO GEVREY-CHAMBERTIN

MARSANNAY

map *page* 505

Chenôve, Marsannay-la-Côte and Couchey are towns at the northern edge of the Côte d'Or, where the bleak outskirts of the city of Dijon, crammed with shopping centers and car dealerships, gradually give way to vineyards. Those communities have more than 240 hectares of vines surrounding them devoted to the Marsannay *appellation* in an area that was planted almost entirely in Gamay before the devastation of phylloxera during the second half of the nineteenth century. The Gamay tradition was largely abandoned as Pinot Noir took over with the first wines dating back to the era between the two world wars. But only in the 1960s did Marsannay begin to appear on wine maps, officially claiming its own *appellation* in 1987 as the northernmost zone of the Côte de Nuits.

Marsannay is the only *appellation* of the Côte d'Or with provisions for the production of three types of wine: white, red and—hear, hear!— rosé. Still, the rosé remains a curiosity on the margins of the Marsannay *appellation*, whose red wines have been attracting growing attention both from producers and enthusiasts. Even if the zone does not yet have any Premier Cru vineyards, a commission of local *vignerons* has submitted a dossier to INAO (Institut National de l'Origine et de la Qualité), presenting the credentials of the best *climats* (about fifteen) for discussion and in-depth study. The aim is to promote them to Premier Cru status, though the outcome of this mission remains to be seen. For the time being, if we may generalize about the quality of the reds of Marsannay, they rate as some of the most fragrant, smooth and easy-drinking wines of the entire Côte de Nuits. Their strong points are acidity and agility as exemplary "food wines" that stand out with local country cooking.

FIXIN

map *page* 503

Fixin is a small *appellation* positioned as a sort of cushion between the vineyards of Marsannay and Gevrey-Chambertin. Its *terroir* is similar to that of Gevrey: deep and fertile red-brown clays, rich in fossils and stones, with an important addition of alluvial soils similar to those of Marsannay. The entire *appellation* covers about a hundred hectares of vineyards of which some 20 percent are designated as Premier Crus. The wines made here are mostly red, generally rich in color and backed by a strong tannic framework. They have good aging potential, even if they are often marked by a certain tannic roughness that has earned them the ungenerous reputation as "rustic cousins" of Gevrey-Chambertin. There are only a few cellars in Fixin, and in general they are not the most competitive. In our experience, the most convincing wines of the *appellation* often come from wineries with headquarters in neighboring towns.

GEVREY-CHAMBERTIN

map *page* 507

The Gevrey-Chambertin *appellation* boasts one of the most extensive spreads of vines of the Côte d'Or (more than 450 hectares), including the region's oldest vineyard sites. The remains of a vineyard dating back to the first century BC were discovered here in 2008, confirming that viticulture was practiced in Burgundy during the period of Roman occupation, as well as under the monks of Cluny. Gevrey is a land of vigorous reds, rich in energy and substance, as well as the home of the largest number of Grand Crus in the entire region: nine total, distributed over 55 hectares. The community of Gevrey was the first to obtain authorization (by order of the King, dated October 17, 1847) to add to its name the adjunct of Burgundy's most prestigious vineyard: Chambertin.

Wafted by the cool currents of five different *combes*, the vineyards can be divided into three distinct groups: to the north, the Côte Saint-Jacques; in the center the parcels around the village of Gevrey extending east to State Route 74 (classified mostly as Villages); and, to the south, the Côte des Grands Crus. In the Côte Saint-Jacques, vineyards reach their highest altitudes at almost 400 meters. Among the several prestigious Premier Crus there (Cazetiers, Lavaux Saint-Jacques) shines the star of Clos Saint-Jacques. This iconic vineyard with its prestigious coat of arms can easily be compared (also in price) to many Grand Crus. In fact, at the time of the classification (1935) Grand Cru status was not given to this vineyard thanks to a whim of the pro-monarchist Conte de Moucheron (who at the time owned the entire *clos*) and who agreed to comply with the classification set out by the commission, either out of spite for the politics of the day, or for tax reasons.

The greatest concentration of prestigious vineyards is in the Côte des Grands Crus. Starting from the north, the first Grand Cru we find is Ruchottes-Chambertin, a small vineyard whose name refers to the several outcroppings of rocks that dot its hillsides. In this well-ventilated area grapes mature later than elsewhere; wines are elegant, balanced and characterized by finesse of texture rather than power. Next comes Mazis-Chambertin divided into two sectors (Mazis-Haut and Mazis-Bas) by a diagonal split of geology. Mazis is noted for robust, vigorous and long-lived reds, with well defined tannic accents. And yet, in the best examples, the concentrated internal density does not detract from floral nuances (notably rosa canina) that evolve with age toward notes of leather and truffle. Then comes Clos de Bèze, extensively described by critics as "the soul of the *terroir*" in wines that combine energy and grace, strength and delicacy, astonishing longevity and delicious precociousness. Chambertin, which is less steeply inclined than the Clos de Bèze, has a cooler microclimate due to its proximity to the Combe Grisard, which channels air currents down through the vines. Chambertin is known for reds of hypnotic charm, powerful energy and royal lineage, having been described as the "King of wines" by Abbé Arnoux (in 1728), and a "champion" by Jules Lavalle (in 1855). Armando Castagno notes that Chambertin "represents perhaps the maximum limit of structure and length a great Pinot Noir wine can achieve." Then come Chapelle-Chambertin and Griotte-Chambertin, the Grand Crus that render the most expressive and sensual reds in all of Burgundy. Though less structured and powerful than others, they embody the most accessible and joyful examples of the wines of Gevrey, suggesting combinations of nuanced aromatics that would be at home in Chambolle-Musigny.

Covering an area of about 30 hectares (second in size only to Clos de Vougeot) Charmes-Chambertin and Mazoyères-Chambertin form a pair of Grand Crus that are often linked, since the law allows producers to use either Charmes or Mazoyères, all to the advantage of the former (the name Charmes itself being, well, more charming). Descriptions of the best wines of those vineyards include the likes of "intensity wrapped in velvet" and "power with an elegant profile," even if on average reds here are simply rather solid and consistent wines. The survey of Gevrey's Grand Crus ends with Latricières-Chambertin, the most enigmatically named *climat* (which Castagno suggests is a reference to its square shape, and not to the scarce fertility of the terrain). As for the wines, they are unusually graceful, exhibiting a remarkable aromatic complexity and a surprising mineral persistence.

The concentration of Grand and Premier Crus threatens to cast a large shadow over the many other parcels of Gevrey: nearly 70, scattered over 350 hectares of vineyards that line the two sides of the main local road between the houses of Gevrey and Brochon. In such a densely-planted area, quality differences between one plot and another are split in a range of vineyards rendering very unequal results. This is especially so in light of the fact that many *domaines* tend to assemble their Villages bottling from grapes derived from multiple *lieux-dits* located far from each other, in every sense. And yet these *lieux-dits* give the reds of Gevrey their reputation as tannic and assertive wines, intense in color and exuberant in aromas of red and black berries, often more powerful than graceful and almost always more autumnal than spring-like.

BART

MARSANNAY-LA-CÔTE

23, Rue Moreau - Tel. +33 (0) 3 80 514976
domaine.bart@wanadoo.fr

21 hectares

Together Martin Bart, his sister Odine, and her son Pierre run this *domaine* covering twenty-one hectares of vineyards located mainly in the territory of Marsannay. The parcels are scattered between seven different *lieux-dits*, all of which are farmed sustainably. During vinification the use of whole-cluster grapes remains rather marginal (only between 10 and 20% on average) and there is no pumping over for the reds. Martin, the cousin of Bruno Clair (see Page 154), is one of the most dynamic advocates of promoting the best parcels of the Marsannay *appellation* to Premier Cru status. Knowing his wines, this is not surprising. His precise and careful attention to the expression of different *terroirs* takes precedence over any possible shortcuts in style that might be more attractive or immediate. Along with a small production of excellent Grand Cru wines from vineyards like Bonnes-Mares and Clos-de-Bèze, the *domaine* also turns out a reliable version of Marsannay rosé, of which more than ten thousand bottles are produced.

Marsannay La Montagne 2015

The vineyard is at the highest part of the hill, close to the woods, with soils similar to those of another Bart property of Longeroies, factors that favor delicate fruit sensations (cherry) and a pleasantly spicy finish on the palate.

Marsannay Les Echezots 2015

To avoid confusion with the much better known Echézeaux, Martin prefers to use a nineteenth-century spelling. Whatever the case, the aromatic persistence recalls a wine of a higher category.

Fixin 1er Cru Hervelets 2015

From reddish soils rich in chipped stones and sand, this is a prompt and expressive red, laden with red fruit and tonic vigor.

René BOUVIER

GEVREY-CHAMBERTIN

Chemin de Saule - Brochon - Tel. +33 (0) 3 80 522137
rene-bouvier@wanadoo.fr

17 hectares

The *domaine* of Bernard Bouvier comprises seventeen hectares of vineyards, distributed mainly in the territory between Marsannay and Gevrey, producing an average of 100,000 bottles a year. Recent vintages have revealed significant changes with a positive influence on the style of wines. Bernard believes the conversion to organic viticulture (certified since 2013) had a direct impact on the texture and tactile quality of the wines, which also reveal less extraction, altering a certain tendency that had at times led to an emphasis on power over finesse. In addition to the more decisive and vigorous reds, which in any case remain the strong point of the *domaine*, we also find more balanced bottlings, capable of directing their notable potential energy to the service of more immediate and enjoyable pleasure.

Marsannay Clos du Roy Vieilles Vignes 2015

The fine gravel of the geological matrix (*grèzes litées*) allied with the remarkable age of the vineyard account for the delicate and soft texture of a red wine, expressive and direct, almost sensual in its fleshiness.

Fixin Crais de Chêne 2015

This stony *climat* runs along the northern border of the *appellation* rendering a delicious wine, playing on whiffs of violet and raspberry; thanks to a warm vintage it suffuses a sense of instant pleasure.

Gevrey-Chambertin La Justice 2015

The use of 50% whole cluster grapes charges the aromatic vivacity by an engaging peppery vein and suggestions of blueberry in the flavor: it tastes very enjoyable and ready to drink.

Bruno CLAIR

MARSANNAY-LA-CÔTE
5, Rue du Vieux Collège - Tel. +33 (0) 3 80 522895
brunoclair@wanadoo.fr | www.bruno-clair.com

21.85 hectares

Bruno Clair comes from a family originally from Santenay at the southern edge of the Côte de Beaune, but for years his name has been the main reference point for Marsannay, the northernmost town of the Côte de Nuits. But it would be remiss to limit his scope to the *appellation* of Marsannay alone; his vineyard possessions exceed twenty hectares, with plots in many prestigious sites, including some of most esteemed of Gevrey (one hectare in the Clos de Bèze, another in the Clos Saint-Jacques). Behind the 24 labels of the *domaine* stand Bruno Clair and his trusted winemaker Philippe Brun, at his side since the beginning, crafting wines full of personality, well-supported by tannic finesse, with solid roots in the *terroirs*. In line with the quality, prices are also quite high, certainly not within everyone's reach, even if they could be considered good value if compared to the staggering prices of many of their distinguished colleagues.

Marsannay Longeroies 2015

From a vineyard planted more than seventy years ago, the oldest of the *domaine*, in a *climat* that is a candidate for a forthcoming promotion to the rank of Premier Cru, this is a red of measured elegance and clear aromatic purity.

Marsannay Les Vaudenelles 2015

From a vineyard planted on white marl, this Marsannay is svelte and breezy in its flavor dynamics. Though it doesn't have the completeness of the Longeroies, nor the tannic finesse of the Grasses Têtes, it does transmit a very pleasant fruity immediacy that invites another sip.

Gevrey-Chambertin 1er Cru Petite Chapelle 2015

Bordering the Grand Cru Chapelle-Chambertin, this *climat* often shares its taste profile, playing on the finesse of its tannins. This version also moves on tiptoe with silky, delicate texture thanks to a well-calibrated extraction.

Gevrey-Chambertin 1er Cru Clos de Fonteny 2015

A layer of white clay around protruding calcareous slabs defines the particularity of the terrain of this *climat*. Bruno Clair's plot is a small *monopole* of three-quarters of a hectare, in the upper part of Fonteny, considered the best area, bordering the stony plot of the Grand Cru Ruchottes. Winemaker Philippe Brun describes this as the most "Chambollian" of his Gevrey wines, with elegance combined with maturity by virtue of a particularly sunny exposure.

Gevrey-Chambertin 1er Cru Clos Saint-Jacques 2015

If, over decades, the wines of Clos Saint-Jacques have merited the critical praise (and prices) of a Grand Cru, it is due in large part to wines like this: so silky and graceful in expressing a wealth of nuances. Of the five producers who own a parcel (others are Armand Rousseau, Sylvie Esmonin, Domaine Fourrier and Louis Jadot) Bruno Clair distinguishes himself in his constant quest for balance and harmony, also in a precocious vintage such as 2015.

Chambertin Clos de Bèze Grand Cru 2015

Bruno Clair's parcel is perpendicular to the slope of the hill, thus benefiting fully from the kaleidoscopic varieties of soils (Bajocian limestone, white marl, brown earth rich in marine fossils). Such complexity makes the Clos de Bèze perhaps less structured and virile than Chambertin, but a wine that is often capable of expressing greater complexity, which translates into subtle nuances. This version exemplifies why this Grand Cru is sometimes compared in terms of delicacy with the most elegant examples of Musigny.

Claude DUGAT

GEVREY-CHAMBERTIN
1, Place de la Cure - Tel. +33 (0) 3 80 343618
claude.dugat@wanadoo.fr

6 hectares

Despite the cultish aura that surrounds his small production (not even 25,000 bottles, booked well in advance by loyal customers all over the world), Claude Dugat remains a humble and smiling *vigneron*. The structure of his *domaine* is strictly within the family; his son and daughter Bertrand and Laëtitia have supported him for some time and, with the return of his daughter Jeanne, his children have begun to manage all the various phases of production. Situated in the small plaza of the church of Gevrey, the winery is housed in the historic complex of the Cellier des Dimes, a former granary of fascinating austerity, whose construction dates back to 1219. The *domaine* owns only three hectares of vineyards (three more are leased) with parcels in the best *climats* of Gevrey. Crafted from completely destemmed grapes, these wines are designed to confront the decades, combining texture and structure in a style that concedes nothing, although recently the wine seem perhaps a little less austere and easier to read.

Gevrey-Chambertin 2015

Made from the grapes of fifteen different parcels (the average age of the vines is over fifty years), this wine is compact and reticent at first, needing time to open, but with aeration it releases surprising juiciness.

Gevrey-Chambertin 1er Cru Lavaux Saint-Jacques 2015

The Dugat plot (less than half a hectare) is located in the upper part of Lavaux, which extends into a combe of the same name, where the layer of topsoil becomes thinner and the stone becomes more compact. Here the benefit of southern exposure is partly compromised by the opposite side of the gorge and the wine retains a certain austerity even in generous vintages like 2015.

Charmes-Chambertin Grand Cru 2015

To define his style, Dugat suggests "*masculin gentil*," which reminds us of the "*puissance veloutée*" dear to Jacky Rigaux. Behind these oxymorons shines the need to simultaneously reinforce both the incisiveness and the expressive grace of the best of Charmes. And if Jasper Morris calls this ' a huge mouthful," this version strikes us for its readiness, its harmonious fusion already completely integrated.

Griotte-Chambertin Grand Cru 2015

Here's a wine that seems to contradict Claude's conviction that 2015 was a year that tends to level the difference between *terroirs*. There is no denying all the sensuality of Griotte. The initial attack on the palate reveals a silky texture and the typical expressive delicacy of the *cru*; then there is harmony in the evolution, a richness of gustatory nuances, and a progressive acceleration on the palate that enriches the finish with promising sapidity.

Chapelle-Chambertin Grand Cru 2015

If you are lucky enough to be welcomed to the cellar of Claude Dugat, in all probability the Chapelle will be the last wine you'll taste. This is no accident, since it's impossible to fit this wine into any place else in the sequence, thanks to its tannic depth and almost "rebellious" character. The 2015 vintage heightens the sensation, if that's possible. The malolactic fermentation finished later than usual, Claude reveals, and having yet to find its balance, the wine is still bustling with energy.

Bernard DUGAT-PY

GEVREY-CHAMBERTIN

Rue Planteligone - Cour de L'Aumônerie - BP 31 - Tel. +33 (0) 3 80 518246
contact@dugat-py.fr | www.dugat-py.fr

10.6 hectares

Perpetuating a tradition that began in the seventeenth century, the Dugat family today represents the thirteenth generation of winemakers. Bernard, at the helm since the seventies, continued to sell the family's wine to *négociants* until his first *domaine* bottling in 1989. His son, Loïc, began working at the *domaine* in the late nineties, and subsequently steps have been taken toward more conscientious viticulture, certified organic (since 2003) and then a full conversion to biodynamic (since 2014, but without certification). These key moves have consolidated the prestige (and prices) of Dugat at very high levels. The nearly eleven hectares of property include parcels in ten of the most prestigious vineyards in Gevrey, equally divided between Grand Cru and Premier Cru. These vineyards give life to deeply colored and potent wines, in which a notable proportion of de-stemmed grapes coexists with a by no means timid use of new wood, meaning that lovers of more rarefied and ethereal reds will need to look elsewhere. These are wines built *pour la garde*, requiring refinement to bring out the differences in *climats* and prove the *savoir-faire* of the Dugat, respected by all for intense dedication. Among reasons to visit the *domaine* are the historic cellars with the fascinating pointed vaults of the Aumônerie clergy, built around the year 1000.

Gevrey-Chambertin Les Evocelles 2015

From a *lieu-dit* overlooking the village of Brochon, the plot with vines more than seventy years old covers a hectare on very stony soils, which the Dugat family works with the help of a horse. In the wine the solidity of the tannic structure coexists with the beguiling cassis-like wildness of the fruit.

Gevrey-Chambertin 1er Cru Petite Chapelle 2015

The wines of Petite Chapelle derive from terrains similar to those of the neighboring Grand Cru Chapelle-Chambertin, boasting a critical literature that exalts the elegance and adds ethereal and floral touches, suggesting similarities with Chambolle.

Loïc's version is remarkably different, matching a concentration of color with energy and fullness on the palate that are a bit the Dugat-Py trademark. The finish, however, reveals mineral vibrations and a more complex and subtly pervasive sapidity.

Mazoyères-Chambertin Grand Cru 2015

Among the few who do not label their Mazoyères with the more attractive name of the neighboring Charmes, Dugat-Py flaunts an uncommon attachment to this less prestigious Grand Cru. Austere and vigorous, poised between earthy notes and more intense spicy aromas, the wine rewards with a generous palate flush with powerful fruit.

Charmes-Chambertin Grand Cru 2015

Barrel tasting at Dugat-Py would test the most experienced of wine critics in confronting the natural concentration of the 2015 vintage, the material style of the *domaine*, the almost chewable intensity of the pulp, the tannic depth of the Grand Cru as well as the prevalent use of new wood (which is nearly 100%). In this embryonic phase of the wine's evolution it was almost impossible to pursue any sense of detail or nuance. It will take time. Time to evaluate the integration of stem-inclusion (this vintage was made with 70% of whole bunches), and time to appreciate the detonating purity of the fruit. More than anything else, it will take time for this wine to reveal its true sense of place and *terroir*.

Gilles DUROCHÉ

GEVREY-CHAMBERTIN

7, Place du Monument - Tel. +33 (0) 3 80 518277

www.domaine-duroche.com

8.5 hectares

The first *mise en bouteille au domaine* was recorded in 1933, but the name Duroché only began to circulate in a lasting way among fans after 2005, with the arrival of young Pierre, who represents the fifth generation of the family to be engaged in viticulture. Starting from the 2009 harvest, Pierre definitively took over the reins of the family *domaine*, which until a few years ago had sold most of its grapes to *négociants*. It was a decisive turnaround in the management of over eight hectares of vineyards (including a large portion of over 60-year-old *vieilles vignes*) with the total abandonment of the use of chemical products. Replanting was carried out using mass selection of the oldest vines, as the soil between the rows began to be worked again, in some parcels also with the help of a horse. This long-term perspective is already bearing its first fruits. The wines reveal a sure hand in proposing convincing examples of the different *climats* and vintages, while showing constant growth in personality.

Bourgogne Pinot Noir 2016

An assemblage of two different parcels (Roncevie and Comble) resulting in a smooth and immediate wine, but not without grace.

Gevrey-Chambertin 1er Cru Estournelles Saint-Jacques 2015

A small *climat* of two-hectares, located above Lavaux-Saint-Jacques in the line of vineyards at opening of the Combe Bossière. Duroché's version features aromas of intense floral cotrasts, as well as a savory, tenacious, engaging palate sealed by a mineral finish.

Gevrey-Chambertin 1er Cru Lavaut Saint-Jacques 2015

The main nucleus of this parcel is rooted in vines planted in 1923. A late-ripening vineyard that offers loads of material from this generous vintage in a powerful and concentrated wine with a very long finish.

Sylvie ESMONIN

GEVREY-CHAMBERTIN

Clos Saint Jacques 1 Rue Neuve - Tel. +33 (0) 3 80 343644
sylvie-esmonin@orange.fr

7.7 hectares

Sylvie Esmonin is a true *vigneronne*, sensitive and determined, hiding behind a smile veined with melancholy a slightly nervous and restless personality. It was she who, after graduating as an agronomist at Montpellier, returned to the *domaine* in the eighties to take over from her father Michel, who had previously sold all the wine to *négociants*. Today she works in her own "radically natural" way even if the fashion of bio wines scares her, while lamenting the tendency of some *domaines* in Burgundy to drift toward a more "Bordeaux" style of wine. She distrusts the proliferation of those richly-colored and concentrated wines that do not leave any space for the nuances of Burgundy so close to her heart. Sylvie's *domaine* includes nearly eight hectares of vineyards, distributed over a few appellations, with a flagship holding in Clos Saint-Jacques of over one and a half hectares. Sylvie loves to recall how her grandfather said that "the Clos Saint-Jacques is a lady, and Chambertin her husband." As a winemaker she translates her femininity into wines of a style that is anything but dainty. Starting with the new millennium, she began experimenting with whole cluster vinification. The wines of her last harvest, despite an elaborate quantity of new oak, demonstrate a decisive *terroir*-driven personality. The *domaine* also produces a tiny quantity of a delicious Aligoté, which is practically unobtainable. "We probably drink more at home than we sell," says Sylvie with a smile.

Bourgogne Cuvée Sylvie 2015

The wine derives from nearly a hectare of old vines in the Pressonnier area, normally the last to be harvested since the deep alluvial soils with high clay content need more time to bring the grapes to complete ripeness. The result is a compact, crisp and tasty red, which confirms Sylvie's skilled hand even with minor *appellations*.

Côte de Nuits-Village 2015

A wine from two different parcels with a high percentage of active limestone, located in the Brochon area (Les Vignois and La Croix Violette). Aromas of violet and blackberries, the wine embodies the warmth of the year in a satisfyingly profound mouthful.

Gevrey-Chambertin 2015

The major portion of grapes comes from Les Crais, on the other side of the *route nationale*, where the land is influenced (not always positively) by debris transported to the plain by the Combe de Lavaux. The result is a precise and solid wine that knots the threads between the vigor of Gevrey and elegance of texture.

Gevrey-Chambertin Cuvée Vieilles Vignes 2015

An assemblage of parcels in several sectors of Gevrey (including one in the Premier Cru Clos Prieur) where most of the vines were planted nearly a century ago between 1919 and 1920. Yields in 2015 were a mere twenty-two hectoliters per hectare, and, in fact, concentration is the fulcrum of this wine, in which the sharpness of structure does not lose tension in the long aromatic persistence.

Gevrey-Chambertin 1er Cru Clos Saint-Jacques 2015

From the vineyard behind her house, the same vines cultivated by Sylvie's grandfather when the *domaine* was still owned by the Count of Moucheron (like the rest of the *clos* which today is in the hands of five different *domaines*). The Esmonin portion extends over an abundant one and a half hectares, following the ground level curve perpendicularly, embracing three different types of soil: high-range marls, the outcropping of mother rock in the middle and clay in the lower reaches. This vintage radiates energy in a sublime expression of the nuances between richness and luminosity.

Jean FOURNIER

MARSANNAY-LA-CÔTE

34, Rue du Château - Tel +33 (0) 3 80 522438
domaine.jean.fournier@orange.fr

16 hectares

A young *vigneron*, highly esteemed by his professional colleagues, Laurent Fournier is a reference point for the Marsannay area. He took over the family *domaine*, one of the oldest of the *appellation*, in 2001, working in vineyards and cellars in an impressively calm, smiling and welcoming way. The *domaine*, which obtained organic certification in 2008, is currently undergoing biodynamic conversion for its sixteen hectares of vineyards, of which fifteen are in Marsannay and most consist of vines over fifty years of age. Vinification is carried out almost entirely with whole bunches, macerations are prolonged (on average for three weeks) and maturation takes place in large barrels *(foudres)* of 20 and 50 hectoliters.

Marsannay Les Longeroies 2015

This ample parcel of over five hectares rests on thick marly soils rich in iron and silicon. The 2015 bottling combines volume and definition in the name of pleasure.

Marsannay Clos du Roy 2015

A candidate for a possible promotion to Premier Cru (along with fourteen *lieux-dits* in Marsannay), this *climat* overlooks the village of Chenôve, on ferrous and reddish soils intersected by veins of sand. Fournier owns three hectares of vineyards for a savory and gritty red, framed by minerality

Marsannay Trois Terres Vieilles Vignes 2015

The flagship wine of the *domaine* comes from an assemblage of three different *lieux-dits*: Les Grandes Vignes, La Charme aux Prêtres and Les Grasses Têtes. Fournier's knowing hands have delivered the vintage's most spherical and delicious profile.

HERESZTYN-MAZZINI

GEVREY-CHAMBERTIN

27, Rue Richebourg - Tel. +33 (0) 6 22 771444
info@heresztyn-mazzini.com | www.heresztyn-mazzini.com

5.5 hectares

The *domaine*, founded in 1959 by the Polish grandfather of Florence Heresztyn, took on new momentum in 2012 when she married Simon Mazzini. Much credit is due to Simon, a *vigneron* who, in spite of a surname echoing the Italian Risorgimento, hails from Champagne, where he continues a parallel activity of making wine in the town of Ville-Dommange. At the *domaine* in Burgundy, the five and a half hectares of vines inherited by the young couple, located mainly in Gevrey, are in conversion to organic farming. Simon has also been using biodynamic preparations to reinforce the vineyards' natural defenses. The wines, streamlined without frills, express easy personality. In our tastings of the 2014 vintage, we greatly admired wines with an extra dimension of dynamic energy.

Gevrey-Chambertin Les Songes 2014

Grapes of two parcels of *vieilles-vignes* (80 and 90 years old) in the northern sector of the appellation went into this assemblage of a wine striking for its freshness and flavor.

Gevrey-Chambertin 1er Cru Les Goulots 2014

This *climat*, rarely cited on labels, is located on the extension of the Combe aux Moines, characterized by steeply sloping vineyards on a thin layer of white marl. The wine has a svelte and streamlined silhouette with generous fluidity, suggesting a possible etymological link between the Goulots site and the term *gouléyant* (drinkable).

Gevrey-Chambertin 1er Cru Les Champonnets 2014

From the right side of the Combe de Lavaux, where the soil is lighter despite an ample quantity of clay, Simon extracts a rich, aromatic red with a solid tannic presence: a wine designed for aging.

Thierry MORTET

GEVREY-CHAMBERTIN
16, Place des Marronniers - Tel. +33 (0) 3 80 518507
domainethierrymortet@gmail.fr | www.domainethierrymortet.fr

7.3 hectares

The *domaine* is relatively young, founded in 1992 by a branch of the family from the ancestral house of Charles Mortet et Fils. After studying enology at the school in Beaune, Thierry (brother of the late Denis Mortet) began working in the family *domaine* in 1983, where he developed a feeling for his craft as *vigneron* reflected in clean linearity and a deft touch with his wines. The vineyards are spread over seven hectares, mainly in the Gevrey-Chambertin appellation, but with important appendages in Chambolle, as well as a parcel north of Dijon (the most northerly vineyard area of the Côte d'Or) from which Thierry derives a pleasantly fresh Bourgogne Blanc. He completely de-stems his grapes, and the *domaine* has been certified as organic since 2007.

Bourgogne 2015
An assemblage of six different parcels gives rise to this agile, pleasurable red.

Gevrey-Chambertin 2015
More than fifteen thousand bottles are produced from these vineyards, aged between ten and sixty years, spread over twenty different plots. In this vintage the combination of internal density and aromatic prominence was entirely convincing.

Gevrey-Chambertin Vigne Belle 2015
A *lieu-dit* with a lovely name, bordering the Premier Cru Petite Chapelle. The soils are markedly calcareous with ample quantities of fine clays, to the benefit of a juicy, well-balanced and inviting wine.

Gevrey-Chambertin 1er Cru Clos Prieur 2015
The vineyard has very thin topsoil layered directly over fissures of calcareous stones. The wine reveals a fleshy concentration, delicious and energized.

Sylvain PATAILLE

MARSANNAY-LA-CÔTE
14, Rue Neuve - Tel. +33 (0) 3 80 511735
domaine.sylvain.pataille@wanadoo.fr

12.5 hectares

Despite the resemblance to a disheveled progressive-rock musician from the seventies, Sylvain Pataille is one of the most clearheaded winemakers of the extreme north of the Côte de Nuits. After graduating as an enologist from the University of Bordeaux in 1997, he took a job in a wine laboratory in Beaune, but soon realized that a career as a technician was not for him. So, in 1999, when a hectare of vines became available for rent in Marsannay, he hurried to lay the foundations of a project that would allow him to leave the laboratory and become a full-time *vigneron*. "I was born to work in the vineyards," admits Sylvain, who today cultivates about twelve hectares (mostly leased) and aligns himself with bio-inspired viticulture. His talent is also apparent in the cellars where he vinifies with extensive stem-inclusion and takes no shortcuts in creating both red and white wines animated by spontaneous energy that are anything but academic.

Bourgogne Aligoté La Charme aux Prêtres 2015

From a plot in the heart of the Marsannay *appellation*, where Sylvain produces both white-grape varieties, but not reds. The Aligoté vineyard, planted in 1949 on poor and stony soils, gives life to a savory white, with a gritty citrus verve.

Marsannay Clos du Roy 2015

This *climat* is rooted in geological matrices composed of fine gravels (*grèzes litées*), which make it little inclined to generate structured and persistent reds. Pataille follows his instincts and produces a soulful version of convincing floral fluency (violets, peonies) and supple drinkability.

Marsannay La Montagne 2015

The vineyards are scattered around at about 300 meters in altitude, producing in 2015 a red wine in a state of grace, which would seem to dispel any doubts about the chances of this *climat* being promoted to Premier Cru.

ROSSIGNOL-TRAPET

GEVREY-CHAMBERTIN

4, Rue de la Petite-Issue · Tel. +33 (0) 3 80 518726
info@rossignol-trapet.com | www.rossignol-trapet.com

13 hectares

Brothers Nicolas and David Rossignol have been running the *domaine* since 1990, after dividing the family vineyards with their cousin Jean-Louis Trapet. Both Nicolas and David are staunch supporters of biodynamic agriculture, evidenced by a conversion that started twenty years ago and led to certification in 2005. The vineyards are spread over ten different *climats*, almost all located in the heart of the *appellation*, as well as additional plots in the areas of Savigny and Beaune. Compared to the refined, nuanced style that made their cousin's reputation, the Rossignol brothers seek greater depth in the wines, but without negating the special personality of each single *cru*. They have chosen to vinify separately each of the various small portions of the vineyards, sometimes in miniscule quantities (Corbeaux, Combottes, Cherbaudes), from their holdings in the many *climats* of Gevrey.

Bourgogne 2015

This assemblage of three different *lieux-dits* (La Burie, Croix des Champs, Grands Champs) exalts the wine's juicy drinkability

Gevrey-Chambertin Vieilles Vignes 2015

Grapes from different parcels over fifty years old, planted on soils of various composition and texture (clays, calcareous stones and silt), give rise to a wine that is rich, austere and full of contrasts, best to be forgotten in the cellar for years.

Gevrey-Chambertin 1er Cru Clos Prieur 2015

The personality of this wine is influenced by the nearby Combe de Lavaux, but the usual severity of the *climat* is mitigated here by a pervasively juicy sapidity.

Latricières-Chambertin Grand Cru 2015

Logistically this is always the last parcel harvested, since ripening is delayed by cool breezes channeled through the Combe Grisard. The calcareous matrix of the soils often gives its best in the hottest vintages, like 2015, imbued with a lively balance between volume, energy and depth on the palate.

Joseph ROTY

GEVREY-CHAMBERTIN

24, Rue Mal de Lattre de Tassigny - Tel. +33 (0) 3 80 341359

9.5 hectares

Far from the Burgundian mainstream of *domaines* dutifully fawned over by critics whose wines are permanent fixtures on the lists of starred restaurants, Joseph Roty is a name unknown to most. Unknown and unapproachable, at least according to the myth that trying to visit the *domaine* is something on the order of breaking into Fort Knox. Well, we somehow managed a visit, not with Joseph Roty, who passed away in 2008, nor his son and successor Philippe, who died in 2015, but with Joseph's widow, Madame Roty, who greeted us with authentic old-school hospitality and no hesitation in recalling the history of a family deeply dedicated to the craft for generations. The *domaine* is now in the hands of Philippe's son Pierre-Jean, who has no intention of changing a thing, in keeping with an eleven-generation family *vigneron* tradition. Our tasting in the cellar of the 2014 vintage was an absolute revelation. If, on the one hand, we've decided to include the *domaine* among our reference points for the best classic Burgundy houses, on the other we're delighted to be able to signal an address off the beaten "label drinker" paths, where even the less noble *appellations* can be highly recommended for their stylistic consistency (and fair pricing).

Côte de Nuits-Villages 2014

From a vineyard in the commune of Brochon, next to the steep and stony *lieu-dit* Les Évocelles, this is a simple but poignant red for freshness and drinkability.

Marsannay Champs Saint-Etienne 2014

A Marsannay dressed as a woman, playing on a delicate amalgam of freshness and elegance.

Gevrey-Chambertin Champs Chenys 2014

Looking at the map you'll notice that this *lieu-dit* borders directly on the Grand Cru Charmes-Chambertin. This wine of Roty is an opulent and luscious version, which dispenses pleasure without sacrificing tension.

Gevrey-Chambertin 1er Cru Les Fontenys 2014

The plaques of *calcaire à entroques* that form the hard substratum of this vineyard favor a wine that deviates from the standards of the *climat* that call for muscular and powerful reds, relying instead on the lightness of floral details, as is the case of the Clos de Fonteny produced by Bruno Clair.

Griotte-Chambertin Grand Cru 2014

The smallest of the Grand Crus of Chambertin displays in Roty's version a fascinating range of notes reminiscent of cherry liqueur (*griotte* is also a variety of sour cherry of acidic flavor, similar to the Italian viscicla). The picture is completed by an aromatic framework of myriad shades of medicinal herbs, and a finish of authentic *fleur de sel*.

Charmes-Chambertin Grand Cru Vieilles Vignes 2014

Madame Roty is keen to point out that the correct indication for this wine should be Très Vieilles Vignes, since more than half of the parcel goes back to the original planting, shortly after 1890, among the first following the devastation of phylloxera. At this point the wine was in a fairly closed and austere state, but also suggests it has all the potential for evolution into complexity in this classic vintage, ready to challenge the decades.

Armand ROUSSEAU

GEVREY-CHAMBERTIN

1, Rue de l'Aumônerie - Tel. +33 (0) 3 80 343055
contact@domaine-rousseau.com | www.domaine-rousseau.com

15 hectares

The parable of Armand Rousseau in the world of Burgundy reads something like this: in the early twentieth century, Armand, the son of small-scale landowners, not yet twenty years old, inherited some vineyards in the town of Gevrey. In the following years he began to shape the ethos of the *domaine* by re-establishing the cellar in its historical space, still active today, and selling his wines to *négociants*. Thus the *domaine* grew enough to sustain itself through both wars and into a period of great expansion and a large increase in its holdings, with parcels in the best Grand Crus of Gevrey. This eventually led to the winery bottling its wines at the *domaine* in 1929, and as a result the base of customers grew worldwide. Armand's son Charles, followed by his nephew Eric, joined the *domaine* in the early eighties and are now flanked by Charles's daughter Cyrielle. In this period of time the *domaine* possesses fifteen hectares of vineyards, all dedicated to Pinot Noir located in the district of Gevrey, with the sole exception of a parcel in the Clos de la Roche. The reputation of the *domaine* has surged, making Rousseau the reference point for more than one Grand Cru of Chambertin (the *domaine* makes six out of the nine, of which it owns over 10% of the vines). A similar hike in prices, skewed towards the exorbitant, makes the wines practically inaccessible, due to the growing gap between supply and demand, and a worldwide clientele increasingly eager to contend for the approximately 65,000 bottles produced each year. However, success is also undoubtedly due to the *savoir faire* the Rousseau family has polished over the years, crafting wines with wonderful balance between energy and elegance, fine tannins and exquisite spice.

Gevrey-Chambertin 2015

A blend from seven different parcels spread in sectors to the south and west of the town of Gevrey, for a total of almost two hectares of vineyards. The result is a savory red with firm and consistent but already well-integrated tannins. Varying from the standard procedure of the *domaine* of almost complete de-stemming, this is the first time 20% of the grapes have been left whole, enriching the generous profile of this wine and accentuating the vintage with additional aromatic vitality.

Gevrey-Chambertin 1er Cru Lavaux Saint-Jacques 2015

The proximity of the *combe* delays ripening and therefore helps to effectively balance early vintages like 2015. Moreover, here as well as in the Clos Saint-Jacques, the rows extend over the whole length of the *climat*, allowing Rousseau to benefit from the texture variations from the brown and clay soils of the lower part, as well as from the well-drained upper part, where the slope rises, the soil becomes thinner and the calcareous matrix becomes more prominent. Vital and dynamic are not the usual qualifiers for Lavaux, which is more often marked by density and structure and sometimes remains a bit short of nuance. This version from Rousseau, however, is animated by a tension and a palate of powerful length.

Gevrey-Chambertin 1er Cru Clos Saint-Jacques 2015

If you are lucky enough to be received at the *domaine* for a tasting in the cellar, you may be surprised to learn that the order of wines doesn't follow the usual hierarchy. The Clos Saint-Jacques, a Premier Crus from a plot of more than two hectares that occupies a third of the entire *climat*, arrives toward the end, when you have already tasted some Grand Crus, and only Chambertin and Clos de Bèze remain. The reason becomes clear at first sip, as the elegance and complexity of the wine strike you. It seems that more than 70% new oak is used, a share that we would never have guessed because it was already impressively integrated and resolved. Even the vintage character tends to linger in the background, leaving up front the austere beauty of a memorable red, among the noblest examples of this fascinating segment of terrain.

Ruchottes-Chambertin Grand Cru Clos des Ruchottes Monopole 2015

This Clos (a monopole belonging entirely to the *domaine*) measures about one hectare and occupies the upper part of the *cru*. The walls and portal are perfectly preserved, framing a vineyard with very weak soils, almost deprived of organic material but, on the contrary, crammed with calcareous stone. The wine is relatively lighter in color and follows a protocol of maturation in new barrels limited to 20%. This translates into an aromatic expression of enchanting vitality, floral and spicy, while fresh, juicy flavors are already prominent in its complex overall configuration. This wine will certainly age well for a long time, though its distinct supplement of finesse can be grasped immediately.

Chambertin Grand Cru 2015

Also in this case, Rousseau's quota is the largest of the *climat*, over two and a half hectares in four different parcels. The vines give life to a literally portentous red, which left us with the sensation of uncontained enthusiasm. Armando Castagno writes of Chambertin: "The impression I am most often left with upon tasting these wines on release to the market is that they possess an unlimited potential." That's exactly how Rousseau's 2015 version seemed to us, with an intensity so pervasive and involving that, after tasting, the reverberations of its incredible persistence of flavor continued to be felt, even hours later.

Marc ROY

GEVREY-CHAMBERTIN

8, Avenue de la Gare - Tel. +33 (0) 3 80 518113
domainemarcroy@orange.fr | www.facebook.com/domainemarcroy

4 hectares

The little *domaine* of Alexandrine Roy proves once again that even without a legacy of noble vineyards (not even one of her parcels is classified as Premier Cru) it is possible to produce wines of personality, stylistic coherence and precision. Alexandrine, fourth generation *vigneronne*, finished her enology studies in Beaune and took over the estate from her father, Marc. Since 2003, she has commanded operations in the vineyards and cellar, taking a responsible and integrated approach to working the four hectares of vines while carrying out vinifications that include total de-stemming of grapes, no selected yeasts and maximum attention to the extraction of tannins. Without mincing words, she confides to doing everything possible to attain from her wines "classicism, elegance and balance," striving to derive from the potential energy of the terrains of Gevrey a complexity that is enhanced over time.

Gevrey-Chambertin Vieilles Vignes 2015

Vines more than sixty years old in ten different *lieux-dits* give life to this perky and fleshy red, one of the most convincing among the ranks of Villages.

Gevrey-Chambertin La Justice 2015

Located on the plain to the east of the state road, this parcel rests on a calcareous fault covered with sandy and well-drained soils. It is the first vineyard that Alexandrine bought (in 2010), convinced that it produces grapes well above the qualitative average of the sector. The wine, with its crisp fruit and bursting energy, seems to prove her right.

Gevrey-Chambertin Cuvée Alexandrine 2015

The result of a selection of the best parcels, from grapes affected by *millerandage* (in which grape bunches develop berries that differ in size and maturity) and which naturally provide a higher concentration of sugar. The 2015 version combines open aromatics, volume and a promising savory-mineral finish with nonchalance.

TRAPET Père et Fils

GEVREY-CHAMBERTIN

53, Route de Beaune - Tel. +33 (0) 3 80 343040
message@trapet.fr | www.trapet.fr

16 hectares

Among the many winemakers we've come to know over the past few years, Jean-Louis Trapet stands out for his warm hospitality and kindness. He is a gentle man, like his wines, which are graceful, even somewhat lyrical, a unique quality that may seem antithetical to the reds of Gevrey. Jean-Louis is also a deep thinker, a man who cherishes self-reflection, and on every visit voices thoughts and ideas that go well beyond the field of wine. "In Burgundy there is a particular *consciousness of the place*, which has its roots in the secular work of the monks." Jean-Louis has taken a philosophical approach to his work from the beginning. After joining his father Jean in 1990, he immediately and resolutely shifted the estate's viticulture to organic methods. The introduction of biodynamics followed, beginning in 1995, thanks to collaboration with influential scholars such as Jean Bouchet and Pierre Masson. These options are aimed at exploring, and exploiting, the nuanced differences and special "aptitudes" of each vineyard to be translated into wines that are always marked by an admirable quest for purity, often enhanced by the gift of grace. Wines of the *domaine* come from about sixteen hectares of vineyards and take in fifteen labels. Each bottling is capable of expressing that fascinating paradox of Burgundy in wines crafted using the barest, stripped-down techniques somehow come together to express themselves with overflowing energy and luxuriant flavor. We can confirm that these reds are among the finest and most commendable of the entire region.

Bourgogne Passetoutgrain "a minima" 2015

Guiding the wine and accompanying it along a path of minimal interventions is the manifesto of "a minima" in the way suggested from the Latin expression chosen for this label. An even split between Gamay and Pinot Noir renders a smooth and juicy wine.

Bourgogne Rouge 2015

You can see Clos-de-Vougeot from this half-hectare vineyard in Gilly-les-Cîteaux, near the parcel that Domaine Roumier also devotes to its Bourgogne. This version from Jean-Louis is noted for delicious freshness and vitality.

Gevrey-Chambertin Cuvée Ostrea 2015

These vineyards are on the border of the village of Brochon (En Derée, Champerrier), on soils whose formation dates back to the Bajocian period, rich in oyster shell fossils (*ostrea acuminata*). The wine has weight and energy in a mouthful of everything one could expect in a red of this category.

Gevrey-Chambertin 1er Cru Petite Chapelle 2015

From a *climat* that many historical documents indicate as an appendage of the Grand Cru Chapelle-Chambertin, Trapet's plot has been a family holding since the end of the nineteenth century. The 2015 bottling, vinified with 100% de-stemmed grapes, shows enviable aromatic contrasts, tension on the palate, and refreshing flavor at the finish, all in the name of elegance.

Gevrey-Chambertin 1er Cru Clos Prieur 2015

The name of this Cru refers to the Prior of the Abbey of Cluny, which owned the property in the tenth century. Critics tend to agree that this vineyard should produce simple and direct wines not at all in line with the usual typology of Gevrey reds. As Armando Castagno put it: "We would call it a sexy wine, were we not talking about Benedictine monks." Jean-Louis has focused this version on dark fruit, a wine more compact than complex, to which time in bottle will hopefully develop some additional details.

Gevrey-Chambertin 1er Cru "Capita" 2015

In the Latin texts of Pliny the Elder, *capita vitis* is a locution indicating that the head of the vine is in its roots. These grapes were selected from three different parcels (aux Combottes, les Corbeaux, en Ergot) assembled in the most ethereal of Premier Crus, light and almost airy to the touch, with a refreshing finish.

Latricière-Chambertin Grand Cru 2015

The affection with which Jean-Louis talks about this wine has a lot to do with the date of the first harvest, done by his ancestors in 1904. The current planting dates back to 1938. The wine shows intensity and consistency along with a silky touch, still revealing only a hint of the remarkable potential minerality that will come with age, though the immediate charm is nonetheless irresistible.

Chambertin Grand Cru 2015

In describing a particularly successful Grand Cru, synthesis is a concept that often serves the purpose. A synthesis of power and elegance, of amplitude and tension, of expression and rigor, and so on. There's no avoiding the term in the case of Trapet's Chambertin, a wine coming from almost two hectares of vineyards planted in 1919. Here the synthesis is between a purity of style and an unfathomable depth of flavor, propitiated by a generous vintage and clay soils, which guarantee stability in the future of this wine.

Domaine des VAROILLES

GEVREY-CHAMBERTIN

11, Rue de l'Ancien Hopital - Tel. +33 (0) 3 80 343030
contact@domaine-varoilles.com | www.domaine-varoilles.com

10 hectares

Swiss-born Gilbert Hammel, an enologist with a degree in economics, became owner of Domaine des Varoilles in 1990. He took over from the Naigeon family and in the process acquired a long and noble repertoire of valuable vines which have been documented back to the twelfth century. Today, from the ten hectares of vineyards distributed over seven different *appellations* (largely centered in Gevrey), Gilbert derives wines inspired by a classic style, shying away from enological shortcuts and with respect for tradition. The *domaine* also maintains a store of some older vintages, offered at very fair prices, available at the winery.

Gevrey-Chambertin Clos du Meix des Ouches 2015

This one-hectare *monopole* at the edge of the city center borders a series of *climats* all characterized by alluvial soil, rich in the debris washing down from a *combe*. The mouth feel is enveloping with spicy notes that brace the palate for a surge of energy.

Gevrey-Chambertin 1er Cru La Romanée 2015

Protected by the woods that frame the cliffs of Combe Chaudron, this vineyard is also a one-hectare *monopole* exposed to the south, planted on thin and stony soils that have broken from the mother rock. The wine displays a tension and tannic depth in a gustatory framework of a certain austerity.

Gevrey-Chambertin 1er Cru Clos des Varoilles 2015

From the small stone house with blue shutters that dominates this ample *monopole* of about six hectares you can enjoy one of the most evocative (and least oleographic) views of the entire Côte de Nuits. The vineyard is affected by the cold air currents that run through the Combe Bossière, so the wine is slower to open up, without however renouncing the elegance that regularly defines this Premier Cru as the most successful of the Varoilles range.

Domaine du VIEUX COLLÈGE

MARSANNAY-LA-CÔTE
4, Rue du Vieux Collège - Tel. +33 (0) 3 80 521243
jp-eric.guyard@wanadoo.fr | www.domaineduvieuxcollege.com

25 hectares

The imminent promotion to Premier Cru of some of the best *climats* of Marsannay helps bring to light the work of a few meticulous *vignerons* who are increasingly aware of the value of their vineyards. One of the most promising is Éric Guyard, who has been running this *domaine* since 2006, a property that has been in his family for seven generations. It is a rather large *domaine* with about twenty-five hectares of vineyards between Marsannay and Fixin, all recently converted to organic viticulture. Vinifications of individual parcels and scrupulous loyalty to the different soils' profiles show Guyard's sensitive approach to the nature of *terroirs*, working, as he does, as the interpreter, rather than the author of his wines.

Marsannay Les Récilles 2015

This Marsannay has shapely tannic texture focused on delicious fruit, a wine that encourages drinkers to empty the glass.

Marsannay Les Longeroies 2015

Among the most accredited *climats* en route to a promotion to Premier Cru, the vineyards of Longeroies cover a series of complex plots composed of a compact layer of clay that tapers toward the highest part at three hundred meters of altitude. The 2015 vintage brought out the epicurean appeal of the wines of Marsannay with a lively balance between fruit, tannins and spicy nuances.

Marsannay Clos du Roy 2015

This vineyard beneath woods in the community of Chenôve boasts full eastern exposure and soils rich in fine gravel not unlike those of Corton-Bressandes, making this *climat* an ideal place to produce fragrant and fleshy red wines. This is a fine example, with a round and creamy palate and a lovely saline finish.

3

FROM MOREY-SAINT-DENIS TO CHAMBOLLE-MUSIGNY

MOREY-SAINT-DENIS

map *page* 508

It's called Morey-Saint-Denis but it could just as well have been named Morey-la-Roche, or even Morey-Tart. A decision was made in 1927 to associate the town with the name of one of its best vineyards. That wasn't an easy choice to judge by the evidence of heated local disputes at the time between devotees and detractors of Saint-Denis (the vineyard, that is, not the patron saint of France). In any case, the reputation of this *appellation*, one of the smallest in the Côte d'Or, owes much of its fame to the four Grand Crus situated in its territory (without considering Bonnes Mares, which lies almost entirely in the community of Chambolle), which together cover some 40 hectares, almost a third of the total vineyards. They apply to four Clos, a legacy of the various abbeys that controlled the best vineyards over the centuries. Coming from Gevrey on the *Route des Grands Crus*, the first you encounter is Clos de la Roche, planted on the same lean brown-calcareous soils of Latricières-Chambertin, of which it is a natural extension. Through two alterations (in 1936 and 1971), Clos de la Roche incorporated a range of contiguous *climats*, which have expanded the original four and a half hectares to almost seventeen. Less extensive, but no less parceled, is Clos Saint-Denis, from which more immediately elegant and finely-textured wines are derived, especially when compared to the ferrous minerality of Clos de la Roche. The delicacy of the wines has earned Clos Saint-Denis the sobriquet of "the Mozart of the Côte de Nuits" (Jean-François Bazin). The situation is quite different for the other two Grand Crus—Clos des Lambrays and Clos de Tart—both lying at the heart of the village of Morey and vinified *en monopole*. Although they are separated only by a road, they give life to distinctly different wines: Clos des Lambrays more spicy and svelte, Clos de Tart more mature and full-bodied. The community also has twenty Premier Cru vineyards. There is also a small enclave (three hectares of vineyards) devoted to white wines, adding a touch of diversity, best expressed in the Clos de Monts Luisants of the Ponsot family who recently reconverted the vineyard to its original planting of Aligoté grapes. Wine enthusiasts, as well as a large share of critics, like to describe Morey-Saint-Denis as balanced between the aristocratic power of Gevrey and the fascinating gentility of Chambolle. If, in the best of circumstances, combining these models results in an original and intriguing amalgam, it should be noted that the continual comparisons of Morey-Saint-Denis to its more established neighbors risks obscuring its wines' true personality.

CHAMBOLLE-MUSIGNY

map *page* 511

The wines of Chambolle have been associated with elegance and sensuality so often, that describing them that way risks sounding mundane. Fragrant, graceful, seductive, these wines are certainly not the most structured reds of Burgundy, nor are they the most deeply colored, due to a marked lack of clay and an overwhelming proportion of calcareous rock in the soil. Spread over 180 hectares, with 24 Premier Crus and only two Grand Crus (Bonnes Mares and Musigny) Chambolle is the home of refined, mineral-driven wines, often more elegant than powerful. Yet one should avoid associating the wines of Bonnes Mares with those of Musigny, since the prestige of the two *climats* is based on distinctly different characteristics. Bonnes-Mares, occupying 15 hectares (one and a half of which is in the territory of Morey-Saint-Denis) forms a large rectangle in which one could draw an imaginary diagonal line connecting the northwestern corner, with most parcels near Morey, to the southeastern corner, near Chambolle. To the west of this virtual line lie the deeper red and clay-based soils that produce wines with more intensity and verve. East of the line the soils are white, rich in pebbles, marl and limestone, rendering wines with a subtler elegance, more in line with the distinctive traits of the *appellation*. That delicate dignity is exalted in the wines of Musigny, a legendary *climat* extending over a dozen hectares and subdivided into Les Musigny and Petits Musigny (the latter a *monopole* of Domaine Comte de Vogüé, whose holdings include also half of Les Musigny). Part of the Combe d'Orveau is customarily included in the Grands Crus of this *appellation*, a *monopole* of Domaine Jacques Prieur. A beautifully positioned vineyard overlooking the Clos de Vougeot, with a moderate slope (up to 15%) and shallow calcareous soils, the Musigny vineyard is as meritorious as any of the more legendary *climats* of Burgundy, producing hypnotic, velvet-textured wines with endless mineral length. For the record, it should be noted that the only white Grand Cru of the Côte de Nuits came from the chalky marls of Chambolle's northernmost strip, even though the wine has been sold simply as Bourgogne Blanc from the date of its last replanting, in 1994. Just a few meters from Musigny, in a setting with the Clos de Vougeot castle in the background, lie the vineyards of Les Amoureuses, an extraordinary Premier Cru that expresses all the magic and delicacy of Chambolle in a way that many associate with the most elegant and long-lived of Grand Crus.

ARLAUD

MOREY-SAINT-DENIS

41, Rue d'Epernay - Tel. +33 (0) 3 80 343265
contact@domainearlaud.com | www.domainearlaud.com

15 hectares

Despite the cold of early December, we spent a pleasant day with Cyprien Arlaud. He invited us to lunch in his historic cellar, filled with charming stone carvings, in the center of Nuits-Saint-Georges, then escorted us to Morey, where we tasted the 2015 vintage at the actual *cuverie*. Since his brother Romain left the *domaine* in 2013, Cyprien has run the winery alone with more than fifteen hectares of vineyards scattered through the communities of Morey, Chambolle and Gevrey. His sister, Bertille, a specialist in equestrian training, assists him with her two horses in working the five hectares of Grand Cru and Premier Cru vineyards. The *domaine*, which ceased the use of herbicides twenty years ago, had been certified as organic since 2010 while converting to biodynamics, completed in 2014. Some 70,000 bottles are produced each year, covering almost twenty different labels. A growing tendency toward stem-inclusion in vinification has contributed to the Arlaud style in wines that are bright, expressive and pure.

Bourgogne Roncevie 2015

From a *lieu-dit* of the southern sector of Gevrey, below the road that runs along the lower side of Charmes and Mazoyeres, this is a juicy and carefree *vin de soif*, of deliciously crisp fruitiness.

Morey-Saint-Denis 2015

In this wine, an assemblage of two different parcels—Clos Solon, near the village of Morey, and En Seuvrey, which borders Gevrey—the gritty wildness typical of the *appellation* bolsters dynamic flavors.

Morey-Saint-Denis 1er Cru Les Blanchards 2015

This small *climat*, with its clay soils and prominent calcareous stones, is bottled by few wineries. Arlaud's version hits the mark by virtue of a conspicuous tang of dark berry fruit that fills the palate with sanguine vitality.

Morey-Saint-Denis 1er Cru Aux Cheseaux 2015

The etymology of this small *climat* stems from the Latin *ex casalis* (from the farmhouses) a term shared with the vast group of vineyards called Echezeaux. The vineyards are at the northernmost limit of the *appellation*, near Gevrey. That may be why the wine recalls the depth of the reds of Gevrey, while reflecting the calcareous dominance of the soils of Morey in a convincingly delicious finish.

Morey-Saint-Denis 1er Cru Le Ruchots 2015

The vineyards lie on a slope facing Chambolle, close to the edge of Clos de Tart, in calcareous soils with no shortage of fossil shells. Despite a tight grip of tannic structure, the wine maintains its energy and vitality.

Clos de la Roche Grand Cru 2015

Arlaud has a parcel of almost half a hectare in this historic *climat* from which he derives a red wine of rare elegance and aromatic complexity. The embroidery of scents coincides with an intensity of flavors that flood the palate with three-dimensional richness.

Ghislaine BARTHOD

CHAMBOLLE-MUSIGNY

4, Ruelle du Lavoir - Tel. +33 (0) 3 80 628016

6.5 hectares

Ghislaine Barthod is a charismatic woman of the wine world, who for thirty years has been running one of the wineries most closely linked to the identity of Chambolle. Her nearly seven hectares of vineyards, inherited from the Noëllat family on her mother's side, are all located within the community and extend over ten different *climats*. Ghislaine is married to Louis Boillot, whose own *domaine* shares the winery with her. She crafts red wines brimming with fragrance and elegance, though she strongly rejects the cliché of dainty and subdued femininity. Instead, with consummate skill, strong determination and a cultivated taste for nuance, she imbues her wines with energy, passion and flavor.

Bourgogne 2015

The vineyard is in the *lieu-dit* Bons Bâtons, on the other side of the Route Nationale. The wine reveals and uncommonly dense texture and juicy flavors full of energy.

Chambolle-Musigny 2015

A quota of the grapes comes from Les Clos, a vineyard facing the Combe Ambin and exposed to the northeast with a microclimate that innervates the wine with aromatic notes of mulberry and Mediterranean brush and flavors of savory vitality with hints of exotic spices.

Chambolle-Musigny 1er Cru Les Véroilles 2015

Located at more than 300 meters of altitude between the Grand Cru Bonnes-Mares and the woods, Véroilles is an ample *climat* of almost six hectares of which only a tenth is classified as Premier Cru. This version shows a lively, somewhat wild streak amended by the herbaceous tendencies and acidic edges that identify the wine from cooler vintages.

Chambolle-Musigny 1er Cru Aux Beaux Bruns 2015

Expressive and inviting, the wine of Beaux Bruns is often *très Chambolle*. Here it releases an irresistible aromatic outpouring of wildflowers, resin and spices from a generous vintage that extols a sensual juiciness on the palate.

CLOS de TART

MOREY-SAINT-DENIS

7, Route des Grands Crus - Tel. +33 (0) 3 80 343091
contact@clos-de-tart.com | www.clos-de-tart.com

7.53 hectares

Founded in 1141 by Bernardine nuns, then surrounded by walls in the fifteenth century, the Clos remained in the same hands until the French Revolution, when it was sold as a *bien national* in 1791. The Mommessin family bought it in 1932 from the Marey-Monge family and ratified its classification as Grand Cru in 1939. The red wine produced here has a centuries-old reputation, based on an expressive completeness, which, in the best examples, draws on both the fleshy depth of a Chambertin and the slender finesse of a Musigny. When the *domaine* was entrusted to the management of Sylvain Pitiot in the mid-nineties, he propelled a surge in quality that heightened the winery's fame. A demanding and meticulous *régisseur*, Pitiot is well known to enthusiasts for his essential work as the cartographer who created the best maps in circulation of the Burgundian *appellations*. Upon his arrival at Clos de Tart, he began preparing detailed maps of the vineyards, according to different types of soil, aided by Claude Bourguignon, allowing targeted harvests of different areas and individual vinification of the parcels in the new *cuverie*. Under Pitiot's management, a new stylistic dimension of the wine emerged, brilliant in its crafting and more refined in its tannic texture, although still demanding in terms of concentration and spiciness. In 2015, Pitiot retired and was succeeded by Jacques Devauges, the former enologist of Domaine de l'Arlot. His arrival coincided with new production guidelines, such as organic certification, the first steps towards biodynamics, and a gradual reduction in the use of new wood for the *élevage*, which, under Pitiot's order had been employed at a full-fledged, 100%. The results of this new direction have yet to be seen, especially in light of the Mommessin family's sale of the property in November 2017. The buyer is multi-millionaire François Pinault, already owner of Château la Tour in Bordeaux and of Domaine d'Eugenie in Vosne-Romanée, who acquired the property at a figure estimated at around 250 million euros—a record sum that has caused considerable discussion.

Clos de Tart Grand Cru 2015

Clos de Tart covers seven and a half hectares of vineyards planted, in an unusual pattern for the Cote d'Or, with the rows oriented in a north-south direction, perpendicular to the contours of the slope with the aim of reducing soil erosion and balancing water drainage. Pitiot's meticulous cartographical plan divided the vineyards into twenty-seven different parcels, which are then vinified in eight distinct *cuvées*, assembled according to balance and ripeness. The 2015 harvest began on September 5, starting with the younger vines, the fruit of which generally goes into the "second wine" of the *domaine*, La Forge de Tart, but instead went entirely into the Close de Tart Grand Cru. In anticipation of the final blend, we tasted six of these *cuvées*, which were vinified with about 50% whole clusters. In each *cuvée* we found a distinct expression. For instance, the parcel of *vieilles vignes* (over fifty years old and bordering on Clos de Lambrays) showed a velvety touch and classic flavors, while that on the edge of Bonnes Mares showed energy and substance, and the parcel from vineyards with soils rich in marl showed freshness and floral nuances. Our "hypothesis" of Clos de Tart 2015 is that the wine will undoubtedly need a long time to liberate its many-voiced energies and attain its true potential, though its intensity and finesse are already quite apparent.

DUJAC

MOREY-SAINT-DENIS

7, Rue de la Bussiere - Tel. +33 (0) 3 80 340100
dujac@dujac.com | www.dujac.com

17.3 hectares

In 1967, Jacques Seysses, then the young scion of a thriving biscuit business with a reputation as a *bon vivant*, purchased a small winery in Morey (Domaine Graillet), changed its name to Dujac, and started from zero. In less than thirty years, the family-run *domaine* had established itself in the upper echelon of Burgundian wine with more than seventeen hectares of vineyards, including seven Grand Cru (two hectares in the Clos de la Roche, one and a half in the Clos Saint-Denis). The wines, vinified largely using whole clusters, are seductively aromatic and monumentally long-lived. A few years ago, control of the winery passed to Jacques' sons Alec and Jeremy (and the American wife of the latter, Diana, an enologist), who gradually converted to an organic regime, certified in 2009. For some years now, to cope with ever-increasing demand, the firm added a *négociant* operation called Dujac Fils et Père with a reliable repertoire of bottlings.

Morey-Saint-Denis 1er Cru 2015

Three quarters of this wine come from the prestigious, stony *climat* Les Ruchots, on the side of Morey facing Chambolle, beneath the Clos de Tart. The aromatics recall wild cherries and the centrality of the fruit enhances a dynamic and delicious palate.

Gevrey-Chambertin 1er Cru Aux Combottes 2015

In his meticulous exploration of the vineyards of the Côte d'Or, Armando Castagno insists on the atypical classification of this *climat*, the one exception in a strip of Grand Crus that connects Ruchottes-Chambertin to Bonnes-Mares. His assertion is based on a number of details, the most important being the proximity of the Combe Grisard, "which wafts cool air on the southern half of the cru almost all year round." In Dujac's version, perhaps the most famous, the wine's aromatic complexity clearly benefits from the use of 80% whole cluster grapes and the finish heralds a promising future.

Vosne-Romanée 1er Cru Aux Malconsorts 2015

The vineyards are situated near those of La Tâche, taking in a portion of a hectare rich in clay purchased in 2005 (from Domaine Thomas) to corroborate the already excellent reputation of this *climat*. While we tasted the wine, Alec told us, "before tasting our Malconsorts, my wife was very fond of me, but after drinking it she fell in love." The most striking features of the wine are the fine-grained tannins and elegant spiciness.

Clos de la Roche Grand Cru 2015

The ferrous nature typical of the *cru* marks this wine with a solid tannic framework. The wine is made from two hectares of vineyards that largely date back to the family's original acquisition. Although a few years in bottle are certainly needed to bring its intensity into focus, even now the wine exhibits a host of aromatics and ample refinement.

Clos Saint-Denis Grand Cru 2015

As Jean-François Bazin put it, "if Clos de la Roche is Beethoven, then Clos Saint-Denis would be Mozart." Finer in texture perhaps, but without losing its tannic grip. There is, in fact, a duality to this wine: on the one hand a more stylized side and on the other something grittier, a spherical souplesse of fleshy fruit and a ridge of tannic-acid. Time will reveal its true potential.

Robert GROFFIER Père et Fils

MOREY-SAINT-DENIS

3, Route des Grands Crus - Tel. +33 (0) 3 80 343153

8 hectares

The winery is based in Morey, but the bulk of its vineyards are in Chambolle: some eight hectares dedicated to Pinot Noir, source of intense and refined wines that have become steadily more prestigious. This is the hallmark of a *domaine* that has passed from father Robert to son Serge, and then to his nephew Nicolas, responsible for his own perfectionist touches. The quest for concentration has resulted in very low grape yields reinforced by the conversion of vine training from *guyot* to *cordon de royat*. The challenge comes in harmonizing such exuberant and fleshy fruit with velvety tannins, wrapping everything in an elegant package but avoiding any hint of flamboyance. A decidedly ambitious bet, which the Groffier family has no intention of losing.

Chambolle-Musigny 1er Cru Les Sentiers 2015

More than one expert considers Groffier to be the reference point for this *climat*, sometimes known as the "poor man's Bonnes-Mares." It might not have the complexity of the best wines of Bonnes-Mares, but it's not missing any of the sweet and savory intensity.

Chambolle-Musigny 1er Cru Les Hauts-Doix 2015

Not even two hectares of vineyards bordering Les Amoureuses on its northeastern flank, of which more than half are owned by Groffier. A small *climat* with a "*très Chambolle*" character, nurturing a red with a fine floral base.

Chambolle-Musigny 1er Cru Les Amoureuses 2015

The aristocratic coat-of-arms of this *climat* owes much to its geology, marked by sandy veins, by small quantities of clays and by an important fissuring of the rocks. Special merit, however, must be reserved for the winemaking skills of talented *vignerons* like Groffier, able to exalt the timeless appeal of its many-faceted aromas.

Henri JOUAN

MOREY-SAINT-DENIS

3, Rue St Roch - Tel. +33 (0) 3 80 343468

4.5 hectares

Since Henri Jouan passed the guidance to his son Philippe a few years ago, little has changed in terms of the structure or strategy of this admirable small *domaine* in Morey-Saint-Denis. The property owns about three hectares of vineyards and leases some historical parcels for a total of less than five hectares, though not all the wine is bottled for the *domaine*. Maison Joseph Drouhin has purchased grapes from the family for more than fifty years, including a portion of their Clos-Saint-Denis. The style of the wines retains a traditional feel. Made from completely de-stemmed grapes, they are intensely aromatic reds with a frank and penetrating palate.

Coteaux Bourguignons Pinot Noir Vieilles Vignes 2015

The Jouan have parcels of old vines to back each bottling, and even the red "entry-level" is no exception. It offers simple and immediate satisfaction, while retaining something particularly frank and honest in flavor.

Morey-Saint-Denis Vieilles Vignes 2015

Obtained from the blending of grapes from three different *lieux-dits*—Les Crais Gillon, Corvée and Le Village—this is a red of a typically masculine nature with vigorous structure complemented by compelling scents of mulberry and spices with tight and tonic flavors, and a tannic bite.

Morey-Saint-Denis 1er Cru Clos Sorbé 2015

From a qualitative point of view, Clos Sorbé is one of Morey's most esteemed Premier Crus. Jouan has two small parcels with eighty-year-old vines for wines that are regularly cited as a reference point for this *climat*, no less successful than those of David Duband. Floral yet fleshy, mature but refreshing, the wine shows solidity and balance on the palate with rich flavors and nuances such as hints of incense.

Domaine des LAMBRAYS

MOREY-SAINT-DENIS
31, Rue basse - Tel. +33 (0) 3 80 518433
clos@lambrays.com | www.lambrays.com

10.7 hectares

A fascinating icon of Burgundian wine, this Clos of almost nine hectares constitutes a slightly wider and less squared off *monopole* than its neighboring Clos de Tart, with a significant difference in altitude of more than sixty meters between its top and base. Strictly speaking, it would be more accurately described as a "*quasi-monopole*" considering that the equivalent of about one barrique of wine comes from an old vegetable garden turned vineyard in 1974, belonging, curiously enough, to Domaine Taupenot-Merme, thus preventing the labeling of the wine as "*monopole*" by Domaine des Lambrays.
The first accounts of the Clos date back to the fourteenth century, but by the early nineteenth century it had been fragmented into more than seventy parcels. Reassembled by a local *négociant* and later sold to the Rodier family, it eventually passed into the hands of a certain Madame Cosson. Thanks to the efforts of the Saier brothers, who acquired the property in the late 1970s, the Clos was formally recognized as a Grand Cru in1981, after which an important vineyard replanting program began. Since 1996, the *domaine* has been owned by the Freund family of Koblenz, but its management remained entrusted to Thierry Brouin, an affable and savvy *régisseur* who today, on the threshold of retirement, can boast almost forty years of service to the Clos.
In April of 2014 the *domaine* saw its latest change of regime with an acquisition (for close to 100 million euros) by the LVMH group of Louis Vuitton, a giant of luxury goods, owner of wine brands such as Krug, Cheval Blanc, Yquem and Dom Pérignon. The repercussions of this new scenario, in terms of vineyard management and the strategy concerning the style (and price) of wines, will obviously be better understood in the future. So far the vineyard has been managed according to organically-inspired principles (*lutte raisonnée*) with extensive use of horses for much of the vineyard work. Vinification has been conducted with stem-inclusion, on the basis of different parcels (from four to seven *cuvées*, depending on the vintage), with the grapes from the younger vines being declassified and diverted to a Morey-Saint-Denis Premier Cru called Les Loups.

The result is a stylized, fragrant and sleek Grand Cru that faithfully translates the vintage through a knowing quest for transparency. A true classic, with loads of personality and admirable dimensions.

Morey-Saint-Denis 2015

This wine is composed of grapes from four *climats* covering an ample hectare of vineyards including Riotte, Clos Solon, Les Larreys and La Bidaude. The nose is still a bit reticent, but on the palate the wine is redeemed by its breadth and depth.

Clos des Lambrays Grand Cru 2015

Among the few vineyards planted in north-south rows, Clos des Lambrays rests on medium-steep terrain somewhat more ferrous than the Clos de Tart. Its splendid aromas are due to a contribution of the stems that innervates the wine's floral finesse with enticing wild spice (pepper) refined by a noble dose of incense. Beautiful also on the palate, the wine already exhibits both maturity and elegance with extreme nonchalance.

Hubert LIGNIER

MOREY-SAINT-DENIS

45, Grande Rue - Tel. +33 (0) 3 80 518740
domaine.hubert.lignier@orange.fr | www.hubert-lignier.com

9 hectares

Founded in 1880, the *domaine* is now firmly in the hands of Laurent Lignier, after the death in 2004 of his elder brother Romain understandably generated some uncertainty. The picture has become clearer since it became apparent that Romain's widow had intended to baptize a new project in the names of their children (Lucie and Auguste Lignier) that has triggered the inevitable division of the most historic and important vineyards pertaining to the family *domaine*. Laurent continues to stress that his brother played a determinate role in building the reputation of the *domaine* admired for the classical style of its wines. Today Laurent seems to have returned to the path toward quintessence and clarity in his wines, renewing their connection with each vineyards' particular expression of *terroir*.

Morey-Saint-Denis "Trilogie" 2015

A blend of three old vineyards (Chenevery, Clos Solon, Porroux), planted between 1936 and 1972 west of the Route Nationale, reveals surprising depth and concentration well supported by vibrant freshness, qualities unexpected in a Villages.

Morey-Saint-Denis 1er Cru Vieilles Vignes 2015

The low yields imposed by the vintage (less than 25 hectoliters per hectare) favor a certain fleshiness, though the venerable age of the over-seventy-year-old vines (Faconnières, Chenevery) guarantees an expressive balance and finesse of high-toned floral notes.

Clos de la Roche Grand Cru 2015

Covering almost a hectare, and with a slope that reaches almost 25%, the historic Hubert Lignier parcel of Clos de le Roche is made up of two-thirds Monts Luisants and a third Fremières. The 2015 bottling has that material richness that announces bright possibilities with age, even if at the moment of our barrel tastings the wine was still partially harnessed by spicy oak.

After the catastrophe of phylloxera, which at the end of the nineteenth century almost completely destroyed the vines of Europe, the vineyard terrains in the stoniest soils were abandoned as unsuitable for growing vegetables, and instead became grazing land for goats and some horses. Jacques Lignier, founder of the *domaine*, had the foresight (and good luck) to purchase for a pittance almost all of the family's current parcel of Clos de la Roche, which would return in the following decades to fully redeem its reputation as a Grand Cru. This anecdote was shared with us by Laurent during a vertical tasting of his Clos de la Roche, which he generously shared with us. Here is a quick review.

2012 The legendary solidity of the *cru* shows in this vintage a precious dose of elegance, which highlights its splendid purity and intensity, followed by a long finish of aromatic herbs.
2011 The literary praise of a vintage that generated sunny and delicious wines is fully reflected in this soft red, with a round and satisfying mouth feel.
2010 Five years after its release (and from tastings for the previous edition of this book) we find this wine in dazzling form, chiseled by an enchanting aromatic purity, overflowing with vitality and freshness.
2008 The "Nordic" quality of the vintage is apparent in the aromatic austerity, though the palate is livelier, marked by citrus, particularly mandarin, and permeated by saline notes.
2007 The power of the *climat* is apparent in a wine that is reticent but still energetic, though it seems to be undergoing a bit of a closed phase.
2001 The last vintage to be vinified by Romain reveals complexity with a twilight tone in a framework of earthy and autumnal notes.
1989 This vintage was made by Hubert (father of Romain and Laurent) releasing a wine that has evolved without any failure; the palate is vivacious and rhythmic with a wonderful saline finish.

Michel MAGNIEN

MOREY-SAINT-DENIS
4, Rue Ribordot - Tel. +33 (0) 3 80 518298
domaine@michel-magnien.com | www.domaine-magnien.com

18 hectares

After Frédéric Magnien joined his father Michel at the *domaine*, now twenty-five years ago, the structure of the winery underwent a critical redefinition. As a first step in the mid-nineties, they decided to bottle the entire production under the property's name. Subsequently the conversion to organic farming began and finally, in 2015, the *domaine* became fully certified as biodynamic by Demeter. The Magnien's many parcels (a total of eighteen hectares) are divided between Gevrey and Chambolle, with an important nucleus in Morey. The grapes are harvested at full maturity, and in most recent years included a variable percentage of stems. With the 2015 harvest, the winery begun using terracotta amphorae for aging, in addition to traditional barrels. Frédéric Magnien has a house dedicated to *négociant* activity, though the wines that offer a bonus of precision and finesse customarily originate in the *domaine* Michel Magnien.

Morey-Saint-Denis 1er Cru Les Millandes 2015

At the edge of the village just below Clos de la Roche, Magnien has about half a hectare of vineyards on reddish soils that recall the texture of Charmes-Chambertin, for a wine exuding energy and ripe tannins.

Morey-Saint-Denis 1er Cru Aux Charmes 2015

The *appellation* Morey-Saint-Denis, like most others in the Côte d'Or, has its own *climat* named Charmes. In this case it is a continuation of the Grand Cru Mazoyères-Chambertin of Gevrey and produces a red where energy and substance interact in animated balance.

Clos de la Roche Grand Cru 2015

The *domaine*'s parcel is located in the Mont Luisants sector, which always distinguishes itself by an aromatic intensity and depth of tannins. The rocky terrain of this vineyard is reflected in the breadth of flavor with a fullness on the palate that is entirely Grand Cru.

Stéphane MAGNIEN

MOREY-SAINT-DENIS

5, Ruelle de l'Eglise - Tel. +33 (0) 3 80 518310
mail@domainemagnien.com | www.domainemagnien.com

4.5 hectares

Stéphane Magnien joined his father Jean-Paul at the *domaine* in 2002, and from 2008 has headed the operation as the fourth generation of the family since its inception in 1897. Their four and a half hectares of vineyard are centered in Morey and are managed in the spirit of careful and balanced viticulture. Stéphane emphasizes that the vines have never been exposed to herbicides. Vinification starts from fully de-stemmed grapes, with macerations that do not exceed two weeks. The wines effectively express the potential of the best red wines of Morey, capable of combining energy with nuance.

Bourgogne Passetoutgrain Cuvée Densité 2015

We were enchanted by this *cuvée* of Pinot Noir and Gamay, which repays its ridiculously low price (just over ten euros) for mouthfuls of carefree lightness.

Morey-Saint-Denis 2015

This blend from four different parcels of old vines reveals a graceful hand in a wine of finesse, even though surprisingly none of the vineyards borders on Chambolle.

Chambolle-Musigny 1er Cru Les Sentiers 2015

The etymology of the vineyard name reminds us that we are on the path between Chambolle and Morey, precisely at the foot of Bonnes Mares. This wine does not deny its origins and shows intensity in color, dark berry fruit (blueberry) mottled with peppery nuances, as well as a tannic structure that marks a strong difference from the more delicate wines of Chambolle.

Clos-Saint-Denis Grand Cru 2015

Few wines of the Côte de Nuits can match the elegance of the wines of this Grand Cru. Notes of wisteria, raspberry, citrus and incense compose a profile of profound aromatic complexity. The palate offers a wealth of fruit and flavor. Like the best of 2015, this wine is already exquisite, but there is good reason to believe that the next few years in bottle will bring out significantly enhanced complexity.

Jacques-Frédéric MUGNIER

CHAMBOLLE-MUSIGNY

Château de Chambolle-Musigny - Tel. +33 (0) 3 80 628539
info@mugnier.fr | www.mugnier.fr

14 hectares

Frédéric Mugnier purchased the Château de Chambolle-Musigny in 1863, with its four hectares of vineyards, and the *domaine* has remained in the family's possession ever since. Born in 1830, Frédéric enjoyed reinvesting the profits from the family's successful Dijon-based liquor company in the winery. In 1880, in the midst of the scourge of phylloxera which caused a major depression in vineyard prices, he astutely decided to expand vineyard holdings by acquiring an important nucleus of parcels in Chambolle from the Marey-Monge family. This was followed in 1902 by the purchase of Clos de la Maréchale at Prémeaux. At that time the wines bottled at the *domaine* with the Château de Chambolle-Musigny label were sold in Paris and the United States, capitalizing on the remarkable commercial success of the family's liqueurs. The deaths of both Frédéric and then his son Ernest led to a period of decline in the *domaine* and conflicts within the family, culminating in the sale of a good portion of the vineyards, almost entirely to the Drouhin family. It took about sixty years to reverse this substantial neglect in the management of the *domaine*, when, in the mid-eighties the third Frédéric of the dynasty, born in 1955 and current owner, took over. A man of many talents, he was an engineer in the oil industry and an airline pilot, but, as he put it, "At one point I got tired of traveling, so I dropped my suitcase at Chambolle and began to try to understand what was happening to our *domaine*." To his credit the *domaine* took a radical turn of direction in its policy of leasing land to *négociants* while completely reintegrating the ten hectares used for tenant farming at the Clos de la Maréchale. Although Mugnier is anything but exuberant, he is certainly not lacking in conviction, and this same purposeful yet introverted and reserved character is reflected in his wines. Wines inspired by a quest for purity and authenticity that enhances their bare, but vibrant profile. It is no coincidence that Mugnier loves to compare the style of his own wines with the inspiration that steers the best Japanese cuisine: a work in subtraction. His approach to organic farming is also pragmatic and personalized. For example, he is somewhat skeptical about biodynamics and completely de-stems his grapes. "I do not have a very romantic idea of winemaking.

I do not consider it a creative process. I'm only responsible for providing the right environment for the grapes to be able to turn into wine." We might add that when the grapes derive from vineyards of this level, there's no reason to worry about the work in the cellars.

Chambolle-Musigny 2015

By declassifying parcels with Premier Cru status (Les Plantes, Combe d'Orveau), Mugnier crafts a juicy and conversational Villages, which pretends to be simple but is anything but.

Chambolle-Musigny 1er Cru Les Fuées 2015

The terrain of this *climat* is a natural continuation of Grand Cru Bonnes-Mares. The wine shows how the most gentle and elegant soul of the reds of Chambolle yet gives way to greater tannic tension and savory-mineral grit.

Nuits-Saint-Georges 1er Cru Clos de la Maréchale 2015

Clos de la Maréchale is the largest *monopole* in Burgundy, located in Prémeaux-Prissey, in the extreme south of the Nuits-Saint-Georges *appellation*. Reviewed in the *classement* of 1855 by Jules Laval as Clos des Fourches (1ère Cuvée), it seems that it was already called La Maréchale, though the origins of the name remain uncertain. Frédéric Mugnier regained possession of the vineyard in 2004, after having rented it to Faiveley for more than fifty years. The 2015 harvest offers a wine that manages to be concentrated and dense without losing its usual energy. Frédéric also produces a white bottling from this vineyard, sourced out of a parcel in the northwest corner of the *clos* planted in Chardonnay. In some years a second selection of red wine is also bottled, aptly baptized Clos des Fourches.

Chambolle-Musigny 1er Cru Les Amoureuses 2015

In a *climat* unanimously considered one of the most fascinating and complete Premier Crus of the entire Côte-de-Nuits, Mugnier's portion contains half a hectare of vines with an average fifty-five years of age. The 2015 bottling does not have the lyrical and quintessential inspiration that we found in 2014, but it is certainly among the most "subtractive" wines of the *domaine*, pushing itself forward in a quest for purity.

Bonnes Mares Grand Cru 2015

Bonnes-Mares is commonly considered to be poised between the tenacious wildness of Morey and the delicate fruit of Chambolle. In this case, the parcel of almost one and a half hectares, whose original nucleus was planted in 1950 and integrated in the eighties, gives life to a wine of chiaroscuro shadings in which balance has yet to be achieved.

Musigny Grand Cru 2015

Planted between 1948 and 1962, Mugnier's vineyards (a little more than a hectare) give a version of Musigny Grand Cru that stresses the aromatic finesse and the complex persistence of the finish in the mouth. The nose is pure and inviting, with hints of pomegranate that return on the palate, where it offers an exciting intensity, revealing a reserve of energy that turns resolutely toward a savory timbre, fascinating in its resonant vibrations. Frédéric couldn't bear to see his Musigny uncorked so young in restaurants and has therefore delayed the release on the market for a few years. Knowing what we do about 2015 and all of its potential for evolution, this seems an especially smart move.

PERROT-MINOT

MOREY-SAINT-DENIS

54, Route des Grands Crus - Tel. +33 (0) 3 80 343251
gfa.perrot-minot@wanadoo.fr | www.perrot-minot.com

13.5 hectares

Christophe Perrot-Minot has been at the helm of his family winery since 1993, though it was only with the acquisition in 2000 of vineyards belonging to the Domaine Pernin-Rossin that the *domaine* assumed its current dimensions. Production today is about fifty thousand bottles per years form thirteen hectares spread over many prestigious *appellations* and farmed responsibly by *lutte raisonnée*. "What interests me in wine is balance and digestibility," says Christophe, always looking for the right mouth feel, with a particular inclination toward the most elegant and silky textures. In the cellar the proportions of de-stemmed grapes change from time to time, according to the vintage and the *climat*. "The goal is to have perfectly mature grapes without leaving much room to intervention in the cellar," he says. In fact, in most cases the quality of different *terroirs* is expressed with sensitivity and precision, although this is less apparent in the so-called *Cuvées Ultra*, which are bottlings of allocated plots from his best vineyards in Nuits and Chambolle (La Richemone e La Combe d'Orveau). We tasted only the 2014 vintage, which had matured in bottle for several months and revealed a convincingly expressive focus, signaling a drift away from a style of the past that sometimes seemed aimed at demonstrative exploits.

Morey-Saint-Denis 1er Cru La Riotte 2014

This little known *climat* is at the exit of the eastern side of town; this version shows a well-defined sculpting of contours with a firm mineral finish.

Vosne-Romanée 1er Cru Beaux Monts 2014

The wines coming from the lower sector of this *climat* have a reputation for exceptional finesse as fully reflected here. The aromatic profile is almost ethereal, the taste both soft and rhythmic.

Nuits-Saint-Georges 1er Cru La Richemone 2014

This steep vineyard (12% incline), is not far from the border of Vosne. A good percentage of the vines dates back to the first planting of 1901: the wine derived from them is austere and slow to evolve, despite the delicate texture and an incisive acceleration at the finish.

Mazoyères-Chambertin Grand Cru 2014

Few wineries bottle this Grand Cru under the name of Mazoyères-Chambertin, since they also have the option to label the wine in reference to neighboring Charmes-Chambertin (generally a more euphonic and commercially palatable option). Perrot-Minot goes against the grain and vinifies his parcels of both *crus* separately, regardless of the name. This bottling flaunts its vivacity with notes of black berries in a wine of uncommon density and energy.

Chambertin Clos de Bèze Grand Cru Vieilles Vignes 2014

A *terroir* of rare personality, here interpreted with the use of a considerable percentage of whole cluster grapes (80%). Even in an embryonic phase the wine reveals remarkable harmony based on velvety texture and typical spicy notes. "A good wine when young, will be much the same when old," says Christophe, citing Henri Jayer.

PONSOT

MOREY-SAINT-DENIS

21, Rue de la Montagne - Tel. +33 (0) 3 80 343246
info@domaine-ponsot.com | www.domaine-ponsot.com

10 hectares

Domaine Ponsot has reached a turning point that will inevitably leave its mark: after thirty-six vintages Laurent Ponsot has decided to leave the direction of the family winery to start up his own *domaine* with the help of his son, Clément. Laurent himself told us the news during our last visit at the end of January 2017. In reality it is not a final exit, since Laurent will retain possession of a quarter of the shares; but three quarters will pass into the hands of his three sisters, with Rose-Marie leading the operations. With the 2017 harvest, a new chapter began and 60-year-old Laurent launched a new brand: Maison Laurent Ponsot, centered on *négociant* bottlings which had already been part of the *domaine*'s activities since 1989 (Chambertin, Clos Saint Denis, Corton- Charlemagne and Mersault Perrières are just some of the more prestigious parcels that will become part of the offerings). As for Domaine Ponsot, we'll need to wait for a better understanding of the future, since increasingly insistent rumors signal potential negotiations in progress for a sale. While waiting to evaluate the developments of this intricate affair, we consoled ourselves by tasting a battery of wines from the 2014 harvest: as usual, all of absolute importance.

Morey-Saint-Denis 1er Cru Clos des Monts Luisants 2014

The black sheep of the Ponsot house, the only Premier Cru Aligoté made in the entire Côte d'Or. This is a brilliant bottling, aromatically precise and tense on the palate.

Chapelle-Chambertin Grand Cru 2014

In classic vintages like 2014 Chapelle-Chambertin best shows its class with a tannic finesse that recalls the best interpretations of Chambolle Grand Cru. The wine's expressive grace is veined with sensuality.

Clos Saint-Denis Grand Cru 2014

This vineyard (planted in 1905) has a yield that barely reaches fifteen hectoliters per hectare. The result is a wine of rare *souplesse* and finesse that from the first sip will help you grasp what François Bazin meant when he called Clos Saint-Denis "the Mozart of the Côte de Nuits."

Clos de la Roche Grand Cru 2014

The 3.5-hectare parcel is situated in the core of the original Grand Cru (before the classification of 1936 incorporated pieces of many neighboring *climats* and increased the few original hectares into what is now almost seventeen). It is difficult to imagine a more closed and austere expression of Clos de la Roche; its complexity is noteworthy, but the wine is clearly still in its infancy.

Gérard RAPHET

MOREY-SAINT-DENIS

25, Route des Grands Crus - Tel. +33 (0) 3 80 518952

12 hectares

This family winery, which has been active for four generations in the village of Morey, in 2002 came under the guidance of Gérard, who took over from his father, Jean. Today Gérard, his wife Sylviane and recently also their daughter Marion, work together. The style of the wines is classic: "elegance and drinkability are the main qualities I look for in a wine," says Gérard. After de-stemming, cold pre-maceration precedes the alcoholic fermentation and a short maceration on the skins. The resulting wines have an enviable aromatic transparency, inspired by a model of Burgundy that respects tradition, but is not at all predictable. The twelve hectares of vineyards are managed by *lutte raisonnée* in fact rather than in word. Among the fourteen *appellations*, Clos de Bèze, Clos de la Roche and Clos de Vougeot stand out, but even among more affordable labels there is no shortage of delights.

Morey-Saint Denis 2015

Here's a Villages wine that pretends to be simple, but the stripped down, almost raw-boned façade can't hide its spontaneous drinkability and markedly saline finish.

Gevrey-Chambertin 2015

Inviting aromas of raspberry and black currant, with slight smoky hints, the wine's flavors are innervated by a current of fresh acidity which then closes with exotic spicy notes. As Armando Castagno wrote, "the Orient on your palate."

Morey-Saint Denis 1er Cru Les Millandes 2015

This *terroir* is located east of Clos de la Roche, with which its wines often share a certain austerity. Raphet's interpretation enhances the floral notes in its composition within a framework of remarkable freshness and incisive flavors.

Gevrey-Chambertin 1er Cru Les Combottes 2015

From a vineyard poised between Premier Cru and Grand Cru classifications, Raphet derives a fleshy, vigorous and energetic Combottes, whose aromatic persistence is worthy of a higher category.

Chantal REMY

MOREY-SAINT-DENIS

1, Place du Monument - Tel. +33 (0) 3 80 343259
domaine.chantal.remy@orange.fr | www.domaine-chantal-remy.com

For visitors to the Côte de Nuits nostalgic for the charm of old Burgundy, 1 Place du Monument in Morey Saint-Denis should be an obligatory rite of passage. In any case it's that way for us, as we gladly return to this elegant pink house in the heart of Morey for the affectionate welcome of Chantal Remy, and also with reasonable expectations of purchasing a few bottles of older vintages, increasingly hard to find. The current vineyard holdings of the historic *domaine* that bore the name Louis Remy—and which included portions of prestigious vineyards, now acquired by Leroy, Ponsot and Duband—is divided into four small parcels owned by her son Florian. The viticulture is careful and calculated, using horses to work some of the land. The style of the wines highlights the differences between the diverse *terroirs* but is faithful to classic Burgundy, expressive and graceful to the core.

Morey-Saint-Denis Clos des Rosiers 2014

This small *monopole* vineyard (which is in fact an appendix to the home garden) was planted in 2000 and shares a border wall as well as soil composition with the lower sector of Clos de Lambrays. In fresh and classic vintages like 2014, this wine shines with commendable elegance and aromatic delicacy. Its promotion to Premier Cru is only a question of time.

Clos de la Roche Grand Cru 2014

Planted on mother rock, Chantal Remy's parcel of Clos de la Roche—almost half a hectare—is at the heart of the original Grand Cru, which was much smaller than it is now due to the 1935 classification. In this vintage the wine's proverbial solidity is embellished by more nuanced tones.

Georges ROUMIER

CHAMBOLLE-MUSIGNY

4, Rue de Vergy - Tel. +33 (0) 3 80 628637
domaine@roumier.com | www.roumier.com

11.8 hectares

Founded in 1924 by Georges Roumier, the *domaine* began bottling its own wine after World War II. Georges' nephew Christophe, who has been with the winery for thirty years, took over direction twenty years ago, showing a talent for optimizing the natural elegance of wines from Chambolle. Credit is also due to the historical family holdings, today encompassing nearly 12 hectares, many of which boast important vineyards in four different Grand Cru sites. Christophe is also an enologist, a graduate of Dijon, and is highly respected by his colleagues. The wines reflect his style, precise and scrupulous, always in search of harmony and expressive balance.

Morey-Saint-Denis 1er Cru Clos de la Bussière 2015

The Roumier family still lives in a house amid the vineyards that have been a *monopole* of the *domaine* since 1950. Despite the immediate proximity to Chambolle, wines from the clays soils of this *climat* are never refined or graceful, but rather tight and vigorous, perhaps the most robust of all the family's wines.

Chambolle-Musigny 1er Cru Les Cras 2015

In a *climat* planted on soils from a geological formation marked by a large calcareous block rich in fossils and active limestone, Roumier produces a fresh and relaxed wine, very elegant, with marked minerality.

Bonnes Mares Grand Cru 2015

The Roumier portion of Bonnes Mares extends over almost one and a half hectares and includes a plot planted on red soils and another on white marls. Christophe vinifies them separately and often uses them as examples of the differences in *terroir* during tastings in the cellar. The red soils render well-rounded wines rich in fruit, while from the white marls of the upper part of the Grand Cru, near Chambolle, wines display a more defined tannic structure that guarantee long aging potential.

TAUPENOT-MERME

MOREY-SAINT-DENIS
33, Route des Grands Crus - Tel. +33 (0) 3 80 343524
virginie.taupenot-daniel@orange.fr

13 hectares

Virginie Taupenot and her brother Romain run a thirteen-hectare *domaine* from their home base in Morey. The winery is easy to spot in the center of town, wedged between the noblest *clos* of the *appellation*. The most valuable legacy of vineyards derives mainly from the division of the Domaine Merme between the Taupenot and Perrot-Minot families. There are also parcels for white wine located between Auxey-Duresses and Saint Romain (their father's birthplace). But the *domaine* is most noted for reds covering various denominations, from the simple Bourgogne Passetoutgrain to Grand Cru bottlings such as Mazoyeres and Charmes-Chambertin. Among the twenty different bottlings, our experience with the 2015 vintage revealed a more calculated pursuit of balance (compared to the slightly more *boisé* style of past vintages) resulting in wines of greater spontaneity in harmony with their respective *terroirs*.

Bourgogne Passetoutgrain 2016

As an example of the new style of the *domaine*, this entry-level wine from the *lieu-dit* Croix Jeanniard, in the community of Morey, provides a light, easy and immediately enjoyable sip.

Morey-Saint-Denis 2015

Fresh, direct, juicy and focused on fruit. In the right years even the reds of Morey have citizenship rights *pour se faire plaisir*, as Virginie rightly claims. This wine comes from a parcel that borders that of Dujac and benefits from *millerandage* that concentrates the flavor while maintaining excellent drinkability.

Chambolle-Musigny 1er Cru La Combe d'Orveau 2015

This flagship label of the *domaine* comes from a *climat* located within the *combe*, benefiting from the generous 2015 vintage in a bottling that complements its usual freshness with a layered, luxurious core of fruit.

Cécile TREMBLAY

MOREY-SAINT-DENIS

8, Rue de Très Girard - Tel. +33 (0) 3 45 836008
domainetremblay@yahoo.fr | www.domaine-ceciletremblay.com

4 hectares

The media hype surrounding her successes over the last few vintages (Michel Bettane has crowned her the heir of Lalou Bize-Leroy) firmly establishes Cécile Tremblay among the most charismatic and talented French winemakers. But all that risks making her seem to be something she is not. Cécile Tremblay is the great-granddaughter of Edouard Jayer, but she is not a diva nor a primadonna. On the contrary, she is a young, dynamic producer, active for about fifteen years, who cultivates four hectares of vines between Nuits and Gevrey. Those vineyards, distributed between eleven labels, have been farmed under certified organic protocol since 2005, with increasing attention to biodynamics. While Cécile waits patiently to reclaim valuable parcels currently leased to other *vignerons*, she works in vineyards and cellars matching rules of common sense to more personal insights. For example, she uses horses to work the land, she employs biodynamic preparations based on herbs and algae to reinforce the defense of the plants, she wisely turn to whole bunch fermentation and uses a small vertical press to finish the maceration. All this in pursuit of a precision that values details without losing sight of natural expression. It may happen (as has happened to us) that in the first few years in bottle, the oak tends to excessively constrict and condition these wines, but it's only a matter of time. Cécile prizes longevity, and the aging potential of the wines is clearly in her favor.

Vosne-Romanée Vieilles Vignes 2015

The main nucleus of this vineyard is a parcel more than fifty years old in the *lieu-dit* Les Jacquines. The floral imprint of the wine is linked to very fine spicy notes, but the vintage also guarantees lasting energy.

Vosne-Romanée 1er Cru Les Beaumonts 2015

In this *climat*, the bulk of the vineyards owned by Cécile will come into her possession in 2021. The limited number of bottles she currently produces come from a few vines planted in 1927 at the upper part of the ridge, still worked by hand and plowed with a horse. The complexity of flavor shines in the lingering finish.

Chambolle-Musigny 1er Cru Les Feusselottes 2015

Within one of the most extensive *climats* of Chambolle, Cécile's parcel enjoys a cool exposure and rests on a calcareous fault *à entroques*. Fleshier than other examples, but without denying that floral trousseau that is the extra dimension of a wine that clearly needs time.

Chapelle-Chambertin Grand Cru 2015

During our tasting in the cellar, Cécile told us that when she became aware of the extraordinary raw material that the 2015 harvest provided, she was almost afraid of it, while imagining how rare it would be to be able to work with such perfect and healthy grapes in the future. To judge from this marvelous "grape juice," pure and graceful but at the same time extraordinarily rich, we'd have to believe that she conquered her fear.

Comte Georges de VOGÜÉ

CHAMBOLLE-MUSIGNY

7, Rue Sainte-Barbe - Tel. +33 (0) 3 80 628625
jlpepin.domainedevogue@wanadoo.fr

12.31 hectares

Few *domaines* can claim such profound roots in Burgundy's history, tracing the foundations to 1450, when Jean Moisson constructed the first building, which is today the winery's headquarters. The name de Vogüé first appeared in 1766, though it was not until 1925, when Count Georges de Vogüé took over, that the groundwork was laid for the most significant phase of the estate's history, beginning with the golden age of the fifties and sixties. Today, the *domaine* is managed by a sort of triumvirate: Jean-Luc Pepin, marketing director, Eric Bourgogne, agronomist, and François Millet, the cellar manager who guided us through a tasting with reverential severity. Appropriately, and especially in their first few years of life, the wines themselves are also quite severe, though eventually they settle into a graceful phase, aligning themselves with the varying complexities of the historic *terroirs*. De Vogüé owns more than seven hectares in Musigny, and just shy of half of that in Bonnes Mares, the Grand Cru plots making up the most noble portions of the estate's twelve-plus hectares. The vineyards are farmed following organic principles, though without certification.

Chambolle-Musigny 2014

This wine comes from the *lieu-dit* Les Porlottes, a parcel on a high hill (320 meters above sea level) near woods that overlook the town from the left side of the *combe*. It is full of nuance and reflects the house style, sensitive to the clear expression of the *terroir*.

Chambolle-Musigny 1er Cru Les Amoureuses 2014

This half-hectare of vines is planted in the upper part of the *cru*, almost identical in size to that of Mugnier, providing a wine with a light and airy quality of superior class and harmony. In a rare rush of confidence, Millet confessed that this *climat* requires a thoughtful approach. "There are concave vineyards that welcome you in, and convex vineyards that push you away. Les Amoureuses is one of those convex vineyards in which the distance between the vine and its cultivator must be respected."

Bonnes Mares Grand Cru 2014

The wine comes from a southeastern portion of Bonnes Mares, enhanced by red clay soils that underline the volume and the roundness of the vintage without losing the precious fruity notes (blueberry) so often found here.

Musigny Grand Cru 2014

Of the almost eleven hectares of this celebrated Grand Cru, de Vogüé owns about two-thirds, including the entire vineyard area of Petits Musigny (over four hectares), as well as a large portion of Les Musigny. The pedigree of these vineyards was confirmed in a first-rate tasting experience. The graceful touch of aromas (pomegranate and raspberry) mingle with spicy tones (black pepper), while on the palate the inner density is apparent without too much muscular power.

Musigny Blanc Grand Cru 2015

After the last bottling in1993, this is the first vintage of the rare Musigny Blanc Grand Cru. The vineyard, replanted between 1986 and 1997, was not considered ready to produce a wine that could meet the uncompromising standards of the *domaine*. For more than twenty vintages the wine had been downgraded to a simple Bourgogne Blanc (also because Chambolle-Musigny as an *appellation* does not include a white Villages). The Chardonnay is planted on white marl in the highest part of the *climat* in a parcel of just two-thirds of a hectare. Only 2,277 bottles were obtained, full of rare energy and uncommon depth that will need to be waited for or, more realistically, dreamed about for a very long time.

4

FROM VOUGEOT TO VOSNE-ROMANÉE

VOUGEOT

map *page* 511

Vougeot is a town where the hierarchy of vineyards, in terms of proportions, is reversed compared to the norm. Of the nearly seventy hectares of vineyards in the community, only three are destined for Villages-level production, while more than fifty belong to the Clos de Vougeot, the imposing Grand Cru celebrated worldwide as a symbol of Burgundy. Although it is not easy to pinpoint the date of its recognition as a vineyard, there were already references in the thirteenth century to a *clausum* (*clos*) at Vougeot belonging to the Cistercian Abbey of Citeaux, founded in 1098 to revive virtues such as austerity and temperance. Ideals, however, which the Benedictines of the mother church (at Cluny) did not seem to hold among their highest priorities. Since the beginning, the wines of Vougeot have been available only to the wealthiest and most powerful customers, an exclusive prerogative of the military and church aristocracies, at least until its confiscation during the Revolution as a national asset. At that point the eventual auctioning and parceling of the Clos began and continued into the last century. At the end of the nineteenth century, there were only six owners. Then, between the two world wars, the number rose to forty, and today there are about twice that number. The soils of the Clos de Vougeot are extremely heterogeneous. The vineyards located at about 250 meters in the highest sector near the chateau, can certainly claim Grand Cru dignity in lean and stony soils with a high percentage of active calcareous stone. That is why wines from the parcels renamed En Musigni (below Petits Musigny) and Grand-Maupertuis (adjacent to Grands-Echézeaux) often share those particular qualities of finesse that are found in the neighboring Grand Crus. Overall, though, elegance is certainly not the most typical feature of these wines. Descending to the east altitudes decline and the percentage of clay in the soil increases (to as much as 40%) as the wines take on more vigorous, assertive and earthy qualities that critics often consider at intermediate levels between the engaging personalities of certain Premier Crus and the more one-dimensional composition of many Villages. Unfortunately, the prices of these wines never reflect qualitative realities, so Clos de Vougeot as a whole risks being one the most overrated Grand Crus of the entire region.

VOSNE-ROMANÉE

map *page* 509

When discussions turn to the most elegant and full-blown of the great wines of Burgundy, the reds of Vosne-Romanée emerge as touchstones. Finesse and tannic depth, intensity and elegance, balance and longevity are the attributes that have made these wines both famous and sought-after throughout the world, often at hyperbolic prices. Behind the reputation of Vosne-Romanée stand the eight Grand Cru vineyards, extending for almost 60 hectares along a central strip planted on brown-calcareous soils with a very complex geological structure. Analyses reveal shallow topsoil shot through by numerous fissures connected to a main fault, extremely diversified in terms of depth and composition (limestone, clays, fossil marls, stones), and with equally varied and differentiated water distribution, all of which translates into ideal conditions for wines of energy and complexity. Moving in a north-south direction, just above the walls of Clos de Vougeot, we find the very extensive surface of Echézeaux. This covers almost 40 hectares (including those in the communal territory of Flagey-Echézeaux, which in practice is considered to be part of Vosne), divided into eleven different, extremely heterogenous *lieux-dits*, similar to those of the Clos de Vougeot. Those vines produce richly colored and long-lived reds of intense flavor. In the central part of the *cru*, among the parcels considered superior to the others, we would specifically point out Echézeaux du Dessus, bordering on the Grand Cru Grands-Echézeaux. Despite the name, Grands- Echézeaux, a nine-hectare *climat*, is only a quarter of the size of Echézeaux, planted on a layer of Bajocian limestone, just like Musigny to which it is sometimes compared, especially for the aromatic refinement and mineral complexity of its wines. Then proceeding toward Vosne, we find the most legendary *climats*. Richebourg (divided into two different *lieux-dits*: Les Richebourgs and Les Véroilles) renders reds with a spirited and intense complexity that a century ago inspired the influential author Camille Rodier to describe as "some of the most sumptuous wines of Burgundy." Romanée Saint-Vivant, with almost ten hectares of iron-rich clay soils, delivers a less imposing wine, but one that is innervated by minerality. La Romanée-Conti, *monopole* of the homonymous *domaine*, covers less than two hectares with a high content of clay (45%) and iron replanted in 1947-48. It has been the subject of numerous publications, achieving revered status from its boundless cult-following. In a monograph dedicated to this Grand Cru, Richard Olney calls it "the most Proustian of all great wines." More prosaically, markets credit it as the most expensive.

As Armando Castagno notes, "15,000 euros may not even get you a bottle of a very good vintage." Then comes La Romanée, the smallest *appellation* in France at only 0.85 hectares, perched on a hillside with a 12% incline, which explains why it is maintained by contour plowing. The soil contains less clay than its neighbor and the wine, a *monopole* of the Comte Liger-Belair, redeems its spicy, youthful bleakness with a fascinating evolution towards finesse and levity on the palate. Promoted to Grand Cru in 1991, La Grand Rue, of just over one and a half hectares, owned by Domaine Lamarche, is a sort of buffer vineyard between La Tâche and La Romanée-Conti. Finally, La Tâche is a *monopole* of six privileged hectares belonging to Domaine de la Romanée-Conti, rendering a wine of velvety texture that combines power and density in the service of absolute elegance. In the opinion of Jacky Rigaux, "This *climat* incites to the point of paroxysm the capacity of Pinot Noir to reveal the transparency of *terroir*, and to transcend it." In an *appellation* such as Vosne, it should be emphasized that the quality level, even outside the realm of the Grand Cru, remains very high. Among the fourteen Premier Crus, it is impossible to ignore Cros Parantoux, forever linked to the memory of Henri Jayer, who, more than any other, was able to collect its impressive minerality into bottles capable of challenging the decades. We must also note Les Suchots, Aux Reignots, Aux Malconsorts, Les Beaux Monts, Les Gaudichots (a good portion of which, was annexed to La Tâche in 1933). To sum up, 300 years ago Claude Courtépée eloquently decreed, "There are no common wines made in Vosne." That observation still rings true today.

Jean-Yves BIZOT

VOSNE-ROMANÉE
9, Rue Grand Velle - Tel. +33 (0) 3 80 612466
les.violettes@wanadoo.fr

3.5 hectares

After abandoning his studies in geology, Jean-Yves Bizot took over his small family *domaine* in 1994. He has increasingly focused his work on the realization of so-called "natural wines," even if this definition appears a bit hasty and incomplete. His vineyards are grassed over and treated with organic products, yet fertilizers are also used. He vinifies whole-cluster grapes without the use of sulfites or pumping over or controlling temperatures or adding yeasts or enzymes, yet he employs entirely new wood barrels. These are just a few of the seemingly contradictory choices that have been part of his winemaking experience over the last few years. Bizot is a free-thinker, exploring the field of winemaking with the strong-willed and open-minded perspective that only a person from another background could bring to it. He also has the privilege of being the life companion of Claire Naudin (see page 278), an inspired and gifted winemaker, who is also clearly opposed to certifications that represent conformity of any sort. Today, after acquisitions in both Chenôve and Marsannay, his total vineyard holdings have risen to 3.5 hectares. Wines from these parcels were among the most exciting we tasted, even in such a fiercely competitive context as Vosne-Romanée.

Bourgogne Le Chapitre 2015

Ten years ago in the commune of Chenôve (beyond the shopping malls on the outskirts of Dijon), Bizot bought two parcels of vines in historically important *lieux-dits*. From one he produces a Marsannay Clos du Roy, scented typically with roses and red fruits, while the other ends up in a Bourgogne that is less supple and sensual but impressively compact and solid in tone.

Vosne-Romanée 2015

Of the four labels obtained from his Vosne vineyards, this bottling uses only grapes from the most recent planting in 1986. If there were a Villages championship, not only would this Vosne play in Ligue 1, but in 2015 it would have been a contender for a top spot, so irresistible are its aromas and unmatchable juiciness.

Vosne-Romanée Vieilles Vignes 2015

This *cuvée* comes from four different parcels, using only grapes from vines planted between 1927 and 1933. The nose offers an enchanting aromatic complexity, with hints of rose and rhubarb, pungently wild. The palate unwinds toward a long and persistent sensation of freshness. A real delight

Vosne-Romanée Les Jachées 2015

Immediately below the village center of Vosne, this gravelly *lieu-dit* is very small (just over a hectare) and Bizot owns more than half. He alone bottles a single-vineyard version, which is right on target with its fascinating amalgam of floral notes and spice. The compact texture of the wine is enhanced by fine-honed tannins in a context of disarming refinement and nonchalance.

Echézeaux Grand Cru 2015

For his Echézeaux Grand Cru, Bizot uses only the parcel of the *lieu-dit* Orveaux. Wine from the younger Treux vineyards is instead bottled as Vosne-Romanée 1er Cru. This is the only Grand Cru of the *domaine* and oddly the first label to be bottled every year, following Jean-Yves' unique belief that such wines don't need long maturing. Yet it seems to us that the new oak is still echoing, and is perceptible here. We suggest to the fortunate few who succeed in procuring a bottle to forget it in the cellar for some time.

CHÂTEAU de la TOUR

VOUGEOT

Clos de Vougeot - Tel. +33 (0) 3 80 628613
contact@chateaudelatour.com | www.chateaudelatour.com

6.5 hectares

Château de la Tour has the privilege of being the only *domaine* that makes wine inside the Clos de Vougeot, of which it also boasts the most comprehensive holdings, with six and a half hectares of vineyards, about 12% of the total. The castle, built in 1890 in a curiously extravagant overlapping architectural style, is owned by François Labet, who has been running the *domaine* since 1986. The vines are on average almost 60 years old (although one hectare dates back to 1910) and come from the massal selection of an ancient Beaune vineyard, the Premier Cru Coucherias, which belongs to the owner's other property, Domaine Pierre Labet. The vineyards are treated only with copper and sulfur and some biodynamic preparations. Yields are always kept strictly below thirty hectoliters per hectare, and the whole cluster vinification is paired with extreme care in the winemaking process and a demanding passage in new oak, as is often the case with a Grand Cru designed *pour la garde*.

Clos Vougeot Grand Cru 2015

The parcels of the *domaine* are located in various areas of the Clos, but the bulk of the vineyards is in the central part, around the château. Grapes of remarkable quality and maturity of fruit result in wines with polished tannins and tantalizingly seductive elegance designed to please all tastes.

Clos Vougeot Grand Cru Vieilles Vignes 2015

A very limited bottling (only eight barrels) from vines over sixty years old, this selection often has an extra dimension in terms of tannic depth and density, without sacrificing the velvety roundness that stands as the hallmark of the *domaine*. When the strong spiciness of new oak (here at 100%) alleviates with time, the wine will gain in vibrancy.

Bruno CLAVELIER

VOSNE-ROMANÉE

6, Route nationale 74 - Tel. +33 (0) 3 80 611081
domaine-clavelier@orange.fr | www.bruno-clavelier.com

6.5 hectares

When he took over the family winery from his maternal grandfather in 1987, Bruno Clavelier was a successful rugby player who had no idea how his new job would go. He was, however, a keen student of the geology of vineyards, who showed personality and skill in following the approach and advice of his grandfather, Joseph, in his early days as a *vigneron*. Today we recommend the estate not only to devotees of organic wines (Clavelier is a true ex-officio considering his long-term organic and biodynamic militancy), but also to lovers of the unequaled *terroir*-based wines of Burgundy. The Clavelier vineyards cover six and a half hectares, located mainly between Vosne and Chambolle, all planted between the two world wars, and replaced on a strategic basis designed to maintain the estate's patrimony. Each parcel is vinified separately with growing reliance on stem-inclusion (in 2015 about half were whole clusters) and very long macerations, followed by refining in *barriques* where the use of new oak has always been carefully restrained.

Bourgogne Aligoté 2015

An eighty-year-old vineyard planted with old biotypes of Aligoté produces a captivating white with agile citric energy and a curious aromatic range that reminded us of muscat, leading to a lengthy finish that is rather extraordinary for the variety.

Bourgogne Passetoutgrain 2015

The vineyard is pretty old, but the expression of this light red wine, which adds to Pinot Noir 10% Gamay grapes is decidedly contemporary. Irresistible in its pure and crisp drinkability.

Vosne-Romanée La Montagne 2015

This minuscule *monopole* of less than a third of a hectare is a natural continuation of the Premier Cru La Combe Brulée, with a higher content of iron oxide in its soils. The wine combines delicate aromas with decidedly intense expressivity on the palate.

Vosne-Romanée La Combe Brulée 2015

This small *lieu-dit* (0.77 ha), planted in calcareous soils with a high percentage of silicon, is exposed to fresh breezes from the Combe de Concœur and a nearby pinewoods. The blend includes an unusual 8-10% of Pinot Blanc (Bruno reminds us that some strains of white grapes were often present amid the old vines of Pinot Noir) in a wine of finesse enhanced by enticing floral nuances.

Vosne-Romanée 1er Cru Les Beaux Monts 2015

The nearly seventy-year-old vineyard of exactly half a hectare rests on reddish, stony and well-drained soils over a substratum interwoven with ooliths and hard calcareous formations (Prémeaux and Comblanchien) dating to the Bathonian stage. The wine is velvety on the palate, revealing breadth and volume in its intense acceleration toward the finish.

Chambolle-Musigny 1er Cru La Combe d'Orveaux 2015

With almost a hectare of vines, of which a good half are now octogenarians, Bruno Clavelier holds the lion's share of this fine *climat*. The position wedged between Grand Crus of the caliber of Echézeaux (En Orveaux) and Musigny (Petits), accounts for its prestige as a Premier Cru. Clavelier's interpretation shows a vertical structure innervated by minerality and cushioned with tannins of rare elegance.

Christian CLERGET

VOUGEOT

10, Ancienne Route Nationale - Tel. +33 (0) 3 80 628737
domainechristianclerget@wanadoo.fr | www.christianclerget-vins.fr

6 hectares

The apparent simplicity of Christian Clerget hides an authentic no-frills man whose reflective nature coincides with a concrete and positive attitude, always open and smiling. His passion for rugby and even more for the mountains (especially the Himalayas and the Andes, where he has already been and dreams of returning) hint at his Spartan tastes, inspired by a deep respect for nature. His wines are also tense and essential, faithful expressions of character. They derive from six hectares of vineyards distributed between Morey, Chambolle and Vougeot, as well as a parcel in the Grand Cru Echézeaux. Work in the vineyards is inspired by simplicity and common sense: no certificates but also no herbicides, insecticides or synthetic products; he is organically oriented with a sincere respect for each individual *climat*. Loyalty to tradition is apparent in the cellars where a natural minimal approach to winemaking starts with completely de-stemmed grapes rigidly selected on the *table de tri*. Respect for natural authenticity results in wines that age exceptionally well, as was apparent after our engaging tasting of old vintages shared with Christian and his wife Isabelle in a recently restored building now used as a tasting room. With an appointment and a little luck, it might be possible to purchase some of these old vintages directly at the *domaine*.

Bourgogne 2015

A perfectly focused version with crunchy fruit fully harmonized with juicy fluidity.

Chambolle-Musigny 2015

Seven different parcels in the lower part of the village of Chambolle contribute to a wine that even from an exuberantly rich vintage displays elegant and balanced flavors.

Vosne-Romanée Les Violettes 2015

This *lieu-dit* comes from the territory of Flagey-Echézeaux, just outside the walls of Clos Vougeot, in the middle part of the vineyard. Christian crafted a surprising red combining depth and elegance.

Vougeot 1er Cru Les Petits Vougeots 2015

The vineyard was designated by the Cistercians as Le Petit Clos Noir to distinguish it from the neighboring Clos Blanc. This *climat* provides a wine noted for density and energy enhanced by a nice saline finish.

Chambolle-Musigny 1er Cru Les Charmes 2015

This parcel of very fine calcareous terrain rests directly atop bedrock. The vineyard, nearly fifty years old, exemplifies the potential of a *climat* often likened to Les Amoureuses, yielding a red wine of extreme finesse, bolstered by dexterity and long, persistent flavors.

Echézeaux Grand Cru 2015

This tiny parcel was planted in 1946 in the shallow terrain of the quadrant known as En Orveaux, part of the extensive Grand Cru. The mineral tension that often distinguishes the wine is conveyed by uncommon concentration, foretelling a promising evolution.

CONFURON-COTETIDOT

VOSNE-ROMANÉE
10, Rue de la Fontaine - Tel. +33 (0) 3 80 610339
domaine-confuron-cotetidot@wanadoo.fr

13 hectares

Brothers Yves and Jean-Pierre, sons of Jacky Confuron, share the work at their family *domaine* while also gathering experience in other wineries. Yves is currently *régisseur* at De Courcel in Pommard, while Jean-Pierre is the enological director at the *maison* Chanson. At home they have always followed the guidelines of traditional agriculture, without herbicides or chemical products of any kind. The age of the vines remains a factor of primary importance, maintained with targeted replanting of individual stocks, to the point that today the Confurons rely on parcels with the venerable age of over seventy years. The privilege of these older vines also limits productivity, with yields constantly among the lowest in the region, and with recent average yields even further reduced in the latest and more complicated vintages. They push grape maturity to the extreme, being invariably among the last to harvest. This choice informs their vinification strategy, conducted using whole clusters with the stems, whatever the vintage. Their wines reveal unmistakable personality starting with the aromas of hypnotic intensity and genuine wildness, even if polished beyond any rusticity. They are always intensely colored, richly extracted and textured by a tannic grip. They are full of fruit that guarantees fleshy texture, as well as promising future evolution. Quality starts from the Villages bottlings, almost didactic in showing the impact of each single vintage on the expressiveness of the different *terroirs*. Their immediate drinkability is also surprising, even in abundant vintages like 2015.

Bourgogne Aligoté 2015

Here is an absolutely recommendable version of Aligoté, to the joy of all of us who are curious about and fond of a variety so often maligned (and mistreated by producers). It is both energetic and fleshy in putting its no-frills intensity at the service of tasty drinkability.

Nuits-Saint-Georges 2015

A winning example of the spicy side of the *appellation*, this mixes black berry fruit with notes of peony and rhubarb, following the contours of an aromatic landscape of captivating intensity. On the palate the wine is rich but not heavy, confirming that in Nuits 2015 is a graceful vintage, even for the less important *climats*.

Vosne-Romanée 2015

The parcels of Porte Feuilles du Clos, bordering Vougeot, and Les Jacquines, on the side facing Nuits, give rise to one of the most seductive Villages wines of the *appellation*. The aromatic complexity is almost intoxicating and precedes a palate of effortless fluency, despite a natural concentration of fruit.

Gevrey-Chambertin 1er Cru Craipillot 2015

This *climat*, which rests on stony ground swept over by cool breezes from the Combe de Lavaux, is year after year among the last parcels harvested by Confuron. The wine has an aromatic vitality with floral tones, showing all the intensity of the best vintages vinified using whole cluster grapes. Opulence on the palate is both dynamic and crisp, with a long finish highlighted by notes of blueberry and licorice.

Nuits-Saint-Georges 1er Cru Les Vignes Rondes 2015

In showing us this parcel, Yves explained that we were almost in the area of the Murgers, on the side facing Vosne. The vineyard planted in 1923 brings to the wine two precious gifts: an amazing tannic elegance, and a bonus of minerality, which complete and enrich that sense of balance and fusion that is anything but normal for a red of this density.

Vosne-Romanée 1er Cru Les Suchots 2015

"Malolactic fermentation ended in September 2016," confirmed Yves, noting that was about six months later than the Nuits-Saint-Georges 1er Cru Les Vignes Rondes. In fact, the wine is still somewhat closed and certainly rather backward in its expression of aromatics. It's a different story on the palate, however, where energy races through on an endless trail of flavor satisfaction.

Charmes-Chambertin Grand Cru 2015

Our experience with this Grand Cru over the years leads us to share, in principle, the opinion of the most astute critics: Charmes-Chambertin is perhaps a bit *too big* to be judged as a whole, including, as it does, vineyards of very different qualities.

And yet, despite a certain resistance to appreciating these wines in their first years in bottle, we noted in this one a totally unusual accessibility and readiness. The brightness of the vintage illuminates the wine and polishes its usual mineral shadings, restoring a soothing sense of harmony and maturity.

Domaine d'EUGENIE

VOSNE-ROMANÉE
14, Rue de la Goillotte - Tel. +33 (0) 3 80 611054
contact@domaine-eugenie.com | www.domaine-eugenie.com

5.3 hectares

In 2005, after the untimely death of Philippe Engel, billionaire François Pinault (already owner of Château la Tour in Bordeaux), bought the René Engel winery and changed its name to Domaine d'Eugenie. Despite this abrupt change of identity, the name René Engel retains a certain interest for us. Engel, who died in 1986 at the age of 92, was an important figure in early twentieth century Burgundy. An enterprising wine merchant, as well as a valued and charismatic university professor, he helped form a generation of *vignerons* and influencers (including Henri Jayer) who would launch Burgundy into the future with an approach to viticulture in step with the times. Engel also endowed the family *domaine* with a valuable heritage of vineyards almost entirely in the territory of Vosne (plus a large parcel of Clos-de- Vougeot). These were taken over by his nephew Philippe, who in the nineties crafted beautifully lyrical wines. Faced with such a demanding legacy, the new property decided to decisively turn the page, initially provoking more than a few worries. The conversion to biodynamics began in 2011, and the wines are now more focused and measured, showing a more discreet approach to winemaking. In November 2017 Pinault officially announced his purchase of the prestigious Clos-de-Tart. What's next?

Vosne-Romanée Clos d'Eugenie 2015

Only a wall and a road separate this half-hectare Clos from La Tâche. Without trying to compare the two wines, this version shines with integrity and elegance.

Grands-Echézeaux Grand Cru 2015

A yield of less than twenty hectoliters per hectare renders a wine of tenacious density and promisingly masculine energy.

Jean GRIVOT

VOSNE-ROMANÉE

6, Rue de la Croix Rameau - Tel. +33 (0) 3 80 610595
domaine.grivot@domainegrivot.fr | www.domainegrivot.fr

15 hectares

“I'm looking for a judicious blend of modernity and tradition.” These are the words of Étienne Grivot, son of Jean and grandson of Gaston, who was one of the first to bottle proprietary wines in the 1920s. After an infatuation with the model of what might be described as pro-Bordeaux, Grivot pursues a more moderate alliance of energy and elegance. The recent arrival of his children Mathilde and Hubert at the *domaine*, has generated more efforts in this direction, resulting in wines with an increasingly sleek and balanced profile. The vineyards are top notch, including more than three hectares of Grand Cru and a range of *climats* between Vosne and Nuits. Grapes are completely de-stemmed, because Grivot claims that the stalks make the wines too ethereal, to the detriment of opulence. And he may have a point.

Vosne-Romanée 2015

Captivating hints of violet and raspberry add graceful details to the freshness in the mouth; the texture is caressing, the pleasure almost weightless.

Vosne-Romanée 1er Cru Les Rouges 2015

This small, rarely-noted *climat* is just above Echézeaux. The wine's severe, almost somber tone does not preclude an appreciable tannic development.

Vosne-Romanée 1er Cru Les Beaux Monts 2015

From a hectare of vineyard split into almost symmetrical parts between Beaux Monts Hauts and Bas, this wine plays on energy, solid on the palate with remarkable flavor and length.

Vosne-Romanée 1er Cru Les Suchots 2015

Les Suchots, between Richebourg, Romanée-Saint-Vivant and Echézeaux, is a *climat* literally besieged by the Grand Crus of Vosne. In this interpretation elaborated by Grivot from a particularly substantial vintage, the palate is overflowing with energy, embellished by a long, savory and spicy finish.

Anne GROS

VOSNE-ROMANÉE

11, Rue des Communes - Tel. +33 (0) 3 80 610795
domaine-annegros@orange.fr | www.anne-gros.com

6.3 hectares

Hailed by critics more than two decades ago as one of the most promising winemakers of Burgundy, Anne Gros has long since established herself in the élite of the Côte de Nuits. With a historically important name behind her, Anne, in the early nineties, guided her father François' small *domaine* to impressive new heights. Currently she has six and a half hectares of vines among the oldest of the Côte (especially in her Grand Cru vineyards), all maintained under a biodynamic regime, if uncertified. Purity of expression has always been the guiding star of her work as a winemaker, though today she seems to pursue it with less rigidity. What the wines have lost in nuance they have gained in density, while retaining notable precision and tannic depth. Anne's daughter Julie is more and more involved in lending her personality to the *domaine*.

Bourgogne Pinot Noir 2015

From the vines of four different parcels planted on clay soils between Vosne and Flagey, this is something more than an "entry-level wine." Compact and dense, it defies presumptions in showing qualities almost like a Bourgogne *de garde*.

Vosne-Romanée Les Barreaux 2015

As Anne puts it: This is a *Vosne d'altitude*. This wine comes from vines more than a century old in a high parcel overlooking Cros Parantoux, exposed to the northeast on soils rich in iron and magnesium. This seemed to us the best wine of the entire lineup, with superior freshness and aromatic vitality (citrus, flowers).

Richebourg Grand Cru 2015

This comes from the highest slope of Richebourg, in a *lieu-dit* known as Verroilles, with east-northeast exposure. Anne fashions a red from elegant fabric, focused on refined fruit (blueberries) and an intriguing spicy vein, with a remarkably long finish.

GROS Frère et Sœur

VOSNE-ROMANÉE
6, Rue des Grands Crus - Tel. +33 (0) 3 80 611243
contact@g-f-s.fr

20 hectares

The Gros dynasty began with Alfonse Gros, who arrived in Vosne from the Hautes Côtes in 1830. He was the first *vigneron* of the area to bottle his wine for direct sale to the public, removing it from the monopolizing mediation of the *courtiers* and *négociants* of the time. Jumping ahead several generations we come to the moment, thirty years ago, when Bernard Gros reinvented himself as a *vigneron* alongside his aunt Colette. Bernard planted the bulk of the vineyards, doubling the winery's holdings with a significant acquisition in the Hautes Côtes. Today the vineyards exceed twenty hectares, taking in many excellent parcels: from Echézeaux to Grands Echézeaux, from Clos Vougeot to Richebourg. Wines are made in a modern style, with an explicit quest for smoothness and roundness and the use of new oak that is anything but timid.

Bourgogne Hautes Cotes de Nuits Rouge 2015

Nine hectares of vineyards recently planted at Concoeur, just above Nuits, provide the ample base of this red wine, whose grapes are harvested a couple of weeks later than average in the Côte de Nuits. The silky tannins, of unusual softness for the *appellation*, exalt the reassuring amiability of a thoroughly polished wine.

Clos Vougeot Musigni Grand Cru 2014

The vineyard is in the northwestern part of the extensive Clos, between the boundary wall and the lane leading to the castle. The name of the *lieu-dit* reveals its proximity to Musigny and Bernard owns here almost a hectare of vines planted in the late eighties. An elegant, spicy wine with a creamy texture.

Richebourg Grand Cru 2014

"Dense but smooth, strong and sweet together," is how Bernard describes the style of his Richebourg. The fine and silky tannins stimulate an enchanting sensation of roundness and harmony.

LEROY

VOSNE-ROMANÉE

15, Rue de la Fontaine - Tel. +33 (0) 3 80 212110
www.domaineleroy.com

21.99 hectares

Even more than her father Henri, a wealthy merchant of brandy and co-owner of the Domaine de la Romanée-Conti from 1942, Marcelle Bize-Leroy (affectionately known as Lalou) deserves credit as the main force behind the wine world's adulation of the estate's extraordinary bottles. Creating a profile of this First Lady of Wine, however, proved to be a task that divided the authors, so we decided to call in a third person as a sort of mediator between our diverse views. Camillo was deeply impressed by the kindness and hospitality that Madame Bize-Leroy showed us, by her aristocratic manners and grace that he perceived as the dainty exterior of an internal core that was otherwise solid and tenacious. He fully agreed with Fabio Rizzari, who wrote a brief but inspired profile of Madame Leroy for the past edition of this book, commenting, among other things, "Not only does Lalou produce some of the most accomplished and prodigious wines in the world, but she is also an unparalleled taster, with almost supernatural sensitivity." Giampaolo, although certainly influenced by the aura of magnetic charisma that surrounds this elderly lady, who is still quite spry and lucid despite her ailments, has some reservations regarding the frankness of her character, asserting that she seemed to know much more than she was willing to reveal. That's nothing new, as Lalou has always divided her audiences. She evokes admiration or distrust with the same intensity: for her detractors she is a calculating and snobbish woman, for her admirers, a legendary winemaker. Despite the partial dissent, however, one thing the authors agreed upon with the same instinctive certainty, and without a shadow of a doubt: the extensive tasting shared in the Leroy cellar in Vosne-Romanée on the morning of Tuesday, November 29, 2016, was an absolute pinnacle of their respective tasting experiences. That reaction is hardly unique. As Fabio Rizzari, in describing his earlier visit, recalled: "The meeting quickly took on the contours of a dreamlike, almost hallucinatory experience, as after taking LSD. At the end of the morning, I rolled up my five-meter-long tongue that was haning to the floor and dragged myself, in a stupefied state, to the hotel, where I was able to re-establish a link to reality only late that evening."

Evidence as powerful and mutually shared as this suggests that we should desist from retracing the highlights of Madame Leroy's career here, and instead concentrate on a review of the wines we tasted with her that morning. Twenty-three wines from 2014, at the time all already bottled (Madame's reluctance to provide barrel samples is well-known). Unfortunately, this will only be a partial account, as there is not enough space here to adequately review the entire program.

Savigny-lès-Beaune Les Narbantons 2014

Irresistible in the charm of its Oriental-like aromas, illuminated by notes of incense. It is also captivating on the palate for the way it combines freshness and grit.

Vosne-Romanée 1er Cru Les Beaux Monts 2014

Though tasted immediately after Aux Brulées, of which Beaux Monts represents a northern extension, this seemed a completely different wine, with much more momentum and tension on the palate, though its vertical dimension is open and free of any rigidity.

Romanée-Saint-Vivant Grand Cru 2014

Madame has a hectare of the *cru* (of the almost ten total), located high up toward the border with Richebourg, on pink calcareous stones of that sector of the *climat* with a geological matrix dating to the Bajocian stage. This vineyard produces a clear and congenial red, which up to a point expresses a sense of balance and measure in its gustatory proportions before showing an impressive acceleration toward the finish, due to an astonishingly intense spicy richness.

Richebourg Grand Cru 2014

A Richebourg more open than a Romanée-Saint-Vivant? Is it possible? We checked several times, fearing that someone had reversed the order of the tasting but in the end we gave in, conceding that 2014 contrasted with most of the critical comments available that would have Richebourg as more closed and reticent in the months after bottling. On the contrary, here the expression of the fruit seemed to us already well integrated with the solid structural form. The vibrations of the wine on the palate feed an interminable persistence, marked by the energy of the tannins and a refreshingly bright acidity.

Musigny Grand Cru 2014

A wine that literally gave us a jolt, so dazzling is its expressive richness and the sharpness of details. The temptation is to rate it among the most complete wines tasted in absolute, in the span of a lifetime, hoping to be able to try it again, maybe in about twenty years. But we also hold a well-founded suspicion that twenty years may not be enough to raise enough cash to afford it.

Clos de la Roche Grand Cru 2014

Leroy's parcel is derived from an acquisition of Domaine Philippe Remy, in 1989. Of the seven *lieux-dits* that compose the Cru, this is located in the original Clos de la Roche proper. The 2014 bottling is irresistible in its beguiling aromatic notes of bitter orange and wild flowers, which were only hinted at in our tasting. It will still take time to propagate its energy.

Latricières-Chambertin Grand Cru 2014

The specificity of Latricières resides both in its microclimate (warmer in respect to vineyards across from it but always ventilated thanks to the breeze through the Combe Grisard) as in soil composition (with a high percentage of oolitic calcium carbonate and excellent drainage). But considering everything, it is difficult to explain the extreme complexity of this version, which shows something enigmatic but displays length and salinity at exaggerated levels.

Chambertin Grand Cru 2014

Madame makes no secret of preferring the 2014 vintage to 2015, pointing out that what she particularly admires in the best wines of 2014 is integrity. Not just in the sense of rectitude, if we understood correctly, but rather in the way the vintage upholds the expressivity peculiar to each *climat*. And what could be more true to character in a Chambertin than concealing elegance in tension, finesse in power?

Corton-Charlemagne Grand Cru 2014

To seal a succession of such fascinating reds, Madame Lalou proposed that we close with a white wine: her rare Corton-Charlemagne. As you may imagine, it was a bottling of a *millésime d'exception*. Confronted with such peerless sublimity, we are left without words to describe its magnificence.

Domaine du Comte LIGER-BELAIR

VOSNE-ROMANÉE

Château de Vosne-Romanée - Tel. +33 (0) 3 80 621370
contact@liger-belair.fr | www.liger-bealir.fr

10.4 hectares

This *domaine* resumed its historically important course in 2000 after about fifty years of oblivion. With more than two centuries of history behind it (founded in 1805), it is rapidly climbing the rigid slope of Burgundian hierarchies, harvest after harvest, thanks to the ambitious and tenacious work of Louis-Michel Liger-Belair. Louis-Michel returned to live with his family in the Château de Vosne-Romanée and began vinifying wines in the ancient cellars of the *domaine* after years of renting out vineyards and working with *négociants*. The current ten hectares of vineyards, worked entirely with horses and with methods strongly inspired by organic protocols, are divided between Vosne, Flagey and Nuits. The most valuable parcels are concentrated in Vosne, including the exclusive *monopole* Grand Cru La Romanée, the smallest *appellation* in France at only 0.85 hectares, which represents a cult wine in the truest sense.

Vosne-Romanée La Colombière 2015

The clay soils of this flat sector of Vosne rarely render wines that live up to the fame of the *appellation*. However, the age of the vines (between sixty and eighty years) helps to ensure an extra dimension in terms of flavor and harmony.

Vosne-Romanée 2015

Twelve parcels from various parts of Vosne deliver an annual production that never exceeds three thousand bottles. The refined house style is very evident in this Villages, with its soft and velvety feel.

Nuits-Saint-Georges 1er Cru Les Cras 2015

Louis-Michel tends to compare this vineyard's features with those of Aux Reignots in Vosne-Romanée for its power and fullness of fruit. A subtle vein of minerality adds complexity to the finish.

Vosne-Romanée 1er Cru Aux Reignots 2015

The workable soil on the steep slope of this *climat* does not exceed twenty-five centimeters in depth and rests on cracks in the calcareous substratum. In vintages like 2015 the vine roots are pushed to seek nourishment at the depths. The result is a solid and severe wine that will take many years to come forth.

Échezeaux Grand Cru 2015

The *domaine* has just over half a hectare in two distinct *lieux-dits* with different characteristics. Les Champs Traversins, with its mixed soil of sand and marl, produces the lightest and most graceful reds of Échezeaux, and Les Cruots, on the poorest stony soils, has a tendency to render sharp, mineral-oriented wines (vines for white were customarily planted here). The resulting blend is finer and tighter than the average Grand Cru, albeit supported by a good reserve of fruit in this vintage.

La Romanée Grand Cru Monopole 2015

Although it had been previously split into six parcels, the family *monopole* was bought in its entirety between 1815 and 1826 by General Louis Liger-Belair, founder of the *domaine*. The rows of this historic *climat* are planted perpendicular to the steep slope in order to limit erosion. The soil, very similar to that of Romanée-Conti, but with a lower percentage of clay, lends the wine a mixture of energy and grace that Benoît France in his *Grand Atlas des Vignobles de France* defines as the synthesis between the severity of Richebourg and the velvety delicacy of La Tâche. Louis Michel told us that when dealing with the grapes of La Romanée, he tends to feel the weight of responsibility that so much history has given him. However, this wine is anything but heavy, and in such a vintage is sure to face a radiant future.

Georges MUGNERET-GIBOURG

VOSNE-ROMANÉE
5 Rue des Communes - Tel. +33 (0) 3 80 610157
dgm@mugneret-gibourg.com | www.mugneret-gibourg.com

8 hectares

Before his premature death in 1988, Georges Mugneret had been preparing to sell the *domaine*. Shortly after his demise, the potential buyer came to his widow Jacqueline and her daughters, telling them: "I will keep my promise to buy the winery, but you should think twice about selling it, it's a very important decision." That noble gesture (by a gentleman who remains anonymous) changed the course of history. The three women, with pride and tenacity, committed themselves to continue Georges' work. After thirty years they have not regretted it, fortified by an entirely female management of the eight hectares of property, which delivers wines focused on aromatic finesse and velvety texture.

Vosne-Romanée 2015

This stylish wine, which derives from totally de-stemmed grapes of five different parcels, has inviting floral notes of rose and violet, surprisingly integrated and ready to drink.

Chambolle-Musigny 1er Cru Les Feusselottes 2015

The etymology of the vineyard name could indicate "small ditches" in a terrain with deep and generous soils. Nevertheless the wine dances gracefully on tiptoes, highlighted by the minerality of the long finish.

Ruchottes-Chambertin Grand Cru 2015

In 1976, Charles Rousseau wanted to buy an ample parcel of Ruchottes of more than two hectares, but his wife, who kept the family budget, opposed the acquisition. So Charles suggested to Georges Mugneret and Michel Bonnefond (Domaine Roumier) that they should each take over a portion. The suggestion was met with approval, and now Mugneret's parcel, just over half a hectare, gives life to this red *tout en finesse,* of which Henri Jayer liked to say, "It's a Chambertin vinified in Vosne."

Georges NOËLLAT

VOSNE-ROMANÉE
1, Rue des Chaumes - Tel. +33 (0) 3 80 611103
mc.noellat@free.fr

5.5 hectares

The name Noëllat has played an important role in the recent past of Vosne-Romanée. In fact, the vineyards that today constitute the backbone of the *domaine* of Madame Lalou Bize-Leroy came from a 1988 purchase of Charles Noëllat's property. The other branch of the family, that of his brother Ernst, founded Domaine Georges Noëllat. But, after control passed to his daughter Marie-Thérese, the *domaine* underwent a long period of inactivity, between 1990 and 2009, when its grapes were sold mainly to Jadot and Drouhin. A breakthrough came in 2010, when Marie-Thérese called her nephew Maxime Cheurlin (born in 1991) to relaunch the estate. Maxime, after studying enology, worked with Domaines Gros and Rouget before taking charge of nearly six hectares of vineyards in important locations. Our recent tastings have confirmed Maxime's talents in emerging as one of the most gifted young winemakers around.

Vosne-Romanée 1er Cru Les Chaumes 2015

The parcel is basically a continuation of the family's garden, on the side facing Nuits. It gives life to a compact and tasty wine, innervated by grit and energy.

Vosne-Romanée 1er Cru Les Petits Monts 2015

This vineyard has an enviable position, at an altitude of three hundred meters overlooking Richebourg, inviting comparisons to the Grand Cru. This bottling reflects some traits of its illustrious neighbor; if more subtle and airy in its aromatic expression, its flavors are more intense, with a richness that is almost sanguine.

Armelle et Bernard RION

VOSNE-ROMANÉE

8, Route Nationale - Tel. +33 (0) 3 80 610531
rion@domainerion.fr | www.domainerion.fr

7.5 hectares

The generous, spontaneous, welcoming character shared by Armelle and Bernard Rion is reflected in their wines: expressive, with strong tannic accents, which prove to be friendly allies at the table. The *domaine*, despite its centuries-old history, has been bottling for just forty years. The range of *appellations* is intriguing, with parcels in Nuits, Vosne, Chambolle and almost a hectare in the Clos Vougeot. In 2010 they expanded into the Côte de Beaune, acquiring a parcel of Meursault in the *lieu-dit* Sous la Velle. Armelle and Bernard are gradually transferring management of the estate to their daughter Alice, who, after finishing studies in enology, seems to have brought a more graceful and measured style of tannic extraction to the wines, as noted in our latest tastings. Under the expert guidance of Bernard, Alice's husband Louis has been working in the vineyards in *lutte raisonnée* since 2010. The winery's strategic position, facing the main road, facilitates direct sales to customers, and the increasingly convincing quality of the wines makes Domaine Rion an easy place to recommend. Also for truffle lovers, who will find various delights made with the *truffe noir* that Armelle and Bernard gather in the woods around Chambolle in the autumn with the truffle hounds that they have bred and trained for many years. To complete the package, the Rion family opened an elegant boutique guest accommodation in 2017, with four apartments available.

Bourgogne La Croix Blanche 2015

Combining freshness with full-bodied cherry flavors, this red on the chalkboard would rake in profits for any bistro.

Nuits-Saint-Georges Cuvée Dame Marguerite 2015

A homage to Alice's grandmother, the wine comes from an assemblage of several parcels for a total of about one hectare in the northern part of Nuits, on the border with Vosne. The silkiness of tannins, more in the style of the reds of Vosne-Romanée, smoothes the edges and adds harmony and roundness to the wine.

Nuits-Saint-Georges 1er Cru Les Damodes 2015

From a vineyard nearly seventy years old on the steep incline of the northern slope of the *appellation*, this is one of estate's wines of most distinct personality. The 2015 vintage produced a wine rich in contrasts, showing a dynamic balance between black berry fruit and ample tannins.

Chambolle-Musigny 1er Cru Les Gruenchers 2015

Wines from the *climats* of this area (such as Les Levrottes and Les Baudes), rather than reflecting the stylized elegance of Chambolle, often express the more compact features of Morey. That's the case in this version by Rion: balsamic, dense and enhanced by an original scent of gillyflower.

Vosne-Romanée 1er Cru Les Chaumes 2015

The Rion parcel of this vineyard consists of almost half a hectare of vines more than seventy years old. The grapes are completely de-stemmed and, after fermentation, the wine matures for fifteen months in barrels, of which more than half are new. The charge of driving energy typical of this *climat* (across the road from La Tâche) in a wine from a generous vintage will require long bottle aging.

Clos de Vougeot Grand Cru 2015

A parcel of old vines in the southern sector of the Clos produces a red notable for its density and tannic depth. At the time of tasting, the wine was still in a closed phase. Given its imposing structure, it will need time to better express its considerable potential.

Domaine de la ROMANÉE-CONTI

VOSNE-ROMANÉE

1, Place de l'Eglise - Tel. +33 (0) 3 80 624880
www.romanee-conti.fr

27.8 hectares

La Bruyère's maxim "*Tout est dit*" could have been conceived with this place in mind. For it seems that everything worth saying has already been said about Domaine de la Romanée Conti. Indeed, before voicing an observation or two about the estate, perhaps based on some low-key personal experience, one might almost feel obliged to ask permission. As Armando Castagno put it in the presentation of the *domaine* he kindly provided us for the last edition of this book: "Anything to be said about the DRC has probably already been said, so it's useless to try to provide an original point of view about its stature." Without venturing anything new, we would at least try to recall some essentials. First, the DRC is a co-ownership belonging in equal parts to two families, De Villaine and Leroy, represented respectively by Aubert de Villaine (since 1974) and Henry-Frédéric Roch (since 1993). Roch is also owner of the Domaine Prieuré-Roch, as well as the nephew of Lalou Bize-Leroy, who had preceded him in his post in a situation marked by incompatibility. Nobody would deny that De Villaine is due much of the credit for the fame and fortune of the *domaine*, starting with changes in vineyard management. Since the mid-eighties the estate has embraced organic practices first, and then biodynamics, with increasing use of horses to work the vineyards. This quest for intimacy with the *terroir* combined with an essential approach to the making of wine identify De Villaine, who makes no secret of his admiration for the labor of monks. And yet, the wines of the DRC are anything but humble. Extremely low yields are imposed, resulting in about 25 hectoliters of wine per hectare (on average, it takes the grapes of three vines to fill a bottle of wine). The *élevage* is carried out in 100% new oak barrels (or 95%, as we were corrected, by the amiable *régisseur* Alexandre Bernier). The author Remington Norman emphasizes the "remarkable dimension of extract and concentration, which is indeed one of the *domaine*'s hallmarks." It has been pointed out, however, that such practices are made possible, if not necessary, by the peculiar array of the vineyards, consisting exclusively of Grand Cru parcels covering nearly thirty hectares, of which more than three-quarters are centered in Vosne-Romanée.

The wines, despite their ungovernable prices, still manage to inspire unanimous agreement around their capacity to age well for a very long time. Never too powerful to annoy proponents of finesse, never too rarefied to disappoint paladins of energy, they seem to push the exploration of the *terroirs* from which they are produced to extreme consequences: to live in a form of symbiosis with those *crus*.

Echézeaux Grand Cru 2015

DRC owns more than four and a half hectares of vineyards in this *cru*, almost entirely included in the *lieu-dit* Les Poulaillères. Grapes from this zone are among the earliest ripening and first to be harvested. Though a bit brusque, the wine doesn't hesitate to express its fruity character.

Grands-Echézeaux Grand Cru 2015

DRC owns more than a third of this Grand Cru area, located in the sector that runs along the enclosure wall of Clos Vougeot. The calcareous substratum dating back to the Bajocian era is the same as that of its higher neighbor Musigny, which is often noted for its subtlety and sensuality. The 2015 vintage seems somewhat out of sync with the reputation of wine. At the time of our tasting, it showed aromatic notes of burnt incense and roasted coffee, penalizing the usual smoothness of the texture, which is generally more graceful and proportionate.

Romanée-Saint-Vivant Grand Cru 2015

The restructuring and replanting of part of the vineyard necessitated a declassification of many grapes which in this vintage will end up in the Cuvée Dauvault-Blochet, a recherché Vosne-Romanée Premier Cru and a unique gem for future collectors. The wine from the rest of the vineyard, on the other hand, seems splendid: clearly influenced by the elegant restraint that is often its nature, but simultaneously animated by an exciting energy in the mouth. We confess to a slight doubt: could writing the term "declassification" in a text dedicated to Romanée-Conti be considered a sin?

Richebourg Grand Cru 2015

About half of the eight hectares of the Cru belong to DRC, which in 2015 offers an interpretation focused on an impressive store of fruit. The palate has volume and tannic depth, accompanied by its usual aggressive undertones.

La Tâche Grand Cru 2015

The name recalls the *tâcheron*, a grapegrower paid according to the area of surface worked. Whatever the case, DRC now has in its proud possession the entire Grand Cru *en monopole* at the end of a novel-like tale. In keeping with the critical line that declares its olfactory profile more or less "stunning" vintage after vintage, we also found it to be the most impressive wine tasted for fullness and aromatic precision. On the palate it reveals the usual marriage of elegance and power with an unfathomable mineral depth.

Romanée-Conti Grand Cru 2015

If Madame Leroy, longtime *co-gérante* of the *domaine*, said it took twenty years to understand why Romanée-Conti is the greatest of all the vineyards in Burgundy, how could we explain it in a few lines? We'll limit ourselves to recalling that the parcel has not even two hectares of land and boasts an ancient reputation, identified as exceptional for at least six centuries. If the vintage's aromatic perfection consists of minutiae, of chiaroscuro shadings, the palate is redeemed by an almost tangible intensity, balanced between texture and persistence. It seems that the 2015 vintage is evolving toward a grandiose future.

Emmanuel ROUGET

FLAGEY-ECHÉZEAUX

18, Route de Gilly - Tel. +33 (0) 3 80 628661

Henri Jayer (1922-2006) was in all likelihood the most influential and charismatic Burgundian *vigneron* of the twentieth century, and his teaching is still very much felt by local winemakers. His presence is perhaps nowhere more alive and tangible than in the *domaine* of his nephew, Emmanuel Rouget, also his student and most direct heir. To interpret the wines of this estate one needs to first understand the essence of Jayer's decisive lessons. At the time they were visionary: the banning of chemical products, short pruning for a drastic reduction of yields, complete de-stemming of grapes, cold pre-maceration, the renunciation of filtering. Considered today, they seem like obvious and established practices of pure common sense, but fifty years ago that wasn't the case. Jayer's voice remained decidedly isolated in his criticism of technically well-made wines short of personality: "A good bottle must always contain a bit of mystery… There is nothing more frustrating than knowing in advance what you will taste in a wine." Rouget remains faithful to the teachings of Jayer, with whom he first went to work in the vineyards at the end of the seventies, and under whose supervision he produced his first wines in 1985. The parcels that were are also Jayer's—Cros Parantoux in primis—have gradually been recovered, boosting the estate's fame and prestige. Some wonder if Rouget's wines would ever have reached their current status without the aura of reverence, of critics and consumers alike, that surrounds the memory of Uncle Henri. That we'll never know, as we go on admiring a range of intense and fruit-forward red wines, elegant in bearing, whose complexity is amplified over time. Among the few variations in the vinification practices encoded by Jayer has been a prolongation of the refining sur lies instead of decanting. Rouget's son Guillaume has become increasingly involved in the estate and the decisions that matter. Among the current crop of wines, it has been noted that they have perhaps lost a bit in spontaneity but gained it back in depth and consistency. In any case, they stand among the most sought after and long-lived examples of excellence in this world epicenter of elegance in wine.

Bourgogne Passetoutgrain 2016

The ample share of Gamay favors a perky and cheerful wine. A quick aeration will relieve the wine of any reduction—about as long as it would take to polish off the bottle.

Savigny-lès-Beaune 2015

From a small vineyard of 0.3 hectares in the neglected *lieu-dit* of *Les Planchots*, this red of cherry-like juiciness and silky and tasty tannins is a real delight.

Nuits-Saint-Georges 2015

Over the last few vintages this wine has been among the most successful of Rouget, and this explosively fruity version is no exception. The tannic base that supports its wide range of flavors is more than solid, and though it's true that it was made in entirely new wood barrels, the oak is well integrated. This is a wine of depth that pushes forth with a primal energy.

Vosne-Romanée 1er Cru Les Beaumonts 2015

The 2015 vintage was precocious in every way: in flowering, ripening and, of course, in harvesting, but also in the maturation in barrels of wines that showed uncharacteristic readiness in a few months. This was true even of the notoriously rebellious Beaumonts, whose wines are usually so closed they beg to be decanted. An elegant touch of oak emphasizes the fruit, the structure is complete without rigidity, and even the notable alcohol level does nothing to upset its composure. In short, a wine to appreciate now for its equilibrium, but which will certainly evolve in harmony for many years.

Echézeaux Grand Cru 2015

Rouget has the fourth largest share of Echézeaux, with vineyards totaling almost one and a half hectares from three of the eleven parcels into which the Grand Cru is divided. These include Les Cruots (a parcel also known as Vignes Blanches, adored by Jayer), Clos Saint Denis (a *lieu-dit* sharing the name of the Grand Cru of Morey, but of inferior value) and Les Treux (with moist, water-retaining soils not really indicative of its status). The substance of the resulting wine is dense and still closed in a certain aromatic austerity. The tannic base supporting this weight is more than solid, but the barrels used in the *élevage* are entirely new oak, so the energy created, however profound and "earthy," in this phase remains compressed. A wine to wait for with confidence.

Vosne-Romanée 1er Cru Cros Parantoux 2015

This one-hectare *climat* is set high on a hill with shallow soils difficult to work. It seems probable that this parcel would have remained an anonymous member of the generic Premier Cru assemblage, had it not been for the stubborn passion of Henri Jayer. After having vinified the grapes for more than thirty years, in 1978 he bottled the wine separately and turned this rawboned red into one of the three or four most sought-after and expensive wines of the world. In 1996, Jayer passed his share of vineyard to Rouget (more than two thirds of the entire *climat*, the remainder of which belongs to Domaine Méo-Camuzet), but continued to endorse a choice few lots until 2001, bottles that today are treasured by collectors. During our winery visit, Rouget made this the last wine to be tasted, in spite of its usual place in the hierarchy. If his Echézeaux is solid and imposing with impenetrable density and consistency, his Cros Parantoux is dynamic, almost *iridescent*, enlivened by an aromatic complexity and a tension on the palate that keep alive the ideals of expressivity decreed by Jayer.

Robert SIRUGUE

VOSNE-ROMANÉE

3, Avenue du Monument - Tel. +33 (0) 3 80 610064

11 hectares

Although based in Vosne-Romanée with parental ties to the Jayer family, the Sirugue family winery is still relatively unknown, despite the quality of wines that deserve greater attention. They are reds of pale color, full of nuanced aromatics, styled without frills but showing discreet elegance. After gaining experience in Provence, Arnaud Sirugue recently joined the *domaine* and is gradually taking over the management from his father Jean-Louis and his aunt Marie-France. Part of the wine produced from the eleven hectares of property is still sold to *négociants*, but the few bottles that carry the Sirugue label are gaining prominence, especially among people who value authenticity.

Vosne-Romanée 2015

The four parcels that contribute to this wine include two in Flagey (Chalandins and Muraille du Clos) and the others in the better known *lieux-dits* of Réas and Barreaux, above Cros Parantoux. The wine offers floral fragrance with hints of small berries and oriental spices and a palate that reveals fleshy fruit and engaging texture.

Vosne-Romanée Vieilles Vignes 2015

This bottling is produced only in certain years, and in very limited quantities from the oldest vines in the *lieu-dit* Les Violettes, just below Clos Vougeot, in a wine of succulent intensity.

Vosne-Romanée 1er Cru Les Petits Monts 2015

Overlooking Richebourg from about 300 meters of altitude, this is the most fragmented *climat* of Vosne. Sirugue owns about a hectare, base of a fascinating red with a taut palate and charged with vibrant energy.

5

NUITS-SAINT-GEORGES

NUITS-SAINT-GEORGES

map *page* 513

As is often the case in the Côte d'Or, the name of a vineyard (Les Saint-Georges) is appended to that of the town, which at the end of the nineteenth century was still called Nuits-sous-Beaune. Despite the absence of any Grand Cru vineyards, Nuits-Saint-Georges holds claim to a strong and distinctive *terroir* which translates into robust red wines—firm, austere, slow to open, often endowed with a "*sauvage*" character that has made them famous worldwide. Obviously, the more we examine the different *climats*, the more we find exceptions and discrepancies outside of this generalization. The area is clearly identified by the valley of the Meuzin stream that neatly divides the hill behind the town center. Clearly distinguishable are the slope to the north of the Combe de la Serrée and the slope to the south. The *climats* of the northern slope show the influence of neighboring Vosne-Romanée in spicy, elegant wines as seen in leading examples from the Premier Cru Aux Boudots and Les Damodes. South of the stream the hills are marked by several small *combes* with a range of very different *terroirs* that proffer wines that are severe, powerful and (especially during their first years in bottle) fairly closed in character. Yet in this area lie the most famous *climats* of the *appellation*. In particular, near the Combe des Vallerots we find a series of excellent Premier Cru, including Les Vaucrains and Les Cailles, already classified as *Tête de Cuvée* by Lavalle in 1855, and, above all, Les Saint-Georges, which a recently submitted proposal would elevate to the rank of Grand Cru. The terrain of this area is characterized by brown soils and reddish clays on a bed of Comblanchien calcareous stones (as evidenced by the nearby quarries). Wines from here tend to be tannic yet fleshy, extremely complex and austere, needing many years of age to express full potential. Further south, in the communal territory of Prémeaux, Clos de la Maréchale stands out as an elegant *monopole* of about ten hectares, recently returned to the hands of Fréderic Mugnier after more than a half century of being rented out. Finally, the Nuits-Saint-Georges *appellation* includes an episodic production of white wines, from a total of about 10 hectares. Parcels planted with Chardonnay are established in the Premier Cru Clos de l'Arlot and Les Terres Blanches, while Pinot Blanc (also called *Pinot Gouges*) is grown uniquely in the *climat* Les Perrières by Domaine Henri Gouges.

Domaine de l'ARLOT

NUITS-SAINT-GEORGES
14, Rd 974 - Tel. +33 (0) 3 80 610192
contact@arlot.fr | www.arlot.com

15 hectares

After being acquired thirty years ago by the wine division of the insurance group AXA (AXA Millésimes), Domaine de l'Arlot integrated the original property of three diverse *clos en monopole* (de l'Arlot, des Forêts Saint-Georges and du Chapeau). With small parcels in some very interesting Vosne- Romanée *climats* (Romanée Saint-Vivant and Les Suchots), thus expanding the *domaine* vineyards to nearly fifteen hectares. Management of the winery was long entrusted to Olivier Leriche, who led the conversion to biodynamics in 2003. Leriche was replaced three years ago by Géraldine Godot, a smiling and talented technical director from *maison* Gambal. Changes soon followed with vinifications by parcel, which inspired a thoughtful reevaluation of the composition of the different *cuvées*, resulting in wines that became immediately more expressive and convincing.

Nuits-Saint-Georges 1er cru Clos de l'Arlot 2015

La *Revue du Vin de France* called this wine "the most original and seductive white of the Côte de Nuits." That demanding investiture was confirmed in the 2015 version, which was less *boisé* than usual, and impressed us with its aromatic complexity and exquisite citric verve.

Nuits-Saint-Georges 1er cru Clos de l'Arlot 2015

The winery's "flagship" label comes only from old Pinot Noir vines, producing a less colored and more elegant red than the *appellation* stereotype. Made from 50% whole cluster grapes, the wine shows fruity exuberance with the customary aromatic complexity.

Nuits-Saint-Georges 1er cru Clos des Forets Saint-Georges 2015

The *domaine* has two vineyards in the community of Prémeaux, the Clos de l'Arlot and the *climat* Les Forêts, which with seven hectares is one of the most extensive *monopoles* in Burgundy. Starting with this vintage, Géraldine elaborated a single *cuvée*, which stands out for internal density and energy.

Robert CHEVILLON

NUITS-SAINT-GEORGES
68, Rue Felix Tisserand - Tel. +33 (0) 3 80 623488
detb@domainerobertchevillon.fr | www.domainercbertchevillon.fr

13 hectares

Heirs of a tradition that goes back to the early twentieth century and the pioneering figure of Symphorien Chevillon, brothers Denis and Bertrand took over fifteen years ago from their father, Robert. Today they manage thirteen hectares of vineyard by *lutte raisonnée*, all within the municipality of Nuits, including eight different Premier Cru. Their red wines, always from entirely de-stemmed grapes, are destined for long aging: today they seem to be much better balanced and graceful than in the past, ready to enjoy even quite young for the fragrant intensity of their fruit, as well as their elegant balance.

Nuits-Saint-Georges Vieilles Vignes 2015

About ten parcels supply the grapes for this *cuvée*. Focused on fruit and on pleasure, the 2015 version is among the winery's most successful ever.

Nuits-Saint-Georges 1er Cru Les Cailles 2015

This eighty-year-old vineyard enhances the reputation of its *climat* in wines of almost feminine finesse. The floral aromas (roses) and silky tannins may not be perfectly in line with the stereotype for the Nuits *appellation*, but the wine is undoubtedly of superior class.

Nuits-Saint-Georges 1er Cru Les Saint-Georges 2015

Thanks to wines like this, Les Saint-Georges has earned its reputation as a *de facto* Grand Cru. The wine shows intensity and elegance, vigor and balance, aromatics of surprisingly fruity vivacity and a lingering saline quality that releases complexity and persistence to the end.

Nuits-Saint-Georges 1er Cru Les Vaucrains 2015

Bertrand served the Vaucrains last in the tasting order, in accordance with a rather widespread practice in the area. The wine does, in fact, have more density, more structure, and more energy than the Saint-Georges, and yet its sauvage intensity is free of any hardness and conveys radiant flavors right to the finish.

Georges CHICOTOT

NUITS-SAINT-GEORGES

15, Rue du Général de Gaulle - Tel. +33 (0) 3 80 611933
chicotot@aol.com | www.domaine-chicotot.com

9 hectares

Descendant of a family of *vignerons* established in Nuits-Saint-Georges for eight generations, Georges Chicotot recently passed control to his young son Clément, who, together with his mother Pascale, run an artisanal *domaine* spread over nine hectares of vineyards. In 2014, small parcels were acquired in the communities of Beaune and Pommard, which add to those in Ladoix and form a nucleus of the winery's most important vineyards in the Nuits area. In fact, thanks to their Nuits reds, Chicotot has built a reputation over time aimed at a succulent, pleasurable drinking experience, free of any inclinations toward muscular or hyper-extractive wines. Inclinations that have proved to be a handicap for a denomination like Nuits-Saint-Georges, already stigmatized by a historic tendency to produce heavily structured, tannic, austere wines. Let us be clear; it is not that Chicotot has abdicated the task of allowing his *terroirs* to shine through in the wines. His special talent, however, consists in the ability to put the structural resources of Nuits reds at the service of previously unexplored enjoyment, also thanks to a masterful use of vinification with stem-inclusion, a method that certainly benefits from a generous vintage like 2015.

Bourgogne Pinot Noir 2015

Always among the most reliable and affordable "entry level" wines of the Côte de Nuits, it's delicious and juicy with persistence of flavors worthy of a category superior to simply Bourgogne.

Nuits-Saint-Georges Aux Alots 2015

The clay-rich soils, fed by small underground springs, thrive in the hot, dry years. Rarely have we found this red to be so graceful, soft and floral.

Nuits-Saint-Georges Plantes au Baron 2015

This minuscule parcel is in a *lieu-dit* just within the area of Prémeaux-Prissey on the edge of Les Saint-Georges. Unlike its noble neighbor, with the resonant voice of a baritone, here we find transparency and finesse, closer to a soprano.

Nuits-Saint-Georges 1er Cru Vaucrains 2015

This Premier Cru is considered among the best of the *appellation*, in obvious discord with an etymology that suggests a link with the expression "*ne vaut rien*" (it's worth nothing). Evidently, the poor and thin soils, as well as the prohibitively steep slopes, have always hampered work in the vineyard, yet it's the ideal terrain for this wine. Chicotot produces a stripped-down version, but one that is also structured and full of energy.

Nuits-Saint-Georges 1er Cru Les Saint-Georges 2015

This is one of those cases in which it's practically impossible not to cite the *hors catégorie* universally bestowed upon this *climat*. While we're aware that an expression like "an iron fist in a velvet glove" is a hackneyed way of putting it, we're at something of a loss for words to describe how this wine's elegant three-dimensional progression on the palate is in all respects worthy of a Grand Cru.

Henry GOUGES

NUITS-SAINT-GEORGES
7, Rue du Moulin - Tel. +33 (0) 3 80 610440
domaine@gouges.com | www.gouges.com

15 hectares

One of the best-known families of Nuits, Gouges bases its reputation on fifteen hectares of medium-large vineyards (by Burgundian standards), located in the best *climats* of the community. Founded in 1920, the winery reached its fourth generation with the entry of Grégory Gouges, son of Pierre, in 2003. In the cellar, gravity is employed in the various stages of processing, with *cuves* in cement designed expressly to enhance the family's precise stylistic vision. Stainless steel tanks are used only for assemblage before bottling. Vinification procedures, beginning with completely de-stemmed grapes, are aimed at rendering greater finesse in the wines, in contrast with the usual notion that associates Gouges with a tradition of producing austere, structured, and unyielding reds. The 2015 harvest, one of the earliest ever, offers several examples of the style. As Grégory told us, "I preferred to use a light hand without pushing for extraction or body." And in fact, despite their typical internal density, our tastings of wines from the vintage have brought to light a general fusion of fleshiness with surprisingly accessible, delicious juice.

Nuits-Saint-Georges 2015

Like the harvest, which was already completed at the beginning of September, the 2015 vintage was also bottled early. "The levels of malic acid were quite low, and fermentation was very fast," explains Grégory. This Villages comes from nine different parcels and has been in bottle since December 2016, a wine focused upon delicious fruit, enviably easy to drink.

Nuits-Saint-Georges 1er Cru Clos des Porrets 2015

This large *monopole* of 3.5-hectares was named for the ancient pear orchard planted on the steeply sloping, gravelly terrain. Critical reviews of the wines have always emphasized concentration and power. "A wine for the very long term," as Jasper Morris put it. Even the 2015 doesn't deviate much from norm—still quite closed on the nose, marked by hints of licorice, and solid on the palate with tight, lively tannins.

Nuits-Saint-Georges 1er Cru Les Vaucrains 2015

Situated in the Combe des Vallerots on soils lacking in organic substance, Vaucrains is nonetheless an excellent *cru*, despite a name that might refer to its worthless status (*vaut rien*) due to the extreme difficulty of working its steep terrain. Gouges has about one hectare, partly replanted in 1980, producing a wine with mineral notes and savory grit that manages to hold an impressive stock of fruit.

Nuits-Saint-Georges 1er Cru Les Saint-Georges 2015

Much like Les Vaucrains, Les Saint-Georges and its slow-to-open, marathon-length wines also have the reputation of performing at the level of a Grand Cru. Gouges' version offers extractive weight, thanks to the depth of the vineyard's dark clays, balanced by tension which adds to the complexity of a wine packed with energy and vitality that develops rhythmically on the palate.

LÉCHENEAUT

NUITS-SAINT-GEORGES

14, Rue des Seuillets - Tel. +33 (0) 3 80 610596
lecheneaut@wanadoo.fr | www.domaine-lecheneaut.fr

10 hectares

Brothers Philippe and Vincent Lécheneaut have been running the domain since 1986, working together in the vineyards, often with a horse, and cellars. In 2000, they ceased the use of any chemical products, employing organic methods of farming, even if not certified. Vinification techniques vary according to the vintage and the *climat*, sometimes using completely de-stemmed grapes and sometimes bunches either whole or in calculated percentages. Currently the *domaine* has ten hectares of vineyards spread over eighteen different *appellations*, all in the Côte de Nuits, with some appendages in the Hautes Côtes.

Bourgogne "Clos Prieur" 2015

The vineyard is located in the lower sector of Chambolle. This sunny vintage year, here as in many nearby *climats*, is expressed in a red wine that is more structured than fine, more spicy than floral.

Nuits-Saint-Georges Au Chouillet 2015

The more than seventy-year old vineyard lends prestige to this *lieu-dit*, on the slope facing Vosne, with soils composed of silt and clay, located in the dejection cone of the *combe*. The terrain retains moisture in the driest years, and in 2015 Lécheneaut produced a red with elegant, aromatic phrasing.

Nuits-Saint-Georges 1er Cru Les Pruliers 2015

This *climat*, located between the Vallerots and Meuzin *combes*, displays soils rich in red clays. There is no lack of personality in this version, which focuses on fruit, backed by a charming and persistent palate.

Antoine LIENHARDT

COMBLANCHIEN

21, Grande Rue - Tel. +33 (0) 3 80 627237
antoinelienhardt.domaine@gmail.com | www.domaineantoinelienhardt.com

4 hectares

Antoine Lienhardt autographed his first harvest in 2011, after gaining experience through internships in Burgundy and South Africa. He now manages his family vineyards, which had been rented out since his grandfather Maurice Guyot retired in 1992. Today, Antoine and his partner Juliette Joblot (owner of the homonymous *domaine* in the Côte Chalonnaise) are converting this four-hectare estate in Comblanchien to organic farming with the plan of being certified by Ecocert from 2018. Using entirely whole cluster grapes, they produce fresh and juicy wines, animated by invitingly spontaneous expressivity at quality levels higher than average for their *appellations*.

Bourgogne Pinot Noir 2015

Here is a joyous example of immediacy and precision in an agile wine that is very pleasant to drink.

Côte de Nuits-Villages Les Essards 2015

The captivating aromas of dark fruit and berries are a preview to the palate with savory, gritty flavors; tension and dazzle by no means preclude pleasure.

Côte de Nuits-Villages aux Vignottes 2015

Across the road from the Clos de la Maréchale of Mugnier, this is the only vineyard segment of the community of Prémeaux remaining outside the perimeter of the Nuits-Saint-Georges *appellation*. Frankly the reason for this isn't clear, given the surprising quality of the wine that Antoine derives from these vines—a wine of creamy texture, punctuated by delicious sweet/savory sensations at a price that is truly a bargain.

Côte de Nuits-Villages Les Plantes aux Bois 2015

These vineyards, almost seventy years old, offer very limited yields (about 3,000 kilos of grapes per hectare), and produce a wine that surprised us by showing the energy and density of a Premier Cru.

Alain MICHELOT

NUITS-SAINT-GEORGES
6, Rue Camille Rodier - Tel. +33 (0) 3 80 611446
domalainmichelot@orange.fr

7.8 hectares

Élodie, the daughter of Alain Michelot, replaced her father at the helm of this *domaine*. She and her husband now manage the eight hectares of vines, including parcels in the best vineyards in Nuits. Faithful to a traditional style, her work favors greater tannic finesse and harmony in the wines, as was particularly evident in our recent tastings of the 2015 vintage.

Nuits-Saint-Georges Vieilles Vignes 2015

Although most *vignerons* assemble grapes from different vineyards in *cuvées* destined for Villages wines, the Michelot family only exploits one single vineyard, located in the northern sector of Nuits facing Vosne, beneath the Premier Cru Les Bousselots. The almost sixty-year-old vines render a fleshy but mellow red wine of pleasing drinkability.

Nuits-Saint-Georges 1er Cru La Richemone 2015

Also in the northern sector of Nuits, this *climat* is rarely mentioned: it is a small (two hectares), steeply sloping vineyard, owned by only two *vignerons* (the other being Perrot-Minot). The obscurity seems a pity, because it is certainly of Premier Cru merit, and, as Armando Castagno describes it, produces "a red wine that can be almost feminine in warm years, perhaps more than any other Nuits *cru*." We found this to be true in Élodie's elegant and spicy 2015 version which is simply a joy to drink.

Nuits-Saint-Georges 1er Cru Aux Champs-Perdrix 2015

In one of the smallest Premier Crus of the *appellation* (just over half a hectare) Michelot has a plot planted in 1937. The vineyard is high and ventilated, guaranteeing very healthy grapes with an incisive acidic freshness; the poor, stony soils lend finesse to the tannins and the sunny vintage provides ripe fruit and velvety texture.

PRIEURÉ-ROCH

NUITS-SAINT-GEORGES

22, Rue du Général de Gaulle - Tel. +33 (0) 3 80 620000
domaine.prieure.roch@wanadoo.fr | www.domaine-prieure-roch.com

15 hectares

Henry-Frédéric Roch was very young when he began to build his *domaine*. In 1988, he bought his first two hectares of Vosne Romanée in four different parcels, and in the early nineties, not yet thirty years old, he already had many first-rate vineyards throughout the Côte de Nuits. This was the result of his decidedly precocious awareness, as well as the privilege of being a nephew of Lalou Bize-Leroy and a descendant of a family involved in the ownership of Romanée-Conti. From the choice of labels with hieroglyphic symbols, it was clear that he felt a need to break with convention and go back to traditional and archaic sources. This archaism also surfaces in the wines, often challenging the conventions of enological rules with a very personal style, which has quickly established itself among lovers of "natural" wines, though not without controversy. The fifteen hectares of vineyards are farmed under organic protocol, with an eye to biodynamics. Vinification is carried out with the stems, foot-stomping, long maturation (the 2015 vintage was only released at the end of 2017) and a drastic reduction in the use of sulfites (only during decanting). These are the most obvious of the options inspired by Roch and coordinated by his right-hand man, Yannick Champ. That the wines take on a prematurely autumnal cast may suggest a decadent style, but that's not the case. The wines remain steadfast, and in the right years become memorable bottles.

Ladoix Le Cloud 2015

With the purchase in 2010 of more than two hectares of vineyards under the hill of Corton, the *domaine* launched itself in Côte de Beaune, in the community of Ladoix, where the 2015 vintage produced ten thousand bottles. This is remarkable, given the difficulties of the most recent harvests and the winery's own selective standards. The result is a crisp and deliciously fruity red wine which will be marketed in an informal way at more affordable prices. Served cool, and paired with a plate of salt cod and chickpeas, a single bottle may not be enough.

Vosne-Romanée Clos Goillotte 2014

In addition to the Clos des Corvées in Nuits, the winery also owns another small vineyard *en monopole* called Clos Goillotte in the heart of the village of Vosne. The half a hectare was sold to Frédéric Roch in 1988 by Domaine de la Romanée Conti. He obtains two thousand bottles of a very original red wine, baroque in style and overflowing with fragrance, a Villages only on paper that is sold at Grand Cru prices.

Vosne-Romanée 1er Cru Les Suchots 2014

This one-hectare plot is rented to Roch by the Marion family. The wine tends to be dark and *sauvage*, requiring substantial aeration to reveal its aromatic makeup, full of violets, black cherry and pepper. On the palate the elegance is more modulated, with a refreshing finish.

Nuits-Saint-Georges 1er Cru Vieilles Vignes 2014

Clos des Corvées, the pride of the *domaine*, is a large vineyard of more than five hectares *en monopole*, on thick, clay soils with notable active calcareous content. The estate derives three different labels from this vineyard, though only one bears the name Clos des Corvées and comes from a selection of the sparsest bunches of grapes. The other two bottlings are defined by the age of the vines. This selection contains grapes from vines on average 80 years old, a factor that enhances the wine's aromatic finesse and foreshadows a palate of a wild nature, animated by contrasts of dynamic energy, on par with the finest reds of Nuits.

REMORIQUET

NUITS-SAINT-GEORGES

25, Rue de Charmois - Tel. +33 (0) 3 80 612484
domaine.remoriquet@wanadoo.fr

9.5 hectares

The wines of Gilles Remoriquet are among the favorite finds of our recent forays through Nuits-Saint Georges. Faithful to a style of declared classical inspiration, the wines are often seen as requiring age. But in a vintage like 2015 they seem to have rounded out the rough edges and have made for enjoyable drinking since bottling. The Remoriquet family, originally from Citeaux, moved to Nuits toward the end of the seventeenth century. Gilles, who studied winemaking in Dijon, has run the *domaine* for almost forty years. His vineyards of just under ten hectares, farmed by *lutte raisonnée*, are dedicated almost entirely to reds for an annual production of around forty thousand bottles.

Nuits-Saint-Georges 2015

This *cuvée* comes from two different parcels and was made using entirely whole grape bunches. The result is surprising for its floral notes and opulent juiciness.

Nuits-Saint-Georges Les Allots 2015

Gilles doesn't hide his affection for this vineyard on a northern slope overlooking Vosne. The first parcel his family purchased and the source of his top wine it tends to give its best in the driest years. The grapes, in this case entirely de-stemmed, derive from the clay-rich soils a fund of greater amplitude, which translates here into a bonus of fruit-forward energy.

Nuits-Saint-Georges 1er Cru Rue de Chaux 2015

This two-hectare *climat*, split among few owners, is located close to the town on the south side of the *combe* and is characterized by reddish soils. The wine is masculine and sanguine, resistant to any smothness, with hints of black fruit and berries and a darkish timbre, unequivocally Nuits.

6

THE HAUTES CÔTES

THE HAUTES CÔTES

maps *page* 502 and 514

The two zones known as Hautes Côtes de Nuits and Hautes Côtes de Beaune together cover a rather large territory of hills and plateaus lying to the west of the Côte d'Or. Often viewed as fringe wine areas, they stand apart from their vaunted neighbors for their generally higher positions and steeper contours, affecting exposure to sun and winds and variations in microclimate. But on close inspection the composition of their soils, consisting of clays and calcareous deposits in various forms and textures is not unlike the rest of the region. And yet it's enough to turn off the state road and start ascending to the west to catapult yourself into a totally different environment, where the usual monoculture of the vine gives way to a landscape of orchards, woods and pastures, much cooler and immediately peaceful. If we consider the area from a point of view of wine, despite the charm of the high hills and the unique atmosphere of its small villages, there has been a tendency to refer to the Hautes Côtes as a "poor man's Burgundy," a place where the *crème de cassis* often outshines the wine.

The vineyards of the Hautes Côtes de Nuits extend over a territory of about twenty communities, between Reulle-Vergy to the north and Magny-lès-Villers to the south. The vineyards of the Hautes Côtes de Beaune are also scattered over about twenty communities, but the territory is more fragmented and less clearly defined. In terms of vineyards, there are about 1,500 hectares distributed almost equally between the two different *appellations* with a strong preference for red varieties. In previous centuries, Gamay had prevailed, but recently the scales have tipped toward Pinot Noir, the ripening of which remains a critical point of discussion. Temperatures here average at least 5°C lower than in the Côte, meaning the harvest usually starts about a week later. That fact can be interpreted in different ways. If we take an optimistic view about global warming and consider the cooler environment of the Hautes Côtes a valuable resource, we shouldn't forget that harvesting up to mid-October at these latitudes can present serious complications. In any case, the potential for wines in both of the Hautes Côtes remains to be seen, though the extraordinary results from talented artisans like Claire Naudin and Emmanuel Giboulot give reason for optimism. Their achievements not only deepen our knowledge about these lesser-known viticultural areas, but shine as examples for *vignerons* of the future, showing that in order to make bright refreshing and expressive wines, you don't necessarily need Grand Cru vineyards.

François BERGERET

NOLAY

15, Rue Franche - Tel. +33 (0) 3 80 218872
contact@domaine-bergeret.com | www.domaine-bergeret.com

7.5 hectares

If you are looking for more affordable alternatives to the classic wines of Burgundy (and who isn't?) a detour into Nolay, on the eastern edge of the Côte d'Or, may be worth the trip. After climbing to more than 400 meters, we were greeted by François Bergeret, a man of gentle manner and reserved character, who calls himself an *artisan vigneron*. We soon realized that the title fits him perfectly. He took us to see his vineyards, which are spread over seven-and-a-half hectares, mainly in the municipality of Nolay, as well as some small parcels between Beaune and Pommard. François Bergeret produces fresh, honest and pleasant wines, always with an eye toward drinkability.

Bourgogne Hautes Côtes de Beaune 2014

There is more to this wine than its fruity character (pear, white melon), as it is also charged with a vein of a refreshing and savory taste.

Bourgogne Hautes Côtes de Beaune "Louis" 2014

From grapes selected in various parcels of Nolay, the wine is vinified entirely whole cluster, and with a very low dose of sulfites. The result is a compelling blend of juiciness and flavor that make it disarmingly drinkable.

Bourgogne Hautes Côtes de Beaune Vieilles Vignes "Rondo" 2014

The vineyard was planted in 1950 at an altitude of 450 meters, facing southeast. The delicacy and expressive purity of the wine, enhanced by inviting floral nuances, would delight any enthusiast looking for slender, svelte reds at absolutely reasonable prices.

BONNARDOT

VILLERS-LA-FAYE

1, Rue de l'Ancienne Cure - Tel. +33 (0) 3 80 629127
domaine.bonnardot@wanadoo.fr | www.bonnardot.fr

20 hectares

Wine didn't figure in Danièle Bonnardot's original plans. The fact that wineries in the Hautes Côtes are less profitable than those of the Côte d'Or, meant that only one of the family's children could be sustained by the domain, and, as often happens, the responsibility fell to the eldest brother. Danièle, after studying economics, had moved to London where she was working in international finance when her brother became ill. This put her at a crossroads: either sell the property or return to Burgundy to help manage the *domaine*. Danièle chose the latter and, in 2005, went back to school to study winemaking. From the 2009 harvest, following the death of her brother, she has managed the estate's twenty hectares herself. Danièle's approach respects the soil, while her winemaking reveals a laudable sensitivity. That means that the shining example of Claire Naudin is being followed by other talented women winemakers in the Hautes Côtes.

Bourgogne Hautes Côtes de Nuits "Clos des Oiseaux" 2015

From a vineyard in the community of Chaux, at high altitudes and on stony soils, this is a dynamic, savory white with a wholesome aptitude for food-pairing.

Bourgogne Hautes Côtes de Nuits "Coup de Foudre" 2015

Light and carefree, but also satisfying and delicious—if there were a championship for red picnic wines this would be a serious contender.

Bourgogne Hautes Côtes de Nuits "L'Age Mûre" 2015

The aromatic array of small black berries and fine spices is alluring, and though the wine spends almost a month macerating on the skins, the palate remains smooth and agile.

Bourgogne Côte de Nuits Village 2015

From old vineyards located in the areas of Corgoloin and Comblanchien, the wine offers an engaging fresh-floral profile. In the mouth the tannins are grittier, translating into a more sapid taste.

Domaine de la CRAS

PLOMBIÈRES-LÈS-DIJON
Domaine de la Cras - Tel. +33 (0) 6 71 680763
domainedelacras@marcsoyard.fr | www.domainedelacras.marcsoyard.fr

8 hectares

In 2013, the city of Dijon purchased a farm of 160 hectares, in line with an urban containment program to preserve the green belt around its periphery. Perched on the rocky ridges west of the town, the estate already included a well-equipped cellar and a single block of eight hectares of vines planted thirty years earlier with almost equal parts of red and white varieties. The trust managing the property sought a young winemaker who did not already own family vineyards, who was interested in organic viticulture and who was willing to make the winery available to the public for educational visits. In return, no rent was required, only the annual contribution of two thousand bottles to be allocated to the city administration. In the end, out of many qualified candidates, Marc Soyard was chosen. Marc is originally from the Jura, and was an apprentice to Jean-Yves Bizot in Vosne-Romanée for six years. It is still early to fully evaluate his work and the quality of the four labels in production at Domaine de la Cras, but our first impression was positive. The wines are fresh and fragrant, energetic and light, and overall delightfully spontaneous.

Bourgogne 2015

Vinified with two thirds stem-inclusion and a semi-carbonic fermentation, this is a red marked by a pleasant aromatic vitality, which offers momentum and smoothness on the palate.

Bourgogne Coteaux de Dijon Cras Monopole 2015

The *domaine* is the only producer allowed to claim the Coteaux de Dijon *appellation*. The wine includes grapes only from the best-exposed and steeply-sloped vineyards, for which an additional time in barrel is provided (up to 18 months). The result is a dynamic and promising red – both energetic and flavorful.

CRUCHANDEAU

CHAUX

4, Rue Robert - Tel. +33 (0) 3 80 621650
contact@domaine-cruchandeau.com | www.domaine-cruchandeau.com

6.5 hectares

Pulling off the heavily traveled roads that run in proximity to Route 74 you may come across wineries that haven't had the luck of belonging to historic families of *vignerons* with parcels in the most prestigious *climats*. Enter Julien Cruchandeau, born in 1978 with no legacy of vineyards behind him, who in 2007 founded a *domaine* in the village of Chaux in the Hautes Côtes de Nuits. After attending the Hotel Institute in Dijon, Julien, then about 20, worked as a waiter in various French cities and in London, while playing music with his electronic band, the Shrink Orchestra, which performed in concerts all over Europe. On his return to Beaune, he enrolled in the school of viticulture and enology and worked as an intern in a cellar in Gevrey, eventually becoming a *régisseur* in the small company of the heirs of France Lechenault at Bouzeron in the Côte Chalonnaise. He soon realized that he could craft a life in wine and started, in 2003, with the purchase of his first vineyards in Bouzeron, before founding his own *domaine*. His wines speak a neat and direct language, linear and well contrasted, especially those produced in the Hautes Côtes de Nuits.

Bourgogne Hautes Côtes de Nuits Vieilles Vignes 2015

A fifty-year-old vineyard planted on white marls with good clay content gives life to a tasty and fresh white, with marked floral overtones.

Bourgogne Hautes Côtes de Nuits "Les Valançons" 2015

The grapes come from Chevannes, at an altitude of 400 meters, and are vinified using half in whole clusters. The wine shows enchanting lightness and drinkability.

Domaine de la DOUAIX

ARCENANT

5, Rue du Moutier - Tel. +33 (0) 6 85 950179
moustie.gilles@orange.fr | www.douaix.fr

4 hectares

Twenty years ago, Mark Moustie, a Belgian, purchased a farmhouse in Arcenant, where he laid the foundations for his dream of moving to Burgundy. In the following years his project took shape with the acquisition of some vineyard parcels in the Hautes Côtes and the construction of a small cellar. Mark then left his previous job as a computer technology consultant and dedicated himself full time to winemaking. He is assisted by his son Gilles, a graduate of the school of viticulture and enology in Beaune. Domaine de la Douaix was thus created, its title inspired by the ancient name for the town of Arcenant. This is a winery to keep an eye on, now reinforced with a large, comfortable bed and breakfast, and vineyards which include new parcels in Prémeaux and Corgoloin, in the Côtes de Nuits Villages *appellation*. Mark also does a bit of work as a *négociant* thanks to grapes purchased between Nuits-Saint-Georges and Pernand-Vergelesses. The vineyards are farmed organically with yields capped at around 30 hectoliters per hectare, producing silky, fresh wines, both red and white, offered at prices that we find to be more than fair.

Bourgogne Blanc En Mairey 2015

This is actually a declassified Hautes Cotes de Nuits, obtained from an equal blend of Chardonnay and Pinot Blanc. The wine shows lively citrus aromas that translate to the palate, adding tension, energy and contrast.

Bourgogne Hautes Côtes de Nuits Le Clos des Fervelots 2015

This parcel is planted on the clay soils of a Clos located north of the village of Arcenant. Moustie obtains a fragrant and tasty red from the vines, refreshing in its spontaneity.

Côte de Nuits-Villages Vieilles Vignes 2015

This comes from a blend of two parcels of the remarkable average age of ninety years old, producing a slender but tense wine with a noticeable tannic grip, enlivened by a saline finish.

David DUBAND

CHEVANNES

12, Rue du Lavoir - Tel. +33 (0) 3 80 614116
contact@domaine-duband.com | www.domaine-duband.com

17 hectares

The name David Duband has come forward, in the course of a few harvests, as a reference point that has inevitably forced the rethinking of Burgundy's hierarchies of wine. The winery doesn't have particularly profound roots. David's father laid the foundations in 1965, planting fifteen hectares of vineyards in the Hautes Côtes, only to sell all the grapes to the local cooperative winery. The breakthrough came in the early nineties, when Parisian lawyer François Feuillet, head of the Trigano Group, hired young David to manage his vineyard properties. This inspired Duband to push Feuillet to create an independent winery in his home town of Chevannes, far from the comfortable surroundings of the Côte d'Or. Duband continues to make wine for both Feuillet and his own family *domaine*, in a well-appointed modern cellar. Following some recent acquisitions of Feuillet, Duband farms seventeen hectares of vineyards organically, contributing to twenty different bottlings. His style, inspired by such models of classicism as Rousseau and Dujac, has always avoided forced extractions or saturated colors, recently experimenting with whole cluster vinifications, always with admirably scrupulous precision.

Bourgogne Hautes Côtes de Nuits "Luis Auguste" 2015

An enchanting bottle, exuding juiciness and freshness with a touch of licorice in the finish that emphasizes its fruity exuberance.

Morey-Saint-Denis 1er Cru Clos Sorbè 2015

The calcareous substrata of the half-century old vineyard are of Bathonian origin. Vinified with more than 75% whole clusters, this is a solid wine of ample structure, integrated by a gripping finish, rich in flavor with spicy nuances.

Nuits-Saint-Georges 1er Cru Aux Thorey 2015

This is a red of absolute value, though its *climat* isn't very well known. Duband's parcel, which covers more than half a hectare of the five hectares in this Premier

Cru, is situated on the east-facing slope, where a Comblanchien calcareous vein intersects with the clay matrices. Rarely so expressive in its first months in bottle, this wine reveals the vintage to be an irresistible amalgam of floral and fruity notes (iris and raspberry).

Echezeaux Grand Cru 2015

This small vineyard nearly eighty years old belongs to a sector known as Les Rouges du Bas, in a parcel whose soils rest on the calcareous rock of Prémeaux, is considered one of the most prestigious of this extensive Grand Cru. Vinified almost entirely with whole bunches, it is a long aging red in which the dense fleshiness of the material and the exuberance of the fruit don't preclude harmony and elegance.

Latricières-Chambertin Grand Cru 2015

The temperature variation and ventilation of the Combe Grisard mitigate the stress this vineyard feels in hot, sunny years, as is apparent in the 2015 vintage, with its marked mineral verticality and its fund of impressive complexities.

Chambertin Grand Cru 2015

Like most Burgundian *vignerons*, David Duband is convinced of the extraordinary quality of the 2015 vintage, which he doesn't hesitate to define as "a year with immense potential for aging." This Chambertin confirms his conviction, though it only hints at its eventual class, since it is still partially compressed by a tightly tannic frame.

Nicolas FAURE

MEUILLEY
6, Rue Gabriel Bachot
n.faure21@gmail.com

Nicolas Faure is a thirty-something *vigneron* from Bordeaux with a CV including an apprenticeship at Domaine de la Romanée-Conti, in whose vineyards he worked from 2010 to 2015, after stages in the Rhone Valley and New Zealand. Lacking the advantage of family vineyards, his debut as a winemaker was rather complicated. He has managed each year (with great difficulty) to bottle his own wines since 2011, while also working simultaneously for other estates and managing to cobble together a mere hectare of property, fragmented into seven minuscule parcels between Vosne and Pernand. With the addition of a few other rows he leases, he is able to produce five virtually "secret" bottlings, all vinified with whole bunches. Yet Faure was immediately noticed and reviewed by some of the most esteemed wine writers—Steen Öhmann has already written of his "mesmerizing" wines. We were surprised and delighted by our visit to his cellar, half-hidden in the village of Meuilley, in discovering one of the most promising young talents in Burgundy.

Bourgogne Aux Argillières 2015

From vineyards in Prémeaux, this is a Burgundy of engaging fruity intensity, unbeatably quaffable.

Coteaux Bourguignons Mes Gamay 2015

In such a precocious vintage, Nicolas picked his Gamay late (September 13), but you'd never know it after tasting the wine he produced. To the contrary, it is an example in fresh, floral aromatics, a pleasure to drink.

Nuits-Saint-Georges Les Herbues 2015

Although this parcel is a hundred meters from the Vosne border on deep clay soils, if tasted blind it would be hard to trace back to Nuits or a generous vintage like 2015. Rather, and more delicately, it enchants us with a feminine grace and a palate devoted to sleek precision.

Claire NAUDIN

MAGNY-LÈS-VILLERS

12, Rue du Meix Grenot - Tel. +33 (0) 3 80 629150
info@naudin-ferrand.com | www.naudin-ferrand.com

21 hectares

When we get bored driving back and forth on State Road 74, one of our favorite diversions is climbing up to Magny-les-Villers, at the junction of the Hautes Côtes of Beaune and Nuits. On our first ascent, at the end of January 2012, a heavy snowfall tried to discourage us. But our stubbornness (and the improbable grit of the Fiat Panda we had rented) proved to be auspicious, rewarding us with the discovery of the engaging wines of Claire Naudin. Her work focuses on wines of the Hautes Côtes, too often dismissed as rustic and simple. She enhances their freshness and juiciness through whole cluster vinifications, and adds no sulfites, but instead calculated doses of carbon dioxide frozen in granules. Claire is an enthusiast of natural wine, but rejects organic labels and certifications, preferring to be free in her approach and deliberate in her work on individual parcels. Carving out her own space within the family domain, she has been experimenting with this line of research for almost twenty years, gradually implementing grassing over in the vineyards and drastically reducing the use of chemical treatments. She has finally begun to receive well-deserved recognition, both from critics and an international clientele. Her wines bear the Latin names of some of the most common wildflowers of these hills, which also adorn the elegant labels. In our view, these are the most accomplished wines ever made in the Hautes Côtes, opening the way for a decisive revival of *appellations* that remain conspicuously underrated.

Le Clou 34 2015

The name and the year of birth of a parcel with an eastern exposure planted more than eighty years ago identify this atypical Aligoté. Atypical not just because part of the vineyard is head-pruned, but also because the wine offers exuberant aromas of tropical fruit along with power and complexity on the palate.

Bourgogne Hautes Côtes de Beaune Bellis Perennis 2015

From a twenty-year-old vineyard of a half hectare facing south within the *lieu-dit* En Daisay in the countryside of Magny, this white pairs fantastically with food.

The wine still needs time to resolve the oak (50% new barrels), but its fiber is tenacious and tasty, and the finish creamy with a grainy redolence.

Bourgogne Hautes Côtes de Beaune Orchis Mascula 2015

After having found the 2010 version enchanting, among the most stunning revelations of our previous edition, we now learn that over a few years Orchis Mascula has become a bit of a cult wine of the Hautes Côtes. With full merit; this is a fascinating wine in every vintage, with its resonant aromatics and palate brimming with nuanced flavors. The 2015, obtained from whole cluster grapes and without added sulfites, has a tannic intensity unexpected in a red that is already so open and forward.

Côtes de Nuits-Villages Vieilles Vignes Viola Odorata 2015

This comes from three different parcels in the community of Corgoloin, where the average age of the vineyards is over seventy and yields fall drastically below twenty hectoliters per hectare. In 2015, the texture of tannins is tighter, and the wine gains in richness of fruit what it loses in aromatic nuances.

Bourgogne Hautes Côtes de Nuits Myosotis Arvensis 2015

An abundant hectare shared between two *climats* (En la Croix and Les Tilles) is the base for a wine with an almost intoxicating aromatic complexity: rosehip, spicy coriander, morello cherries, and bitter rhubarb mingle in a wild and seductive bouquet. The palate is just as lively and juicy. Enchanting.

Claude NOUVEAU

CHANGE-PAR-NOLAY
Lieu-dit Marcheseuil - Tel. +33 (0) 3 85 911334
domaine@claudenouveau.com | www.claudenouveau.com

14 hectares

If you know where to look, the Burgundy of the Hautes Côtes teems with small wineries where the bulk of the work is done by hand, by true artisans. As noted, these little-known and undervalued zones provide some of the finest translations of *terroir*. As Armando Castagno writes, the best wines of the Hautes Côtes are "exceptionally clean and true, as well as being spectacular "*gourmand*" wines: decidedly fresh, fragrant, well-defined and delicious to drink." Claude Nouveau's *domaine* fits into this still undiscovered landscape, offering a range of labels at unbeatable prices obtained from vineyards in an extensive stretch of almost five hectares in the Hautes Côtes plus parcels located between Santenay and Maranges.

Bourgogne Hautes Côtes de Beaune Vieilles Vignes 2015

A red wine made from completely de-stemmed grapes shows lively aromatics, including inviting nuances of moss and spices. The flavors come across in a generous and compact mouthful and a finish with a streak of cheerful rusticity.

Bourgogne Hautes Côtes de Beaune 2015

This fifty-year-old vineyard, situated at over 400 meters, covers half a hectare with a western exposure. From this *terroir* Nouveau produces a distinctly floral white wine of modulated linearity that pairs perfectly with food.

Santenay Le Chainey 2015

Le Chainey is a *lieu-dit* located at the summit of one of Santenay's best known Premier Crus, Grand Clos Rousseau. Its high and well-ventilated position translates into a taut, fresh and juicy white, whose biting acidity is not at all weakened by the warmth of the vintage.

Agnès PAQUET

MELOISEY

10, Rue du Puits Bouret - Tel. +33 (0) 3 80 260741
contact@vinpaquet.com | www.vinpaquet.com

11 hectares

In the Paquet family, vineyard owners since the 1950s in the *appellation* of Auxey-Duresses, nobody seemed interested in winemaking. But the decision to sell the *domaine* stirred something in Agnès Paquet's consciousness, so she decided to set aside her economics studies to become a *vigneronne*. After her first harvest in 2001, she expanded holdings in the Hautes Côtes up to the eleven hectares of vineyards she currently farms organically, but without certification. Her wines are fresh and light, immediately drinkable, and always offered at very advantageous prices.

Ali Boit Boit et les 40 Buveurs

This is a sparkling wine made from Aligoté, refermented in the bottle according the ancestral method, with a playful and light-hearted name and a tart, fresh palate, deliberate in its simplicity. Eight degrees of alcohol, and sold locally for eight euros. Need we say more?

Auxey-Duresses 2015

The grapes come from a parcel in the hamlet of Melin, at the edge of Saint-Romain. The calcareous soils, constant ventilation from the northeast, and remarkable age of the nearly ninety-year-old vineyard, account for a surprisingly complete white wine. Agnès fashioned an Auxey-Duresses that is not only taut, contrasted and textured, but has a well-defined acidity and closes on a refreshing savory note—and it's a real bargain.

Bourgogne Pinot Noir 2016

The grapes come from Meloisey in the Hautes Côtes, not far from the winery, and are entirely de-stemmed. Agnès produces a red wine vinified and refined (for ten months) in stainless steel: fresh and fragrant, light and smooth it's as pleasant as it is drinkable.

RECRUE DES SENS

MESSANGES

11, Rue des Vignes - Tel. +33 (0) 3 80 625064
recruedessens@gmail.com

3 hectares

In French *Recrue* means recruit, or, in a more popular sense: freshman, beginner, neophyte. So, at first glance, Yann Durieux seems to be referring to himself as a recruit of the senses, the latest *vigneron* to arrive, a harmless dilettante of sensations. But that's hardly the case: Yann has the sensitivity of a cultivated palate, which is anything but novice. He worked for several years in the cellars of Prieuré-Roch and Julien Guillot at the Clos des Vignes du Maynes, where he got to know wine, exploring vinifications without sulfites from a prestigious array of *crus*. You don't need to be a linguistic whiz to realize that *recrue* contains the word *cru*, past participle of the French verb *croître* (to grow), essential in the language and culture of Burgundy and its wines. Chatting with Yann, we found all of the deeper meanings imbedded in his project, and much more. In particular in his urgency to separate himself from the *appellation* system, and to rethink the spontaneous, natural expressiveness of his free-rein, dynamic and delectable wines. His prices may be high, but his level of awareness is extraordinary.

Bourgogne Hautes Côtes de Nuits Manon 2015

There's a handprint on the label of this gritty and distinct Chardonnay. Since Yann is the producer, it's best not to accept the obvious but to look for a hidden meaning. And, in fact, it turns out that the name (and the handprint) are from Manon, his young daughter who lends a new dimension to the wine as an all-encompassing life project.

Bourgogne Hautes Côtes de Nuits Les Ponts 2015

The main assets of this wine are the aromatic profile of flowers, herbs and spices, even more than the focus on fruit on the palate, where tactile delicacy is well integrated with doses of tension and flavor.

SAINT-MARC

PARIS-L'HÔPITAL

1, Rue de Nolay - Tel. +33 (0) 3 85 911314
domaine@saint-marc.fr | www.domaine-saintmarc.fr

8 hectares

This little winery was created almost by chance in 1980. Two old friends met for lunch and, after a few glasses of wine, decided to found a *domaine* that for its first vintage would draw on, well, half a hectare of vines. One of the two at the table was Jean-Claude Mitanchey, the director of Château de Meursault and its winemaker for more than 30 years. Over time, thanks to his connections and knowledge of the area, he was able to acquire other vineyards to bring the total to the current eight hectares, located mainly in the Hautes Côtes de Beaune, Maranges and Santenay. Today the *domaine* is led by his son, the young and determined Arnaud Mitanchey. To taste wines this delightful, it's well worth a trek up the hills of the Hautes Côtes to the lost village of Paris l'Hôpital.

Hautes Côtes de Beaune 2015

This wine's totally de-stemmed grapes come from a two-hectare, forty-year-old vineyard on marl soils. It is a true *vin de soif*, agile and rhythmical.

Santenay Les Chainey 2015

Located above the Grand Clos Rousseau on steep slopes with very poor soils, the vineyard tends to suffer in the hottest years. Yet the resulting wine lacks none of its usual citrus-like freshness, combined with wild flavors of surprising vitality.

Maranges 1er Cru Clos Rousseau 2015

This was Arnaud's first experimentation with stem-inclusion, using the fruit of this seventy-year-old vineyard. The result is more than encouraging: tannins are tight but tasty, and leading to an engaging evolution over the palate.

7

BETWEEN CORTON AND BEAUNE

THE HILL OF CORTON:
LADOIX-SERRIGNY, ALOXE-CORTON PERNAND-VERGELESSES

map *page* 517

The entry into the Côte de Beaune is marked by the hill of Corton, locally called *montagne* more out of deference than for any real altitudinal justification. A semicircular hill, carpeted with vines and crowned by dense woods of juniper and boxwood, has established itself in the general consciousness as the promised land for exceptionally age-worthy, deeply mineral and crystalline white wines, more so than reds. It is a rather diversified area, with a large portion of Grand Cru vineyards (about 160 hectares, the widest in Burgundy), including the only Grand Cru reds of the entire Côte de Beaune. To begin to understand its peculiarities, it's necessary to explore the three communes that divide the vineyards: Ladoix-Serrigny, Aloxe-Corton and Pernand-Vergelesses.

Ladoix-Serrigny is the first of the villages you come to as you descend from Nuits, and the only one of the three whose double name does not derive from a reference to a vineyard. Vines here extend for about 170 hectares, taking in every level of the pyramid of *appellations*, even if only a minor part of the vineyard area (not even a third) is occupied by Grand and Premier Cru, many of which are marketed as Aloxe-Corton Premier Cru. Most wines of the commune of Ladoix are classified as Villages in both white and (a majority) red versions. It's hard to sum up the identity of these wines in few words, since the terrain itself is so diverse. You'll find wines that are simple and robust, tonic and austere, delicate and tannic, with no shortage of rather ordinary wines, rustic blends of different parcels, which fare best in matches with the rich and spicy local cuisine.

Continuing along the main road, you will soon be flanked by the vineyards of Aloxe-Corton, or rather engulfed by the *lieux-dits* of lesser quality, since most of the town's vines are classified as Grand Cru and are situated elsewhere. This is the most important of the three communes, in terms of both the total vineyard area (almost 250 hectares) and overall quality. Alongside sites with a distinct white wine vocation (notably Le Charlemagne), Aloxe includes a central core of Pinot Noir vineyards on the Corton hill, 120 hectares of Grand Cru, including acclaimed *climats* such as Clos du Roi, Bressandes, Renardes, as well as other parcels, whose status is often open to discussion. Leaving aside the Grand Crus, which we will consider later, the general impression of the wines of Aloxe typifies them as deeply-colored reds, solid, tannic, in which it is not uncommon to detect tones that are vegetal or on the wild side.

At the back of the hill, half hidden on the western-facing side, the village of Pernand-Vergelesses occupies the basin of a vast *combe* in a secluded, shaded position. The commune has more than 220 hectares of vineyards, equally distributed through the hierarchy of *appellations*, though defined by distinct zones. The area south of the village, toward the border with Savigny-lès-Beaune, is dedicated to red wines. Here we find the largest and most famous Premier Cru of the *appellation* (Les Vergelesses), chosen in 1922 by the inhabitants to complement the town's name. Wines here are delicious, fresh and fruity, though occasionally with rigid tannins. Northeast of the village of Pernand, the area is steeply sloped and especially well-suited to white wines. Of the various *climats* here, three were promoted in 2000 from Villages to Premier Cru, but only for the whites. These white wines of Pernand are noted for a Nordic character: reticent and sometimes a bit angular when young, guaranteeing notable longevity and often taking on an intriguing flinty touch.

Focusing on the area's core Grand Cru vineyards, regardless of their communes, we detect a substantial bipartition of the hill. The circuit of the upper part, fifty hectares at about 300 meters of altitude below the woods, rests on marly soils ideal for whites, taking in the vineyards of the legendary Corton-Charlemagne (or simply Charlemagne). The lower area, descending to about 200 meters, is about twice as large and consists of brownish calcareous soils rich in iron and silicon, conditions well suited to red wines. Solid in weight and tannic structure, the wines are often quite hard when young and benefit from several years of aging. In terms of finesse and complexity, they present a rather mixed picture, supporting the widespread belief that the general quality level of the Grand Cru reds of Corton is similar to that of Premier Cru wines elsewhere White wines are certainly more uniform in class, and more lustrous in their best examples. Vines exposed due south in the portion called Le Charlemagne highlight the elegance of texture and aromatic finesse. Those exposed to the west, and sometimes even northwest behind the hill, in the commune of Pernand (En Charlemagne) are the latest ripening parcels, resulting in wines that are more austere but over the years take on a savory mineral complexity that is truly unique.

SAVIGNY-LÈS-BEAUNE
CHOREY-LÈS-BEAUNE

map *page* 515

Covering more than 370 hectares, Savigny-lès-Beaune is a vast and varied basin of vineyards, producing wines that are not easily characterized, and actually critics offer opinions on the identity of Savigny that are often so profoundly discordant that they risk confusion. However, the majority of the wine produced here is red, the best versions coming from the south-facing sector between the Combe d'Orange and the Combe de Barbaron below the two small woods of Noël and Chenôve. Situated here is the nucleus of the most consistent of the commune's 22 Premier Cru, among which at least Les Lavières, Aux Gravains and Aux Serpentières deserve special mention. These *climats* produce often elegant reds, energized by an inviting aromatic expression and an unsuspected touch of delicacy, perhaps favored by the quantities of sand and calcareous slabs found in the soils. The gap between prices of Villages and Premier Cru wines of Savigny is generally less than average, meaning some bargains can be found.

Moving east, beyond State Road 74, we find the vineyards of Chorey-lès-Beaune distributed over about 150 hectares. Here, too, red wines make up the overwhelming majority, but, unlike Savigny, the *appellation* does not include any Premier Cru—only 19 Villages *lieux-dits* rarely cited on labels. Here it is common to assemble multiple parcels into a single *cuvée*, and label the wines simply as Chorey-lès-Beaune with no indication of a specific vineyard or, even more often, to download it to the regional *appellation* Bourgogne. Don't expect to be especially moved by the wines of Chorey, as they are often quite simple. Still, well-drained soils here favor fresh and fruity wines, whose lack of aging potential is offset by a "food-friendly" nature, the reds being in best cases reliably fluent and the whites surprisingly savory. All at very competitive prices.

BEAUNE

map *page* 519

Beaune is one of the most extensively planted *appellations* of the Côte d'Or, with over 470 hectares of vineyards covering hills adjacent to the city. It is no coincidence that Beaune was the capital city of Burgundy until the sixteenth century, since it was the commercial center of the wine trade upon which centuries of extraordinary wealth was built (the per capita income here is still among the highest of France) and headquarters for all of the greatest Burgundian *maisons de négoce*, from Bouchard to Chanson, from Latour to Drouhin, from Champy to Jadot, and beyond. Those businesses greatly influenced the structure of the Beaune *appellation*, unique in Burgundy in that it boasts a record 42 Premier Cru *climats* (over two-thirds of the total planted areas) but not one Grand Cru. The wines of Beaune are mostly red (90%) and, as Armando Castagno describes them, "solid and reliable." They tend to be compact with ripe fruit rather than delicate or floral, animated by energy and ample flavors and show unexpected potential for long lives. A number of *climats* merit special interest. Starting from the north we'd cite Les Bressandes, which produces colored, tannic, spicy reds which are often a little in the shade in their early years, but with great ageing potential. Then there is Les Grèves, a large *climat* noted for finely perfumed red wines of clearly established but still surprising longevity. Lavalle's initial mapping of this *climat* included Bouchard's famous *monopole*, the excellent Vigne de l'Enfant Jésus as a sort of *tête de cuvée*. Not to be ignored are Les Teurons in the center of the zone, nor Les Vignes Franches and Clos des Mouches, not far from the Pommard border. These last *climats* of the southern slope of the *appellation* register a different expressive orientation: their whitish fossil-rich soils render more delicate, svelte reds which do not give up on aging even if they can show incomparable finesse when young. As for whites, from the 50 hectares of vineyards dedicated to Chardonnay the general profile of the wines is ripe and often suggestive of exotic fruits and honey, integrated on the palate with captivating flavors. Although generous and rich, they have little prospect of evolution. A few kilometers to the south you will certainly find better.

BONNEAU du MARTRAY

PERNAND-VERGELESSES

2, Rue de Frétille - Tel. +33 (0) 3 80 215064
contact@bonneaudumartray.com | www.bonneaudumartray.com

14 hectares

We've had the good fortune of meeting with Jean-Charles de la Morinière, a real old-time gentleman, several times over his years of managing the family *domaine*. His leadership was appreciated by all, for how it changed the vineyards, converted to biodynamic farming nearly fifteen years ago, as well as for the style of wines, uniquely elegant and long-lived.
Not even a month after our last visit, in November 2016, we learned that the winery had been acquired by an American businessman, Stan Kroenke, with holdings in numerous sports franchises (including the Los Angeles Rams of the NFL, the Denver Nuggets of the NBA and England's Arsenal football club) as well as the California winery Screaming Eagle. Like everyone else, we were stunned and incredulous. The exorbitant increase in land-values, which have reached astronomical levels in the Côte d'Or, persuaded Jean-Charles' family to sell the *domaine* against his wishes, for a figure rumored to be close to a hundred million euro. We'll have to wait a few harvests to adequately assess the impact this change may have on the wines, although Jean-Charles' decision to remove himself completely from the operation gives us pause. For now, it's worth remembering that the *domaine* counts on eleven hectares of vineyards, which form a central core of Corton-Charlemagne (Grand Cru, in name and in fact), though it makes only two wines from it. Corton-Charlemagne is the source of a classic, luminous white wine, vinified parcel by parcel (as many as eighteen) and sought after by enthusiasts worldwide, despite its prohibitive price. The *domaine* also releases a red Corton, produced from a 1.5-hectare portion of the vineyard, limited quantities of anything but a small wine, though over time it has been overshadowed by the Chardonnay.

Corton-Charlemagne Grand Cru 2015

Jean-Charles praised the sunny, Mediterranean character of the 2015 harvest, which gives life to a more generous and ready version with respect to the winery's usual releases, although it is vibrant and marked by that mineral imprint that has helped define its reputation.

Corton-Charlemagne Grand Cru 2014

Fine, vibrant, tense and with an interminable almost saline finish: probably one of the best interpretations of this vineyard we have ever tasted. Jean-Charles described it as "powerful but reserved," inviting comparison to the paintings of Jan Vermeer.

Corton Grand Cru 2015

2015 vintage was marked by an unusual peak of heat in late spring, in the middle of flowering, which led to a high rate of *millerandage* and finally to a 50% down yield. Traditional severity of this red loses here any stiffness. On the contrary, the wine shows such an intense stock of fruit to both soften and envelop tannins, so that you can enjoy it since next months, even if it's supposed to age (and improve) for many years.

CHANDON de BRIAILLES

SAVIGNY-LÈS-BEAUNE

1, Rue Soeur Goby - Tel. +33 (0) 3 80 215231
contact@chandondebriailles.com | www.chandondebriailles.com

14 hectares

If you are looking for wines that are more elegant than muscular, sometimes even slimmed down in their fluency but uniquely and classically Burgundian, this is the address. Housed in a historic mansion with a vaguely dusky aura, Chandon de Briailles has remained in the same family since its founding in 1834. Today it is managed by Countess Claude de Nicolay and her brother François, who oversee their fourteen hectares of vineyards between Savigny, Pernand-Vergelesses and Aloxe-Corton. The *domaine* has been organic since the early 1990s and then converted to biodynamics (certified in 2011). Work in the vineyards is increasingly done with the help of three horses, each of which ensures coverage of nearly five hectares. In the cellar, the equipment is spare. There's a vibrating sorting table, useful for isolating dried berries damaged by hail; a vertical press best suited to whole cluster grapes, used here with increasing frequency; and a wide range of concrete *cuves*. "They require less care than stainless steel and guarantee a more natural, spontaneous expression in the wine," says Claude. It is precisely because of this natural spontaneity, expressed in a fresh and graceful style, that the wines never cease to enchant us.

Savigny-lès-Beaune 2015

The grapes come from two different parcels (Aux Fourneaux, Les Saucours) and in this vintage were completely de-stemmed. The wine is fresh, juicy, fluent and full of flavor, the best that a Villages can offer.

Savigny-lès-Beaune 1er Cru Les Lavières 2015

From a large vineyard of more than two and a half hectares, planted in the mid-1950s in soils consisting of calcareous slabs (*laves*). The wine shows felicitous expressiveness in its open floral aromatics and very tonic palate, finishing with a refreshing saline streak.

Pernand-Vergelesses 1er Cru Ile des Vergelesses 2015

From a *climat* noted for erratic ripening, this version from Chandon de Briailles deserves to be better known and appreciated. It comes from an ample plot (more than four hectares), situated at mid-slope on very poor terrain but with a south-eastern exposure that reduces the negative effects of the shadow of the hill of Corton. Here citrus and floral notes mingle with an intriguing chiaroscuro of peppery spices and licorice. The palate has a velvety feel, while retaining the usual momentum and energy.

Corton Les Bressandes Grand Cru 2015

These four parcels extend over a hectare at mid-slope on deep soils. The grapes, vinified 80% whole cluster, release a conspicuous amount of fruit. The mouth has an enveloping texture and the finish reveals energy despite the wine's compact weight.

Corton Grand Cru 2015

The Chardonnay for this wine is planted on land almost exclusively reserved for Pinot Noir (mainly in Bressandes and Chaumes). The *domaine* offers about six thousand bottles, pleasant and drinkable and from this hot vintage rounder and more generous than usual.

CHANTERÊVES

SAVIGNY-LÈS-BEAUNE

Chemin de la Grande Chaume
idee@chantereves.com

As you might guess from her name, Tomoko Kuriyama is not a native of Burgundy. Japanese-born, she studied enology in Germany at the renowned University of Geisenheim, followed by an important experience in Rheingau with Friedrich Altenkirch. Together with her husband, Guillaume Bott, who worked earlier at Domaines Etienne Sauzet and Patrick Bize, she decided to stay in Burgundy, where the couple has been running a small *négociant* house based in Savigny since 2010, known for genuine, *terroir*-driven wines, even though all the grapes are purchased. The whites exhibit an expressive transparency bordering on nudity, which the wine writer Steen Öhman has compared for purity of fruit to certain expressions of the Moselle. Tomoko's touch is also evident in the reds, surprising for their delicacy and range of nuances. If you're looking for an original voice in the chorus of small *négociant* houses, a visit to Chanterêves is highly recommended.

Saint-Romain Combe Bazin 2015

The Saint-Romain whites are particularly in the style of Tomoko and Guillaume, both for the subtlety of aromatics, and for their refreshing salinity in the mouth. The *climat* in question faces southwest, with a truly remarkable view of the ancient village center, source of a wine whose citric notes contribute to a purity that bears comparison to spring water.

Bourgogne Pinot Noir 2015

Two thirds of the grapes come from the granitic soils of Paris-l'Hôpital, near Maranges, while the rest originate in the calcareous matrices of Puligny. The wine is light and fleeting and spontaneously expressive with notes of dark fruit and berries in its fascinating chiaroscuro of aromas.

Louis CHENU Père & Filles

SAVIGNY-LÈS-BEAUNE

12, Rue Joseph de Pesquidoux - Tel. +33 (0) 3 80 261396
juliette@louischenu.com | www.louischenu.com

9.5 hectares

This all-female *domaine* is particularly close to our hearts, run by two sisters, Juliette and Caroline, daughters of Louis Chenu, following an organic protocol in the almost ten hectares of vineyards in the commune of Savigny. Caroline, who heads operations in both vineyards and cellars, produces wines that combine natural expression with a bright, slim silhouette: they may seem simple only on the surface.

Savigny-lès-Beaune 1er Cru Les Talmettes 2015

The name of this vineyard, exposed to the south on soils crossed by sandy veins, appears rarely on labels of the Savigny *appellation*. A shame, because Chenu's version is irresistible with its delicate but juicy flavors and textures and its captivating notes of raspberry.

Savigny-lès-Beaune 1er Cru Les Lavières 2015

The stony shallow soils of this parcel rest on flat limestone slabs (*laves*, source of the name of this *climat*). The floral notes are embellished with violets and coexist with a mouthful of promising minerality.

Savigny-lès-Beaune 1er Cru Aux Clous 2015

Located in the narrow part of a *combe*, this parcel is marked by clay soils of intense reddish hues due to a strong presence of iron oxide. Noted for early ripening, the grapes render a wine that is supple and seductive on the palate, surprisingly forward and expressive.

Savigny-lès-Beaune 1er Cru Hauts-Jarrons 2015

The deep clays of this vineyard recall those of the *climat* Les Bressandes of Beaune, with similarities expressed also in the wines. This is often the latest to mature of Chenu's reds, opening slowly due to taut tannins. In a vintage like 2015, it shows an abundance of substance and grit, and a promising potential to age well for years in the cellar.

Domaine des CROIX

BEAUNE

2, Rue Colbert - Tel. +33 (0) 9 65 234688
contact@domainedescroix.com

6.5 hectares

In 2005, Domaine Duchet, with more than five hectares of vineyards in the best *climats* of Beaune, was bought by a group of American investors, and David Croix, a young winemaker from the Loire region, was hired to direct the project. At the time he was technical director for the *maison de négoce* Camille Giroud. In launching the *domaine*, the owners not only engaged David Crois as their *régisseur* but decided to name the company after him. And, in fact, David who since a couple of years began collaborating with Jean-Marc Roulot, got involved in the project as if the *domaine* were his. Currently the property controls six and a half hectares of vines in eleven different *appellations*, having annexed parcels in the communes of Savigny and Pommard, as well as small shares of Grand Cru on the hill of Corton. Our latest tastings, conducted in the winery in Beaune, once again highlighted David's sensitivity and talent. The reds, vinified without sulfites, are focused on nuance in a rather delicate, even understated way, described as almost "silent" by Becky Wassermann (perhaps in contrast to the "noisy" wines of more flamboyant winemakers). But this silence can't hide the admirable way these wines express the voice of their *terroirs*.

Aloxe-Corton Les Boutières 2015

This *lieu-dit* rests on very deep soils in three different communes, Aloxe, Savigny and Pernand. David's interpretation is based on delicacy and has nothing to do with the often taut and rather rough-hewn traits of other reds of Aloxe.

Beaune 2015

In its simplicity, this seemed to us the most explicit and persuasive red of what David called the "magic" 2015 vintage. Maturity, sweetness and alcoholic warmth benefit the flavor dynamics and drinkability of a wine whose delicate floral notes contribute to freshness on the palate.

Beaune 1er Cru Les Bressandes 2015

The wine comes from one of the best *climats* on the Beaune hillside, in a parcel at three hundred meters of altitude with ample quantities of brown clay and calcareous gravel. David's version is rather austere with marked mineral tones, yet intensely colored with tight tannins and a fleshiness that translates into energy.

Beaune 1er Cru Les Grèves 2015

This Premier Cru in the heart of Beaune, on well-drained reddish soils rich in iron oxide, is considered to be among the best of the *appellation*. The 2015 version is immediate and releases a fascinating aromatic purity, which might make it difficult to leave it in the cellar, as most experts suggest, to enhance its enormous potential for complexity over time.

Corton La Vigne au Saint Grand Cru 2015

This small parcel is exposed to the south between Les Chaumes and Les Combes, in the lower part of the hill of Corton. Half of the wine was vinified with whole clusters, feeding a wonderful balance of density and freshness, elegance and energy. Detractors of the red wines of the hill of Corton may find that this version refutes some of those prejudices (which, however, are not always unfounded).

Alex GAMBAL

BEAUNE

14, Boulevard Jules Ferry - Tel. +33 (0) 3 80 227581
info@alexgambal.com | www.alexgambal.com

12 hectares

In 1993, Bostonian real estate businessman Alex Gambal took a trip to Burgundy that would radically change his life. By 1997, he was already at the helm of his *maison de négoce*, after a fast learning period beginning with a course at the Lycée Viticole in Beaune and three years of experience alongside Becky Wasserman, esteemed export consultant and Burgundian by adoption. To understand the evolution of the *négoce* system in a quality perspective, a visit to the Gambal headquarters on Beaune's *boulevard* is highly recommended. In twenty years, Alex has reduced his acquisition of grapes and increased his acquisition of vineyards up to the current twelve hectares, all farmed organically until a definitive biodynamic conversion in 2011. He has continued to improve the quality of the wines, and their precision and elegance. The arrival of Alexandre Brault in the role of *régisseur*, has consolidated the domain's efforts, adding energy and rigor to this period of transition and growth.

Beaune Montagne Saint-Désiré 2015

This vineyard is among the highest of Beaune, at more than three hundred meters, on sandy and calcareous soils that produce an inviting aromatic array of flowers and herbs, elegant and finished with a breath of balsamic notes.

Saint-Romain 2015

Among the latest acquisitions of 2015, this parcel is part of a core of seven hectares acquired from Domaine Christophe Buisson. The white marl soils translate into a delicate floral range, followed on the palate with creamy texture and crisp acidity.

Savigny-Lès-Beaune Les Grand Picotins 2015

This rarely cited *lieu-dit* has a fifty-year-old vineyard near the border of Chorey, providing a surprising red whose winning cards are soft tannins and a long spicy finish.

Emmanuel GIBOULOT

BEAUNE
4, Rue de Seurre - Tel. +33 (0) 3 80 229007
emmanuel.giboulot@wanadoo.fr

10.3 hectares

Today the practice of biodynamics has many followers who like to compete about who was first to join the movement. A competition Emmanuel Giboulot has no intention of entering, since he doesn't like being an easy winner. As far back as 1970, Emmanuel's father began working organically, and the family completed its transition to biodynamics in 1996. The estate covers ten hectares, six of which are in the commune of Beaune, including an admirable endowment of old vines. Emmanuel's priorities in the vineyard include strengthening the vines' natural resistance to pests and stimulating the microbiological activity of the soils. In the cellar he is committed to enhancing acidic freshness, proving something of an allergy to showy extractions in wines with sweet tones or overtly *boisé*. His are wines of extreme spontaneity, which stand out for their essence and palatability, and for a vertical structure that is not without hard edges. Even more convincing than the individual wines, is the humanity of the *vigneron*, his polite and gentle manner, and the depth of his philosophy that continues to impress us. In 2013, he risked jail when he refused to apply chemicals to his vines to combat *Flavescence dorée*. In an unprecedented response by the media and public opinion, he won international support for his stance, becoming a world figure for responsible farming. Emmanuel is a man of considerable culture and sensitivity, always available for dialogue and debate. Label drinkers should look elsewhere, but for those who come to Burgundy in search of deeper knowledge and broader horizons, Giboulot and his *domaine* are warmly recommended.

Bourgogne Hautes Côtes de Nuits Sous le Mont 2015

We preferred the "no sulfite" version of this wine, which was juicer and less concentrated, with its fresh and fragrant fruitiness, as well as showing a subtle and infiltrating salinity.

Beaune Lulunne 2015

This vineyard is the highest of the *appellation*, more than 350 meters above sea level, on the border of Pommard, below the woods of the Montagne Saint Desiré. Giboulot produces a pale quintessential red wine, even in such a generous vintage. The tension on the palate, an indispensable quality of the house style, doesn't deny a charming blend of floral and fruity notes, conveyed by a long aromatic persistence.

Côtes de Beaune Les Pierres Blanches Rouge 2015

This *appellation* is one of the rarest and least known of Burgundy. Of the sixty-six hectares of potential vineyards, not even half are claimed for production (in 2015, only thirty-one hectares were accounted for, as Armando Castagno reminds us with his usual, implacable precision). The seven *climats* of the *appellation* are still fairly evenly divided between Pinot Noir and Chardonnay, but perhaps no other producer matches the success of Giboulot with both red and white. This dual role is inscribed in the earth with the name Les Pierres Blanches Rouge since the stones in the soils of this *lieu-dit* are white, but when the small iron nodules they contain break, they release a reddish color. Innervated with freshness and acidity, this red claims both citric vitality and gorgeous vertical structure.

Côtes de Beaune Combe d'Eve 2015

Subtle and discreet aromatics, but with a charge of extraordinarily refreshing juiciness and a flavor dynamic that offers the savory energy and sweeping persistence of a Premier Cru.

Saint-Romain En Chevrot 2015

From a *climat* in the upper part of the vineyard, windy and cold, and almost never vinified by itself, Giboulot fashions a version enlivened by traces of chalk and saline ruffles, with an enchantingly svelte finish.

Benjamin LEROUX

BEAUNE
5, Rue Colbert - Tel. +33 (0) 3 80 227106
contact@benjamin-leroux.com

7.5 hectares

We admired Benjamin Leroux's talents during his years as *régisseur* at Comte Armand in Pommard, where he landed in 1999 at the age of twenty-three, following an already full bag of experiences in New Zealand and Oregon, in Saint-Estephe at Cos d'Estournel and in Beaune with Jadot. Alongside his role at Comte Armand, with the support of financial partners, Benjamin launched a *maison de négoce* under his own name, which today has become his exclusive occupation. The winery avails itself of about twenty hectares of vineyards, of which seven are owned. The parcels and labels continue to increase, but the style remains faithful to the habitual search for purity and definition, with little time for oaky wines in his quest to focus on fresher expressions.

Auxey-Duresses 2015
Agile and saline, this is one of Benjamin's signature wines, obtained from two hectares of vineyards influenced by the cooling currents of a *combe*.

Meursault Les Vireuils 2015
This forty-year-old vineyard is one of the most "Nordic" and fascinating *climats* of Meursault. Crystalline in its definition, the wine's minerality exalts its verticality.

Savigny-lès-Beaune 2015
Derived from a quartet of *lieux-dits* located in various sectors of Savigny, the wine, vinified with 40% whole clusters, combines energy and tension with juicy flavor.

Volnay 1er Cru Clos de la Cave des Ducs 2015
Over half a hectare *en monopole*, farmed biodynamically in the heart of the village, provides a red of admirable purity, in the spirit of the most seductive Volnay.

Volnay 1er Cru En Caillerets 2015
A notable quota of active calcareous terrain accounts for the tension and energy of this wine, essential to releasing dynamic flavors, notable from such a sunny vintage.

MAILLARD Père & Fils

CHOREY-LES-BEAUNE

5, Rue Joseph Bard - Tel. +33 (0) 3 80 221067
contact@domainemaillard.com | www.domainemaillard.com

19 hectares

Pascal Maillard comes from a long tradition of *vignerons*, even if Domaine Maillard was founded by his father Daniel only in 1952. Before that the family followed the usual practice in rural Burgundy of growing grapes and other crops. Pascal notes that only in the most recent years have consumers been interested in the so-called minor *appellations*, either for reasons of price, or due to new curiosity about the areas outside the tourist havens of the Côte d'Or. But, he adds, "If I weren't making good wines, I'm sure nobody would come looking for me here." Pascal's savvy pragmatism translates into trusty wines of special interest to gastronomes. He has nineteen hectares of vineyards, managed under *lutte raisonnée*, mainly in Chorey but also with numerous parcels in Ladoix, Savigny, Beaune and Aloxe-Corton (he is the only growers to produce a white Corton Grand Cru in the *climat* Les Renardes).

Chorey-Lès-Beaune 2015

A Chorey blanc of note? Absolutely yes: agile, fresh and with a pleasant savory finish.

Chorey-Lès-Beaune 2015

Production exceeds thirty thousand bottles of a wine laden with palate-pleasing fruit that reflects scrupulous work in the vineyards and a clear vision in the cellar.

Ladoix Les Chaillots 2015

This vineyard parcel laps the vast archipelago of the Grand Cru of Corton, and favors a solid wine, in which energy tends to brings out the best of its nuance.

Savigny-lès-Beaune 2015

Chicken and guinea fowl make ideal food-pairings for this essential, juicy red, obtained from almost two hectares of forty-year-old vines planted on brown soils rich in calcareous pebbles. The aromatics recall peony and currants; the flavors exalt silky, tasty tannins.

Catherine et Claude MARÉCHAL

BLIGNY-LÈS-BEAUNE
6, Route de Chalon - Tel. +33 (0) 3 80 214437
marechalcc@orange.fr | www.bourgogne-marechal.com

12.8 hectares

The pleasure of meeting a mild and gentle person was the first thing that struck us about Claude Maréchal. We were apologizing for a delay in arrival, to which he responded: "Without you writing about our wines, many customers who became fans over time would never have passed by here." And indeed, if you arrive at Bligny-lès-Beaune, it's because you really wanted to get there, isolated as it is from the usual wine routes of the Côte de Beaune. But the detour is brief and certainly worth the trip. The *domaine* offers ten wines from less noted, but not necessarily minor, *appellations* (there is only one Premier Cru) coming from almost thirteen hectares of vineyards, cultivated for thirty years without herbicides or pesticides. The diligence of Claude's work is reflected in the maxim: "Pinot Noir can't stand mediocrity." Yet prices remain fair and the fragrance and flavor that sustain the "food friendly" nature of these wines is free of any hint of rusticity.

Bourgogne Cuvée Gravel 2015

Color and aromas of a solar vintage, lush in the mouth, overflowing with energy, the wine has all the traits that set it apart from lesser examples of Bourgogne: thirty thousand bottles of absolute pleasure

Savigny-lès-Beaune Vieilles Vignes 2015

Two total hectares composed of many different parcels, provide a red focused on fruit with a tannic reactivity that releases energy.

Volnay 2015

A few minutes of aeration serve to bring the aromatics into focus, though the Maréchal brand guarantees frankness and flavor. This should be listed among the least "ethereal" Volnays we have tasted, but at the table it will hold its own with a range of food matches.

Albert MOROT

BEAUNE

20, Château de la Creusotte - Tel. +33 (0) 3 80 223539
albertmorot@aol.com

8 hectares

Albert Morot was fifty years old in 1880 when he took over the *maison de négoce* started by his father and gave it his name, gradually purchasing parcels planted in the best *climats* of Beaune. Jumping to the present day, the *domaine* with its eight hectares of vines is managed by Geoffroy Choppin, who inherited it from his Aunt Françoise. Choppin has introduced important changes, such as lengthening macerations for more delicate extractions of tannins and converting his vineyards to organic, certified since 2015. The wines have obviously benefited in terms of aromatic finesse and balance, inspired by a classic style. Some of the best *terroirs* of Beaune (including eight Premier Cru) are represented here in wines that exalt their individuality.

Beaune 1er Cru Marconnets 2014

The *climat* is in the northern sector of the Beaune area, where most of the wines are made by *négociants* of the caliber of Bouchard and Chanson. Choppin strives to make the most of his oldest vineyard (planted in 1955) and the wine rewards him with its funds of juicy fruit and exquisite freshness.

Beaune 1er Cru Teurons 2014

The aromatic spectrum covers a wide range, from cherry to incense. On the palate it is less fleshy than expected, but the relative austerity sags on the finish with an appreciable harmony supported by the plush texture of tasty tannins.

Beaune 1er Cru Bressandes 2014

The brown soils of this *climat* contain sand that facilitates drainage. The wine's tannic depth is concealed by its dynamics articulated in energy and sapidity, adding to a sense of completeness confirmed by an intense and persistent finish.

Philippe PACALET

BEAUNE

12, Rue de Chaumergy - Tel. +33 (0) 3 80 259100
contact@vins-philippe-pacalet.fr | www.philippe-pacalet.com

14 hectares

Philippe Pacalet went through an impressive apprenticeship before setting up his own *maison de négoce* in 2001. Starting with his uncle Marcel Lapierre, in Beaujolais, he moved on to Domaine de la Romanée-Conti in the last years of Lalou Bize-Leroy's direction, and then on to a decisive ten-year association with Henry-Frédéric Roch at the Domaine Prieuré-Roch of Nuits-Saint-Georges. As a *négociant* he took an original approach to his calling with a range of wines of many different types—currently nearly thirty labels—following a protocol of renting old parcels from *vignerons* who work with him as a team. A chemist by training and a craftsman by vocation, Pacalet left biodynamics in the mid-1990s, saying that he felt closer to the spirit of the medieval Templars than to the modern theories of Rudolf Steiner. He is a cerebral type with a love of metaphor, who compares his work to that of a cheese-refiner ("My wine is a raw milk Camembert"), as well as to a musician who needs to clean up his score to find deeper and purer "resonance." His wines are direct, spontaneous and immediate in their natural conveyance of the matrix terrains expressed with pluck and discretion. He takes little interest in the fruity components of wine, pointing out that the appreciation of fruitiness is an "adolescent" pleasure. How can we blame him?

Gevrey-Chambertin Bel Air 2015

This comes from the shallow, calcareous soils of a steeply sloped *climat* at around 350 meters of altitude in a clearing of the woods that dominate the Clos de Bèze. The wine is strongly marked by acidity mixed with notes of cassis.

Nuits-Saint-Georges 2015

The *climats* of origin are Au Bas de Combe, on the border with Vosne, and Longecourt, just below Les Saint-Georges. The tone is decidedly mineral with tannins, copious and well aligned by aging *sur-lie*, that support its juicy qualilties.

Chambolle-Musigny 1er Cru Les Sentiers 2015

Don't expect the usual feminine grace associated with the wines of Chambolle, since this comes from a plot on the border of Morey, just below Les Bonnes Mares but on deep, dark clay terrains. A wine defined by intensity and energy.

Ruchottes-Chambertin Grand Cru 2015

In the words of Pacalet, this is "a simple wine but with everything it needs." In all honesty, we have a somewhat different idea of "simple" in a wine that has the stuff, the tannic depth, the salinity and the freshness of a truly complete and three-dimensional Grand Cru.

Echézeaux Grand Cru 2015

Philippe has great expectations for the 2015 vintage, which he compares to 1985 but with double the yield. Here energy and purity seem to be channeled precisely in the same direction. If you'd like to check it out, get ready to break the bank.

RAPET Père & Fils

PERNAND-VERGELESSES
2, Place de la Mairie - Tel. +33 (0) 3 80 215994
vincent@domaine-rapet.com | www.domaine-rapet.com

20 hectares

It's worth remembering that the origins of the *domaine* date to 1765, preceding the French Revolution. The winery has always been in Pernand-Vergelesses, run by Vincent Rapet, who produces wines from an ample spread of about twenty hectares of vineyards, scattered through several *appellations* between Beaune and the Corton hill. About 60% of the vineyards are dedicated to Pinot Noir, though the range of labels also takes in impressive white wines from prestigious vineyards of Pernand. In short, a safe address, offering precise and reliable wines with an always cordial and smiling welcome.

Pernand-Vergelesses 1er Cru En Caradeux 2015

The *climat* is large, facing east on a rather steep slope, source of one of the most elegant whites of the whole *appellation*. Tending more toward slender than fleshy and always a bit reticent in aromas, on the palate the wine has bracing tonic flavors and notable persistence.

Pernand-Vergelesses 1er Cru Sous Frétille 2015

Promoted to Premier Cru in 2000, the *climat* covers the hill rising from the village to the east, overlooking an area of sheer cliffs. This white shows admirable *droiture* even in such sunny years with resinous tones in the aromas and a reassuring potential for aging.

Pernand-Vergelesses 1er Cru Île des Vergelesses 2015

This singular vine-covered islet of elongated shape acts as a watershed between the extremities of Pernand and Savigny and the *climat* Les/Aux Vergelesses. Many consider this the most suitable site for the red wines of Pernand. Rapet elaborates a version of enchanting aromatic grace, in which notes of violet mingle with hints of menthol. The palate is equally expressive, with firm and tasty tannins aligned with flavors reminiscent of chokecherries and blueberries.

Jean-Claude RATEAU

BEAUNE
26, Route de Bouze - Tel. +33 (0) 3 80 229891
jean-claude.rateau@wanadoo.fr

10 hectares

Jean-Claude Rateau has a mustache worthy of Asterix framing the sly smile of a very knowledgeable man. And it is indeed *savoir faire* that lies behind his reputation as one of the most savvy interpreters of the wines of Beaune. That reputation is even more firmly rooted among colleagues than critics, due to the tenacity and talent of a sixty-something who has always defended and valued his *vigneron* status. A pioneer of biodynamics, since 1979, and an expert without peer of his *terroir*, Rateau today heads a *domaine* with ten hectares of vineyards, equally split between reds and whites, producing extraordinary wines in the so-called minor *climats*.

Hautes Côtes de Beaune 2015

Grit, tension and freshness innervate a dynamic and expressive red, obtained from a terraced vineyard trained with a *lyre* system to optimize exposure to sunlight.

Beaune Clos des Mariages 2015

Jean-Claude knows well this *lieu-dit*, from which he also produces a white wine after having recently replanted the vineyard *en complantation* (with Pinot Blanc and Pinot Gris vines to complement the Chardonnay). Compared to the versions we've tasted at other wineries, this stands apart: the aromatic vitality more inviting, the floral embroidery more refined, the spice more elegant, the taste more delicious.

Beaune 1er Cru Les Reversées 2015

In a *climat* situated at the base of the Clos de la Mousse, on dark clay soils at rather low altitude, Rateau owns almost a hectare of vines, about a third of which are very old. The red that comes from it is often enhanced by generous vintages and, in fact, this version reveals splendid substance amassed in a mouthful of irresistible juiciness.

Nicolas ROSSIGNOL

BEAUNE
22, Rue JF Champollion - Tel. +33 (0) 3 80 243552
stephanie.domainerossignol@gmail.com | www.nicolas-rossignol.com

20 hectares

Nicolas Rossignol started his winemaking career early with internships around France (Vieux Télégraphe, Chateau La Cardonne) and the world (Boschendal in South Africa). In 2011, he took charge of the family *domaine*, and today, at just forty, works with an impressive nucleus of almost twenty hectares of vineyards. Between the *domaine* and a *négociant* activity he bottles wines with about thirty different labels, seven in Volnay and six in Pommard. Ambitious and driven by a vision of Burgundy focused on a strong need for change, Nicolas recently moved to a new location in the industrial outskirts of Beaune. In moving from the poetic ambience of cellars of stone to larger and more functional surroundings for processing wines, he also put aside his youthful demonstrative ambitions to focus on emphasizing the character of the different *climats* with greater sensitivity to nuances.

Volnay 1er Cru Cailleret 2015

Here is all the natural elegance of one of the most beloved *climats*: "Cailleret never yields showy wines," says Nicolas. The grapes are completely de-stemmed and the ample scents of small black fruits and berries puts the wine's captivating potential at the service of flavor complexity.

Volnay 1er Cru Chevret 2015

The vineyard lies just a few meters below Cailleret, but the wine doesn't have the same richness of mineral nuances. The 50% of whole clusters helps to innervate the more fleshy and substantial roundness remindful of the neighboring Santenots.

Pommard 1er Cru Epenots 2015

Obtained from two different parcels with an important share of old vines, Nicolas proposes this as a sort of compendium of all his wines. The extraordinary wealth of details of aroma and flavor illustrate his point.

8

POMMARD, VOLNAY AND SURROUNDINGS

POMMARD

map *page* 520

The vineyards of Pommard appear ahead with little advance notice after the fork in the D973 road a couple of kilometers south of Beaune. They surround the inhabited center of the small commune on all sides, spreading over 320 hectares, of which more than a third is classified as Premier Cru. They are usually grouped into three sectors. The first and most extensive lies to the right of the road heading south from Beaune and its most valuable portion can be seen in an initial cluster of *climats* around the large vineyard of Épenots, whose name suggests the widespread presence of thornbushes before vines took over. Divided into Grands Épenots and Petits Épenots, both noted as *tête de cuvée* in the pioneering classifications of 1855 and 1920, they incorporate two notable *monopoles*, Clos des Épenaux (Comte Armand) and the Grand Clos des Épenots (De Courcel). From these vineyards come some of best reds of the Côte de Beaune, whose "noble elegance is cloaked in crystalline light," as an inspired Giancarlo Marino wrote. The second sector includes the Premier Cru vineyards to the southwest beyond the town in the direction of Volnay, taking in the *climat* Les Rugiens. From its most valued vineyards of Les Rugiens Bas come reds of extraordinary gustative persistence, unanimously considered worthy of the status of Grand Cru. In fact, in 2013, the dossier for promotion to Grand Cru was submitted to the INAO national commission, concerning not only Les Rugiens (both Hauts and Bas) but also the whole group of Épenots. The third sector takes in a flat strip of vineyards classified Villages to the southeast of the town in an area directly affected by the dejection cone of the Grande Combe, the long and narrow canyon crossed by the Avant-Dheune stream that runs through the village, and over the millennia has deposited alluvial materials and assorted debris.

The soils of Pommard contain clay and ferrous elements that make the wines somewhat more austere and slow to open than others, especially those of Volnay, influencing the reputation of deeply colored and tannic wines in which hardness prevails over elegance. But that notion is often contradicted. For example, considering wines from *climats* such as Les Fremiers and Les Pézerolles, we discover fragrance and finesse, sleek elegance and incisive flavor, whose tautness does not preclude fascinating nuance. To fully appreciate them, there's no need to leave them long in the cellar.

VOLNAY

map *page* 521

Long considered the home of the finest reds of Burgundy, Volnay claimed historic prestige in eras when the light touch (so dear to the abbot Claude Arnoux in the early eighteenth century) was considered an absolute value, when roseate pallor and "eye of the partridge" tints overcame fragility in terms of stylized elegance. But with the decline of the Dukes of Burgundy, who had a summer residence here, along with growing competition from the Côte de Nuits and the inexorable progression of tastes, fashions and commercial trends, the hierarchy changed among the reds of Burgundy, bringing the primacy of Volnay increasingly into question. Still, the image of clarity and grace, the time-honored sensual elegance associated with Volnay make it "the southernmost outpost of Pinot Noir of authentic grandeur" (Armando Castagno). In fact, on close inspection, the Burgundy of the great reds does end here and the chances of finding wines from Pinot Noir of similar stature south of Volnay become rare, if not entirely out of the question. A quick look at the *climats* of Volnay reveals more than 200 hectares of vineyards registered under the *appellation*—all destined for red, as in Pommard—of which more than half of the surface is dedicated to some thirty Premier Cru. In the vineyard nucleus of the northern slope, toward the border with Pommard, wines noted as tannic and colored (Pitures) share traits with those of its neighbor, while certain other plots (Frémiets) give rise to reds of aristocratic delicacy and elegance. Then there's a group of very stony vineyards, often conducted *en monopole* and almost completely walled in, around the town and sometimes inside it. Excluding the *climats* of noted value (Clos des Ducs, Clos de la Barre), the other vineyards, including some as small as a half hectare, are sources of Villages wines. Before the establishment of the *appellation* system, it was customary to refer to historical names of the vineyards. In this area, finesse is the rule, even if profound differences are to be found in the styles and interpretive sensibility of producers, leading to a certain disparity of results. South of the town of Volnay, bordering on the Meursault and Monthelie districts, we find some of the most appreciated Premier Cru. Consider the sharp minerality of Taillepieds, the harmonious classicism of Champans, the fresh floreality of Clos des Chênes (especially in the upper part of the *climat*), the refined tannins of Caillerets, and the solid vigor of Santenots. These are ample vineyards, covering an area of about eighty hectares of great value, with wines that, in the best of cases, are certainly comparable to those of many Grand Cru.

It is well worth noting that the 1855 classification drawn up by Jules Lavalle identified three of these *climats* with the privileged rank of *tête de cuvée* (Champans, Caillerets and Santenots), recognition that for various reasons never resulted in their investiture as Grand Cru.
Singular in this context is the situation of the *climat* Santenots, which actually lies within the commune of Meursault. Yet the reds produced there are labeled Volnay Premier Cru Santenots, in the name of a kind of courtesy convention, ratified in 1924 by a pronouncement of the Tribunal of Beaune. Thus the already ample array of vineyards producing the fine red wines of Volnay annexed a further addition, of about thirty hectares total, whose indisputable capacity to generate robust and long-lived reds is exalted in the *lieu-dit* Santenots du Milieu. Another "unique case" of singular interest and yet another exception that gives the rules even more strength, credibility and legitimacy.

SAINT-ROMAIN AUXEY-DURESSES, MONTHELIE

maps *page* 522, 523 e 524

Overwhelmed by the celebrity of neighboring *appellations* (Volnay and Meursault, above all), the wines of these three small communes rate less visibility on the market, as well as rather intermittent, if not scant, critical consideration. A shame, because it is not at all rare to find authentic expressions of *terroir* at prices well below demanding Burgundian standards. Promoted to an autonomous *appellation* in 1947, Saint-Romain has some of the highest altitude vineyards of the entire Côte d'Or (all above 300 meters with some rises over 400). White wines have dominated from the start, today representing about two-thirds of total production. They reveal distinctive character, thanks to a high percentage of active calcareous terrains and cool, well ventilated exposures. Though subtle in their floral and citrus aromas, not without some harshness and rigidity, the wines are animated by dynamic flavors whose "rocky" vein is described by Burgundians as "*goût de caillou*" (pebble flavor). Of the approximately one hundred hectares of vineyards, no parcel can yet boast the title of Premier Cru, but a commission is working in this direction, to verify the candidacy of the most suitable sites.

Auxey-Duresses boasts a dozen Premier Cru distributed over about 130 hectares of vineyards of which almost two-thirds are destined for reds. The area is influenced by cool air currents from the Hautes Côtes, which, coupled with the significantly diverse expositions of the vineyards, with a large portion facing north, results in complex patterns of ripening. This is reflected in often incisive and sharp acidity in the wines, and sometimes also in tannins marked by a certain hardness (Duresses is the name of the most prestigious *climat*). On the other hand, in the ever more frequent years with high summer temperatures, areas like this have everything to gain, reason to believe that the wines of Auxey will rise again. It's interesting to note that experiments with the "lyre" form of low density espalier training aimed at improving the concentration of sugars and polyphenols in grapes more fully exposed to the sun show promise in vineyards with northeastern exposures in the shadows of nearby Montagne du Bourdon.

The wines of Monthelie also often show a certain tendency toward rigidity, though exceptions can be made for those from vineyards near the border of Volnay, which in the best cases match the quality of their neighbors. Those vineyards, which lie to the north of the main road, are dominated by reds, accounting for about 90% of the total 140 hectares, of which almost a third are classified as Premier Cru. Some of these reds when young seem a bit rustic, though with age—some have remarkable longevity—they tend to gain in refinement of aromas and flavors and show an admirable knack to match well with foods.

Marquis d'ANGERVILLE

VOLNAY

Clos des Ducs - Tel. +33 (0) 3 80 216475
info@domainedangerville.fr | www.domainedangerville.fr

14.9 hectares

Following the line traced by his grandfather Sem and his father Jacques, a key figure of Burgundian wine in the second half of the twentieth century, Guillaume d'Angerville has been at the helm of the historic family *domaine* for about fifteen years. He is aided by the agronomic experience of his brother-in-law Renaud De Villette and the energy of the *régisseur* François Duvivier, who led the conversion to biodynamics, carried out between 2006 and 2009. With vineyards in the best *climats* of Volnay, from whose graftings was selected the prized variety "Pinot d'Angerville," the estate today extends over about fifteen hectares, more than three-quarters of which are Premier Cru. The wines come from completely de-stemmed grapes and express Burgundian classicism like few others: slow to open without ever losing finesse, summarize the qualities of a great Volnay.

Volnay 2015

Guillaume d'Angerville is not going to write off the 2015 vintage in the name of sunshine. This is a Volnay of appreciable smoothness, which lacks neither dynamism nor freshness.

Volnay 1er Cru Champans 2015

This comes from the largest vineyard of the house of Angerville, four hectares distributed over two different plots, covering more than a third of the total area of the *climat*. The stony soils, rich in iron and clay, often back the wine's reputation as a marathon runner, though this interpretation also puts dark colors and a slow pace at the service of a convincing tannic depth.

Volnay 1er Cru Fremiet 2015

One and a half hectares on poor soils, very stony and thin (just 20 centimeters) which give rise to elegant and powerful wines. Like this 2015, stripped down and mineral in spite of the rich vintage, distancing itself from the cliché of neighboring Pommard (where the *climat* becomes Fremiers) in showing unbeatable juiciness.

Volnay 1er Cru Taillepieds 2015

Stony to the point of cutting the feet (therefore the name), the soils of this *climat* are lighter in color than the adjacent Champans, with a higher percentage of active limestone. The d'Angerville vineyard covers about a hectare and favors a wine of extraordinary gustatory tension, where aromatic analogies with small black fruits and berries mark a flavor profile that seems suspended, ethereal, vivified by the mineral vibrations of the long finish on the palate.

Volnay 1er cru Clos des Ducs 2015

This historic parcel *en monopole* of more than two hectares on the steep slope rising from 190 to 330 meters of altitude above the village of Volnay is one of the most admired *climats* of the entire Côte de Beaune. Its value depends to a large extent on the white marls of the stony soils, the magnificent exposure of the double slope, the average age of vines close to fifty years, and veins of water guaranteeing reserves to the roots even in dry years like 2015. A Volnay of vertical attitude, if there is such a thing, showing once again the nonchalance of a true champion.

Domaine du Comte ARMAND

POMMARD

7, Rue de la Mairie - Tel. +33 (0) 3 80 247050
epeneaux@domaine-comte-armand.com | www.domaine-comte-armand.com

9 hectares

As proprietors of the Clos des Epeneaux since 1828, the Counts Armand have turned this historic *domaine*, with its classical ambience, into a sort of experimental laboratory for young and talented *régisseurs*. After Pascal Marchand, who steered the company into biodynamics, and Benjamin Leroux, who decisively corrected the tendency toward overtly stylish wines, the direction has passed on to another debutant, Paul Zinetti, who had worked alongside Leroux since 2010. Upon taking the helm, none of these three winemakers had yet turned twenty-five. That said, the *domaine* owes its reputation to the *monopole* of the Clos des Epeneaux, an iconic Pommard of timeless elegance, as well as to the vineyards of Volnay and Auxey-Duresses, which produce notable wines full of substance and verve.

Auxey-Duresses 2015

The cold and windy village of Auxey is certainly not renowned for the production of graceful red wines. This bottling is aimed at challenging that notion in a wine from a parcel exposed to the south and planted on the richest active calcareous soils of the entire Côte (over 30%). It shows a certain tension, naturally, but also enjoyable vitality in the fruit.

Volnay 1er Cru Fremiets 2015

Compared to the adjacent vineyards of Pommard (where it is known as Fremiers), Fremiets has the same clay and iron-rich soils, but grapes ripen earlier. Floral aromas and delicate texture define this Volnay with its mellow character and tasty tannins.

Pommard 1er Cru Clos des Épeneaux 2015

A *monopole* of more than five hectares at the intersection of Grands Epenots and Petits Epenots, this is an exceptional *climat* for geological complexity and age of vines (the main nucleus dates back to the thirties). The dark fruit and tight tannic density are integrated by a driving energy that extends the length on the palate.

Domaine d'AUVENAY

SAINT-ROMAIN
Village Bas - Tel. +33 (0) 3 80 212327

3.9 hectares

Under the sign of the d'Auvenay brand, about four hectares of vineyards, almost entirely consecrated to white wines, are grouped as the exclusive property of Lalou Bize-Leroy, who organized the winery following the same viticultural and winemaking strategies which built the success (and the cult) of Domaine Leroy at Vosne-Romanée (see Page 234). Given the drastic selectivity of yields, the production is minuscule, on average less than 10,000 bottles among a dozen rare and almost priceless labels. But beyond the prestige of such nonpareil Grand Crus as Chevalier and Criots-Bâtard, what impresses us most about the whites of Domaine d'Auvenay are the interpretations of second and third ranked *climats*, proposed in versions of intensity and precision well beyond the norm, thanks to interminable persistence.

Auxey-Duresses Les Boutonniers 2015

The *lieu-dit* borders the prestigious *climat* of Meix Chavaux of Meursault, but were it not for d'Auvenay few would have heard of it. The vineyard's northeastern exposure usually confers rigidity to the vigorous saline acidity of the wine, but the hottest harvests, such as 2015, enhance its fullness and momentum.

Meursault Les Narvaux 2015

After a year of grace like 2014 for the whites of Meursault, which enhanced the classicism of the Gouttes d'Or *climat*, from 2015 we were struck by the white of an extreme place like Narvaux, which by virtue of being the northernmost vineyard seems to have interacted better with the radiance of the vintage. Still reserved in fragrance, it reveals a sapid energy of impressive progression, which takes over the palate and holds it hostage for hours.

Jean-Marc et Thomas BOULEY

VOLNAY

12, Chemin de la Cave - Tel. +33 (0) 3 80 216233
jeanmarc.bouley@wanadoo.fr | www.jean-marc-bouley.com

8.8 hectares

Harvest after harvest, we have the feeling that this small family *domaine*, represented by the strong personality of young Thomas Bouley, is entering the list of the most interesting and inspired wineries of the Côte de Beaune. Meticulous work in the vineyards and ever fewer interventions in the process of winemaking has led to the shaping of wines that are rich in character and substance, but also in spontaneous expression. The vineyards are distributed over just under nine hectares, almost all between Volnay and Pommard, and divided into 29 different parcels. They are not certified as organic, but in recent years the use of chemical products has been limited to extreme situations. "My priority in working the land is to have living soils," Thomas points out. There are no strict cellar protocols, but rather an agenda designed to enhance each *terroir* on a case by case basis. The use of the stalks in vinfications changes from one vintage to another and above all from one *climat* to another. As Thomas points out, "in some cases the use of stalks is likely to become a technique that masks the *terroir* rather than exalts it." We were received in the new and functional *cuverie*, adjacent to the old cellar, in the highest part of the town of Volnay, where Thomas led us through a detailed survey of the 2015 harvest. Beyond the remarkable quality level, the vintage also guaranteed those yields that were lacking in the previous three years, partially or drastically reduced by hailstorms that hit the Côte de Beaune.

Bourgogne Hautes Côtes de Beaune 2015

The vineyards are all in the commune of Volnay, at the highest part of the ridge, just beyond the boundaries of the *appellation*. The expression of fruit is defined and engaging, enriched by the clear mineral ascendance. For its type, this is a highly recommendable purchase.

Volnay Vieilles Vignes 2015

The assembly of the grapes of four different parcels with on average fifty-year-old vines make a wine of promising evolution of structure and energy on the palate, in addition to that touch of floral complexity that remains the mark of the best Volnay.

Volnay 1er Cru Les Caillerets 2015

Thomas does not hide a weakness for the *climat* Les Carelles, but has no trouble in recognizing that the greatest *terroir* of Volnay is Les Caillerets, in deference to the adage that says, "He who has no vineyards in Caillerets, doesn't know how much a Volnay is worth." The tannic finesse, the elasticity and the length of this version confirm this once again.

Pommard 1er Cru Les Fremiers 2015

In imagining the prospect of the evolution of the 2015 harvest, the inevitable search for comparisons with other years pushed us into suggesting some similarity with 2009. That prompted Thomas's observation that, "in 2009, the volume of the vintage tended to overwhelm the expression of *terroir*; in 2015, the exact opposite is true." The vineyards are located right below the Pommard cross, but concentration coexists here with a delicacy that is almost more typical of a Volnay.

Pommard 1er Cru Rugiens 2015

The plot of almost half a hectare is included in the Rugiens-Hauts sector (on paper not the most suitable) but the Bouley version, made from grapes for three quarters not de-stemmed, has nothing to envy in the complexity of the best Rugiens.

Henri et Gilles BUISSON

SAINT-ROMAIN

Impasse du Clou - Tel. +33 (0) 3 80 212222
contact@domaine-buisson.com | www.domaine-buisson.com

19 hectares

Henri and Gilles Buisson are respectively grandfather and father of the brothers Frédérick and Franck, eighth generation of *vignerons* today at the helm of a *domaine* of considerable extension, based in Saint-Romain. From nineteen total hectares, almost two thirds dedicated to Pinot Noir, they derive a wide range of labels, covering all the main *appellations* of the Côte de Beaune. But, in our opinion, the wines of Saint-Romain are the most convincing. The conversion to organic farming, in 2009, and the vinification of some *cuvées* without sulfites reveals an attitude open to research but always based on a certain pragmatism, reflected in the disciplined style of wines, notably in excellent whites.

Saint-Romain Absolu 2015

A small portion of Pinot Noir from a large parcel in the *lieu-dit* Sous Roche, among the few *climats* exposed to the west, in recent years has been diverted by the Buisson brothers into a wine made without sulfites: two thousand bottles of a red of dynamic balance between fleshiness and lightness, grit and precision, to which the proportion of grapes not de-stemmed (in this year around 40%) releases a charge of aromatic personality.

Saint-Romain La Perrière 2015

A wine more expressive in aromas than the standard of a *climat* not generally known for fragrance, this offers a sharp but elegant mouthful of clear and captivating persistence.

Saint-Romain Sous le Château 2015

Intriguing candied lemon scents enhance the most successful white of the vintage, vibrant with a perfect posture and a long refreshing finish.

CHÂTEAU de MONTHELIE

MONTHELIE

Château de Monthelie - Tel. +33 (0) 3 80 212332
desuremain@wanadoo.fr | www.domaine-eric-de-suremain.com

10.5 hectares

Unlike in Bordeaux, Burgundy's wine elite does not live in castles. Indeed, we've found that those estates that call themselves *châteaux* rarely produce wines above the average. That of Eric de Suremain is therefore the classic exception that proves the rule. A *domaine* of about ten hectares (half of which are located in Rully, in the Côte Chalonnaise) was among the first to embrace biodynamics in the nineties and today stands as the most recommendable address in this half-hidden village between Volnay and Meursault. But one should not be deceived by appearances. It's called Château de Monthelie for the eighteenth-century origins of the construction, but Eric and his wife Dominique run it more in the spirit of a farmhouse, with hens pecking around the yard and a sense of naturalness and rustic disregard present in every detail. Naturalness and nonchalance also reflect in the style of wines, all characterized by a trim and fresh profile, with convincing juicy fragrance and a capacity for aging that is often surprising. Among the many good reasons to visit the *château* is the opportunity to buy a few bottles of old vintages, still incredibly listed at the same reasonable prices as current bottlings!

Rully 1er Cru Pillot "l'Intemporelle" 2015

"Timeless" in its tenacious resistance to the wear and tear of time. That's how Eric envisions the centenary vineyard planted in 1920 on the brown and stony terrain of this small *climat*. It renders a white wine of remarkable expressive vitality, which opens its inviting aromatic range on notes of rhubarb and citrus and coasts into a long and salivating finish on the palate.

Monthelie 2015

Just over two hectares distributed in almost equal parts of three different *climats* (Romagniens, Riottes and Barbières). You don't need a crystal ball to foresee that the reasonably priced 7,000 bottles produced in 2015 of this fleshy and spicy red will be swept away in record time.

Monthelie 1er Cru Clou des Chênes 2015

Not even a hectare of vineyard, planted twenty-five years ago to occupy about half of the entire surface of this small *climat*, on the border with Volnay. De Suremain made a tonic and slender red, beautifully reactive and energetic in the 2015 version that is simply enchanting.

Monthelie 1er Cru sur la Velle 2015

Velle is a dialectal term for village, in this case Monthelie whose habitat is overlooked by the vineyard, which continues in line with the Clos des Chênes of Volnay. The parcel of Eric de Suremain extends for about two and a half hectares, divided into four portions of vines planted in different years, between 1960 and 1997. The 2015 vintage recalls the aromas of small red berries and combines elegance and suppleness.

Eric generously provided an impromptu mini-vertical tasting in the cellar at the beginning of December 2016 that demonstrated the class of earlier vintages of Monthelie 1er Cru sur la Velle, still available for purchase. From **2010**, the wine shows a lush aromatic amalgam of flowers, red oranges and damp earth, svelte and overflowing with nuances, with a finish of iridescent sapidity and remarkable persistence. From **2008**, a wine with floral and citrus scents, a bit lean on the palate but invitingly fresh. From **2004**, a slim wine marked by its aromatic embroidery. From **1999**, an intense yet somehow relaxed wine with full dimensional development on the palate.

Domaine de COURCEL

POMMARD

29, Place de l'Eglise - Tel. +33 (0) 3 80 221064
courcel@domaine-de-courcel.com | www.domainedecourcel-pommard.fr

10 hectares

This historic *domaine*, which has belonged to the De Courcel family since the seventeenth century, is now owned by Anne Bommelaer and Gilles De Courcel, who work from ten hectares of vineyards entirely and exclusively in the commune of Pommard. The key figure in the operation is Yves Confuron, *vigneron/régisseur* in charge of the entire production chain, who has enhanced the winery's potential to a level of interpretative sensitivity never before realized. Yves, who is also the owner of Domaine Confuron-Cotetidot in Vosne-Romanée, has been with De Courcel since 1996, when he immediately directed vineyard management toward organic practices, albeit with a certain skepticism about the "certification mania" as about what he calls a "sectarian" attitude of the movement. He's a firm advocate of vinifications with the stalks, although embarrassed by the fashionable airs that surround it. "The stalks are not a vehicle of freshness or tannic prominence, but rather the keeper of the integrity of the grape, preserving the complexity and aromatic finesse during alcoholic fermentation." Confuron relies on a range of vineyards distributed in the best *climats* of the *appellation*, among which shines the star of the Grand Clos des Épenots.

Bourgogne 2015

In generous vintages like 2015, finding simple Bourgognes that are fresh and tasty is obviously easier. This one, bearing the De Courcel label, was simply irresistible.

Pommard Les Vaumuriens 2015

The only Villages of the *domaine* comes from a vineyard on white marl soils at a height of four hundred meters. This wine contrasts with the *appellation* stereotypes in that it shows less in the way of color and tannins than in floral fragrance and flavors of an earthy quality with tones of autumn.

Pommard 1er Cru Les Frémiers 2015

The 2015 vintage will be remembered in this *domaine* for severely low yields, due to hail that reduced the average crop to thirteen hectoliters per hectare.

The few available bottles of Les Frémiers are in any case delicious with fresh flavors that recall marasca cherries and a finish that dispenses spicy elegance.

Pommard 1er Cru Les Rugiens 2015

The plot covers more than a hectare of fifty-year-old vines planted on a very steep slope in the upper part of the *climat*, the less valuable on paper. The terrain differs between the shallow marls in the upper part and deeper brown soils in the lower part, next to the Rugiens-Bas sector. The wine shows ferrous complexity that translates into energy and tension. Time is all on its side.

On a cold Saturday morning in early February 2017, we met Yves Confuron in the historic building overlooking the Place de l'Eglise in Pommard, an occasion for an extensive retrospective of the Grand Clos des Epenots, monopole of almost five hectares, flagship of the De Courcel house. Here is a quick review.

Pommard 1er Cru Grand Clos des Épenots 2015

Compressed and austere, it highlights a structure of great breadth and complexity, the *physique du rôle* of a great wine, but without any showy tendencies. On the contrary, the more it remains in the glass, the more the desire grows to drink it.

2014 The impact of hail on the harvest was devastating, 80% of the crop lost. Behind the tenacious reduction on notes of cassis, it reveals keen energy, which at least partially compensates for the slightly bitter base.
2013 The vintage was late, with grapes harvested in mid-October and a complicated maturation, which emphasizes the varietal traits. The texture is thin, the floral *côté* has an almost wilted essence, but in the mouth there is more energy and verticality and the acid freshness releases a vibrating tension.
2012 More resolved in the aromatic mix, while the palate reveals balance between the centrality of the black berry fruit, floral finesse and well-integrated spice.
2011 In a jubilant phase, this is a rather unusual *vin de plaisir* by *appellation* standards: open and sunny, combining freshness and ease of drinking.
2010 The great wine we predicted is confirmed, for us undoubtedly the best of the battery, vital, dynamic, three-dimensional, it releases an exciting energy. If on the one hand we never tire of tracing details and nuances of flavor, on the other hand the lively drive on the palate suggests a long and radiant evolution.

2009 This has a warm tenor voice, supported by an imposing stock of fruit. Today the power seems better melded than in the early years in bottle and the sapid verve brings unexpected pleasure.
2008 The cold, damp vintage accounts for the reserved character of a wine with a bold tannic grip, though it remains a red that is somewhat bland and moody.
2007 Surprising for maturity and balance, this shows character that suggests comparisons with the 2015 and 2010 vintages. At the time of release few would have predicted a similar progression, and today its drinkability is literally uncontainable.
2003 Evolved without flaws, this is an example to remind us that even hot and precocious vintages can dispense pleasure and nonchalance of surprising tenacity over the years.

Alain GRAS

SAINT-ROMAIN

Sous la Velle - Village Haut - Tel. +33 (0) 3 80 212783
contact@domaine-alain-gras.com | www.domaine-alain-gras.com

14 hectares

The dean of Saint-Romain, Alain Gras has continued for years to be the best known and most representative *vigneron* of the *appellation*. And it is no coincidence that of the 27 French restaurants with three Michelin stars, as many as 21 today have his wines on their lists. In 1979, he took over the family business, interrupting the sale of wine to neighbors to bottle his own. Alain has expanded to 14 hectares of vineyards, distributed almost entirely in the best *climats* of Saint-Romain, with a felicitous reach into Auxey. He nourishes a certain skepticism toward organic farming, coupled with a lack of enthusiasm for the promotion to Premier Cru of the best vineyards of Saint-Romain, which actually concerns a single *climat* (Sous le Château). He believes he contributes more to the Saint-Romain *appellation* by assembling wines (one red, one white) from the grapes of forty vineyards, thus guaranteeing constant quality in the 90,000 bottles produced a year. The wines are appreciated both for their fresh vitality of style and their prudent prices.

Saint-Romain 2016

Produced in quantities of almost 40,000 bottles and vinified at 80% in stainless steel, the 2016 version from Alain Gras is a textbook white. The clear mineral tract innervates the fruit in a fascinatingly sapid vein, propitiating rhythmic tasting dynamics and a finish on the palate that is tonic and pure.

Auxey-Duresses Très Vieilles Vignes 2015

If the red of Saint-Romain comes from young vines, that of Auxey-Duresses originates in centenary vineyards planted by Alain's great-grandfather. The yields per hectare fall below thirty hectoliters as the wine gains in complexity and nuances, while retaining an unbeatable juiciness.

Michel LAFARGE

VOLNAY

15, Rue de la Combe - Tel. +33 (0) 3 80 216161
contact@domainelafarge.com | www.domainelafarge.f

12 hectares

The winery has belonged to the family for a couple of centuries. At the beginning, in the nineteenth century, it bore the name of Gillotte, but it was Lafarge who inaugurated the bottling part of the production as early as 1934. Old Michel had been at the helm since 1949, consolidating the reputation with expansions of vineyards and a decision to bottle the entire crop already in the sixties. Today his son Frédéric, who joined his father in 1978, conducts operations. As he puts it, "In a world of speed and gigantism, I'm happy to have a *domaine* of human dimensions and to work in harmony with the land." Frédéric introduced biodynamic farming in 2000 over the entire vineyard area of twelve hectares, about half of which are in the commune of Volnay, where Lafarge has plots in five Premier Cru. The sight of roosters and hens foraging in the house's most precious vineyard, the Clos du Château des Ducs, tells of a *domaine* based on no-frills country authenticity with wines vibrating with tension and rich in flavors designed to last in time.

Bourgogne Passetoutgrain l'Exception 2015

Obtained from seventy-year-old vineyards, in open contrast with the custom of using only grapes from recent plantings (hence the *exception*), this is a *vin de plaisir* where the presence of Gamay, harvested and vinified together with Pinot Noir, plays up the peppery notes and juicy vibrancy.

Volnay 2015

Each area of the *appellation* is represented in the assembly of these five parcels, so as to summarize from one harvest to another an exemplary profile of Volnay Villages. Here the drastically lower yields do not coincide with excessive concentration in a wine of faultless *droiture*, closing with an engaging, savory persistence.

Volnay Vendanges Sélectionnées 2015

This differs from the Volnay *tout court* because its grapes come from four parcels in the center of the *appellation*, right under the Premier Cru. The floral expressiveness and the menthol nuances release momentum and freshness on the palate.

Volnay 1er Cru Mitans 2015

Silky and tasty tannins, sleek and rich on the palate, a perfect example of an original Lafarge interpretation which places the 2015 vintage in line with that of 1929, that is to say not so much under the sign of solar radiance as of expressive purity.

Volnay 1er Cru Clos du Château des Ducs 2015

To understand the tannic and austere expressions of this wine, you need to enter the *clos*, a *monopole* of about half a hectare, surrounded by houses on three sides. The brown soils, rich in clay and poor in iron, half a meter deep, are factors behind a wine that still seems contracted, but is well focused on fruit.

Volnay 1er Cru Clos des Chênes 2015

The most masculine of the Lafarge Volnays, as confirmed every year, to the point of inducing the phlegmatic Frédéric to open up with an uncharacteristically happy prediction: "This awaits a radiant evolution, to be appreciated in the coming decades." Message received.

LAFOUGE

AUXEY-DURESSES

1, Rue du Pont Boillot - Tel. +33 (0) 3 80 216817
domainelafouge@orange.fr

11.5 hectres

We'd been missing from Auxey-Duresses for a few years. The village, after all, remains a bit off the tested wine-lovers' routes and the wines of the *appellation* that are worth the trip are, frankly, quite rare. We therefore gladly took the advice of Jean Baptiste Bouzereau and decided that a new visit to Auxey might be worthwhile, to meet his brother-in-law Gilles Lafouge and taste the wines he makes from almost twelve hectares of vineyards, almost entirely in the Auxey valley. A valley oriented east-west, where the further up you go the more difficult the ripening, but the vineyards of Lafouge are all planted at the beginning of the valley and benefit from better exposure. And if the wines retain the slightly acidulous touch typical of the *appellation*, they remain completely liberated of the rustic features that have often penalized the Auxey reputation. To round out the story on a happy note: reasonable prices and an extremely warm reception.

Auxey-Duresses Les Hautés 2015

The *lieu-dit* is located at the top, on red and ferrous soils, on the border with Meursault's Vireuils *climat*. Gilles derives a white of clear floral vitality.

Auxey-Duresses 2015

Made from seven different *lieux-dits* with over ten thousand bottles produced, here is a light and flowing red, dangerously drinkable, which combines fruit and spices in dynamic synthesis.

Auxey-Duresses 1er Cru La Chapelle 2015

The *climat* is tiny, just over a hectare, and Lafouge has two-thirds of it. The south-eastern exposure and the white marls of the soils favor a tannic and gritty wine, which combines open aromatics (cassis) and gustatory tension.

Auxey-Duresses 1er Cru Les Duresses 2015

The name of the *climat* certainly does not suggest roundness and softness, but Gilles' version surprised us with its harmony and lenght in taste.

LEJEUNE

POMMARD

1, Place de l'Eglise - Tel. +33 (0) 3 80 229088
domaine-lejeune@wanadoo.fr | www.domaine-lejeune.fr

10 hectares

The building that houses the winery dates back to 1740 and was bought by the Lejeune family in 1793, after the revolutionaries requisitioned it to the ancient Confraternity of the Sacred Sacrament at the end of the eighteenth century. After the death of Maxime Lejeune in 1864, the *domaine* was handed down through the family's female lineage, and was conducted for thirty years by François Jullien de Pommerol, former professor of enology at the Lycée Viticole of Beaune. His son-in-law Aubert Lefas took over several years ago, following artisanal methods of winemaking. The entire crop is vinified with the stalks, though most is simply whole cluster, while about a third comes from whole clusters pressed by foot and fermented in large trunk-conical vats of unknown age (probably among the oldest in the region still in use). The wines have aromatic momentum and freshness, though, despite competitive prices, they perhaps do not yet enjoy the critical consideration they deserve. The *domaine* can count on about ten hectares of its own vineyards, to which another four hectares can be added for use in a recently created *négociant* business.

Bourgogne Passetoutgrain 2015

Two thirds Gamay and a third Pinot Noir are the simple recipe for this *vin de soif* of soaring fluidity. Be advised that you can buy it at the winery for less than ten euros.

Bourgogne "Les Grandes Carelles" 2015

In the best years, certain wineries are able to make exciting wines even in the simplest *appellations*. Here is a glowing example: a delicious drink with an articulation of aromas and flavors that are anything but trivial.

Pommard Trois Follots 2015

Opinions are divided on the etymology of Follots, which some say is a dialect term for the almond tree and others that it refers to fog in the guise of elves, rising from the small stream that runs through the village of Pommard. Unable to decide, we focused on the crispness of the fruit—a joy for the palate.

Pommard 1er Cru Les Argillières 2015

The clay soil matrix of this *climat*, located north of the Grands Epenots, appears more than evident from the name (also known as En Largillière). The 2015 vintage offers us a less fleshy version than expected, yet it is fully equipped with aromatic finesse, tasty tannins and a convincing flavor progression.

Pommard 1er Cru Les Poutures 2015

The deep and humid soils (Poutures derives from *pâtures*, or *pastures*, i.e. muddy terrain) in the torrid summer of 2015 maintained a precious reserve of freshness in a wine more noted for energy than nuance and dashing drinkability.

Pommard 1er Cru Les Rugiens 2015

The red soils of the lower part of the *climat* are the base of the reputation Pommard has established over the centuries for tannic wines, slow to open, with an innate propensity for aging. It is there that Aubert Lefas produces Les Rugiens with an interpretation of the vintage that loses nothing in depth, while retaining that more delicate and almost "airy" aromatic character that marks the winery s style. Character that we found unfolded with an even greater array of nuances than the 2014 version, in order to increase its captivating elegance.

Domaine de MONTILLE

VOLNAY

Rue du Pied de la Vallée - Tel. +33 (0) 3 80 213914
sales@demontille.com | www.demontille.com

23 hectares

"Where there are wines, there is civilization," were the unforgettable words of the aged Hubert de Montille, in front of the cameras of the film Mondovino by Jonathan Nossiter. Hubert, who died in November 2014, decided in the post-war years to stop selling wine to *négociants*, taking on himself all the risks involved. He always showed a binding loyalty to the different *climats*, in the name of an idea of elegance centered on aromatic purity and moderate alcohol. Founded in Volnay in the mid-eighteenth century, the *domaine* has carried the family name for a century and a half. In the early nineties, Hubert passed on direction of the winery to his son Etienne, not without some sparks flying between the two strong personalities. Since then the De Montille style has gained something in terms of charm. "A change of style, but not of philosophy," explains Etienne. "Both my father and I have always sought the same qualities in wines: authenticity, purity and balance." Sister Alix follows the entire chain of white wine production, with precious help from American *chef de cave* Brian Sieve, taking in the four *appellations* of the property (including a couple of hectares divided between Corton Charlemagne and les Caillerets in Puligny), and in the *négociant* activity started with her brother in 2003 under the name Deux Montille. The family also bought the Château de Puligny in 2011, bringing the total of vineyards between the properties to thirty-seven hectares, a truly remarkable figure compared to the average of the Côte d'Or. The *domaine* has practiced organic farming since 1995, followed by biodynamic certification for a dozen harvests. In 2015, almost all the wines were vinified using whole bunches.

Beaune 1er Cru Greves 2015

Already a *tête de cuvée* in the classification of Dr. Lavalle, this is the wine that Etienne De Montille prefers among all the Premier Cru of Beaune, to the point of labeling it like a Grand Cru. The remarkable aromatic finesse is already at the service of the powerful energy that will challenge the decades.

Volnay 1er Cru en Champans 2015

This *climat*, which was already mentioned in correspondence from 1252, rests on a geological substratum that dates to the Oxfordian stage. The seventy-year-old vineyard extends over about a hectare where the more markedly calcareous matrix of the upper part combines with the clay rich soils of the lower part. De Montille's interpretation comes off delicately and crosses the palate with enchanting grace.

Volnay 1er Cru Les Taillepieds 2015

The ample vineyard of De Montille (one and a half hectares) is high, above three hundred meters, on soils with a high percentage of active limestone. It renders a Volnay of insidious charm, starting with a seductive velvety feel, then opening to sapid-mineral persistence. A wine worth a long wait

Pommard 1er Cru Les Rugiens-Bas Cuvée Hubert 2015

Hubert's favorite wine, this vintage will be bottled only in magnums. We were struck by the three-dimensionality, the "grip" on the palate, as well as a truly enchanting radiance. For us, without hesitation, this is among the best reds of 2015 tasted in Côte de Beaune.

REBOURGEON-MURE

POMMARD

6, Grande-Rue - Tel. +33 (0) 3 80 227539
contact@rebourgeonmure.fr | www.rebourgeonmure.fr

7 hectares

The *domaine*, founded in the sixteenth century, has remained the property of the same family over time, while maintaining an innate touch in wines that are full of charm and free of any sense of rusticity. Located essentially between Pommard and Volnay, the seven hectares of vineyards are almost entirely dedicated to Pinot Noir. David Rebourgeon elaborates wines of uncompromising tension, sometimes even a bit rawboned and lean, but animated in the best cases by a supplement of vibrantly sapid minerality. Wine drinkers who don't look for the immediate impact of fruit in a red, perceived as predictably comforting, should keep this address in mind.

Pommard 2015

Four different *lieux-dits* combine in an assemblage of convincing incisiveness, gritty and very flavorful.

Pommard 1er Cru Clos des Arvelets 2015

This comes from the original parcel of the *climat* Les Arvelets, located in the innermost part of a *combe* at about 300 meters, steep and cool but well exposed to the south. For Armando Castagno: "This is perhaps the most tenuous and feminine wine of Pommard at the Premier Cru level." With delicately peppery aromas, the 2015 version seems to confirm his statement.

Volnay 1er Cru Caillerets 2015

If the best interpretations of the *climat* are noted for graceful aromas and resolute flavors, here the opposite is true. The wine has intense aromas, with a wild mix of earthy notes, yet it manages to become delicate and fine on the palate with enticing nuances of flavor. The finish is marked by firmer tannins but not rigid and losing nothing in terms of nuance.

Fanny SABRE

POMMARD
12, Place de l'Europe - Tel. +33 (0) 3 45 631653
laciefanny@gmail.com

4.5 hectares

The winery has only been active since 2005, but the name Fanny Sabre quickly established itself as one of the most accredited sources for wines of natural inspiration produced between Beaune and Pommard. A word of caution: if you heed the Pommard legend of colored, tannic reds whose hardness prevails over elegance, you have the wrong address. Formed at the school of Philippe Pacalet, Fanny owes her fame to perfumed and fresh wines of refined expressive spontaneity. These are produced mainly in micro-vinifications made with whole cluster grapes from small plots under organic conditions from a total vineyard area that does not arrive at five hectares. Fermentations often start with semi-carbonic macerations, the use of sulfites is reduced to homeopathic doses, no decanting is foreseen and the aging takes place mainly in extensively used barrels. The deliberate absence of enological assistants does not preclude attention to detail in fashioning wines that often enchant for seductive nonchalance, overflowing with nuances.

Bourgogne 2016

Flowing with vital aromatic wildness (hibiscus, black pepper), here is a red that dissolves into enviable fluency.

Pommard 2015

Fanny ironically defines this Pommard as *trapu*. We beg to differ: his wine offers a lot of fruity *souplesse* and it might seem just a bit curvy, but not stocky at all, anything but overweight.

Beaune 1er Cru Vignes Franches 2015

The potential of aromatic and tactile finesse associated with the *climat*, one of the most admired of the entire *appellation*, is enhanced in this version from Fanny, refined in texture and deliciously juicy.

SARNIN-BERRUX

MONTHELIE

23, Rue de Beaune - Tel. +33 (0) 3 80 261596
www.sarnin-berrux.com

The project took off in 2007, thanks to the partnership between Jean-Pascal Sarnin, a former financial broker in Paris, and Jean-Marie Berrux, an enologist already active in the vineyards of the Jura. After just a few vintages, Sarnin-Berrux stood out as one of the most convincing in Burgundy's vibrant ranks of wine of natural inspiration. The base is in Saint-Romain and the activity is articulated as an original form of *négoce*, based on the purchase of grapes exclusively from certified organic vines. The result leads to almost twenty labels vinified without sulfites in accordance with the lunar calendar, starting from un-stemmed grapes, with slow pressing and long macerations in large truncated cone barrels. The wines reveal lively dynamics and incisive acid levels with a strong point of expressive spontaneity.

Bourgogne 2015

The fascinating wildness of the aromatic spectrum prepares the palate for a play on smoothness, though not without a touch of fragrant rusticity.

Saint-Romain 2014

To the nose the wine flaunts grit and personality in an original amalgam of floral and citrus notes. The palate is free rein, electric and nervous, marked by the incomparable vitality of acidic freshness. Almost like a white camouflaged in red.

Saint-Romain 2014

The aromatic verve of peat-like scents enlivened by refreshing iodized streaks is original, predicating a slender, vertical taste structure that still needs to be fully expressed. This once again confirms that the white wines of Saint-Romain guarantee an ageing potential often superior to the reds.

VAUDOISEY-CREUSEFOND

POMMARD

16, Route d'Autun - Tel. +33 (0) 3 80 224863
vaudoisey-creusefond@wanadoo.fr | www.vaudoisey-creusefond.fr

8 hectares

The label graphics have recently been renewed, but otherwise the *domaine* remains linked to a traditional approach. And even today as the young Alexandre Vaudoisey takes the place of his father Henri, a few months into retirement, everything retains an old school atmosphere: vineyard management in *lutte raisonnée*, fermentations in old wooden vats, long macerations and maturations with the use of new barrels reduced to a minimum, enological interventions limited to bare essentials. The result is equally traditional wines, sometimes a bit austere in their youth, but always tasty and long-lived. The eight hectares of vineyards mainly involve the *appellations* Pommard, Volnay and Auxey-Duresses, with prices always very competitive.

Auxey-Duresses 2015

Half a hectare of vines in two different parcels (La Macabrée, Les Fosses), for a balanced white of sweet-savory harmony, faithful to the extroverted character of the vintage.

Pommard 2015

Alexandre jokingly defines this as the Pommard of the four cardinal points, since the grapes come from one and a half hectares of vineyards located in six different parcels at the four corners of the *appellation*. They compose a profile of extreme consistency, which fully expresses the house style: a *sauvage* nature, savory grit, tight tannins. If you are looking for a *vin de soif* that emphasizes the delicious character of the vintage, you'll have to look elsewhere. Villages is on the label but it might as well read: wine for aging.

Pommard 1er Cru Charmots 2015

The *climat* has two different exposures, southeast and full south. Alexandre has vineyard on both sides for an austere but by no means dour red, vertical but not rigid, showing promising tannic tension.

Thierry VIOLOT-GUILLEMARD

POMMARD

7, Rue Sainte-Marguerite - Tel. +33 (0) 3 80 224998
contact@violot-guillemard.fr | www.violot-guillemard.fr

6 hectares

"*Authentiquement bourguignon, passionnément vigneron*," is how Thierry Violot-Guillemard defines his approach to wine. A translation would be superfluous. Indeed, if one had to invent a figure bringing flesh and bone to the image of a *vigneron* it might look just like him: hands of a consummate worker, Obelix mustache, good-natured smile and an irrepressible desire to tell the story of his land. We arrived at the winery at four in the afternoon and left three hours later, after having tasted an unknown number of wines. During each, he was ready to rummage through the family reserves to pick the right bottle to illustrate that specific episode, to offer concrete examples of his thoughts. Reflecting on the possible parallels between the years 2009 and 2015, he opened a Pommard 1er Cru Rugiens 2009 with overflowing citric energy and yet of an unmatchable, almost angular freshness. To emphasize how hot vintages can give life to long-lived wines as well as luscious ones, he uncorked a rare white Beaune 1er Cru Clos des Mouches 2011 of radiant drinkability. His wines are steeped in tradition and classicism: "I want to do exactly what my father and my grandfather did. I never considered changing anything in my way of interpreting this work," admits Thierry. The winery was founded by his great-grandfather in the early twentieth century, producing wine and distillates. Thierry began working in the family *domaine* in the late seventies, gradually assuming its management. For almost twenty years, the six hectares of vineyards have been cultivated under organic conditions with complete working of the soils, officially recognized only in 2014. He depends on spontaneous fermentation without the use of selected yeasts and vinifies using at most 50% of whole cluster grapes, though only in the best years. His wife Estelle manages a *maison d'hôtes* with four elegant rooms, complete with a swimming pool, all inside the *domaine*, which takes in the small Clos de Derrière Saint-Jean. As Thierry likes to clarify: "It's the only Premier Cru pool in Burgundy!"

Beaune En Montagne Saint-Désiré 2015

In a *domaine* with an evident red-wine tendency, it's a pleasure to find a delicious white that is so precise and freshly natural.

Bourgogne Les Maisons-Dieu 2015

From the name of an old inn for hosting pilgrims, this is a *lieu-dit* whose wines until 1937 were classified as Villages. Then they were relegated to lower status due to the proximity of the national highway. Still, the position doesn't seem to have penalized the wine's appeal animated by a sapid fluency.

Monthelie 1er Cru Les Duresses 2015

In contrast to the conviction that the wines of this *climat* are the most powerful and muscular of the *appellation*, Thierry's version surprises for its finesse and fine-honed floral nuances.

Pommard 1er Cru Clos de Derrière Saint-Jean 2015

This Clos is really the home garden, a tenth of a hectare a part of which has been devoted to the swimming pool of the *maison d'hôtes*. The miniscule area under vines, however, gives life to a soft and graceful red with a persistent saline finish.

Pommard 1er Cru La Platière 2015

The *climat* facing south within the Grande Combe, owes its name to flat stones scattered through the thin terrain in close contact with matrix rock. The vineyard, planted in 1935, renders a vertical and tapered red, vital in tannic grip without giving up finesse.

Pommard 1er Cru Rugiens 2015

A parcel on the edge of the two sectors of the *cru*, this confirms the superior rank of its *climat*. The wine is supported by an austere, almost skeletal structure, which disguises a complexity that will need a long time in bottle to show its best.

Joseph VOILLOT

VOLNAY

4, Place de l'Eglise - Tel. +33 (0) 3 80 216227
joseph.voillot@wanadoo.fr | www.joseph-voillot.com

10 hectares

Started by Jean-Baptiste Voillot at the end of the nineteenth century, the *domaine* first passed into the hands of his son Marius and then his nephew Joseph, who in 1945 was just fourteen when he did his first harvest. Devastated by frosts and hail, the vineyard diaries recorded that grapes from seven hectares produced hardly eight *pièces* of wine, or just over two thousand bottles. Joseph Voillot set about upgrading the family *domaine*: ending the custom of selling all the wine to *négociants*, introducing the use of stainless steel cuves for vinification and releasing the first bottlings with the Voillot label at the beginning of the fifties. Joseph's son-in-law, Jean-Pierre Charlot, formerly a *courtier* and then professor of enology at the Lycée Viticole of Beaune, has been at the helm since 1995. Today he offers seventeen labels from about ten hectares of proprietary vines, worked by limiting treatments to the essentials, according to the dictates of *lutte raisonnée*. The most important parcels are distributed between Volnay and Pommard. From completely de-stemmed grapes he makes wines of exemplary fidelity both to the vintage and to the particular *climat*. Short macerations, low percentage of new wood and a built-in hostility to any form of enological intervention can make the wines seem a bit lean and austere, but time is on their side as the matrix of the *terroir* is always perfectly transparent.

Bourgogne Pinot Noir Vieilles Vignes 2015

A snack wine if ever there was one, overflowing with juiciness, a perfect match with salami and bread, though a single bottle on table risks not being enough.

Volnay Vieilles Vignes 2015

Those who like the wines of Volnay graceful and essential, even in a generous vintage like 2015, will be enchanted by so much fluency of flavors.

Beaune 1er Cru Aux Coucherias 2015

As Armando Castagno writes, the *climat* is "little known but original, located high up on a hill in a wooded and isolated spot with challenging slopes." The 2015 vintage displays a red with ripe fruit (cherry), mottled by a sweet spice that recalls cinnamon.

Volnay 1er Cru Les Frémiets 2015

Paradoxically, the vineyard closest to the border with Pommard is the winery's finest Volnay. Backed by a vineyard planted in the thirties, the wine is free of any redundancy in putting its mineral vitality at the service of almost compulsive drinkability.

Volnay 1er Cru Les Champans 2015

Already mentioned in 1252, this vineyard was included in the list of *tête de cuvée* in classifications of both Lavalle (1855) and Rodet (1920). It is a stony and well-drained *climat*, of which Jean-Pierre works a parcel of about a hectare. The wine, as the exact opposite of a delicate and welcoming Volnay, has more grit than grace, more sapidity than floreality, with a chiaroscuro of officinal herbs and a tonic and vital final, very promising. "Why buy wines for aging to drink young?" asks Jean-Pierre.

Pommard 1er Cru Les Pézerolles 2014

The *climat* has earned the reputation of the "Pessac-Léognan of Burgundy" and in this version of Voillot is the antithesis of the most tenacious and corpulent Pommards. Lean and supple, it proves depth and great charme.

Pommard 1er Cru Les Rugiens 2014

From the Grand Cru *in pectore* of Rugiens-Bas, this red shows almost monastic austerity, with a supply of tension, grit and freshness that guarantee the prospect of a long evolution.

9

MEURSAULT

MEURSAULT

map *page* 527

Meursault, with a winemaking tradition that dates back to the Romans, is the gateway to the so-called Côte des Blancs, a sequence of vineyards that produce some of the world's most esteemed white wines. It has been said that the lack of a star vineyard to challenge the undisputed supremacy of Montrachet has not only prevented the recognition of a Meursault Grand Cru, but has perhaps hindered Meursault's reputation as a wine town when compared to Puligny and Chassagne. It seems to us, however, that the reputation, which was greatly strengthened when *vignerons* stopped selling the bulk of the crop to *négociants*, has further consolidated in the last twenty years, revitalizing the culture of *terroir* and affirming the status of certain producers in the global élite of white wine. In the process, the taste model of the wines of Meursault has become increasingly complex and multifaceted, a far cry from the popular image of a fat and opulent white disparaged as "*beurre et noisette*." Today the expressive richness of Meursault wines is different, translating into a plurality of styles that has never been so vital.

Looking at the details of the *appellation*, the area under vine extends over nearly 400 hectares, of which about a quarter is divided between the 17 Premier Cru—which then become 29 if we take into account the subdivisions of the different *climats*. Taking a schematic view, we find the block of vines between the village and the northern border with Monthelie and Volnay where wines from Pinot Noir come from parcels of Les Santenots. These are excellent red wines, which are not surprisingly incorporated into the Volnay *appellation* due to a singular exception to the rules in this land of whites that we have already discussed in Volnay (see Page 314). On the ridges behind the village we find a second nucleus of *climats*, almost all of extreme interest: from Meix Chavaux to Luchets, from Vireuils to Tesson, from Tillets to Narvaux. None of these is classified as Premier Cru, but on close inspection it becomes clear that the average quality of the many Villages wines, which seems higher than in any other commune in the region, is an outstanding merit of the wines of Meursault. "We're probably dealing with the best communal category in all of Burgundy" writes Armando Castagno. For what it's worth, we agree. And so we continue to be won over by the floral and mineral vitality of these whites, innervated by flavor tension and surprisingly long-lived.

A third block of vineyards to the south of the village forms the nucleus of the Meursault Premier Cru: a strip of parcels exposed to the east, running parallel to the main road and including all the most prominent vineyard realities, from

Gouttes d'Or to Porusots, from Genevrières to Charmes and Perrières. These *climats*, long exalted in critical reviews, are enhanced by the complex nature of calcareous soils, of extreme mineral richness, with significant percentages of magnesium, very important for harmonizing the different qualities of white wines. Here shines the star of Perrières, in the view of many experts (including the worthy Dr. Lavalle, who indicated it as a *tête de cuvée* in 1855) the most entitled Premier Cru of Meursault. The white wines are anything but easy to drink in their youth, hard and reticent, but with extraordinary complexity that translates into a marked aptitude for aging, appreciable over decades. Whatever the outcome of the age-old dossier that supports its promotion, Les Perrières should be considered a Grand Cru *in pectore*, as it is universally recognized.

Rounding out the survey are the vineyards of the extreme southwest, under the Mont Mélian, about 50 hectares situated high up on the hill of the village of Blagny. The production of white wines in this sector is divided between the denominations of Meursault and Puligny, while for the reds Blagny has its own *appellation*, with vineyards classified as both Premier Cru and Villages. The situation is to say the least cumbersome and this is not the place for detailed investigations. We'll limit our observations to stating that the best *climats* of the Blagny *appellation* give rise to reds of a certain finesse and tenacity over time.

BALLOT-MILLOT & Fils

MEURSAULT

9, Rue de la Goutte d'Or - Tel. +33 (0) 3 80 212139
charles.ballot@ballotmillot.com | www.ballotmillot.com

10 hectares

Since the entry of Charles Ballot in 2000, first alongside his father Philippe, then gradually taking over from him, the *domaine* has shown a significant progress. In the ten hectares of vineyards, more than two thirds allocated to whites, the intensive working of the soils allows reduced treatments and increasing interest in the organic regime. The range of labels has further expanded, with a selection of some of the most convincing wines of Meursault, always with integrated *droiture* and *souplesse*, and always very reasonably priced.

Meursault Les Criots 2015

Here is a *lieu-dit* about which little is said. We are in the northern sector, under the Santenots block, on deep and rich soils, but Ballot's parcel covers an unusual rock ripple, where soils change radically. The anomaly may be propitious in a wine with a higher than average impact of freshness underlining its juicy clarity.

Meursault 1er Cru Perrières 2015

The plot of over half a hectare is located in the lower part of the *climat*, near the Clos des Perrières. Charles obtains a white of rare completeness and balance, rich and powerful but of greater gustatory tension than Genevrières, with a mineral imprint that releases a long persistence on the palate.

Volnay 1er Cru Taillepieds 2015

While we were tasting together, Charles admitted to have deeply changed his way of vinifying red wines in recent years, favoring much slower macerations and more delicate extractions, renouncing inoculation of yeasts and filtrations. In this vintage there is also a proportion of whole cluster grapes, icing on the cake for a fragrant (raspberry) and gritty version, with an intact and tonic fruit lining and coating the tannins.

Michel BOUZEREAU & Fils

MEURSAULT

5, Rue Robert Thénard - Tel. +33 (0) 3 80 212074
michel-bouzereau-et-fils@wanadoo.fr | www.michelbouzereauetfils.com

12 hectares

Jean-Baptiste Bouzereau is probably the most "Italian" of the Burgundian *vignerons*: smiling and friendly, hospitable, generous and irresistibly *simpatico*. To spend a few hours with him, his wife Sylvie, and their wonderful family inspires a warm and peaceful feeling of home. We've had the good fortune of knowing him for some time, and thanks to these many shared moments in his home and cellar, we've been able to better understand how deep is the Côte d'Or renovation over the last few years. As part of the seventh generation of Bouzereau family *vignerons*, Jean-Baptiste is well aware of his role in a vital heritage of the Meursault *appellation* (he also has parcels in Puligny, in particular holdings in the premier cru Le Cailleret), he likes to talk about his wines in a direct manner, without rhetoric, linked to his profound respect for *terroir*. Grapes of uncompromising quality, traditional vinification, *élevage en fûts de chêne* for periods ranging from twelve to eighteen months, very light clarification and a lot of common sense. That's all. His wines are a faithful mirror of this demanding linearity: clean, enjoyable, elegant and accented by vibrant minerality. This *domaine* should be a point of reference for anyone who loves the classic white wines of the Côte de Beaune.

Bourgogne 2015

Jean-Baptiste often says about this wine with a smile: "*c'est parfait en apéro*." You hardly need a translation to intuit that it's gloriously quaffable.

Meursault Les Grands Charrons 2015

From a vineyard of one-and-a-half hectares, covering much of the hill behind the town, the upper part planted in calcareous soils and the lower part in alluvial terrain. Ample and eminently drinkable with a saline vein true to the vintage.

Meursault Les Tessons 2015

The faded red cottage that stands in the middle of this beautiful parcel is recognizable from afar and identifies a label confirmed from year to year as one of the most consistent wines of the *domaine*. Even 2015, with its typical combination of precision and freshness, is destined for a certain longevity.

Meursault 1er Cru Charmes 2015

In the extensive *climat* of Charmes, where altitudes and soil compositions show notable variations, Bouzereau's parcel is located in the upper portion called Charmes-Dessus, noted as the sector best suited to production of rich and complex whites. The pedigree is summarily confirmed by this version, which includes a bonus of elegance and energy.

Meursault 1er Cru Genevrières 2015

Critics often refer to this *climat* as the most complete and balanced *appellation*. The happy hand of Jean-Baptiste, always seeking the maximum in purity and precision, gives us a surprisingly refined version from a vintage noted for a sunny Mediterranean disposition.

Meursault 1er Cru Perrières 2015

Two parcels are assembled: the first higher up, planted in 1939 on the stones of the Perrières-Dessus, the second in the deeper terrain of the Perrières-Dessous, adjacent to Clos des Perrières. Critics often describe these wines as combining the minerality of Genevrières with the rotund plasticity of Charmes, a duality exemplified by Bouzereau's chiseled interpretation.

BUISSON-CHARLES

MEURSAULT

3, Rue de la Velle - Tel. +33 (0) 3 80 212232
www.buisson-charles.com | dombuissoncharles@wanadoo.fr

6.4 hectares

Appearances often mislead, which is why people may get the wrong idea about Patrick Essa, a heavy-set gym teacher with a Maserati Ghibli parked under his home. To get a true perspective of the man, it's enough to scroll the pages of his blog—www.degustateurs.pro—to understand the seriousness and rigor of his insights into vineyards and *climats*. A visit to the winery confirms that we are dealing with an accomplished producer, who manages with his wife Catherine, daughter of Michel Buisson, the five hectares of properties centered mostly in Meursault, to which a small *négociant* activity was integrated in 2011 for wines sold under the same brand.

Bourgogne Pinot Noir Hautes Coutures 2016

Grapes, which are vinified with the stalks, come from three different parcels in the commune of Meursault (Hautes and Petites Coutures, plus Magny), though this version also incorporates a plot of Pommard Village A skilled hand can be noted even in the few reds of the *domaine*, not only the Volnay Santenots, an intense and promising Premier Cru, but also in this Bourgogne appreciated for its prompt drinkability.

Meursault Les Tessons 2016

Patrick considers Les Tessons the best *climat* of the Meursault-Villages *appellation*, and he is not alone. From his small parcel he makes a sculpted white, noted for a bracing intensity.

Meursault 1er Cru Bouches Chères 2015

Better known as Bouchères, the *climat* offers considerable potential, largely unrecognized by local *vignerons*, who often prefer to bottle the wine with the names of more famous neighboring *crus*. But Buisson has always believed in it, already using the nineteenth-century Bouches Chères name on bottles of the early 1960s. The focus is on extremely fine texture in a wine with the surprising tenacity of a *blanc de garde*.

Jean-François COCHE-DURY

MEURSAULT

9, Rue Charles-Giraud - Tel. +33 (0) 3 80 212412

10.3 hectares

It's not easy to portray a cult *domaine* like that of Jean-François Coche-Dury, producer of some of the most sought-after and disputed wines of all Burgundy. He is widely known as a rough and secluded man, immune to any form of media flattery and notoriously hostile to anything aimed at image rather than substance. Even more widespread is the fame of his wines, produced in a context of austere dedication to work. The whites remain unmistakable for their micrometric precision, for their *droiture* and gustatory tension, for the fascinating aromatic nuances of hazelnut. Even the reds, if more episodic since they come from a quarter of his ten hectares of vineyards, show silky texture and enviable complexity. In other places, a similar level of fame might have prompted the engagement of a "star architect" for a self-celebratory winery of pharaonic scope. That you certainly won't find at number 25, Rue Charles Giraud, practically anonymous in a neighborhood of simple buildings, shunning any suggestion of ostentation. The only recent construction came in 2015 with the enlargement of the *cuverie*, but always with a view to improving the quality of vinification. Today Jean-François has officially handed over management to his son Raphaël, who has worked alongside him since 2003, but the music hasn't changed. The routine of self-denial is still at work in the vineyard, drastic pruning and rigorously selective yields, organic farming with no certifications. Grapes are vinified on a parcel by parcel basis, in quest of the different inflections taken by the "voice" of the territory of Meursault, from one vineyard to another, from one season to another. Not even fifty thousand bottles are produced and sold immediately by reservation to loyal and carefully selected customers, though that doesn't prevent hyperbolic price speculation approaching the limits of decency. In any case, if you are lucky enough to open a Coche-Dury wine at the table, you won't soon forget it.

Bourgogne 2014

It is rare to find a base wine of such compelling complexity. If you could manage to find a bottle on the wine list of a restaurant whose prices are not yet influenced by the Dow Jones index, we advise you to not let it escape.

Meursault 2014

The tenacious cliché that the whites of Meursault are fat and ripe, buttery and soft, must come to terms with an increasing number of praiseworthy exceptions. At the time, Coche-Dury was among the first to show that elegance is more a matter of purity than opulence. In line with these premises, the interpretation of the 2014 vintage goes in the sense of an appreciable classicism: the impact on the palate releases caresses of citrus freshness, but the stretch to the finish redeems tension and sapid grit.

Meursault 1er Cru Perrières 2014

Praising Perrières is all too easy; the belief that this *climat* possesses the value of a Grand Cru is now known to all and risks becoming a cliché. Anything but obvious is to find yourself in face of such a prancing thoroughbred whose radiant energy brings together density and lightness in a brilliant dynamic balance.

Corton-Charlemagne Grand Cru 2014

The plot of a third of a hectare, planted in 1950 and exposed to the southwest, is located exactly at the foot of the cross that marks the portion of this large Grand Cru known as Le Charlemagne. Coche-Dury produces a wine of extraordinary sapid-mineral complexity, stony and saline, with an impressive return of wild strawberries in the retro-nasal passage, as sometimes happens in the case of certain memorable Champagnes.

Sylvain DUSSORT

MEURSAULT

12, Rue Charles Giraud - Tel. +33 (0) 3 80 212750
contact@sylvaindussort.com | www.sylvaindussort.com

6.5 hectares

Sylvain Dussort took over the family *domaine* in 1982, and, with the help of his wife, has run it full time since. A careful acquisition strategy has increased his vineyards to six and a half hectares, all in the territory of Meursault and managed agronomically in integrated culture (*lutte raisonnée*). Although he has no vineyards in the *climats* of greatest reputation, Sylvain knows how to make the most of his grapes, meaning that his Bourgogne keeps pace with a Meursault Village, or his Limozin has all the stuff of a Premier Cru. With the not inconsiderable exception that they are offered at more affordable prices.

Bourgogne Aligoté 2015

Dussort appreciates the *sucrosité* or natural sweetness of precocious vintages. The usual nervous and sharp character of Aligoté concedes to a version more prone to pleasure.

Bourgogne Blanc Cuvée des Ormes 2015

Of the four *lieux-dits* that supply it, a couple are classified Villages plots (en l'Ormeau and Pellans) declassified here in a blend that benefits in terms of vitality by a vibrant grip on the palate.

Meursault Vieilles Vignes 2015

The almost seventy-year-old vines (of Pelles Dessous and Les Forges) are a key to complexity, vertical posture, savory grit enhanced by the expertise of Dussort.

Meursault Limozin 2015

From the only *lieu-dit* of Meursault that borders on three different Premier Cru (Charmes, Genevrieres and Porusots), comes a white fragrant with aromatic herbs, acacia flowers and lime peel. Powerful and dense on the palate, it closes innervated by an astringent salinity.

Arnaud ENTE

MEURSAULT

12, Rue de Mazeray - Tel. +33 (0) 3 80 216612
arnaud.ente@wanadoo.fr

3.65 hectares

"*A. Ente viticulteur*" reads the small plaque on the wall next to the entrance gate, providing a hint to the character of Arnaud Ente, a secluded and discreet man little concerned with appearances. Arnaud, originally from a small village in northern France, is however a very meticulous, intransigent and perfectionist 50-year-old winemaker. The vineyards are certified organic and for years have been managed with biodynamic preparations, with grass often left between rows to enrich the soil microbiology. Careful observation of vine behavior and reading of old agronomic treatises (in particular one by René Lafon in 1921), allowed Arnaud and his wife Marie-Odile to recover the Poussard method of pruning, based on a peculiar technique that promotes the prevention of some diseases of the vine. In the winery the constant search for elegance and harmony results in soft and slow pressing, meticulous cleaning of the musts before fermentation and *élevage* in barrels of different sizes. Yields are drastically contained, around thirty hectoliters per hectare, but the fleshy style at the limit of opulence that made the fortune of the *domaine* in the nineties has long been redimensioned. Earlier harvest times with a view to a more subtle balance between maturity and acidity, has resulted in wines of fresh and tasty complexity.

Bourgogne Aligoté 2016

A vineyard planted in 1938 gives rise to a white of sparkling freshness. Tasted blind, it might hold some surprises.

Meursault 2015

Here is a Villages at antipodes of the anachronistic cliché that wants Meursault whites opulent and buttery. This shows maturity, but it is balanced by a vibrant sapidity that revives the dynamics and depth on the palate.

Meursault "Clos des Ambres" 2015

In the *lieu-dit* En l'Ormeau, on the plain extending to the east of the town, Arnaud has the largest plot of land, though with its deep clay soils it is not a prestigious site. And yet this *cuvée*, based on a vineyard planted in 1952, has a luminous stylistic purity.

Meursault "La Sève du Clos" 2015

Remaining in the *lieu-dit* En l'Ormeau, this section was largely ignored before Ente came on the scene. This is a further selection of old vines, some over a century old, which Arnaud defines as "a precious library of pruning history and culture." The wine reveals natural concentration and truly powerful internal energy, rating among the most surprising tasted for this edition.

Meursault 1er Cru La Goutte d'Or 2015

The only Meursault Premier Cru on the Ente list comes from relatively young vineyards, planted in 1992. Still we find the distinctive features of the *climat*, modulated in floral perfumes, tea rose in a classic balance with the vibrations of an almost chalky minerality.

Volnay 1er Cru Les Santenots du Milieu 2015

It is not at all obvious that a ranking white wine specialist has a similarly deft touch with Pinot Noir. The undisputed qualities of the *climat* certainly help, but here there is also high-class *savoir faire* behind a red that is a creamy amalgam of strength and finesse.

Henri GERMAIN et Fils

MEURSAULT
4, Rue des Forges - Tel. +33 (0) 3 80 212204
domaine.h.germain-et-fils@orange.fr

8 hectares

Henri Germain, originally from Chorey, moved to Meursault in 1973 when he owned only a hectare of vines and faced a few years of experience before wine became his main occupation. Today the winery has expanded its vineyard area to eight hectares, three-quarters for whites, and has been run by his son Jean-François since 2000. Jean-François received us in the cellar to guide us through a reconnaissance of the 2015 vintage. Classic seems to us the right word to define the style of the *domaine* with a fine sequence of expressive and harmonious wines, of long flavor persistence, able to explore with sensitivity and precision the many facets of the Meursault *terroir*.

Meursault Clos des Mouches 2015

Exceptionally vinified with 25% of whole bunches, when complete de-stemming is the rule of the *domaine*, here is a red from a small triangular *climat* of half a hectare, that Germain possesses *en monopole*, in the area that faces Volnay. Finesse is its usual strength, and even in such a generous vintage it guarantees balanced flavor rich in nuances.

Meursault Chevalières 2015

The somewhat hasty definition of "baroque" wine does not seem to do justice to the white of this *lieu-dit*. It lies in the sector of the various Tessons, Vireuils, Luchets and Meix Chavaux, that is to say the best the commune has to offer at the level of the Villages *appellation*. Jean-François made a wine of extraordinary aromatic vitality, innervated by citric and delicate smoky notes.

Meursault 1er Cru Charmes 2015

If you love whites of enveloping but not cloying qualities, round but not soft, elegant but not showy, here is a wine for you. The palate develops broadly, with elegant hints of hazelnut and a long and tasty finish.

Albert GRIVAULT

MEURSAULT
7, Place du Murger - Tel. +33 (0) 3 80 212312
albert.grivault@wanadoo.fr

6 hectares

Albert Grivault was not yet twenty years old in 1875, when he began to work the vineyards received as an inheritance. Then in 1879, while phylloxera devastated the vineyards of half of Europe, Grivault proved to be a visionary with the purchase of the famous Premier Cru Clos des Perrières, *monopole* of a hectare in the heart of the finest Meursault *climat*, which became the emblem of the *domaine*. Michel Bardet, a descendant of the founder who remains sprightly and amiable despite his advanced age, would have promoted Clos des Perrières to Grand Cru, and even today when he welcomes us to the cellar with the same enthusiasm as ever, his hope remains unchanged. He is devoted to uncompromising classicism in the style of wines, confirmed by an inspired quest for expressive purity and longevity.

Meursault Clos des Murgers 2015

The nearly fifty-year-old vines propitiate balance even in a sunny and precocious *millésime*. The wine is fleshy on the palate, more weighty than tense, but on the finish it revives with a refreshing spark.

Meursault 1er Cru Perrières 2015

The parcel of Grivault is the largest of the *climat* (1.7 ha) and guarantees an average of ten thousand bottles a year. Though not far from the Clos, the vineyard is older (1971) with less clay in the soils. The wine shows delicate floral notes, while the palate redeems grit and tension.

Meursault 1er Cru Clos des Perrières 2014

Reserved to the point of reticence, the wine seizes upon an enormous potential of purity and minerality. This is an authentic *blanc de garde*, in which the classic vintage enhances the equally classic style of the *domaine*, and like all classics, it shows exceptional vitality.

Patrick JAVILLIER

MEURSAULT

9 bis, Rue des Forges - Tel. +33 (0) 3 80 212787
contact@patrickjavillier.com | www.patrickjavillier.com

10 hectares

After generations of serving as *courtiers*, the Javillier family diverted activities from trade to production, as expressed by Patrick Javillier, *vigneron*. The shift, begun in the seventies, was gradually realized through an articulated strategy of acquisitions, leading to the current configuration of about ten hectares of vineyards, 80% for white wine. It also affirmed the precise style and identity of the wines of Javillier in the fierce competition between Meursault's white wine specialists. As advocates of long *sur lies* refinements, Javillier continues to prefer the porosity of concrete tanks to those of stainless steel, even though they recently abandoned the old Vaslin press for pneumatic processing. After a long apprenticeship, Patrick's daughter Marion has replaced her father in managing the *domaine*.

Bourgogne Cuvée Oligocène 2015

The parcel is in the *lieu-dit* Les Pellans (more than half of which is classified as Villages) on the slope that faces Puligny. The wine translates the calcareous soils into tension and flavor.

Meursault Cuvée Tête de Murger 2015

Crasis may be the figure of speech that best represents the selections of the house of Javiller. Tête de Murger is in fact a fantasy name that refers to the mix between the *climats* Les Casses-Têtes of Meursault and Les Murgers of Monthelie, constituents of the *cuvée*. The citric notes announce a responsive white that stimulates salivation with its long flavor persistence.

Savigny-lès-Beaune Les Grands Liards 2015

Marion argues that 2015 is a red wine vintage, which, coming from a white wine specialist, is to be believed. We took it seriously in reviewing this vital and savory red with lively aromas of pepper and raspberry and a refreshing finish.

Antoine JOBARD

MEURSAULT

2, Rue de Leignon - Tel. +33 (0) 3 80 212126
antoine.jobard@orange.fr

6 hectares

Antoine Jobard, who has run the winery since 2007, cultivates six hectares of vines for artisanal wines produced at an average of thirty thousand bottles a year. Vineyard management is traditional in the use of sulfur and copper, while in the cellar Antoine advocates long aging *sur lies*, so on average the wines remain on the fine lees for a period of twenty months. Decanting, *bâtonnage* and clarifications are foreign to his way of working. Jobard views his wines in the long term, so don't look for wines with slim silhouettes and limber agility. Without renouncing the internal dynamics, Jobard's wines show a tendency to greater density and amplitude, designed as they are for a medium-long aging.

Puligny-Montrachet 2015

Antoine's vineyard is in the *lieu-dit* Le Trezin of the hamlet of Blagny, a parcel planted at a height of about four hundred meters, near the border with Saint-Aubin. Even from this precocious vintage, the wine remains fresh and taut, a Villages that tends to preserve its quality beyond the average of the *appellation*.

Meursault Les Tillets 2015

Another high-altitude *climat* above the Premier Crus of Meursault. Yet, despite the lean soils, the wine shows a richness derived from the grape skins, with a savory grit of somewhat tannic ascendancy, stimulating salivation.

Meursault 1er Cru Genevrières 2015

The Jobard vineyard is located in the lower part of the cru (Dessous). Antoine makes a complete wine, able to combine the richness of fiber and matter typical of his whites with a more pervasive flavor articulation, enhancing the texture and length at the finish.

Rémi JOBARD

MEURSAULT

12, Rue Sudot - Tel. +33 (0) 3 80 212023
remijobardvins@orange.fr

9.5 hectares

The Jobard dynasty dates back to grandfather Pierre, who in the sixties divided his vineyards between his two sons François and Charles. François passed control to his son Antoine and Charles to his son Rémi, who as a youth took an active role in the winery in the late nineties. The current configuration of the *domaine* is fragmented, with nine hectares of vineyards divided into different *appellations*, though the core remains the whites of various areas of Meursault, which have contributed most to the winery's reputation. Rémi vinifies them in Austrian oak barrels (a rather unique case in the area) in search of aromatic purity, convinced as he is that those woods better respect the original taste of wines. Though the 2015 crop was reduced by 40%, wines of the vintage show a happy balance between creaminess and clarity.

Bourgogne Blanc 2015

From a hectare and a half of vineyards split into different parcels, but all in Meursault neighborhood comes a white that is unusually rich for its category, to the point that Jobard proudly treats it in all respects as a Meursault.

Meursault Les Narvaux 2015

The recent purchase (2008) of a large parcel of three quarters of a hectare, planted in the early sixties on the calcareous stones of this fascinating *climat*, results in a very fresh, tense and slender wine, of exciting mineral progression.

Meursault 1er Cru Le Poruzot-Dessus 2015

The Dessus (upper) portion is usually considered the best *lieu-dit* of the *climat*, showing geological similarities with the neighboring Genevrières Dessus. Rémi produces an enchanting white with almost peppery spiciness in its precious touches of aromatic originality, while the fruit's pulp is innervated with freshness and it leads to a finish that retains an enthralling dynamism.

Domaine des Comtes LAFON

MEURSAULT

5, Rue Pierre Joigneaux - Tel. +33 (0) 3 80 212217
comtes.lafon@gmail.com | www.comtes-lafon.fr

16.4 hectares

A man of rare charisma, with thirty vintages of experience behind him, Dominique Lafon is a leading light in the Burgundy of wine. Behind that slightly ruffled air of a veteran navigator, he reveals himself as a sincere and authentic interpreter of his land: ironic, brilliant and profoundly human. After taking charge of the *domaine* in the late eighties, Dominique was among the first, to totally abandon the use of chemicals in the vineyards (1992), to start the conversion to organic farming (1995) and to introduce the principles of biodynamics for all of the estate's vineyards (1998). Sensitive to the teachings of the late Henri Jayer, Dominique today controls nearly 17 hectares of vines, for which he never ceases to thank his great-grandfather Jules, who in marrying a woman of Meursault, bought the best vineyards with the spirit of a collector. The wines are never harnessed by technology, but are increasingly animated by the quest for an authentic expressive transparency. Parcels are distributed in the most valuable *climats* of Meursault, with extensions to Volnay for the reds plus a small plot (a third of a hectare) in Montrachet. To complete the range, he also has a large *domaine* of about twenty hectares in the Mâconnais (Les Héritiers du Comte Lafon, see Page 449) vinified with little regard for the opulent and overripe versions of Chardonnay.

Volnay 1er Cru Santenots du Milieu 2015

Even if we are in a white fiefdom, there is no ignoring this red so generously endowed with color, rhythm and energy and the tannic texture of a thoroughbred. It comes from an important parcel of almost four hectares, exposed to the east on heavy, though not very deep, clay soils. Much more powerful than most Volnays, it would pay to forget this for a time in the cellar.

Meursault Clos de la Barre 2015

A *monopole* of more than 2 hectares on stony, shallow soils, it seems a bit like the Lafon home garden on the side facing Volnay, where a recent coring revealed a calcareous layer sixty meters deep. The flowering is always rather precocious, the ripening rather late. The production of about 15,000 bottles of a wine of hearty flavor is among the least expensive in the range of a high-priced *domaine*.

Meursault 1er Cru Genevrières 2015

Dominique has a weakness for this *climat* and makes no secret of it: "The greatest wine of Meursault is Perrières, the best is Genevrières." From half a hectare on the upper slope (Dessus), unanimously considered the most valuable area, comes a three-dimensional and complete version, heralded by inviting citrus notes and closed by a long finish of irradiating minerality.

Meursault 1er Cru Perrières 2015

Assembling three different parcels, all under the sign of calcareous marl, the Perrières of Lafon is confirmed as a white of luminous intensity, able as few other white wines are to bring together power and reactivity. The palate of interminable length is innervated by tension and flavor.

Montrachet Grand Cru 2015

This comes from the extreme south of the *climat*, in the territory of Chassagne, where wines are noted as even richer and denser than those from the slope of Puligny. The vineyard, planted in 1953 by Auguste and Pierre Morey, renders only about a thousand bottles, contended for at prohibitive prices. The complexity of this version consists of thrusts and counter-thrusts, energy and details, viscosity and freshness, with the new oak already incorporated—a monumental wine, destined for long aging.

Thierry et Pascale MATROT

MEURSAULT
12, Rue de Martray - Tel. +33 (0) 3 80 212013
info@domaine-matrot.fr | www.matrot.com

23.2 hectares

Thierry Matrot remains very attached to the town of Meursault, to its wines and his winemaker friends. And even now that his daughters Adèle and Elsa are progressively joining the company (the third daughter is involved in the management of the restaurant Le Chevreuil, also at Meursault) Thierry continues to oversee all operations, including guiding us through tastings, never stopping for a minute. The *domaine* has twenty-three hectares of vineyards, managed with the utmost respect for soils, under organic conditions for over fifteen years but without certifications. The house range of about twenty labels shows a prevalence of whites, representing 60% of the total production, distributed between Meursault and Puligny. But the list also includes an interesting quota of reds, from entirely de-stemmed grapes, often capable of surprising positively. Matrot has completely renounced the use of new wood, no recent decision. He says his father used to buy new *pièces*, "lend" them to Michelot and resume using them not before a year. That explains why the style doesn't emphasize sweet and *boisé* tones, but rather exalts the fiber and substance of the wines. Wines that shine with intensity of which Thierry emphasizes the dense and fleshy aspects without renouncing balance. This was demonstrated by a tasting battery of 2015, a vintage finally abundant after a string of harvests harmed by hail (and before an unlucky 2016, with losses of over 80%). The concentration of the material is complemented by a good measure of acidity in a series of impressive whites that carried over to some successful reds.

Meursault 2015

Fully thirteen parcels from eleven different *lieux-dits* covering over six hectares provide the grapes for this basic Meursault, produced in thirty thousand bottles (though in 2016 not even five thousand) of a round and enveloping wine, well contrasted by a bright citrus vein.

Meursault 1er Cru Charmes 2015

The vocation of the *climat* to produce soft and plush wines of good alcoholic tenor is confirmed by this recent version from Matrot, rich and tasty.

Meursault 1er Cru Perrières 2015

This comes from half a hectare of vines in the lower part of the *climat*, near the plot of Jean-Marc Roulot. The 2015 marks a return to the list after an absence caused both by hail of previous years and by the demanding shipments to the American market. It surprised us with a stripped-down intensity, vertical structure and a long finish of fascinating minerality.

Meursault 2015

This label had also been missing for three years, but the absence was forgiven when we tasted Thierry's deft reading of the *millésime*: "Malolactic fermentations were quick since there was very little malic acid, but tartaric acid guarantees freshness." The wine is focused on black berries and fruit, fleshy and round, with juiciness that gives it momentum.

Blagny 1er Cru La Pièce sous le Bois 2015

Almost one and a half hectares of vineyard in a steep and stony *climat*, similarly suited to both Chardonnay and Pinot Noir. This is one of Thierry's preferred wines, a red showing notes of blueberry and licorice in aromas, gliding onto the palate with a delicately exotic touch of spiciness that is a bit the stylistic code of the *cru*.

MICHELOT

MEURSAULT
31, Rue de la Velle - Tel. +33 (0) 3 3 80 212317
contact@domaine-michelot.com | www.domaine-michelot.com

19 hectares

A decade ago, in 2008, during the biennial preview of the Grands Jours de Bourgogne, we had the pleasure of being received by Bernard Michelot, born in 1926, histrionic personality and historical *mémorialiste* of the land of Meursault, its traditions and its secrets. That tasting went on for several hours, with about twenty old bottles generously uncorked by Bernard and regularly drained by the group, which hour after hour had become more numerous. Michelot left us in 2016, but his wines will talk about him and his work for years to come. In old age he was joined by his son-in-law Jean-François Mestre, who in turn has left more room to his son Nicholas, who, after studies in enology at Montpellier and a long internship in New Zealand, returned to manage the family *domaine*. Among the nineteen hectares of vineyards, practically none of Meursault's best *climats* is missing.

Meursault Clos Saint-Félix 2015

This small *monopole* surrounds the house and cellar and takes its name from Thiroux de Saint Félix, farm manager of King Louis XV who owned it in the early eighteenth century. Partially vinified in *tonneaux*, this graceful white expresses delicate notes of acacia flowers and a slender but incisive palate.

Meursault Les Narvaux 2015

We confess to a weakness for this stony *climat* located high up in a secluded gap near the woods of Montmellian. The Michelot version is animated by a juicy mineral verve of engaging tension.

Meursault Charmes 1er Cru 2015

Those who expect the "usual" large and voluminous Charmes, have picked the wrong bottle. The substance is rich, but the red soils of the parcel facing Puligny innervate the palate with a vibrant iodized freshness.

Francois MIKULSKY

MEURSAULT

7, Route Nationale 74 - Tel. +33 (0) 3 80 212511
contact@domainemikulski.fr | www.domainemikulski.fr

9.5 hectares

After taking over from his uncle Pierre Boillot, François Mikulski during last ten years has expanded vineyards to nearly ten hectares between properties and rents. The winery's more than reliable reputation has been built on fresh and slender wines, exact opposites of those fat and buttery Meursaults that some consider typical. François pays particular attention to the sugar-acid balance, keeping his wines under 13 degrees of alcohol. He is always among the first to harvest. "With Chardonnay, just wait two or three days too long and you lose your balance, slipping into excess. It happened in 2006 and 2009, but I learned the lesson." His reds are agile and poised, on the same stylistic trajectory that favors drinkability.

Bourgogne Pinot Noir 2016

From completely de-stemmed grapes, François derives a Pinot of pleasant aromatic vivacity, inviting, fresh and juicy. He advises drinking it after a few years, but to us it already seemed eminently enjoyable.

Bourgogne Aligoté 2016

The one and a half hectare plot, planted in 1929 and 1948, provides an expressive white that would be a shame to drink only as an aperitif.

Meursault 2016

The largest *cuvée* of the *domaine* derives from several parcels covering all the different types of soils of Meursault and translates into about ten thousand bottles of surprising freshness. As Bill Nanson put it, "Not many words needed here, just a super wine!" We agree.

Meursault 1er Cru Les Poruzots 2015

Sharpness and aromatic clarity are the guiding lights of the work of François, who considers Poruzots the most feminine and graceful of his Premier Cru. Energy and elegance come together in the mineral trail of the long final.

Pierre MOREY

MEURSAULT

13, Rue Pierre Mouchoux - Tel. +33 (0) 3 80 212103
www.morey-meursault.fr | contact@morey-meursault.fr

10 hectares

Auguste Morey, father of Pierre, laid the groundwork for the estate in 1935, when he obtained a sharecropping contract from the Lafon family to manage small parcels in Meursault, between Perrières and Genevrières. In 1971, Pierre replaced his father, but in the mid-1980s, when Dominique Lafon took over the family *domaine*, the contract was not renewed. That gave Pierre an opportunity to collaborate with Domaine Leflaive of Puligny, which he managed for twenty years, until 2008, when he decided to retire to the winery that bears his name. His daughter Anne, who joined him years ago, today manages in first person the ten hectares of vineyards, cultivated organically since the beginning of the nineties. Morey was among the first in Burgundy to use biodynamic preparations changeover was completed in 1998 and certified since 2001. The many wines listed are centered essentially on Meursault. Anne vinifies them with a sure and graceful hand, revealing a fascinating sensitivity in her interpretations. A small *négociant* business complements the range, under the name Morey-Blanc.

Monthelie 2015

In describing the wide range of *domaine* labels, we sometimes neglect that about a third of the vines are dedicated to reds. We recommend one in particular, obtained from nine vineyard parcels spread over six different Monthelie *climats*. Its luminosity won us over, an aspect that Anne considers the most peculiar trait of the 2015 harvest, with crisp and juicy black berry fruit and drinkability that is simply unique.

Bourgogne Aligoté 2015

Grapes come from almost two hectares of a vineyard planted at Meursault in 1957 for a wine vinified at 80% in stainless steel. Those are the background notes of a gritty and refreshing wine that is anything but the ugly duckling of Burgundy's whites. The wine's versatility in pairings at the table would make it the envy of many a Premier Cru.

Meursault Les Terres Blanches 2015

This small *climat* is bordered by Les Gouttes d'Or, from which come wines usually quite fat and voluminous. Morey bought his plot (about half a hectare) in 2006 and was the first to propose a labeled bottling, which here shows volume teeming with energy and a flinty nuance that adds a supplement of elegance.

Meursault Les Tessons 2015

Considered among the best *lieux-dits* in the context of Meursault Villages, Anne Morey's Tesson comes from almost a hectare of vines over forty years old and often takes favorable nods when compared to *climats* of much more noble lineage. We had evidence of this during an impromptu mini-vertical in the winery last February: **2015** offers aromas of pastry wrapped in a creamy texture with frequencies tuned to a wave of long aging; **2012** evolves more rapidly, but in the mix of earthy and stony notes reveals an original personality; **2010** shows off a tense and rocky minerality and a final of enchanting fruit purity; **2008** simply marvelous, with an almost intoxicating aromatic complexity, and crisp liveliness on the palate, sealed by a long iodized finish.

Meursault 1er Cru Perrières 2015

About half a hectare of vineyard in the most coveted *climat* of Meursault, and precisely in the most valuable southern part, between the Clos des Perrières and the border with Puligny. The proximity to the quarry and the complexity of the soils (reddish earth, hard calcareous stones and marls), translate into a tense and mineral wine, vertical and deep, with the pace of a marathoner.

Jean-Marc ROULOT

MEURSAULT
1, Rue Charles Giraud - Tel. +33 (0) 3 80 212165
roulot@domaineroulot.fr

16.3 hectares

Jean-Marc Roulot might have pursued a promising career as an actor and theater author, but instead, in the late nineties, he decided to take control of his father's estate, already appreciated for the class of its Meursault. Over the years he continued to improve quality and the *domaine* became recognized as a cult destination for admirers of the most tense and mineral versions of Meursault, then as the home of one of the most inspired producers of *vin blanc d'auteur*. His pursuit of purity and transparency of expression has distinguished Jean-Marc Roulot as a genuine interpretative talent, not so much for his work with prestigious *climats*, of which the *domaine* possesses little of note, as for his wines from certain *lieux-dits* of the *appellation* Villages, of which the winery has become a point of reference in recent years. In the vineyards, the *domaine* has been organic since 2000, while approaching the goal of biodynamic. In the cellars, the use of new oak has been reduced, as well as the practice of *bâtonnage*. The wines, once noted as austere with a tendency to "fill out in the bottle," seem to have gained in terms of *droiture* and delicacy, gaining over time far more gratifying breadth and harmony. Jean-Marc, after some thirty years, has been anticipating a less dominant role in the winery with his hiring of David Croix, a talented *régisseur* (Domaine des Croix), already appreciated for his work at the Maison Camille Giroud. What some have described as an unexpected *coup de théâtre*, given the histrionic character of Roulot, we have interpreted as a farsighted move that would help the winery to explore even further margins for growth.

Bourgogne Blanc 2015

Produced in twenty-five thousand bottles, this is a calling card for the scrupulous work of Jean-Marc with less noble parcels. Open and fragrant in its notes of white fruit, it leaves the palate impregnated with luminous vitality.

Meursault Luchets 2015

The vineyard is exposed to the northeast, on the border with Auxey-Duresses, and is customarily harvested last. As is sometimes the case with less gifted children,

Jean-Marc has cultivated a fondness for his Luchets, dedicating to it "nothing less than a *pièce* (in the sense of the show, not the barrel)," as Armando Castagno recalls amused. The sunny vintage helped him to develop a wine less "razor-thin" than his standards. If minerality is expressed with more delicacy, the aging potential should not be underestimated.

Meursault Vireuils 2015

This *climat* on the slopes of Mont Mélian at over three hundred meters, has the curious feature of leaner soils in the lower part with outcroppings of calcareous mother rock at several points. While retaining vertical posture, the character appears less severe than usual and this greater harmony translates into terms of elegance.

Meursault Tillets 2015

Half a hectare of forty-year-old vines exposed to the southeast on shallow soils at over three hundred meters—these are background notes of the most "disheveled" of the Roulot Meursaults. Critical literature is kinder to it in hot years—as is the case—when the usual austere and thin traits are enhanced by a lively floral vivacity and smoothness on the palate.

Meursault Clos du Haut Tesson À Mon Plaisir 2015

Here is a *climat* that tends to break the hearts of winemakers and enthusiasts alike, due to its obvious qualifications for a boost to a higher category. Roulot owns almost a hectare of a vineyard 55 years old enclosed by walls. The 2015 shows disarming purity and aromatic complexity, with notes of acacia and mandarin mingling with a smoked touch and a palate of almost lyrical delicacy.

Meursault 1er Cru Perrières 2015

We rarely taste the same version of Perrières more than twice over the course of a few months, all the more difficult in the case of the Roulot, given the limited edition and very demanding prices. Due to a mysterious turn of events between March and December 2017 we were able to add a third occasion to our two earlier visits to the winery. This time we were in Italy with our friend Giancarlo Marino, animator of engaging Burgundy evenings as well as a "pusher" of precious bottles. Well, if you already have two clues to go on, the third can only confirm the earlier so we surrendered to the evidence. This is a magical vintage, heralded by intriguing peppery and *fumé* notes, which decline with surprising precocity as the finesse becomes "ethereal" and the pervasive minerality weaves its way into a sweet-savory amalgam of uncontrollable energy.

Arnaud TESSIER

MEURSAULT

2, Allée des Amandiers - Tel. +33 (0) 3 80 212536
domainetessier@hotmail.fr

7.5 hectares

Interrupting the custom of selling the grapes to *négociants*, Arnaud Tessier began to vinify and bottle wines just ten years ago, after the death of his father. At the time he was just over twenty, but he showed remarkable foresight in developing a winery that in a very short time has been greeted by critics such as Neal Martin, Armando Castagno, Steen Öhman and Jancis Robinson as one of the new names of greatest talent of the entire Côte des Blancs. Priority to the vines has been the mantra of the years in which Arnaud has expanded his vineyards to seven and a half hectares, almost entirely in the commune of Meursault. Vineyards are managed in the spirit of organic, but without certification, for a range of whites of classic style, inspired by purity, flavor and balance.

Bourgogne Champ Perrier 2015

Arnaud's only vineyard outside of Meursault is in Puligny and is allocated to his basic white. Alluring in its aromas of acacia flowers, it has a juicy palate with suggestions of fragrant white melon.

Meursault Les Casse-Têtes 2015

Climbing between Tillets and Tessons, vineyards of more than fifty years old on rocky soils render a wine of tense and nuanced character with engaging vitality on the palate.

Meursault 1er Cru Le Poruzot Dessus 2015

If Arnaud's Charmes is often the softer and more enveloping white, Genevrières the most powerful and long-lived, Poruzot holds the record in terms of mineral complexity and spicy exuberance. The generous 2015 version confirms the rule, with aromatic openings of considerable breadth, from pepper to candied lemon, and an pervading flavor persistence.

10

FROM SAINT-AUBIN TO PULIGNY-MONTRACHET

PULIGNY-MONTRACHET

map *page* 528

In the best whites of Puligny the structure necessary for long aging coexists with aromatic grace and the most nuanced and delicate flavor finesse. This is especially true of the Grand Cru. It should be noted that more than half of the over thirty total hectares of legendary Montrachet Grand Cru vineyards are included in the territory of Puligny. In particular, all of the vineyards of Bienvenues-Bâtard-Montrachet and Chevalier-Montrachet are in Puligny. If the wines obtained from Bienvenues share with those of Bâtard (with which the parcel borders on two sides) greater structural strength and internal density, those labeled Chevalier reveal a decidedly original profile, which translates into more nervous, fresh and mineral whites rather than broad and fleshy. Microclimates are influenced by altitude with cooler conditions at the highest points (up to 300 meters) where soils are thinner. The geological composition of the terrain changes by virtue of a fault line that separates the two *climats*; the mother rock of Chevalier is similar to certain matrices of the Côte de Nuits with a strong presence of oolitic limestone.

Montrachet represents the absolute excellence of white wine, with an exuberant and majestic expressiveness that has inspired praise from experts since the eighteenth century. The *climat* is divided into two distinct parts: one of four hectares in the commune of Puligny, called Montrachet; the other of the same size (differences are micrometric) in the commune of Chassagne, called Le Montrachet, distinguished by the "Le" as an indication of greater merit in vintages that are less hot where ripening is slower. As Armando Castagno summarizes: "Where in Puligny the basic factor that makes itself felt is acidity, in Chassagne in most cases the salinity commands the 'minerality' of the final."

The Puligny-Montrachet *appellation* covers a total area of about 300 hectares—almost entirely dedicated to white wines—of which about 100 hectares are classified Premier Cru. Among the 17 Premier Cru, Le Cailleret and Les Pucelles stand out and are often aligned with the neighboring Grand Cru, with whose wines they often share finesse and complexity. But truly all of the Premier Cru are commendable for white wines that convince, whether they are dynamic and intense, or taut and mineral, or mellow and vital.

SAINT-AUBIN

map *page* 525

Saint-Aubin is without a doubt one of the *appellations* that provides the best quality/price ratio among white wines of the entire region. Located at a distance from the main routes through the Côte d'Or, its vineyards are situated largely within the basin of the *combe* that acts as a watershed between Puligny and Chassagne. Altitudes are higher than average and the morphology of the territory is rather irregular, with significantly cooler microclimates and more pronounced temperature excursions. The best whites often come from the *climats* behind Montrachet, from vineyards facing south on soils rich in calcareous pebbles on a base of white marls. Among the *climats* the Premier Cru En Remilly and Les Murgers des Dents de Chien are the qualitative reference points for the denomination, with tense and mineral wines capable of positive evolution over time. If perhaps less elegant in aromas than the best of Puligny and Chassagne, they are noted for freshness that makes them particularly well suited to matching with food. Production of red wines has been sharply reduced, here as in Chassagne (see Page 392). At the beginning of the seventies, two-thirds of the vineyards were planted in red wine varieties, where today no more than 40 hectares of the 160 total are allocated to reds.

Jean-Claude BACHELET et Fils

SAINT-AUBIN

1, Rue de la Fontaine - Hameau de Gamay - Tel. +33 (0) 3 80 213101
info@domainebachelet.fr | www.domainebachelet.fr

10 hectares

The winery is based in Gamay, a hamlet of stone houses unchanged through the ages. Benoît and Jean-Baptiste took over the *domaine* from their father Jean-Claude Bachelet, who started bottling and marketing on his own in the seventies. They produce eighteen different wines from ten hectares of vineyards. The most successful are undoubtedly the whites, notably those of the *appellation* Saint-Aubin, which reflect meticulous care in the vineyard (converted to biodynamic in 2016). Cellar interventions are kept to a minimum as wines remain in wood for over a year and a half with long refinement on the lees and no decanting. Upright and tense, the best whites conjure an inviting aromatic array of floral and citric scents. Lean and agile in body, they are enlivened by a refreshing saline finish.

Bourgogne Aligoté 2015

Citrusy vitality, acid freshness, tension and *droiture*, this certainly ranks among the vintage's best Aligoté wines.

Saint-Aubin 1er Cru Les Champlots 2014

The *climat* of heavy clay soils faces southwest overlooking the village of Gamay. On the palate, the wine is gracious and snappy.

Saint-Aubin 1er Cru Les Charmois 2014

The Bachelet parcel of almost a hectare, near Chassagne, is exposed to the east on red and calcareous soils. The wine has amplitude and *souplesse* on the palate, while maintaining a sleek finish.

Saint-Aubin 1er Cru Les Murgers des Dents de Chien 2014

Here the soils are thinner but the age of the vineyard is greater. The aromatic expression remains discrete, almost reticent, but on the palate it surprises with a pervasive mineral trace that releases energy and flavor.

François CARILLON

PULIGNY-MONTRACHET

2-3, Place de l'Église - Tel. +33 (0) 3 80 210080
domainef.carillon@free.fr | www.francois-carillon.com

6.5 hectares

The Carillon family, which has resided at Puligny since the sixteenth century, is now represented by the sixteenth generation of *vignerons*. François is one of two sons of Louis Carillon, a well-known figure behind some of the finest whites of Puligny, who, a few years ago, split the property in two, dividing the family heritage between François and his brother Jacques. After more than twenty years of working alongside his father, François has put his *savoir faire* at the service of the new adventure. Vineyards are maintained with respect for the soil, so in all plots where conditions permit, he works the land with the use of a horse. Most of the six and a half hectares of property fall within the Puligny-Montrachet *appellation* and favor well-defined wines with clear expressive personality.

Puligny-Montrachet Les Einseignères 2015

This *lieu-dit*, bordering the Grand Cru vineyards of Bâtard and Bienvenue, is the largest among those included in the municipal *appellation*. The wine shows floral notes that are the common denominator of the whites of Puligny, with a welcome complement of intensity and volume.

Puligny-Montrachet 1er Cru Champ Gain 2015

The vineyard is in the highest sector of the *appellation*, at around 350 meters at the edge of a wooded area where soils are poor and thin. Yet the wine shows density and breadth on the palate balanced by a dynamic finish, played on refreshing flavor notes.

Puligny-Montrachet 1er Cru Les Combettes 2015

The proximity of the border with Charmes-du-Dessus in the commune of Meursault inspires this sort of "frontier white" in which finesse of the best Puligny is allied with the generous fleshiness of the Premier Cru of Meursault.

Jacques CARILLON

PULIGNY-MONTRACHET
1, Impasse Drouhin - Tel. +33 (0) 3 80 210130
carillon.jacques@free.fr | www.jacques-carillon.com

5.25 hectares

The quiet, almost timid character of Jacques Carillon hides a sensitiveness that is regularly found in his wines, free of any redundancy, among the most accomplished expressions of the Puligny district. In the background was the division of the Domaine Louis Carillon in 2010, in which Jacques and his brother François shared the legacy of an enviable spread of twelve hectares of vines, and pursued different paths. Jacques had been active since 1980 in the family *domaine*, years spent alongside his father Louis that have left him a priceless fund of experience and *savoir faire*. Today this maturity translates into a fine range of labels, linked by a quest for nuance and elegance without shortcuts as expressed in the wines' dimensions.

Puligny-Montrachet 2015

Round and enveloping, the wine derives from the assembly of different parcels spread over more than two and a half hectares. The forty year old vines and the cautious use of new wood (around 15%) make this an exemplary white in tune with the *appellation*.

Puligny-Montrachet 1er Cru Les Perrières 2015

This comes from a plot with forty year old vines on soils composed of marls and clay on an outcropping of mother rock. The wine does not yield to softness of any sort, but relies on a promising supply of energy and minerality, to be assessed in perspective.

Puligny-Montrachet 1er Cru Les Referts 2015

The wine combines scents of aromatic herbs (mint and thyme), with elastic fiber of remarkable *souplesse* and a long finish with chalky notes.

Bienvenues-Bâtard-Montrachet Grand Cru 2015

The deep and well drained soils of these two Grand Crus rest one after another. The proverbial power is articulated by an interminable sapid-mineral trail.

Jean CHARTRON

PULIGNY-MONTRACHET

8 bis, Grande Rue - Tel. +33 (0) 3 80 211999
info@jeanchartron.com | www.jeanchartron.com

14 hectares

The *domaine* was founded in 1859 by Jean-Edouard Dupard, who contributed decisively in changing the name of his town Puligny into Puligny-Montrachet (1873). The winery is in its fifth generation of *vignerons* with Jean-Michel Chartron, who has worked his vineyards organically for over a decade without worrying about certification. His basic choices include no chemical treatments in the vineyards and modern and rational winemaking techniques with a moderate use of new oak. Spread over fourteen hectares, the range of *climats* is enviably complete and includes several prestigious parcels in Puligny, such as Clos de la Pucelle and Clos du Cailleret. In recent years, Chartron has focused on a style more faithful to the matrix *terroirs* in whites marked by definition and sharpness.

Saint Aubin 1er Cru Les Murgers des Dents de Chien 2015

As fans of this *climat*, situated just above Montrachet, we greatly appreciated this wine of Chartron, which shows bright elegance and freshness.

Puligny-Montrachet 2015

The grapes come from the *lieu-dit* Les Levrons, adjacent to Premier Cru of Meursault Les Charmes, with which it shares broad and fleshy qualities, especially in such rich vintages.

Puligny-Montrachet 1er Cru Clos du Cailleret 2015

The notably stony plot of Le Cailleret is a direct continuation of Montrachet and Chevalier-Montrachet, though it doesn't share their magical expositions. Chartron's share is no longer *en monopole*, yet he considers the Clos his prime wine due to its internal density and long flavor persistence.

Alain CHAVY

PULIGNY-MONTRACHET

5, Rue des Creux de Chagny - Tel. +33 (0) 3 80 213927

10 hectares

Alain Chavy, who worked in the company of his father Gérard for over thirty years, started his own winery in 2003, separating from his brother Jean-Louis a few years after his father's retirement. Today he runs a *domaine* centered entirely in Puligny, with the cellar a stone's throw from the town square, and ten hectares of vineyards dedicated largely to local whites. Vineyard management in *lutte raisonnée* has led to gradual change of approach with increased working of the soils and reduced treatments. In the cellar, however, his priorities have remained the same: to enhance the clarity, precision and elegance of whites.

Puligny-Montrachet 2015

The largest *cuvée* of the *domaine* draws from as many as eight different parcels of origin for twenty thousand bottles on average a year, almost a third of the entire production. Alain was pleased with his interpretation of the hot vintage by anticipating the harvest, and the wine backs his choice: maturity and *souplesse* remain well harmonized and the overall balance does not lack dynamics.

Puligny-Montrachet 1er Cru Les Champs Gains 2015

The vineyard is high, above three hundred meters, with a light layer of reddish earth and a tendency to suffer in dry summers with the risk of water stress. Alain managed the situation with sensitivity in a wine that translates the calcareous vitality of the soils without losing tension.

Puligny-Montrachet 1er Cru Les Folatières 2015

In the largest *climat* of the *appellation*, Chavy's parcel is on a challengingly steep slope, source of a white innervated with minerality and flavor, and at the same time ethereal and enveloping, without losing the clarity of detail that marks the *domaine*'s style.

Marc COLIN et Fils

SAINT-AUBIN
9, Rue de la Chatenière - Tel. +33 (0) 3 80 213043
damien@marc-colin.com | www.marc-colin.com

19 hectares

The name Marc Colin is well known to fans of white Burgundy. Not so much to the label drinkers as to authentic enthusiasts, able to recognize talent and quality even when the wines come from second-hand *appellations*, as Saint-Aubin was long considered. Today, fortunately, the picture has changed, and thanks to the work of producers like Colin, Saint-Aubin has become recognized for authored whites by a growing audience of consumers. For more than a decade, Marc has left the winery in the hands of three of his four children: Caroline, Joseph and Damien (the eldest, Pierre-Yves, has been running his own *domaine* since 2005, based in Chassagne, see Page 400). The range of vineyards remains very respectable, with nearly twenty hectares accounting for some thirty different labels, with a strong emphasis on whites.

Saint-Aubin 1er Cru La Chatenière 2015

The Colin portion, which extends over an abundant hectare exposed to the south-west on steep slopes, is worked with the help of a horse. Half of the wine was refined in large barrels (twenty-five hectoliters). Though rich in substance, the weight doesn't penalize the articulation on the palate.

Saint-Aubin 1er Cru En Montceau 2015

The small *lieu-dit* that dominates the hamlet of Gamay is actually part of the *climat* Les Champlots. Though notoriously late in ripening, from this sunny vintage the wine has maintained the finesse and tension of cooler years.

Saint-Aubin 1er Cru En Remilly 2015

The thin and chalky soils of this fine *climat* often cause some vine stress in dry vintages like this. Yet the wine has vital tension and a range of floral nuances that refers to the proximity of Puligny.

Benoit ENTE

PULIGNY-MONTRACHET

4, Rue de la Mairie - Tel. +33 (0) 3 80 219373
www.benoit-ente.fr

6 hectares

With the 1999 harvest, Benoît Ente officially began his adventure as a *vigneron* with a knack for white wines of the Puligny area. The younger brother of Arnaud Ente, Benoît worked for a few years in the *domaine* of his grandparents, who until 1997 sold the grapes almost entirely to a *négociant* of Beaune. His first years were marked by a quest for expressive identity, which at that time often translated into terms of softness, density and spiciness. Then a radical change occurred with the 2003 harvest, here as elsewhere marked by wines of excessive weight, persuading Benoît to reassess his winemaking style. By the following year his wines showed greater equilibrium, focused on freshness and delicacy, an equilibrium that has remained his lodestar.

Puligny-Montrachet 2015

The assembly of two different *lieux-dits* (Les Tremblots and Les Houillères), home of the oldest vines planted by Benoît's grandfather in 1943, renders a white wine in which flavor embraces the enticing floral notes.

Puligny-Montrachet 1er Cru Clos de la Truffière 2015

The *climat* is usually noted for whites among the most floral of the *appellation*, but this version instead shows aromas of flint and variations on *fumé*, before relaxing on the palate in a more convincing gustative extension.

Puligny-Montrachet 1er Cru En la Richarde 2015

As far as we know, Benoît Ente and the Domaine d'Auvenay are the only *domaines* to claim En la Richarde on the label, one of the four *lieux-dits* that make up the nearly eighteen hectares of the renowned Premier Cru Les Folatières. Somewhat reticent in aroma, the wine is more vital and tense on the palate with an innervated final of minerality.

Hubert LAMY

SAINT-AUBIN

20, Rue des Lavières - Tel. +33 (0) 3 80 213255
hubertlamydomaine@gmail.com | www.domainehubertlamy.com

18.5 hectares

Olivier Lamy's reserved and introspective nature hides a deep passion for his work. A tireless experimenter with a meticulous knowledge of the land, Olivier joined his father Hubert in 1995 and today leads with confidence a *domaine* with more than eighteen hectares of vineyards. The whites of the *appellation* Saint Aubin remain the strong point of the *domaine*. Olivier has integrated or replaced the traditional 228-liter *pièces* with larger *tonneaux* (of three to six hectoliters), which guarantee greater balance in the wines. The vineyards have been entirely worked without the use of chemical treatments for twenty years. Olivier has been experimenting, by now over several vintages, with high-density planting, which in a portion of the plot Derrière Chez Edouard reaches levels of 28,000 vines per hectare. This may appear to be forced, but tastings of different vintages have revealed a texture of great complexity and naturalness on the palate.

Saint-Aubin 1er Cru Derrière Chez Edouard 2015

The high density vines favor intensity without sacrificing precision: the palate is broad and combines warmth and delicacy.

Saint-Aubin 1er Cru Les Murgers des Dents de Chien 2015

The small parcel of Lamy was planted in the eighties on the reddish soil of the *climat*, which at up to 350 meters of altitude, dominates the high sector of the Premier Cru of Puligny. Heightened minerality and pronounced freshness are its strengths.

Saint-Aubin 1er Cru Clos de la Chatenière 2015

The *clos* includes an abundant hectare of vineyards over the age of fifty, on a steep slope facing southwest. In the Lamy version, breadth and energy coexist with admirable aromatic purity.

LARUE

SAINT-AUBIN

32, Rue de la Chatenière - Tel. +33 (0) 3 80 213074
dom.larue@wanadoo.fr | www.larue-vins.com

17 hectares

The base is in Saint-Aubin, off the beaten track of the Côte des Blancs, and the *domaine* is run by the brothers Didier and Denis Larue with the help of their children Vivien and Bruno. Production emphasizes number 17, both in terms of hectares of vineyards (two-thirds dedicated to whites) and number of labels, of which more than half refer to the *appellation* Saint-Aubin, where the Larue family is among the leading performers.

Saint-Aubin 1er Cru Vieilles Vignes 2015

This is not an assemblage of multiple *crus*—as is almost always the case in Burgundy when the reference to the Premier Cru remains generic—but comes from the *climat* Sur Gamay, a name omitted to avoid confusion with homonym red variety. This is perhaps the most proportioned and classic Saint-Aubin of the winery with floral aromas preparing the palate for lively flavors that recall fruit with white pulp, beautifully crunchy and tasty.

Saint-Aubin 1er Cru Les Cortons 2015

The vineyards are in the *climat* En Remilly, which overlooks Montrachet and comes off as one of the noblest places of the entire *appellation*. The portion closest to the hamlet of Gamay is called Les Cortons, where the Larue have about half a hectare for a vital and engaging white with enticing contrasts between harmonious array of aromas and vibrant flavors.

Saint-Aubin 1er Cru Murgers des Dents de Chien 2015

The outcropping of sharp pointed stones on the steep slope suggested the image of "dog's teeth" for the name of the *climat*. The Larue have a wide parcel of more than a hectare dedicated to a white of intense iodized notes, almost saline, with pervasive minerality stimulating an interminable persistence on the palate.

LEFLAIVE

PULIGNY-MONTRACHET

Place Pasquier de la Fontaine - Tel. +33 (0) 3 80 213013
domaine@leflaive.fr | www.leflaive.fr

24 hectares

It is impossible to write about this *domaine* without paying tribute to Anne-Claude Leflaive, who passed away in the spring of 2015. A convinced interpreter of biodynamics, under her leadership the vineyards were converted to this type of agriculture in the mid-1990s. It was Anne-Claude who, in 2008, founded *L'École du Vin et des Terroirs* in Puligny, to motivate winemakers from all over the world to an approach both ecological and "humanistic" to winemaking. The Leflaive family has been active in the Puligny area since the early eighteenth century. It was Vincent Leflaive, father of Anne-Claude, who originated production of an impressive series of legendary white wines that over the last fifty years came to rank with the best of Burgundy. Yet it seems likely that the heritage of Anne-Claude is going to be appreciated in coming decades. The reorganization carried out after her death has kept the *domaine* in the hands of the Leflaive family in the name, at least in theory, of a certain continuity. The direction has passed to Brice de La Morandière, great-grandson of the founder Joseph Leflaive, who lived for almost thirty years in China, Turkey and United States, holding strategic roles in the management of large industrial groups. The modus operandi in vineyards and cellars has remained the same as consolidated by Anne-Claude, even if from the 2017 harvest control has passed to Pierre Vincent, after a decade of directing the Domaine de la Vougeraie. Here as elsewhere in Burgundy, the times are changing. We shall see.

Puligny Montrachet 1er Cru Les Pucelles 2015

Leflaive's prime wine comes from three hectares of vineyards that represent almost half of the *climat*. With no special reverence for the neighboring Grand Cru, even in a year so abundant as 2015, the wine maintains incisiveness and contrast.

Bienvenues-Bâtard-Montrachet Grand Cru 2015

The wine shows a decidedly feminine *allure*, in terms of grace and precision. The old vines planted in 1958 certainly offer an important contribution to the complexity of an expansive palate that is a model of harmony.

Bâtard-Montrachet Grand Cru 2015

The reputation of the wines of this Grand Cru for generosity and almost opulent richness is not immune to clichés, even if it finds full confirmation here. We bet this version will seduce fans of the genre for many years to come.

Chevalier-Montrachet Grand Cru 2015

We're not alone in our weakness for this star of the Montrachet constellation, always in balance between depth of flavor and momentum of evolution, solidity and vertical extension, richness and minerality *hors-catégories*. This interpretation once again confirms the value of a *terroir* among the most fascinating and complete of the Côte de Beaune.

Etienne SAUZET

PULIGNY-MONTRACHET

11, Rue de Poiseul - Tel. +33 (0) 3 80 213210
etienne.sauzet@wanadoo.fr | www.etiennesauzet.com

10 hectares

This admired winery of Puligny has been guided since the mid-seventies by Gérard Boudot, husband of the founder's granddaughter, who has been joined by his daughter Emilie and her husband Benoît Riffault, *vigneron* from Sancerre. The range of labels produced is complete, taking in all the most prestigious *climats* of Puligny, thanks also to a *négociant* activity that relies on grapes from the ten hectares of property. The agronomic management has been biodynamic since 2010, although not certified, and the wines reflect an extremely precise *savoir-faire*, with appreciable peaks of elegance.

Bourgogne La Tufera 2015

The combination of a generous and early ripening harvest and vinification without frills (no new *pièce* is used for this *cuvée*) renders a luxuriant wine with notes of white fruit (melon, pear) and enjoyable immediacy

Puligny-Montrachet 1er Cru Champ Canet 2015

A continuation of Meursault Perrières, this is among the vineyards favored by Gérard Boudot, who obtains a white that collects in one sip the best prerogatives of Puligny: aromatic definition of floral and citric notes and an extra touch of class on the palate, which closes with promising mineral vibrations.

Puligny-Montrachet 1er Cru Les Combettes 2015

The *climat* of ancient and original geological texture borders Les Charmes Dessus of Meursault, with which it shares the breadth and generosity of the wines. In Sauzet version, a tasty backlash enlivens the sip.

Puligny-Montrachet 1er Cru Les Folatières 2015

In Puligny's largest Premier Cru, Boudot works with grapes from two different parcels. His 2015 shows off an engaging palette of floral details along with full and enveloping flavor.

11

FROM CHASSAGNE-MONTRACHET TO MARANGES

CHASSAGNE-MONTRACHET

map *page* 528

In sharing with Puligny the Grand Cru Montrachet, one might expect the wines of Chassagne to share a similar profile with that of their prestigious neighbors. On the contrary, only part of the area of the *appellation* is suitable for white wines. The remaining slice of *climats* has traditionally been more congenial to reds, which in the nineteenth century were in an overwhelming majority and only fifty years ago still accounted for two-thirds of production. Today, however, the proportions have been reversed and the reds account for only a hundred hectares of vineyards, or less than a third of the total area, which is around 320 hectares. Commercial reasons are obviously at the base of this asymmetry. After a long period of lassitude, the seventies signaled an inversion of tendency and a clear recovery in the market for whites, which today are easier to sell and command far higher prices. That's why 80% of the grapes coming from the 15 *climats* of Chassagne classified in Premier Cru today are white. If the reds of Chassagne tend to be tannic, robust and ripe, showing a certain hardness in flavor (allowing for some important exceptions), the whites represent on the contrary "munificent examples of the concept of intensity of expression in a wine." (Armando Castagno). They are undoubtedly more sapid and austere than whites of Meursault and Puligny, often evoking scents of yellow flowers and cereals while evincing chalky minerality that lends persistence to the flavor. These qualities are exalted in wines from the Grand Cru: half of Montrachet, and a little less than half of Bâtard-Montrachet and the entire portion (1.57 hectares as the smallest white Grand Cru of Burgundy) of Criots-Bâtard-Montrachet, for a total of a few dozen hectares. Elegance is the key with complexity that unfolds over time in a fascinating texture.

Among the Premier Cru, the first point to record concerns the cumbersome classification system, which allows labels to claim an exaggerated number of sub-parcels. Best whites often come from *climat* Cailleret, where they show brilliant minerality and a potential for longevity of a higher level, though La Grande Montagne and La Maltroie also show harmony in Chardonnay. Better suited to Pinot Noir, on the other hand, is the Clos Saint-Jean whose red was already recognized by Lavalle as a *tête de cuvée* in the mid-nineteenth century and especially appreciated for its expressive finesse.

SANTENAY MARANGES

maps *page* 530 e 531

The wines of Santenay come from a large area of vineyards: about 400 hectares, of which 140 are classified as Premier Cru. They are well exposed and sunny vineyards, on terrains with efficient drainage favoring the production of red wines, which today account for over 80% of the total. Many reliable observers consider the reds of Santenay underrated. Wines that are ready and expressive young, they can amaze as much for their aromatic vivacity as for their durability. The different geological matrices are twisted in composing a particularly confused picture (J. Wilson, *Terroir*), but by schematizing a bit we can distinguish three macro-zones. To the northeast, near the border with Chassagne, the *climats* of greatest qualitative interest extend to the first houses of the village and sometimes offer surprisingly complete and long-lived wines, as is the case of the Premier Cru Les Gravières, combining intensity and elegance. To the northwest of the village, the approximately thirty hectares of vineyards in Premier Cru are divided between the two *climats* Beaurepaire and La Maladière for wines that are focused more on fruit than on structure. Finally, to the south of the village, the vineyards of the Clos Rousseau (Grand and Petit, though curiously the latter is larger) favor more tannic and intense reds whose character is also shaping the bulk of wines produced in the 250 hectares for Santenay Villages.

Under the name Maranges (dialectal version of *murgers*, or low stone walls), the wines of the three districts have been grouped since 1988, each with its respective name: Cheilly-lès-Maranges, Dezize-lès-Maranges and Sampigny-lès-Maranges. These are rather complicated names to remember, which have only recently acquired greater visibility. They remain in theory on the margins of the Côte d'Or, which from an administrative point of view ends in Santenay, while in fact, it extends south into Saône-et- Loire. Although this area was planted mainly in Chardonnay in the late nineteenth century, today production is balanced toward red wine. Covering less than 200 hectares, almost half classified as Premier Cru, they render rather colored versions of solid tannic framework, sometimes short of finesse but always trusty companions at table, especially in pairing with local food.

BACHELET-MONNOT

DEZIZE-LÈS-MARANGES

15, Grande Rue - Tel. +33 (0) 3 85 911682
bachelet-monnot@wanadoo.fr

20 hectares

Brothers Marc and Alexandre Bachelet have been at the helm of the family *domaine* based in Dezize-Les-Maranges since 2005. Taking over from their father Jean-François, they further expanded the vineyard holdings and now find themselves managing a demanding estate with 20 hectares. These parcels are distributed throughout the Côte de Beaune, with a slight prevalence for Pinot Noir. They produce more than 100,000 bottles covering about twenty labels, most already sold before bottling, thanks to a wide and diversified offer. Results are particularly notable in whites that are fresh and zesty rather than intense and fleshy.

Chassagne-Montrachet 2015

An early harvest (on August 28) of grapes from seven different *lieux-dits*, allowed Bachelet brothers to produce 12,000 bottles of a very successful white wine. Open aromatics, tactile *souplesse*, tasty harmony all combined in a wine of extreme pleasure.

Meursault Clos du Cromin 2015

Half of the plot was planted in 1927, grapes from the old vines help to integrate a precious mineral edge into the vigorous energy of a wine of aromatic vitality (citrus, sage) and savory freshness in a dynamic balance.

Bourgogne Rouge 2015

In this blend of grapes from the Hautes Côtes and Maranges, the 2015 version incorporates a small, un-stemmed portion that enhances the aromatic *finesse*, while the amalgam of fruit and spices on the palate is captivating and stimulating.

Maranges 1er Cru Clos de la Boutière 2015

Bachelet owns half of the Clos, with almost one and a half hectares of 70-year-old vines on the stoniest terrain of the entire *appellation* (as well as the longest rows at about 400 meters). They produce a classy red wine, with aromas of oriental flowers and spices and a gritty and savory palate.

BACHEY-LEGROS

SANTENAY
12, Rue de la Charrière - Tel. +33 (0) 3 80 206414
domaine.bachey-legros@orange.fr | www.bachey-legros.com

18 hectares

The *domaine* in its sixth generation is emerging with a range of reliable and well-designed wines. Christiane Bachey-Legros, assisted by her sons Lénaïc and Samuel, has 18 hectares of vineyards mainly in Santenay, as well as parcels in the *appellations* of Chassagne and Maranges. The prevalence of old vines (mostly planted between 1935 and 1955) and effective work in the vineyards help to give depth to the entire production, almost equally distributed between whites and reds. If the expressive personality is not yet so pronounced, the wines still reveal an appreciable balance between territoriality and precision.

Santenay Sous la Roche 2015
The *lieu-dit* on the thin soils directly over the mother rock is the source of a wine of clear mineral ascendancy, fleshed out by tasty notes of ripe white fruit.

Santenay Clos des Hâtes 2015
Looking at the map of Santenay, it is not easy to understand why this *lieu-dit*, flanked by a band of Premier Crus, does not enjoy the same classification. Jasper Morris claims that the cause is the greater depth of soil. But the fact remains that the parcel of Bachey-Legros, planted with vineyards over 80, from this vintage rendered an elegant and velvety wine that assuages the usual tannic stiffness thanks to rich and mellow fruit.

Santenay 1er Cru Clos Rousseau Vieilles Vignes 2015
This is an assemblage of three different parcels: Les Fourneaux (planted in 1914), Le Grand Clos Rousseau (in 1980) and Le Petit Clos (in 1955). Often considered the producer's prime red, in this vintage it shows more energy than finesse without sacrificing dynamism or gustative persistence.

BLAIN-GAGNARD

CHASSAGNE-MONTRACHET
17, Route de Santenay - Tel. +33 (0) 3 80 213407
domaine-blain-gagnard@wanadoo.fr

8.7 hectares

Jean-Marc Blain, a native of the Loire, founded the *domaine* in 1980, after marrying Claudine Gagnard, daughter of *vignerons* living in Chassagne for generations. The estate vineyards are located mainly in the *appellation* Chassagne-Montrachet, from which come a wide range of Premier Crus (also in red) and three Grand Crus in the enclave of Montrachet. Jean-Marc has always made the pursuit of elegance his top priority: elegance moderated by a careful dosage of new oak, between 15 and 30%, and by a thrifty use of *bâtonnage*. Thanks to this the wines reach a fine balance between density and freshness, without giving up the antioxidant contribution of yeasts. Today their son Marc-Antonin has joined the operation after significant experience between Australia and New Zealand.

Chassagne-Montrachet 2015

The so-called Villages of the Chassagne *appellation* often have more energy than originality, as in this white, savory and creamy, of captivating conviviality.

Chassagne-Montrachet 1er Cru La Boudriotte 2015

The base parcel is located in the *lieu-dit* Champ Jendreau, and again in this vintage renders a full and enveloping wine, but without heaviness or redundancy.

Criots-Bâtard-Montrachet Grand Cru 2015

In the smallest of the Burgundian Grand Crus allocated to white wines (about one and a half hectares), the Blain-Gagnard parcel is a fifth of a hectare, producing a little more than a thousand bottles of a well-focused wine of almost tropical sweetness of fruit (papaya, peach) embellished by a lively spicy touch, which recalls ginger in the full flavor.

CHEVROT et Fils

CHEILLY-LES-MARANGES

19, Route de Couches - Tel. +33 (0) 3 85 911055
contact@chevrot.fr | www.chevrot.fr

17 hectares

The brothers Pablo and Vincent Chevrot are heirs of a line of winemakers active in the area since the mid-nineteenth century. Today they manage a *domaine* of 17 hectares of vineyards, more than two thirds dedicated to Pinot Noir and scattered over 15 labels that include some of the best *climats* between Santenay and Maranges. Since 2011, vineyard management has been certified as organic and all wines (even the few whites) now seem to express themselves with greater spontaneity and originality, thus gathering more and more support.

Bourgogne Aligoté Cuvée des Quatre Terroirs 2016

Here is an Aligoté with a southerly temperament, warmed by enveloping fruit maturity (apricot) and rich substance, while remaining natural and energetic on the palate.

Maranges 1er Cru La Fussière 2015

La Fussière looks something like a terracotta vase among iron containers, given the clear prevalence of reds obtained from the large *climat*. But it shows surprising grace, with a lively saline twist to enliven the final flavor.

Santenay Vieilles Vignes 2015

Half a hectare of 45-year-old vines renders a red wine with enticing aromatic nuances, including hints of wild strawberries and a delicate spicy trace (cumin) lending vivacity to the flavor.

Maranges 1er Cru Le Croix Moines 2015

The small *climat* of just a hectare is very steep and represents a portion of vineyard on its own within the Premier Cru La Fussière. Facing south and located above the village of Dezize, the tiny parcel of Chevrot renders a charming red, where the usual endowment of small red fruits is matched by more original aromatics, flavors of oriental spices (curry, ginger) and balsamic touches of refreshing delicacy.

Bruno COLIN

CHASSAGNE-MONTRACHET

3, Impasse des Crêts - Tel. +33 (0) 3 80 247561

contact@domainebrunocolin.com | www.domaine-bruno-colin.com

9 hectares

Bruno Colin "signed" his first vintage in 2004, after a long apprenticeship in the family business following his father Michel. From the start, the critical approach to his work has been very high: always seeking precision and clarity of expression. The wines of Bruno are particularly modern and pleasurable whites that with time gain points in terms of complexity. From about nine hectares of total vineyards, cultivated according to the principles of integrated pest control, today there are about twenty different labels, more than half of which are issued from the commune of Chassagne-Montrachet (with seven Premier Cru), providing the enthusiast a range as complete as any of the *appellation*.

Chassagne-Montrachet 1er Cru Les Vergers 2015

From about a third of a hectare in the *lieu-dit* Les Pasquelles, oriented to the northeast on shallow soils with outcropping rocks, Bruno provides a wine of lovely fruit, with enticing citrus nuances and hints of almond and hazelnut.

Chassagne-Montrachet 1er Cru La Boudriotte 2015

The wine comes from a quarter of a hectare of vines over 40 years old, planted in the *lieu-dit* Champ Jeandreau, though the label bears the name of the neighboring *climat*. The floral character and the luscious ease of drinking combine with a certain *droiture*, with appreciable balance between amplitude and tension.

Chassagne-Montrachet 1er Cru Blanchot-Dessus 2015

This micro-parcel of a tiny Premier Cru among the most prestigious of the *appellation* (located at the foot of Montrachet) translates into a wine of great concentration, but also complexity and tonic freshness, due to the sunny character of the vintage.

Philippe COLIN

CHASSAGNE-MONTRACHET

ZA le Haut Des Champ - Tel. +33 (0) 3 80 219049
domainephilippecolin@orange.fr

13 hectares

Philippe Colin's *domaine* represents about half of the former property of Colin-Deléger. When in 2004 their parents retired, Philippe and his brother Bruno decided to take different paths, dividing in half the approximately eighteen hectares of the family winery, almost entirely in the territory of Chassagne. Today Philippe has increased his vineyard to 13 hectares, managed under integrated cultivation for wines represented by 28 different labels. A brilliant businessman and tireless worker, Philippe started a new adventure in South Africa in 2014, taking over the Topiary Wines company in the Stellenbosch district. We have no doubt that he'll succeed in this challenge too. In the meantime we admire his whites, defined and stylized, but always focused on drinkability with a polished refinement that never represents an end in itself.

Chassagne-Montrachet 1er Cru Les Chaumées 2015

The vineyard with steep stony soils is located in the northernmost sector of the *appellation*, on the border with Saint-Aubin. Philippe fashions a white based on balance, whose tension does not detract from immediate pleasure.

Chassagne-Montrachet 1er Cru Chenevottes 2015

The *climat* tends to render wines that are more soft than tenacious, yet this juicy version proposed by Colin is nicely balanced between the delicacy of the pulp and the freshness of the citrus notes.

Chevalier-Montrachet Grand Cru 2015

The potential of substance and energy is considerable and intended to a progressive refinement in the coming decades. In line with what is claimed by the most accredited wine critics, the mineral tone is there at the service of fascinating three-dimensional flavor.

Pierre-Yves COLIN MOREY

CHASSAGNE-MONTRACHET

4, Rue de la Murée - Tel. +33 (0) 3 80 219010
contact@pierreyvescolinmorey.fr

6 hectares

Pierre-Yves is the eldest son of Marc Colin, a prominent name in Saint-Aubin (see Page 383). His career as a soloist took a first step in 2001, when, while working in the family *domaine*, he began a small activity of *négoce* (which continues today) along with his wife Caroline Morey. But only in 2005 did the project begin to take shape, thanks to the detachment of a portion from prized family vineyard holdings. Considered among the most talented winemakers of his generation, Pierre-Yves now manages six hectares of property, to which must be added a variable quota of grapes purchased for the *négoce*. He focuses clearly on the *élevage*, which occurs in barrels of 350 liters (*demi-muids*), without *bâtonnage* and with a limited use of new oak, often extending refinement beyond 18 months to avoid clarifications and filtration. The clear style and the *droiture* of his whites are increasingly appreciated, both by the press and by consumers whose palates are attuned to the pure expression of *terroir*.

Saint-Aubin Le Banc 2015

From the highest part of the *appellation* in the most extensive *lieu-dit* of Saint-Aubin, the *domaine* derives a white which in the beginning is a little reticent on the nose but soon revealing an open palate rich in substance and tension.

Saint-Aubin 1er Cru En Remilly 2015

A wine of vibrant flavor that reinforces the widespread opinion that En Remilly rates among the most complete *climats* of the *appellation*. This version from Pierre-Yves has the stigmata of a *blanc de garde*: time is on its side.

Chassagne-Montrachet 1er Cru Les Baudines 2015

The vineyard with lean and marly soils is adjacent to the woods of Chassagne, in a sector that remained uncultivated until the 1960s. Prompt and almost nervous on the palate, the wine shows a truly engaging dynamism.

FONTAINE-GAGNARD

CHASSAGNE-MONTRACHET

19, Route de Santenay - Tel. +33 (0) 3 80 213550
domainefontainegagnard@wanadoo.fr | www.domaine-fontaine-gagnard.com

12 hectares

Following an intricate story of inheritance and successions, Laurence Gagnard is the current owner of this esteemed *domaine* along with her husband Richard Fontaine, a former French airline pilot. The assortment of parcels is among the most complete of the entire *appellation* and includes vineyards in Montrachet, Bâtard and Criots-Bâtard, as well as a dozen Premier Crus in Chassagne, to complete the picture. The daughter Céline, who is more and more involved in the management, welcomed us to the cellar and guided us through a detailed exploration of the over 20 wines obtained from 12 hectares of property, white for two thirds. The style of the wines is rooted in classicism and is appreciated for resources of aromatic clarity and gustatory persistence.

Chassagne-Montrachet 1er Cru Clos des Murées 2015

The *clos*, a small *monopole* of a third of hectare near the center of the village, has shallow and very stony soils. Céline has obtained a white that is mature but not static, faithful to the vintage but with no concessions to excessive softness.

Chassagne-Montrachet 1er Cru La Romanée 2015

The vibrant minerality that often animates wines from this *climat* also applies to this version, tense and tasty.

Criots-Bâtard-Montrachet Grand Cru 2015

The smallest of the Grand Cru of Montrachet (one and a half hectares) is the prerogative of only eight producers. The interpretation of Fontaine-Gagnard exalts the fleshy power of 2015, showing *souplesse* and ductility.

HEITZ-LOCHARDET

CHASSAGNE-MONTRACHET

24, Rue Charles Paquelin - Tel. +33 (0) 3 80 213319

8 hectares

By gradually regaining control of the family vineyards, which were leased to Drouhin and other companies for almost thirty years, Armand Heitz recomposed the structure of a *domaine* founded in the mid-nineteenth century, but subsequently dismembered as a result of the phylloxera epidemic. The new Heitz-Lochardet brand debuted with the harvest of 2013, a challenge for a man who is not yet thirty, fresh from wine studies and immediately called upon to prove himself with parcels of the highest quality, located in some of the best *climats* of the Côte de Beaune. But beyond the good vineyards, Armand has a clear and precocious talent reflected in the quality of the first bottling that seems anything but what one might expect from a novice. Expressiveness, definition and elegance have been from the very beginning the hallmarks of his wines, all vinified with the stalks and enlivened by felicitous gustatory dynamics in both whites and reds. Discerning wine critics noticed immediately and recognition was not long in coming, as he was proclaimed a "bright new star on the Burgundy horizon" (Steen Öhman). But Armand isn't moved. "I go at my own pace," he commented as he conducted a tasting of the 2015 vintage. Judging from the quality of the tastings, that pace seems rapid indeed. There was not a wine among them that was less than exquisite, from the almost lyrical purity of Chevalier-Montrachet, to the tannic tension of the surprising Pommard. Others will follow soon, as the *domaine* regains possession of all the other vineyards it owns. Vineyards are managed under biodynamics, for the moment covering eight hectares. He also started a small *négoce* activity that carries the brand Armand Heitz, in whose range shines the carefree and smooth succulence of a Coteaux Bourguignons made without sulfites and simply delicious.

Bourgogne Chardonnay Les Durots 2016

Vital and snappy, this white comes from Meursault, from the homonymous *lieu-dit* classified Villages, on the slope facing Volnay.

Meursault 1er Cru Les Perrières 2015

From almost half a hectare of land, this wine in its early life seems less elusive and reticent than the average young Perrières, certainly thanks to a vintage that propitiates aromas of acacia flowers and a gustatory fullness of lingering persistence.

Chevalier-Montrachet Grand Cru 2015

The portion owned by Heitz is not even a tenth of a hectare, so about the size of a home garden. Yet, despite the limited production, once tasted this wine could not be exempted from the review, so enchanting is its finesse.

Pommard 1er Cru Clos des Poutures Monopole 2015

A little more than half a hectare *en monopole* of a *climat* that doesn't usually render wines so graceful. Heitz's version is another story, both for the original aromatic touch and the firm but silky tannins.

Pommard 1er Cru Pézerolles 2015

While accompanying us in the tasting, Armand confessed his own weak for the wines of this *climat*, which express Pommard reds of more slender and elegant profile, without however renouncing the remarkable potential of evolution.

Bernard MOREAU et Fils

CHASSAGNE-MONTRACHET

3, Route de Chagny - Tel. +33 (0) 3 80 213370
domaine.moreau-bernard@wanadoo.fr

14 hectares

The Moreau *domaine* is now run by Bernard's sons, Alexandre and Benoît, still relatively young but self-confident when they talk of their work and valuable teachings of their father. The company vineyards have increased to 14 hectares, almost all located in the district of Chassagne and spread over thirteen different *appellations*. Vineyard management is inspired by a biological approach, both in working of the soils and contained yields. Refinements in the cellar always last between 12 and 18 months. The style of the wines shows a rather modern interpretation with precision and clarity as fundamental values.

Chassagne-Montrachet 2015

Production of this Villages exceeds 20,000 bottles, making it widely available. It's an assemblage of different parcels coming from the *lieux-dits* Masures (east of the town) and Les Houillères (on the border with Puligny). The wine combines a satisfying fullness on the palate with a long finish of tasty mineral persistence.

Chassagne-Montrachet 1er Cru Les Grandes Ruchottes 2015

Enhanced by rocky soils of marl matrix and perfect exposure to the east, this *climat* has proven to be one of the most suitable for Chardonnay. The Moreau parcel was planted in 1939 and, in our opinion, is the source of the most profound and articulate wine among those tasted here. The structure is vertical, but the wine retains a spontaneity free from of any sign of rigidity: a truly gorgeous white.

Chassagne-Montrachet 1er Cru La Cardeuse 2015

In this small *monopole* in the *sub-climat* of Les Brussonnes, Pinot noir has always coexisted with Chardonnay. Delicacy and delicious flavor make it a surprisingly pleasant red.

David MOREAU

SANTENAY
4, Rue de la Bussière - Tel. +33 (0) 6 85 963028
contact@bourgogne-david-moreau.com | www.bourgogne-david-moreau.com

9 ettari | *importato in Italia da: deGustate*

David Moreau took over the family winery in 2009, after gaining experience in New Zealand and in Rhône, and through highly educational internships at Olivier Lamy in Saint-Aubin, as well as at the Domaine de la Romanée-Conti. Taking over from his grandfather, who emphasized vigor and productivity, David reversed the course, returning to manual work in the vineyard with a craftsman's spirit. Today, with his wife Blandine, he manages nine hectares of vineyards distributed essentially in the commune of Santenay, and through very meticulous work produces a dozen wines that have won us over for their freshness and gustatory tension.

Bourgogne Pinot Noir 2016

"Wine should not be drunk, but tasted and appreciated." If a *vigneron* who makes a red so pleasantly drinkable and refreshing, asserts a similar claim, one might mention Dr. Jekyll and Mr. Hyde. No fear, contradiction is only apparent.

Maranges 2015

While tasting in the cellar, Blandine confessed to a weakness for this red, made from three small parcels, one of which is classified as Premier Cru. The small bunches and the recurrent *millerandage* of irregular grapes in the bunches, impose a natural selection to the advantage of a finely spicy flavor without losing the more savory and *sauvage* touches of mouth finish.

Santenay Cuvée "S" 2015

The flagship wine of the *domaine* is a tribute to grandmother Simone and comes from a historic parcel of poor productive vigor, located in the center of the village, in the *lieu-dit* Les Cornières. It is a splendid wine, introduced by inviting notes of blueberry and capable of combining a complex tannic framework with a light touch of enviable nonchalance.

Marc MOREY & Fils

CHASSAGNE-MONTRACHET
3, Rue Charles-Paquelin - Tel. +33 (0) 3 80 213011
domaine.marc-morey@wanadoo.fr

10 hectares

This *domaine*, which deserves a place among the most reliable wineries of the Chassagne-Montrachet area, is about to celebrate a century of activity. It was founded in 1919 by Fernand Morey, taken over by his son Marc in the 1950s, and elevated with full merit to international success in the 1990s by Marc's son-in-law, Bernard Mollard. About ten years ago, Mollard ceded the direction to his daughter Sabine, who chose to continue the solid tradition of Morey. Vineyard management is in *lutte raisonnée,* relying on the experience of Bernard, long retired but always full of advice, to minimize the use of chemicals. From ten hectares of vineyards, planted 80% in white, the *domaine* produces wines that are decidedly more noted for freshness and minerality than for flesh and fruit.

Chassagne-Montrachet 1er Cru Chenevottes 2015

The cool, deep soils of this sector, not far from the Saint Aubin *appellation*, mitigated the heat of 2015, giving the wine softness and harmony.

Chassagne-Montrachet 1er Cru Les Vergers 2015

The *climat* is bordered in part by Chenevottes, from which it differs with shallower soils with outcrops of mother rock on the surface. The Mediterranean character of the vintage shaped a white of bright vitality with enticing notes of aromatic herbs.

Chassagne-Montrachet 1er Cru En Virondot 2015

Located in the highest part of the *appellation*, at over 300 meters above sea level, at the edge of the Chassagne woods, this *climat* is a sort of *monopole*, given that Sabine also vinifies the (small) portion of grapes not owned by the domain. Lean soils are at the source of a vibrating gustatory tension and of almost chalky minerality.

Vincent MOREY & Sophie

CHASSAGNE-MONTRACHET
3, Hameau de Morgeot - Tel. +33 (0) 3 80 206786
morey.vincentetsophie@club.fr | www.morey-vins.com

20 hectares

Vincent Morey has created a large *domaine* by putting together the portion of vines inherited from his father Bernard with the conspicuous dowry of his wife Sophie Belland (12 hectares in the territory of Santenay). The more than twenty hectares total are cultivated according to the principles of *lutte raisonnée*. As is often the case with wineries based in Chassagne, whites are overall more interesting than reds. Sometimes more ripe and generous, sometimes more tense and reactive, they show inviting aromatic vitality, and immediacy in the development of incisive and persitent flavors.

Chassagne Montrachet Vieilles Vignes 2015
Like almost all of the vineyards owned by Vincent in Chassagne, the three parcels that render this Villages are located in the southern sector of the village, facing Santenay. In the usual expressive mode of extreme clarity and definition, the wine reveals itself as broad and enveloping with no loss of tension.

Chassagne Montrachet 1er Cru Les Baudines 2015
The vineyard is close to the woods of Chassagne, above three hundred meters, but here the white clays soils do not translate into the usual broad and buttery white. *Au contraire*, the wine shows pervasive sapidity and minerality in an expanse of flavors innervated by tension.

Chassagne Montrachet 1er Cru Les Embrazées 2015
More than four and a half hectares of the abundant five of the entire *lieu-dit* belong to Morey, for about 90% of the total. Paradoxically, though located beneath Les Baudines, Les Embrazées has much poorer reddish soils with little clay and many stones. In fact, the taste of the wine is not marked so much by richness of fruit than a rather leaner but tasty mineral vein.

OLIVIER

SANTENAY

5, Rue Gaudin - Tel. +33 (0) 3 80 206135
www.antoineolivier.wine | domaineolivier@orange.fr

12 hectares

Antoine Olivier is admired as a white wine specialist with an able and inspired hand, even though the vineyards of the Santenay area are mostly planted in Pinot Noir (more than 80% of the total area). But Antoine continues to go his own way, while not always hiding a certain impatience with generally accepted clichés and conventions. Thus the innovative designs of his labels, the fanciful names chosen for some of his wines and even screw caps on a pair of Premier Cru bottles. And yet the style of his wines does not accept shortcuts, or techniques aimed at softness. On the contrary, he works in reduction and permanence on the yeasts, always using new wood at less than 20%. From 12 hectares of vineyards, Antoine makes on average almost 70,000 bottles, of which more than two thirds are Santenay.

Rully Saint-Jacques 2015

Among the few labels outside the orbit of the Santenay *appellation*, we'd signal this happy excursion into the Côte Chalonnaise: friendly and colloquial, a white wine to drink freely.

Santenay Les Coteaux sous la Roche 2015

The vineyard is located on a steep slope at the exit of the narrow Combe de Saint-Jean: the soft and mature character of the vintage does not exclude a snappy twist.

Santenay Le Bievaux "L'Air de Rien" 2015

As a kind of subtitle for this *cuvée*, "L'Air de Rien" underlines the *nonchalance* of its faux-simple character. It may seem to pretend nothing, but how you feel that grit and that juice.

Santenay 1er Cru Beaurepaire 2015

From the hazel-colored clays of this *climat* with challenging slopes and well-drained soils, Antoine produces a successful version in red, as well as a full-flavored, full-bodied white with a long and incisive finish.

Paul PILLOT

CHASSAGNE-MONTRACHET

3, Clos Saint-Jean - Tel. +33 (0) 3 80 213191
contact@domainepaulpillot.com

13 hectares

The brand of Paul Pillot, linked to the smiling face of Thierry Pillot, is increasingly synonymous with precision and *droiture* in the crowded panorama of the wines of Chassagne. The *domaine* was founded in the late nineteenth century by Jean-Baptiste Pillot, a former barrel maker, and his two sons who started marketing bottled wines as early as the twenties, well ahead of other producers in the area who began appearing on the market only after World War II. Substituting his father Henri in 1968, Paul Pillot consolidated the vineyard area with the acquisition of other excellent parcels of the Chassagne *appellation*, up to the current 13 hectares. For several years, Thierry and Chrystelle, Paul's son and daughter, have been running the winery, heirs to a style devoted to subtlety and expressive transparency.

Chassagne-Montrachet 1er Cru Clos Saint-Jean 2015

Clos Saint Jean is considered one of the best red wine vineyards of Chassagne, but Pillot regularly makes a white version of appreciable completeness, with pervasive flavor.

Chassagne-Montrachet 1er Cru Les Grandes Ruchottes 2015

A parcel located at the highest part of the slope, over 250 meters above sea level, on marly soils rich in limestone, renders a white rich in nuances, in which elegance, amplitude and energy merge.

Chassagne-Montrachet 1er Cru La Romanée 2015

This comes from a 60-year-old *vieille vignes* of almost half a hectare, planted on a steep slope on shallow soils, in a cool and ventilated area. Even from such a sunny year, we are struck by the intense minerality, which leaves no room for softness.

RAMONET

CHASSAGNE-MONTRACHET
4, Place Noyers - Tel. +33 (0) 3 80 213088
ramonet.domaine@wanadoo.fr

13 hectares

The winery dates back to the 1920s and the eccentric figure of Pierre Ramonet, from whom the property passed to his son André and finally to his nephews Jean Claude and Noël, owners for about thirty years. Working with old vines and lowering yields have always been guidelines for the identity of a *domaine* that in the Chassagne area is also among those to watch for its few red wines. Reds focused on an intense expression of fruit, often able to keep tannins in line with quality standards of the Côte de Nuits. They have drawn applause from more than one critic, including Jasper Morris, who called them "consistently exciting." Taking nothing away from the reds, we remain convinced that the main attraction here is the enchanting character of the whites of Chassagne: elegant and expressive wines, designed to age for a long time.

Chassagne-Montrachet 1er cru Clos de la Boudriotte 2015

One hectare of vineyards over fifty years old on stony soils of pink-orange color, rich in iron oxide and manganese, is the source of a red refined in tannins, while giving away nothing in savory fragrance.

Chassagne-Montrachet 1er cru Les Ruchottes 2015

The *lieu-dit* is part of the La Grande Montagne, which, as Armando Castagno rightly points out, "more than a *climat* is a puzzle." The vineyard dates back to the 1930s and Ramonet obtains a white of rich texture and internal density, marked by substance and amplitude.

Montrachet Grand Cru 2015

From vineyards in Puligny area and vines almost 90 years old—partially replanted in 1990—here is a Montrachet of sumptuous expressive intensity, three-dimensional and tonic, with no pretension of being showy.

Domaine des ROUGES-QUEUES

SAMPIGNY-LÈS-MARANGES

10, Rue Saint-Antoine - Tel. +33 (0) 3 85 911869
rougesqueues@gmail.com | www.domaine-rouges-queues.com

5 hectares

Call it love at first sight. One day, after returning from a tiring marathon of tastings, we stuck our noses into the wines of Jean-Yves Vantey, and sparks were set off. The expressive style, the graceful feel and the bright vitality set them apart from the average reds from Maranges, sometimes anonymous and not entirely immune to rustic accents. Jean-Yves is Burgundian, his wife Isabelle comes from the Swiss Valais. In 1998, very young and with only a hectare of vines, they embarked on the adventure of a new *domaine*. From the start choices were very clear: no herbicides and pesticides, tilling of the soil and no enological interventions in vinifications, save for those suggested by common sense and experience. Today the *domaine* has five hectares of vineyards located in the Maranges and in the Hautes Côtes de Beaune; organic certification dates back to 2008 and biodynamic principles have been applied for several years.

Hautes Côtes de Beaune 2014

Two different *lieux-dits* give life to a fast-paced red, all rhythm and flavor.

Maranges Vieilles Vignes 2014

The original Vantey vineyard, acquired in 1998, covers about a hectare with a good portion of vines planted in 1934 on clay soils of Pleistocene origin. The wine combines delicacy, contrast and depth, conveying a spontaneous sense of completeness on the palate.

Maranges 1er Cru La Fussière 2014

This is the largest Premier Cru of Maranges, covering more than forty hectares, known by the critics as propitiating wines with generous supplies of fruit but with tannins not inclined to finesse. The knowing hand of Jean-Yves manages to challenge this cliché, delighting us with a tonic and slender wine of admirable reactivity and energy.

12

CÔTE CHALONNAISE

CÔTE CHALONNAISE

maps *page* 533, 534, 535, 536, 537

Côte Chalonnaise is the natural extension to the south of the Côte d'Or with marked similarities in geological formations. It extends for thirty-five kilometers along a north-south axis to the west of the city of Chalon-sur-Saône. Along the route heading south we come, one by one, to the towns of Bouzeron, Rully, Mercurey, Givry and Montagny-lès-Buxy at the core of the five communal *appellations*. If geography seems to have favored the vineyards of the Côte Chalonnaise, the same can't be said for history. This area of the Burgundy of wine suffered a long negative backlash between the nineteenth and twentieth centuries, due to a series of particularly critical and unfortunate events. First the ravages of phylloxera, then the Great War, then the crisis of the mining district of Montceau-lès-Mines with the collapse of wine markets in the area and finally World War II and the German invasion, with the demarcation line of the occupied territories traced right next to the village of Mercurey.

A survey of the vineyard areas starts at the village of Bouzeron, the northernmost *appellation* with an intriguing element of originality. Promoted only twenty years ago to communal Villages status, Bouzeron represents a unique case in Burgundy in that Aligoté is the only variety permitted in the approximately 50 hectares of vineyards in production. To obtain quality results, leading local *vignerons* have focused on Aligoté Doré, a biotype much less productive than the better known and widespread Aligoté Vert, but also much more expressive and engaging in aroma and flavor, as well as surprisingly well suited to aging.

Just to the south of Bouzeron is the town of Rully, which gives its name to an *appellation* devoted for two-thirds to Chardonnay, whose grapes tend to ripen slightly later, and offer excellent bases for sparkling wines, as well as still whites of pleasant freshness. Jasper Morris calls them "light, fresh and friendly," though it must be noted that the 23 *climats* classified as Premier Cru aspire to superior quality. About a third of the approximately 350 hectares of vineyards is allocated to Pinot Noir, but that doesn't guarantee Rully the same quality levels obtained a few kilometers to the south, in the Mercurey *appellation*, favored by stony soils on a hard calcareous base. Mercurey should be considered the doyen of the Côte Chalonnaise, both for quality and scope, with almost 650 hectares of vineyards dominated by Pinot Noir (over 85%) and 32 *climats* classified as Premier Cru. Red wines are noted for discreet tannic structure and, in the best examples, also for appreciable qualities of complexity and persistence.

Moving south from Mercurey we come immediately to the vineyards of Givry: not quite 300 hectares, devoted 80% to Pinot Noir, with 38 *climats* as Premier Cru. In retrospect, the most admired reds of the Côte Chalonnaise were often found at Givry, at one time capable of rivaling even the reds of Beaune. But times have changed, and it might be said that the primacy of Givry is to be found in the quality of its raw material, the grapes, rather than in its wines. We've noted that overall wines seem to lack original and distinctive character traits, but what is really missing from the scene is an exceptional interpreter, a winemaker capable of shaking up the status quo by creating exemplary wines to inspire the others.

Leaving the last foothills of the Mont Saint-Vincent ridge, another twelve kilometers to the south we come to the commune of Buxy and the Montagny *appellation*, which closes this brief review of the Côte Chalonnaise. Montagny has about 300 hectares of vineyards in Chardonnay, for an *appellation* entirely devoted to white wine, with some 50 *climats* as Premier Cru (over 60% of the entire area). Here the slopes crinkle and climb up to 400 meters, signaling a high potential for wines of territorial identity, but three-quarters of production is processed by the local cooperative winery, and the artisans who have mastered their craft can be counted on the fingers of one hand.

Stéphane ALADAME

MONTAGNY-LES-BUXY
20, Rue du Lavoir - Tel. +33 (0) 3 85 920601
contact@aladame.fr | www.aladame.fr

7.7 hectares

At the age of forty-five, Stéphane Aladame has already accumulated the experience of a veteran *vigneron*. He was just eighteen, with a fresh diploma in enology, when he met an aging Montagny producer who was about to retire and offered him the chance to rent three hectares of vineyards. He didn't think twice about it and plunged into the work, though his first harvest in 1992 proved to be a challenge. "The fermentations didn't want to take off," he recalled, "but it was a valuable lesson." In the meantime, he's completed twenty-six harvests and, with his wife Julie, heads a *domaine* with more than seven hectares of vines, between property and rentals, with eight plots in Premier Cru, all in the Montagny *appellation* and managed mainly organically. He's proven to be a meticulous and perfectionist crafter of white wines that combine freshness and elegance and are sold at judicious prices.

Bourgogne Mon Blanc 2015

This is Montagny, not Chamonix, but Stéphane's lighthearted play on words reveals his predilection for the purity of mountain whites. Aged in wood for only 20%, it is a coolly refreshing aperitif.

Montagny 1er Cru Sélection Vieilles Vignes 2015

From the over fifty-year-old vines of different parcels, here is an effective blend of maturity and gustatory dynamics.

Montagny 1er Cru Les Vignes Derrière 2015

Stéphane sees the whites of Montagny as closer to the Chablis than to Meursault, and the exemplary nature of this *cru* supports his view. The vineyard faces northeast and like the profile of the wine, chalky and tense.

Montagny 1er Cru Les Coères 2015

The largest *climat* of Montagny renders sunny and round whites that in the Aladame version has mineral tones and complexity adding tension, energy and contrast.

CHÂTEAU de CHAMILLY

CHAMILLY

7, Allée du Château - Tel. +33 (0) 3 85 872224
contact@chateaudechamilly.com | www.chateaudechamilly.com

25 hectares

Framed by a verdant rural landscape, the castle was built in the seventeenth century by Noël Bouton, officer of the army of Louis XIV, on the foundations of fortified farm of the fourteenth century. For about two centuries the property has belonged to the Desfontaine family, with Veronique Desfontaine currently at the helm, flanked in the last ten years by sons Arnaud and Xavier. The estate has 25 hectares in the Mercurey and Montagny *appellations*, equally divided between Pinot Noir and Chardonnay (with a balance of Aligoté). The vineyard approach is organic and vinifications are carried out with a low intake of sulfur and a year and a half of *élevage* for the reds and for most of the whites. The wines are spontaneously drinkable, aimed at satisfaction more than complexity and proposed at decidedly reasonable prices.

Bourgogne Aligoté 2016

The vineyard parcels are located at the two ends of the Côte Chalonnaise: one to the north, in the Chamilly area, the other at Buxy, close to the Premier Cru of Montagny. The result is a white aperitif wine, easy to approach but vital and tasty.

Montagny Les Bassets 2016

Thirty thousand bottles a year are produced from the four hectares of vineyards. Vinification in cement tanks propitiates *droiture* in a wine that combines conviviality and digestibility at a more than affordable price.

Bourgogne Côte Chalonnaise 2016

The carefree smoothness on the palate and the availability of some fifty thousand bottles at about ten euros each epitomize the concept of everyday wine at its best.

Mercurey 1er Cru Les Puillets 2015

The vineyard on a steep slope with thin soils and hard calcareous rock close to the surface transmits into the intense personality of the wine, which allies aromatic finesse in nuances of peony and raspberry with an appreciable tannic grit.

CHÂTEAU de CHAMIREY

MERCUREY

Rue du Château - Tel. +33 (0) 3 85 445320
contact@chateaudechamirey.com | www.chamirey.com

37 hectares

After taking over the property of this elegant eighteenth-century residence from his father-in-law, the Marquis de Jouennes d'Herville, Bertrand Devillard has considerably expanded the vineyards, acquiring parcels in Mercurey's best *terroirs* while also expanding the wine business to other areas of Burgundy. In addition to the thirty seven hectares of vineyards of Chamirey (of which fifteen are Premier Cru), the dynamic Devillard family also owns Domaine des Perdrix in Nuits-Saint-Georges, Domaine de la Ferté in Givry and Domaine de la Garenne in the Mâconnais. The role of *régisseur* of the entire lot is entrusted to Enrico Peyron, a winemaker from Turin who combines expertise with passion. Since his arrival in 2008, the wines speak a more direct language, reflecting attention to detail but not enological extravagances while expressing interpretive clarity of *terroir*. A note to visitors: Château de Chamirey is also a refined hotel, complete with *table d'hôtes*.

Mercurey 1er Cru La Mission 2015

A *monopole* of vineyards nearly seventy years planted on a calcareous plaque and framed by a fascinating landscape are at the origin of this white with scents of acacia and iodized suggestions, combining finesse and personality.

Mercurey Clos de la Maladière 2015

Fluidity and precision define a wine that shows spontaneity on the palate with a saline lift at the finish.

Mercurey 1er Cru Clos des Ruelles 2015

A *monopole* of two and a half hectares on calcareous red earth rich in iron oxide, source of a solid, masculine red with dynamic flavors and an incisive finish.

Mercurey 1er Cru Champs Martin 2015

The use of 40% of whole bunches in vinification contributes to an inviting floral delicacy in a wine whose winning ways include juicy flavors on the palate.

Les CHAMPS de l'ABBAYE

ALUZES

9 Rue des Roches Pendantes - Tel. +33 (0) 3 85 455932
alainhasard@wanadoo.fr

6 hectares

Originally from the Ardennes, Alain Hasard had been a sommelier in a restaurant in Montpellier, had done seasonal work in cellars in the south of France, as well as in wine shops in Paris and Limoges. But his passion for wine possessed him with a "physical" urgency to produce, so he and his wife Isabelle decided to move to Burgundy with their three children and become winemakers. After a false start in the misunderstood Côte du Couchois, in 2001 they moved to the Côte Chalonnaise. Convinced supporters of environmentally friendly agriculture, they follow the principles of biodynamics and today manage six hectares of vineyards between Rully and Mercurey, certified organic, to which they have added a small slope in the Côte d'Or and a leased plot in Monthelie. The wines have momentum, sometimes with more energy than design, but always with personalized character and an engaging expressive naturalness.

Mercurey La Brigadière 2015

The *lieu-dit* is north of the town, above the Premier Cru area, planted on a rounded slope that resembles a crown with vines exposed in all directions. Alain obtains a tonic and salivating white with a long and savory persistence.

Rully Les Cailloux 2015

The sunny vintage made the whites more open and amiable with a fund of salty taste evoked by the name of the parcel (*cailloux* are the limestones scattered through the vineyard) and soft, fruity flavors that stimulate the palate.

Bourgogne Pinot Noir 2015

A sixty-year-old vineyard renders a wine that teeters between the fragrant and the rustic with incisive acid freshness and engaging juicy grit.

Mercurey Les Marcoeurs 2015

From the northeast sector of the *appellation* comes a red of overflowing energy, combining firm and tasty tannins with appreciable gustatory dynamics.

CLOS SALOMON

GIVRY

16, Rue du Clos Salomon - Tel. +33 (0) 3 85 443224
clos.salomon@orange.fr

9,5 hectares

A *domaine* of noble tradition, founded in the fourteenth century when it was among the suppliers to the captive papal court of Avignon, it has been owned by the Du Gardin family in its various ramifications for over five centuries. At the beginning of the nineties, a change of pace took place in terms of quality with the arrival as *régisseur* of the enologist Fabrice Perrotto, who remained in company with the current owner Ludovic Du Gardin until 2016. The estate is based on the large parcel of Clos Salomon, a Premier Cru of almost seven hectares en monopole, with a peculiar geological originality, from which comes a red wine among the longest-lived of the *appellation*.

Montagny Le Clou 2015

From the southernmost *appellation* of the Côte Chalonnaise, entirely devoted to Chardonnay, this is a jaunty but by no means trivial white appreciated for agility, substance and flavor.

Givry 1er Cru La Grande Berge 2015

From a parcel of almost half a hectare, marked by a strong percentage of active limestone (30%), comes a white that combines the vitality of citric freshness with delicate and elegant hints of toasted almonds.

Givry 1er Cru Clos Salomon 2015

The extensive *monopole* of almost seven hectares can boast an original geological matrix since it is situated on the dejection cone of a small overlying *combe*, which over time deposited a peculiar mix of alluvial elements (calcareous stones, clay and silt) in the soils. In the 2015 version, the generous supply of small black berried fruits provides a lining for soft tannins with incisive peppery flavors and a promising finish on the palate.

Vincent DUREUIL-JANTHIAL

RULLY

10, Rue de la Buisserolle - Tel. +33 (0) 3 85 872632
vincent.dureuil@gmail.com

20 hectares

"If I find a Vincent Dureuil wine on a restaurant list, I order it right away, without thinking twice." We repeat this quote from a French wine magazine, since it was written by one of the most esteemed (and least complimentary) white wine producers in the world, a certain Jean-François Coche, who commands attention. Beyond such endorsements, the wines of Dureuil-Janthial have become authentic ambassadors of the Côte Chalonnaise, with labels that have been winning recognition and calling attention to the potential of Rully finally coming to light after being too long underestimated. Vincent Dureuil is a man of the vineyard, deeply attached to the life of soils, for which he renounced pesticides in 2001 and converted to organic in 2005 with certification in 2008. During the vegetative cycle it is not unusual for him to spend twelve hours a day among his vines, convinced as he is that sustainability in agriculture can only be achieved through sensitive observation, meticulousness manual labor and the precision of the artisanal approach. Nevertheless, in the summer of 2016, a year that caused considerable problems in the vineyard, he had no choice: to combat peronospora he was forced to resort to synthetic treatments. "In more than twenty harvests I had never seen anything like this," recalls Vincent. "The pressure was very strong and I was confronted by several colleagues, including Sylvain Pataille, always among the most rigorous, but he also advised me to change course, so as not to lose the entire harvest. So in the end I used a product considered bio in Germany but not by us. I put aside my convictions and considered the welfare of an estate of almost twenty hectares, of the six salaries to be paid, of mortgages and rents to be honored." Vincent has resumed with a conversion period that will take three years to become certified again. In the meantime, his wines remain the same as ever, solid, genuine and tough in textures, they speak their own language and do not tell lies.

Rully 2015

If it's true that the happy hand of a *vigneron* is revealed in his simplest wines, here Vincent plays his ace immediately in a white of precision and strength that exalts the pleasure of drinking.

Rully 1er Cru Margotés 2015

White marls interspersed with the oolitic limestone of the Oxfordian era make this *climat* one of the most suitable of Rully for the production of white wines. Vocation confirmed by a spindly and agile version with an inviting array of aromatic herbs.

Rully 1er Cru Gresigny 2015

Southeastern exposure and white soils with a high content of active limestone give life to a wine of proportions modulated between white fruit, incisiveness and flavor.

Rully 1er Cru Le Meix Cadot Vieilles Vignes 2015

Almost half a hectare of vineyard with most of the vines dating back to the original planting by Vincent's great-grandfather in 1920. The nose evokes the floral delicacy and elegance of the best Puligny, the palate gains traction with a supplement of energy and contrast.

Rully 1er Cru La Fosse 2015

A red that smells of rose and wild strawberry, with dynamic and spontaneous flavors. Simply delicious.

GOUFFIER

FONTAINES

11, Grande-Rue - Tel. +33 (0) 3 85 914966
domaine@domainegouffier.fr | www.domainegouffier.fr

6 hectares

After eight years as administrative director of La Chablisienne cooperative, Fréderic Gueugneau returned to Fontaines, his birthplace in Côte Chalonnaise, to collaborate with the *domaine* of the Gouffier family, historic brand of Mercurey. Gueugneau began a gradual restructuring of the winery, which he acquired in 2012 without changing its insignia, given his affection for his longtime mentor Jérôme Gouffier, who had just died. Under his management, the area under vines has been reduced to six hectares, while the working of the land was resumed and harvest logistics were redesigned. The winery has extensively renewed its barrels with the aim of improving the quality of maturations and succeed in bottling the entire production. To this end, Gueugneau hired Benoît Pagot, to direct vinifications and to join him in a small *négociant* activity, which completes the range with some white labels between Bouzeron and Rully. Anticipating a conversion to organic farming, the *domaine* is back on track with wines of immediate and agile pleasure, focused on the fragrant juiciness of the fruit.

Mercurey Les Bussières 2015

Captivating in the scents of yellow flowers and resins, the wine is more vital on the palate, spontaneous and refreshing without sacrificing precision.

Mercurey Les Murgers 2015

The delicately vegetal fragrances set the stage for a gustatory progression of extreme fluidity and smoothness.

Mercurey 1er Cru Champs Martin 2015

From the highest part of the *climat*, on a thin layer of white marls exposed to the southwest, comes a red with a mineral vein, both stylish and solid.

JAEGER-DEFAIX

MILLY

17, Rue du Château - Tel. +33 (0) 3 86 424075
contact@jaeger-defaix.com | www.jaeger-defaix.com

4.5 hectares

A crystal ball isn't needed to envision a future of increasing popularity and success for the wines of the Rully *appellation*. This is one of those places that combines *climats* of certain value, scrupulous and talented *vignerons*, and reasonable prices to trigger a crescendo of interest. Among the cellars to be cited, we enthusiastically endorse that of Jaeger-Defaix, a *domaine* with a relatively new name, but with profound roots in the history of the *appellation*. In 2002, Hélène Jaeger-Defaix (wife of Didier Defaix, producer in Chablis) inherited from her great-aunt a hectare of vines in Premier Cru. That opened a link to the *domaine* of her great-grandfather Henri Niepce, who, between the wars, was among the most determined *vignerons* to push for classification of Rully. Thanks to subsequent acquisitions, Hélène managed to recover the original property of four and a half hectares among the best Premier Cru vineyards of Rully. The *domaine*, which has been organic since 2012, devotes extreme attention to the vineyards, which translates into wines of energy and flavor, with promising potential for evolution.

Rully 1er Cru Mont-Palais 2015

The first parcel recovered by Hélène has become the source of a sunny wine rich in scents and flavors of white pulp fruit.

Rully 1er Cru Rabourcé 2015

The *climat* is on a steep slope whose white clays favor the early ripening of grapes, among the first to be harvested. The *savoir faire* in vinification and a long refinement in *fûts* (about eighteen months) shape a white of rich substance, overflowing with power.

Rully 1er Cru Clos du Chapitre 2015

More than a hectare *en monopole* right behind the family home is the source of a robust structured red, of sure perspective.

Paul et Marie JACQUESON

RULLY

12, Rue Saint Laurent - Tel. +33 (0) 3 85 432605
marie@jacqueson-vins.fr | www.jacqueson-vins.fr

13 hectares

Rully is one of the places in Burgundy that suffered most from the devastation of World War II. At the end of the nineteenth century there were about six hundred hectares of vineyards in Rully; in 1945, less than a hundred remained. "In the commune only four *vignerons* out of eighty returned from the front, and of those only two resumed work in the vineyards," recalls Paul Jacqueson, whose father Henry was one of those two. By 1946, amid innumerable difficulties in rebuilding the family business, Henry Jacqueson made a decisive commitment to the rebirth of the Rully *appellation*. In 2006, Marie Jacqueson joined her father Paul in the winery and, with increasing astuteness, continues the meticulous work focused on the essentials of elegance and drinkability. Together with her brother Pierre, she manages thirteen hectares of vineyards divided between Rully, Bouzeron and Mercurey, producing a range of wines of fine expressive harmony, equally impressive in whites and reds that can also be purchased directly at the *domaine*.

Rully 1er Cru Gresigny 2015

A *climat* for white wines only, which enjoys a favorable southeastern exposure on terrain with a high content of active limestone. The 2015 version combines inviting floral finesse with a long and tasty finish.

Rully 1er Cru La Pucelle 2015

A vineyard where grapes arrive early at full maturity, yet the wine shows substance and energy trailed by citric scent that enlivens the palate.

Rully 1er Cru Les Cloux 2015

Marie often emphasizes that this red shows an immediate gourmand character instead of a tendency toward power and longevity. Here is a glowing example of a parcel suited to white that renders a red as an appealing alternative with, of course, a spontaneous epicurean bent.

JOBLOT

GIVRY

4, Rue Pasteur - Tel. +33 (0) 3 85 443077
domaine.joblot@wanadoo.fr | www.domainejoblot.com

14 hectares

A trustworthy address for more than twenty years in the Côte Chalonnaise, this *domaine* shifted gears toward a decisive pursuit of quality, thanks to Jean-Marc Joblot, who in 1979 joined his father in the company founded in the post-war period. "Ever since my arrival at the winery, I've been convinced that *climats* with soils very similar to those of the Côte de Nuits could not do less than produce excellent wines," says Jean-Marc. That conviction led him to renew the plant material in the vineyard, inserting superior clones of Pinot Noir, while changing the vinification protocol and drawing inspiration from the work of the icon Henri Jayer. Since he was joined by his daughter Juliette in 2012, the styling of the wines has undergone a renewed quest for pleasure based on crisp, fresh and expressive fruit, without neglecting territorial origins.

Givry 1er Cru "Mademoiselle" 2015

The assemblage of grapes from two distinct Premier Cru (En Veau and La Servoisine) results in a well defined and enjoyable white of immediate pleasure.

Givry 1er Cru Les Bois Chevaux 2015

The first written record documenting the *lieu-dit* is dated 1285, and it seems that even Henry IV, at the end of the sixteenth century, was a convinced admirer. There's reason to believe that he would also enjoy this red with a velvety touch, laden with fruit (cherry and raspberry) that emerges in the name of freshness.

Givry 1er Cru Clos du Cellier aux Moines 2015

The scenic beauty of the *climat* is alone worth a trip. The 2015 version from Juliette retains agility despite the tannic structure, extending into a fruity and complex impact on the palate.

Bruno LORENZON

MERCUREY

14, Rue du Reu - Tel. +33 (0) 3 85 451351
contact@domainelorenzon.com | www.domainelorenzon.com

7 hectares

Bruno Lorenzon began his career as a producer in 1997, taking over management of the family vineyards after experience as a consultant in South Africa and then as commercial director of the Mercurey *tonnellerie*. Today, the *domaine* can count on seven hectares of vineyards, with a slight prevalence of the Pinot Noir over Chardonnay, distributed in the best sectors of the Mercurey *appellation* and cultivated in certified organic conditions. With the latest vintages, Lorenzon has gone beyond being a promising name to become a consistent quality reference point for the entire Côte Chalonnaise. The use of increasingly large portions of whole bunches in vinifications is a factor in the style of wines that become ever more convincing for lightness, balance and expressive spontaneity.

Mercurey 1er Cru Clos des Barraults 2015

This L-shaped *climat* of exceptionally stony soils fully exposed to the south is devoted mainly to production of Pinot Noir. But Lorenzon made a white of enveloping flavor and persistent mineral verve.

Mercurey Le Chapitre 2015

The sunny harvest left a stamp of pleasure on this fleshy and ripe red, fragrant with blackberries and a palate combining spicy notes with generous tannins.

Mercurey 1er Cru Carline Clos des Champs Martin 2015

The vineyard in the heart of Les Champs Martin *climat* has reddish soils rich in ferrous veins that intertwine with gray marl of the Oxfordian stage. Bruno directs only the oldest vines of this large parcel into the *cuvée* dedicated to his sister Carline: a deep and contrasted red, of remarkable tannic finesse and sure perspective.

François LUMPP

GIVRY
36, avenue de Mortières - Tel. +33 (0) 3 85 444557
domaine@francoislumpp.com | www.francoislumpp.com

9 hectares

At the end of the seventies, at the tender age of seventeen, François Lumpp was already at work in the family *domaine* with his brother Vincent. In 1991, he decided to go on his own, founding the *domaine* with his wife Isabelle: "It's a career that I only really chose at the age of thirty," François explained. "I realized that I was a *vigneron* only by accumulating the experience of many harvests and many tastings of the wines of others." Today the winery, managed with the help of the eldest son Pierre, can count on nine hectares of vines in the Givry *appellation*, mainly dedicated to reds and managed with the criteria of organic agriculture (but without certification). This is one of the most recommendable addresses of the entire Côte Chalonnaise, thanks to wines of class and longevity that exalt the important heritage of old vines. "If Burgundy produces exceptional wines, it is not just due to *terroir* but also to the plant material," says François. "In all these years, of my nine hectares I've replanted less than half a hectare."

Givry 1er Cru Crausot 2015
The matrices of soils of Bathonian origin contain an important quota of active limestone, which transmit to the wine a valuable supply of savory freshness, despite the pronounced maturity of the fruit.

Givry 1er Cru Clos du Cras Long 2015
Lean and well-drained soils contribute to the character of a red focused on the pleasurable fruit, ready and enjoyable in harmonious fusion.

Givry 1er Cru Clos Jus 2015
The unique Premier Cru in the commune of Dracy-le-Fort is characterized by steeply sloping terrain of reddish color due to the strong presence of iron oxide. The result is a red with satiny tannins and lovely aromatic vivacity, based on notes of cherry and wild berries, combining intensity and finesse in the long, spicy finish.

Jean-Baptiste PONSOT

RULLY
26, Grande-Rue - Tel. +33 (0) 3 85 871790
domaine.ponsot@orange.fr

8.5 hectares

In the year 2000, Jean-Baptiste Ponsot convinced his family to cut off ties with the *négociants* who had been buying their grapes since the 1950s. Jean-Baptiste was twenty years old at the time, but he was a determined boy, with very clear ideas. That break was just the beginning of a more profound renewal: construction of a new *cuverie*, planting new vineyards, renting other plots, stopping chemical treatments in the vineyard and returning to working the land. On the threshold of forty years, Jean-Baptiste has become a scrupulous and perfectionist *vigneron*, with the enviable experience of seventeen vintages producing wines among the most reliable of the *appellation* (as well as among the most affordable in price). The *domaine* has more than eight hectares of vineyards, of which two thirds are classified as Premier Cru and located in the most suitable sectors of Rully.

Rully en Bas de Vauvry 2016

The parcel is a Ponsot *monopole* of almost three hectares from which Jean-Baptiste makes a white fermented partly in wood and partly in stainless steel, lean and balanced, an ideal aperitif.

Rully 1er Cru Molesme 2015

The *climat* is characterized by a steep slope and reddish soils, from which the *domaine* also makes a red of proven aging potential. This white is full but graceful with rich structure that does not affect the sapid tension or agility.

Rully 1er Cru La Fosse 2015

The generous 2015 harvest was dealt with deftly by Jean-Baptiste, who with this Premier Cru plays his ace card in a fragrant red that combines concentration and elegance with persistence on the palate.

RAGOT

GIVRY

4, Rue de l'École - Tel. +33 (0) 3 85 443567
givry@domaine-ragot.com | www.domaine-ragot.com

9 hectares

Among the young *vignerons* who are giving new life to the Côte Chalonnaise, Nicolas Ragot is due consideration. He has been running the family *domaine* since 2008, continuing an activity whose roots date to the nineteenth century. The nine hectares of vineyards, all in the Givry *appellation* and dedicated mainly to Pinot Noir, are worked in part with grassing over and managed without the use of herbicides or synthetic products. Vinifications are carried out with completely de-stemmed grapes, fermentations are started with spontaneous yeasts, and refinement takes place partly in cement tanks, as well as in oak *fûts*, with no more than 20% of new wood. The wines are immediate and enjoyable, with elegant aromatic nuances and marked personality—all at very reasonable prices.

Givry Vieilles Vignes 2015

A plot of more than a hectare of vines over fifty years old renders a red with aromatic nuances of roots and blueberries and a palate with a creamy touch that combines momentum and finesse.

Givry 1er Cru La Grande Berge 2015

The *climat* near the southern border of the *appellation* is among those recently promoted to Premier Cru. The Ragot plot extends over more than two hectares on the calcareous matrixes of a rather steep slope, facing southeast. From it comes a fleshy and flavorful red, which shows savory grit, energy and personality.

Givry 1er Cru Clos Jus 2015

From one of the most prized *climats* of the *appellation*, and the only one in the commune of Dracy-le-Fort, Nicolas Ragot makes an ambitious wine, with fine tannic texture if still not fully expressive aromatically, but with a bonus of gustatory complexity that proves it's well worth waiting for.

François RAQUILLET

MERCUREY

19, Rue de Jamproyes - Tel. +33 (0) 3 85 451461
www.domaine-raquillet.com | contact@domaine-raquillet.com

12.55 hectares

The Raquillet family, active in the vineyards of Mercurey for several generations, found its point of reference in 1990 when François Raquillet took over management of the *domaine*. An enterprising and dynamic man, with a noted mania for golf, François Raquillet over nearly thirty years has aligned the winery with the elite of Mercurey. The *domaine* has some twelve hectares of vineyards, about two-thirds dedicated to red wines. Carefully controlled yields, along with studied vinification and refinement techniques, have resulted in mature and balanced wines with discreet packaging that have attracted customers to the point that the *domaine* bottles its entire production.

Mercurey Vieilles Vignes 2015

Vines nearly seventy years old give life to a compact and fragrant red, focused on the harmonious amalgam of fruity (blueberry) and spicy notes, and made even more pleasant by a savory vein that nourishes contrasts and stimulates the palate.

Mercurey 1er Cru Les Veleys 2015

The *climat* has a felicitous southeastern exposure that favors relatively early maturing. Raquillet makes successful versions in both colors. The white expresses scope, density and volume, but our preference is for the red, which even in a generous and exuberant vintage like 2015 loses none of its juicy, dynamic verve.

Mercurey 1er Cru Les Vasées 2015

South facing and planted on clay soils, this parcel of Raquillet measures over a hectare. It renders a red of appreciable finesse and momentum that will gain further rhythm with bottle refinement.

THEULOT JUILLOT

MERCUREY

4, Rue de Mercurey - Tel. +33 (0) 3 85 451387
contact@theulotjuillot.eu | www.theulotjuillot.eu

11 hectares

Nathalie Juillot inherited the *domaine* from her grandmother, along the rather obsolete female hereditary lines of Burgundy, and today manages it with the help of her husband Jean-Claude Theulot. They have expanded the property vineyards to eleven hectares all in the Mercurey *appellation*, of which only a couple are destined for whites, committing themselves to more selective control of yields following the parameters of *lutte raisonnée*. Grapes are vinified always completely de-stemmed, favoring fleshy and tasty wines, enviably food friendly and always reasonably priced.

Mercurey 1er Cru Les Saumonts 2015

The orange-hued marls of a precipitous *climat* littered with marine fossils render a white with beautiful citrus scents (cedar, bergamot) and enveloping creaminess on the palate.

Mercurey Château Mipont 2015

Here is a red that shines on the palate, allying spontaneity, dynamics and harmony with the delicacy of the tannic grain and the quality of gustatory persistence.

Mercurey 1er Cru Les Croichots 2015

Nathalie counts on four separate parcels covering more than a hectare for a red wine enlivened by an aromatic mixture of flowers and earth, with a lively spicy vein and, above all, a convincing expansion on the palate, of surprising amplitude.

Mercurey 1er Cru Les Combins 2015

The vineyard at the edge of the town center has full southern exposure, though the Oxfordian marls of the soil tend to suffer from drought. Still, despite the intense maturity of the fruit and a velvety touch of *boisé*, the palate reveals civilized tannins that are juicy and refreshing.

Domaine de VILLAINE

BOUZERON

2, Rue de la Fontaine - Tel. +33 (0) 3 85 912050
contact@de-villaine.com | www.de-villaine.com

24.5 hectares

Coming from the north, Bouzeron is the first commune of the Côte Chalonnaise: a village of 150 souls so secluded from the main lines of communication that you really have to want to get there to arrive. The location, far from any worldly temptations and oblivious to most, seduced Aubert de Villaine and his wife Pamela, who as newlyweds bought a small farm here in 1971, not long before Aubert was appointed *co-gérant* of the Domaine de la Romanée-Conti in 1974. Little by little, they acquired vineyards of Aligoté in the area of Bouzeron, annexing them to form a *domaine* completely independent of DRC. Since 1986, cultivation has been oriented toward organic farming. In the nineties they acquired new plots in the areas of Mercurey and Rully, expanding the property to nearly twenty-five hectares. The core of production remains Aligoté, to which the *domaine* has allocated almost ten hectares, providing a decisive impulse to the promotion of the Bouzeron *appellation* from regional to communal (1998). From the 2000 harvest, management of operations has been entrusted to Aubert's nephew, Pierre de Benoist, who guided the conversion to biodynamics, extended to the entire property since 2006, and has been busy making the wines known around the world. Even today that production exceeds 120,000 bottles, it must be said that quality continues to improve over the entire range. The Aligoté wines set the standard of the Bouzeron *appellation*. But also among the reds, each harvest seems to come up with a particularly successful wine, by virtue of a defined and captivating style based on extreme care and precision.

Bouzeron 2015

A unique case in Burgundy, in Bouzeron the prince of vines is Aligoté: a tyrranical prince, on closer examination, since no other grape is permitted in the production. Aubert de Villaine, who was also mayor of the commune from 2001 to 2008, decided from the beginning of his time in Bouzeron to focus on Aligoté Doré. That biotype is much less productive than the better known and widespread Aligoté Vert, but it is also far more expressive and engaging in aromas and shows superior quality also in its surprising disposition toward aging. Today the *domaine* possesses parcels of *vieilles vignes* in different *lieux-dits*, but everything is merged under a single label, with vinifications always inspired by a calibrated dosage of stainless steel vats and oak barrels, in various formats. The white from this vintage guarantees the usual clarity and aromatic intensity of citric notes also sensed on the palate in a refined finish of almost creamy consistency.

Rully Les Saint-Jacques 2015

The planting of this parcel of Chardonnay—over one and a half hectares—dates back to 1990, a *lieu-dit* exposed to the east, right below the namesake Clos classified as Premier Cru. The wine refined in large casks, and it shows a sleek and tapered silhouette.

Bourgogne Côte Chalonnaise La Digoine 2015

Not without a certain taste for hyperbole, Jasper Morris writes, "This is one of the world's most stylish Pinot Noirs from humble origins." Coming from two hectares of vineyards facing south on the deep terrain of the homonymous *lieu-dit* in the commune of Bouzeron, the wine alternates the carefree charm of cherry flavors with a more graceful and rounded elegance, but it is always intimately delicious and quaffable.

Mercurey Les Montots 2015

Two parcels located at different levels of the slope are home to vineyards of Pinot Noir selected in Nuits-Saint-Georges. Well structured and long-lived, this red from a sunny year that rounded and softened the tannins, usually somewhat sharp at this stage of development.

13

MÂCONNAIS

MÂCONNAIS

map *page* 539, 540, 541, 542, 543

To the south of the Côte Chalonnaise, the Mâconnais is the southernmost sector of Burgundian wine, occupying a territory to the west of the river Saône in hills to the north and west of the city of Mâcon. A few kilometers beyond and calcareous-clay soils give way to the granite matrices of Beaujolais, and Chardonnay ceases to be the reference grape variety. In the Mâconnais, however, Chardonnay remains the principal variety, distributed over an area of more than five thousand hectares of vineyards for a production that exceeds 40 million bottles a year. Production that long remained the preserve of an industry in wines of little qualitative interest amassed by a network of cooperative wineries. In recent years a decisive change has taken place as the quality of wines has improved along with the growing awareness of the value of vineyards and renewed interest in environmental priorities. A new generation of *artisan vignerons* has emerged, committed to the revival of wines of *terroir* inspired by the sustainability of work in the vineyards, of selective vinifications and targeted refinements in the cellars, managed with the sensitivity necessary to enhance their expressive transparency.

Among the wines of the Mâconnais, the best known is certainly Pouilly-Fuissé, an *appellation* established in 1929 which covers about 800 hectares of vineyards spread over four different communes (Fuissé, Solutré-Pouilly, Vergisson and Chaintré). The area is dominated by the profiles of the Roche de Solutré and Roche de Vergisson, rocky massifs that stand out on the horizon like prows of ships. The white wines, at their best, show elegance and personality, with an enthralling sapid-mineral vein and little to envy in the whites of the Côte Chalonnaise and Côte de Beaune. This quality is indicated by the dossier for the promotion of the best *climats* of Pouilly-Fuissé to Premier Cru status, a bid that after a long and laborious gestation is about to reach completion. Next to the Pouilly-Fuissé zone, a wide range of *appellations* covers the territory north toward Tournus, extending for about forty kilometers in a gentle hilly landscape, more open and broad than in the Côte d'Or. It is here that the whites of *appellations* such as Viré-Clessé and Saint-Véran originate, along with the wines of the Mâcon, Mâcon-Villages and Mâcon followed by the name of one of the 26 communes in the jagged archipelago of the Mâconnais. White wines dominate, but our research has shed light on some reds from Gamay, which will delight fans of lighter and more drinkable wines noted for versatility at the table.

BRET BROTHERS LA SOUFRANDIÈRE

VINZELLES

125, Rue aux Bourgeois - Tel. +33 (0) 3 85 356772
contact@bretbrothers.com | www.bretbrothers.com

10.95 hectares

If you produce wine by trade and your last name is Bret, using it as a company header may not seem to be the best of ideas, given the similarity to the term Brett, the Brettanomyces mushroom that alters the taste of wines and keeps winemakers awake at night. That doesn't seem to bother the brothers Jean-Philippe and Jean-Guillaume Bret, who sleep soundly and go their own way, running for years a *négociant* activity under the name Bret Brothers in addition to producing wines at the family *domaine* La Soufrandière. Among the many companies that list wines produced on their own and wines made from purchased grapes, the Bret Brothers seem to have an edge. They surprised us positively with a very high and homogeneous quality level in the "*haute couture*" segment, inspired by a sort of "he who loves us, follows us" strategy behind the *négociant* wines. From the last harvest, in fact, they bought only grapes certified as organic or in the process of conversion. La Soufrandière vineyards were certified as organic in 2000 and have been biodynamic since 2006. The estate vineyards take in parcels of the historic core of four hectares in the prestigious *climat* Les Quarts, surrounding the winery at Vinzelles, as well as important acquisitions in the *appellations* of Saint-Véran and Pouilly-Fuissé, which bring the total to more than ten hectares, almost entirely dedicated to whites. Paradoxically, surpassing the fateful quota of 100,000 bottles a year seems to have actually improved the quality of wines, never so focused on the individual characteristics of the many different *climats*. This is due to acertain intransigence in managing the ambitions of a winery expanded to deal with wines that are now issued under some 30 labels. Meticulous care is reflected in the vineyards, where some parcels are worked with horses. In the cellars, vinfications are precisely managed with long refinements in *pièces* that are never new.
In short: steadily improving quality at an address that offers an almost complete range of the many-faceted whites of the Mâconnais.

Mâcon-Cruzille 2016

The age of the vines ranges up to eighty years on white calcareous soils in the northwestern quadrant of the Mâconnais, not far from the Clos des Vignes du Mayne of Julien Guillot. The white has the fragrance of tangerines with a generously pleasing touch on the palate.

Saint-Véran Climat "En Combe" 2016

From the Chasselas area, in the southwestern area of the *appellation*, the Bret Brothers buy the grapes of a parcel of land rich in iron oxide, exposed to the south at an altitude of 350 meters. The whole cluster pressing and refining of eleven months results in white balanced in dynamics with a long salivating finish.

Pouilly-Vinzelles 2016

Selected according to the age of the vines, in this case between the thirty-five and fifty years, this label takes us back to the original core of the *domaine* in a tiny *appellation* of only fifty hectares total. Two-thirds of the final blend is vinified in stainless steel, contributing freshness to a food-friendly wine of surprising versatility.

Pouilly-Vinzelles Climat "Les Quarts" 2015

The so-called "beacon" *cuvée* of the *domaine* comes from the highest parcel of the *climat*, boasting eighty-year-old vines on very stony red soil webbed by ferrous veins. The 2015 version, striking for its candied lemon notes, exalts the maturity of fruit in a generous mouthful innervated by minerality.

Frantz CHAGNOLEAU

PIERRECLOS
Le Carruge, 18 Chemin Des Prés - Tel. +33 (0) 3 85 387817
domaine.chagnoleau@orange.fr | www.domainefrantzchagnoleau.fr

8.5 hectares

If we were to name a winemaker of the Mâconnais, only one, still not as well known (especially abroad) or appreciated as he deserves to be but a sure bet for the future, it would certainly be Frantz Chagnoleau. A graduate of enology in Bordeaux in 2004, Frantz chose to move to Burgundy "because it's the region that pushes the expression of *terroirs* to the extreme." After an internship with Olivier Merlin, in 2009 he became a *vigneron* on his own, with no second thoughts. Today, between purchases and rentals, the winery exceeds eight hectares of vineyards (all in organic management). Frantz has been joined by Caroline Gon, his companion in life as well as an enologist (Les Héritiers du Conte Lafon). Together they form a solid and close-knit team of winemakers driven by boundless passion and determination. Despite the many difficulties related to the rogue climate, the latest harvests record a truly remarkable qualitative surge. The white wines are tense, precise and soaring with a surprising freshness of fruit.

Viré-Clessé Les Raspillères 2016

This comes from the only parcel saved from the terrible hail of mid-April, which decimated production in 2016. The vineyard is exposed to the east on a steep slope with light and well-drained soils, favoring slow maturation. Frantz has drawn from it a tense wine, with vibrant minerality and interminable persistence.

Pouilly-Fuissé Pastoral 2015

The vineyard at an altitude of 350 meters near the Roche de Vergisson has soils rich in active limestone and scattered with pebbles. This is a white of perky citrus notes with tonic and salivating freshness on the palate.

Saint-Véran La Roche 2015

The composition of the soils reveals important portions of iron oxide, which this vineyard of almost eighty years old transmits to a wine of vitality and savory grip on the palate.

CHÂTEAU de LAVERNETTE

LEYNES

La Vernette - Tel. +33 (0) 3 85 356321
chateau@lavernette.com | www.lavernette.com

13 hectares

Château de Lavernette, at the crossroads of the Macônnais and Beaujolais, is owned by Xavier de Boissieu, who represents the thirteenth generation of wine producers at the *domaine*. After studies in viticulture and enology between Beaune and Montpellier, Xavier returned home in 2004, after field training as an intern in New Zealand (Margrain Vineyard) and the Napa Valley (Saintsbury). In California he met his wife Kerrie, an enologist trained at the University of California Davis, a national champion taster and today aspiring Master of Wine. In 2005, Kerrie joined Xavier at Leynes, where they gradually took over the family winery. They immediately converted the thirteen hectares of vineyards to organic, laying the foundations for the next step of biodynamic, completed in 2007 and certified Demeter. They gave new impetus to the *domaine* with wines sold under a dozen labels, among Gamay reds stand out.

Pouilly-Fuissé Vers Châne 2015

The parcel of about a hectare at an altitude of 350 meters is exposed to the east and located in the same sector as the *lieu-dit* Les Rontets. The 2015 version, refined for more than twenty months before bottling, is a white of discrete *souplesse*, which holds in check the heat of the vintage.

Beaujolais-Leynes Le Clos 2016

The fifty-year-old vineyard consists of almost two hectares of head-trained vines facing south. Xavier obtains a prompt and easy drinking Gamay of enchanting fluency.

Saint-Amour Le Châtelet 2016

The deliciously brimming flavors of small black berries and peppery notes conceal rich substance and an unexpected tannic grip, suggesting it could thrive on further time in bottle.

CHÂTEAU des RONTETS

FUISSÉ

Château des Rontets - Tel. +33 (0) 3 85 329018
base@chateaurontets.com | www.chateaurontets.com

6.7 hectares

Claire Gazeau and Fabio Montrasi are both architects. As recent graduates, they met in the late eighties in Milan, his hometown, during a stage in the studio of the famous architect Vittorio Gregotti and, following the inscrutable paths of life, they soon ended up at the property that from the mid-nineteenth century belonged to her family, Gazeau-Varambon. There they decided to reinvent themselves as winemakers, bringing new life to the fascinating château located in the *lieu-dit* Les Rontets in the commune of Fuissé, atop a hill of 350 meters overlooking the village. The property is near the geological fault that divides the granitic terrains of Beaujolais from the calcareous clay soils of Burgundy proper, resurfaced from a remote past of seabeds. The place is magical, surrounded by woods yet bright, cool and always breezy. The almost seven hectares of vineyards, with the exception of one parcel, are grouped around the house and winery, inside a Clos that dominates the landscape of Pouilly-Fuissé. That *appellation* applies to three of the four whites produced here, now regularly found among the most popular and sought after labels in the region. The reasons are simple, starting from the high quality of the vineyards, certified bio since 2005. They are historical vineyards of a Premier Cru *in pectore*, with a remarkable nucleus of old vines that the couple destines for their "sprightly" selections of Les Birbettes. But style also plays a decisive role, inspired by sober and discreet elegance and a quest for complexity that translates into a wealth of detail in wines that retain an admirable sense of spontaneity and expressive naturalness. The range is completed by a Bourgogne Blanc, made from the most recent plantings, and a few bottles of Saint-Amour, a red from Gamay of awesome smoothness, simply delicious.

Pouilly-Fuissé Clos Varambon 2015

The basic *cuvée* is obtained from vines planted mostly in the fifties and sixties at a density of 9,000 vines per hectare. The 2015 vintage is a white focused on the soft maturity of the fruit, expressive and open with a harmony that reflects the character of an early harvest.

Pouilly-Fuissé Pierrefolle 2015

The parcel is half a kilometer from the Clos, planted in the early seventies. The substantial difference compared to the other whites is due to the soils on a mother rock of granite origin. The impact on the palate is agile and supple in line with the enveloping effect of the natural amplitude of a hot vintage, but the wine shows surprising acceleration to close on a pleasant saline note.

Pouilly-Fuissé Les Birbettes 2015

The assonance with the Italian language is evident in the French (argot) of the noun *birbette* corresponding to *birbante* or little rascal in Italian vernacular. The fact is that the age of the vines destined for the Birbettes selection is venerable, having been planted behind the château, on the eastern slope of the Clos, between 1910 and 1920. Bottling without filtration after more than twenty months of refinement, Fabio and Claire have fashioned a classy white, a Premier Cru *in pectore* for its deep roots in the territory and the measured elegance of the wine, very relaxed in bringing the sweet maturity of the fruit into line with the gustatory dynamics.

Saint-Amour Côte de Besset 2016

The grapes come from a vineyard located in the Côte de Bessay, in Saint Amour, six kilometers south of the *domaine*, in one of the most "beloved" *crus* of Beaujolais. Vinification is carried out in stainless steel: cold carbonic maceration without added sulfites and aging in used barrels for about six months. The aromatic vitality is seductive, with scents of freshly ground black pepper and notes of roots and damp woods. On the palate it combines lightness and juiciness and impulsive drinkability.

CLOS des VIGNES du MAYNE

CRUZILLE

Rue des Moines, Sagy-le-Haut - Tel. +33 (0) 3 85 332015
info@vignes-du-maynes.com | www.vignes-du-maynes.com

7 hectares

The origins of the Clos des Vignes du Maynes date to the year 910, when the abbey of Cluny was founded. Leaping through the centuries to approach modern times, Pierre Guillot bought the property in 1952 and, for health reasons, resolved to produce wines without chemicals: no herbicides or insecticides in the vineyards, as well as no sulfites or filtrations of any kind in the cellar. That caused a break with *négociants*, as well as expulsion from the cooperative winery of Cluny. But Guillot's health-minded gesture proved to be fruitful in the long run, since forty years later his son Alain became president of the Fédération Nationale de l'Agriculture Biologique (FNAB), and propitiated the agreement with the minister of agriculture to officially recognize the AB logo, for organic agriculture, in 1995. In those years the École d'Agrobiologie de Beaujeu was founded, giving impetus to the movement toward natural wines in Burgundy, inspired by the need to put the notion of "living" at the center of the debate, in full conflict with the agricultural policies of the time. Alain Guillot's nephew Julien, born in 1974, assumed the task putting these ferments into effect in the family *domaine*. After a promising early career as an actor, Julien abandoned the theater to assume command of the winery in the 1990s, determined to immediately turn toward biodynamics. He also introduced a different winemaking strategy, based on the alternation of de-stemmed and uneven bunches (*à mille-feuilles*) of grapes, with slower and longer semi-carbonic fermentations, following the lunar calendar in the timing of decanting and bottling. Hostile to new wood, which in his opinion penalizes the length of the wines and disperses the contribution of minerality, Julien employs only used and neutral barrels for refining. "I do not make wines for tasters, but for those who drink them," he responded abruptly when we asked for a spit bucket. But he's due full credit for his methods and his views, which have also been recognized on the market as his wines have achieved global success. In all frankness, we confess to admiring them too, especially the reds obtained from a core of seven hectares, of which two-thirds are planted in Pinot Noir and Gamay. Overflowing with aromas, they are luminous examples of juicy and svelte *vins vivants*, perfect companions at the table.

Bourgogne Cuvée Auguste 2016

The aromatic profile of herbs and spices, even more than the centrality of the fruit, is the typical characteristic of this peculiar variety of Pinot called Pinot Fin. Iron rich soils integrates its delicacy with an infusion of tension and sapidity.

Mâcon-Cruzille Cuvée 910 2016

The date of the first enclosure of the Clos des Vignes du Maynes coincided with the foundation of the abbey of Cluny in 910. Julien has cited that year with his assemblage of equal parts of Chardonnay, Gamay and Pinot Noir of the *domaine*. The share of white grapes enhances the lightness of the color and taste and releases a boost of floral freshness.

Mâcon-Cruzille Manganite 2016

Vinified with 90% of whole cluster grapes, this wine from the Gamay à Petits Grains variety is a house specialty. We shared our latest round of tasting with wine writer Tim Atkin, who, while sipping the Cruzille Manganite, kept repeating, "simply delicious!"

Mâcon-Cruzille Aragonite 2016

A white dedicated to the geology of the Clos, whose calcareous soils are rich in silicon and manganese. The name recalls the calcium carbonate crystals that translate into minerality in terms of gustatory dynamics and flavor personality.

GUILLEMOT-MICHEL

CLESSÉ

664, Route de Quintaine - Tel. +33 (0) 3 85 369588
sceadequintaine@wanadoo.fr | www.domaineguillemotmichel.net

6.5 hectares

Marc Guillemot and his wife Pierrette, both enologists, should be considered among the forerunners of the artisanal movement that drives the Mâconnais of wine today. With their daughter Sophie, they conduct a small *domaine*, which boasts a pioneering organic certification (1992), closely followed by conversion to biodynamics. The six hectares of vineyard are located in the area around the village of Quintaine, halfway between Viré and Clessé. The family cultivates them with almost monastic devotion, in search of harmony with the environment that deeply involves the life of the soil. They have always produced a single wine, a white with a white label that illustrates a clear and defined style that conveys with precision all their attention and dedication to vineyards. For those who associate biodynamics with opaque and approximate wines, the *domaine* is clearly off limits. From 2014, they list a new label, a sparkling wine called appropriately "Une Bulle" (A Bubble) vinified according to the ancestral method with a fifteen-month contact on the lees.

Viré-Clessé Quintaine 2015

Made from an assemblage of grapes from all the estate vineyards since 1985 without interruption, Quintaine is now the signature label for the white *vins d'auteurs* of the Mâconnais. The early character of this latest vintage on the market, harvested on August 30, is focused on the centrality of ripe fruit, without yielding too much to amplitude or exotic aromatic nuances. Instead it releases pleasing flavor that harmonizes spontaneously with the warmth on the palate.

Les HERITIERS du Comte LAFON

MILLY-LAMARTINE

4, Rue Lamartine - Tel. +33 (0) 3 80 212217
comtes.lafon@gmail.com

26 hectares

The growth pattern of the Mâconnais, both in the quality of the wines and in the awareness of the winemakers, has deep roots in the agricultural history of the region and its socio-cultural fabric. It would be a mistake, however, not to consider the decisive impulse generated (also at the media level) by the investments made here by two charismatic "outsider" entrepreneurs, both—in different ways—true champions of wine. Of the two, the Belgian Jean-Marie Guffens was the precursor, a pioneer in the eighties of the first affirmation of authored white wines traced to their terrains of origin at the Domaine Guffens Heynen. Yet his example has remained largely ignored by local producers who seem to no longer relate to it in any way. Dominique Lafon, an icon of Burgundian wine of another level of humanity and depth, is quite different. He has propitiated a more stimulating and profitable interaction with the work of the *Artisans Vignerons de la Bourgogne du Sud*, of which his estate has embraced the ideals, sharing its path thoroughly. That's why Les Héritiers du Comte Lafon was immediately accepted as a project that was much more than a simple local branch of the parent company of Meursault. It is precisely a demanding and meditated investment in vineyards, launched in 1999 and now centered on twenty-six hectares of property, entirely consecrated to Chardonnay, managed under organic and biodynamic principles (but without certification) and applying, for the most part, to lesser known appellations of the zone. It would be a mistake to think of the wines as "signed" by Lafon, since Dominique has always declined to ride the wave of his celebrity. Instead, the mission here is to explore the resources of *terroirs*, still little known to the *vignerons* who work them. The headquarters are in Milly-Lamartine and the direction is entrusted to a talented 35-year-old, Caroline Gon, partner of Frantz Chagnoleau in life (as at his *domaine*). The range of labels is vast for a total production of around 150,000 bottles a year, while prices remain balanced though quality never stops growing.

Mâcon-Milly-Lamartine 2016

Coming from two large vineyard parcels (four and a half hectares) planted about thirty years ago at around 400 meters of altitude and exposed to the east, the wine is vinified in large barrels and reveals tension and vitality. Its vertical structure might make one think of a white from Chablis.

Mâcon-Milly-Lamartine Clos du Four 2016

The one and a half hectare Clos was planted at the beginning of the eighties and renders a wine whose aromatic contours show crystalline precision. The palate has sparkling energy, without losing a beat in terms of definition.

Mâcon-Chardonnay Clos de la Crochette 2016

It should be remembered that in these parts Chardonnay is not only the name of a grape, but also of a small village nestled in the vineyards. Lafon has bought a Clos of two and a half hectares, from which he derives the most solar of his whites.

Saint-Véran 2016

This comes from parcels in the communes of Prissé and Davayé, in both cases with deep clays, that account for consistency, energy and amplitude.

Viré-Clessé 2016

Here the extent of vineyards is a total of six hectares distributed over different parcels, with a share of old vines at higher levels than the rest. The 2016 version seemed to us the most successful ever, by virtue of a magical balance between the floral elegance of the aromas and the savory persistence of the long finish on the palate.

Nicolas MAILLET

VERZE
291, Route d'Ige - Tel. +33 (0) 3 85 334676
vinsnicolasmaillet@orange.fr | www.vins-nicolas-maillet.com

7.5 hectares

Nicolas Maillet is a bearded and shaggy man, but, as we Italians put it, he has no hair on his tongue. A winemaker who is honest, frank and outspoken as few others, Nicolas plays the role of co-chairman of the consortium of *Artisans Vignerons de la Bourgogne du Sud* with combative passion even though he's near the end of his mandate. His winery is in Verzé, a wine zone in which more than 80% of the grapes end up at the local cooperative winery, a practice followed by his father Gérard until Nicolas entered the company. He set out by rethinking the work in the vineyards, orienting it toward organic (since 2008), with a growing interest in biodynamics. He increased the vineyards to the current seven hectares, the source of wines that Nicolas ferments at low temperatures for a long time, and refines in enameled iron vats, without resorting to wood.

Bourgogne Aligoté 2016

From a sixty-year-old vineyard in the commune of Igé, this is one of the best Aligotés of the Mâconnais. Citric notes intertwine with notes of pear and white melon composing an aromatic panorama of engagingly fruity vitality. On the palate the wine is more sapid, sealed by a long finish with hints of white pepper.

Mâcon-Verzé Le Chemin Blanc 2016

Agility is allied to elegance in the most successful white of the range. The mineral stamp has an almost chalky character, accounted for by the calcareous and stony soils of a vineyard more than eighty years old.

Mâcon-Verzé Rouge 2015

Gamay enthusiasts will appreciate the refreshing delicacy of this red, vinified using carbonic maceration and overflowing with floral and fruity tones.

Olivier MERLIN

LA ROCHE-VINEUSE

305, Route de la Boisserole - Tel. +33 (0) 3 85 366209
contact@merlin-vins.fr | www.merlin-vins.com

14.7 hectares

More than thirty years have passed since Olivier Merlin, originally from Charolais, took over the Domaine du Vieux Saint-Sorlin with his wife Corinne. From those first vines at La Roche-Vineuse, the *domaine* has never stopped growing, now counting on about fifteen hectares of vineyards, to which must be added a dynamic *négociant* activity. Sons Théo and Paul have joined their parents at the winery that produces about 150,000 bottles a year, though with no concessions to quality. They offer a range of calibrated wines that reflect both the meticulous manual work in the vineyards and deft management of vinifications and refinements conducted with uncommon sensitivity. But Olivier continues to show the restless spirit of the entrepreneur, as evidenced by the recent purchase of the Clos des Quarts in Chaintré, in the Puilly-Fuissé *appellation*, in partnership with his friend Dominique Lafon. A project on the launch pad that deserves to be followed carefully.

Mâcon-La Roche Vineuse 2016

A white from an assembly of fifteen different parcels, refined entirely in steel, reveals a convincing balance between sweetness of fruit and depth of flavor.

Mâcon-La Roche Vineuse Les Cras 2015

Broad, fleshy and powerful, the passage of this white wine in oak contributes to softness and roundness, though the high rate of active limestone in the soils guarantees an intense minerality in the long finish.

Moulin-à-Vent La Rochelle 2015

In 2006, Merlin expanded to Beaujolais with the purchase of two hectares in the zone of Moulin-à-Vent, on sandy soils of granitic matrix with a significant presence of manganese. The head-pruned vines of this prized *climat*, planted almost entirely in 1937, are worked in organic conditions and with the use of a horse. The result is an intensely spicy and complex red, aged for twenty months in barriques and destined for a long evolution.

Jacques et Nathalie SAUMAIZE

VERGISSON
746, Route des Bruyères - Tel. +33 (0) 3 85 358214
nathalie.saumaize@wanadoo.fr | www.saumaize.com

9 hectares

In the early eighties, Jacques Saumaize was twenty years old when he decided to start his own business, with the first two hectares of vineyards nicely situated under the Roche de Vergisson. Jacques comes from a family of *vignerons*, but he preferred to leave the orbit of his father Léon and his brother Roger (Saumaize-Michelin) to follow a path of gradual expansion, assisted by his wife Nathalie. After more than thirty-five years, with their son Anthony active in the winery, the *domaine* has acquired a well-defined style in wines highly admired by consumers and critics. Their nine hectares of vineyards are entirely dedicated to Chardonnay, in plots distributed essentially between the *appellations* Pouilly-Fuissé and Saint-Véran. The whites are clear and flavorful, inspired by a quest for balance and in the expressions of the different *terroirs*.

Saint-Véran La Vieille Vigne des Crêches 2015

The vineyard almost sixty years old in the commune of Davayé is dominated by calcareous soils, rendering a white that shows tension and savory grit.

Pouilly-Fuissé La Maréchaude 2015

The *climat* is always sunny, exposed full south under the Roche de Vergisson, on very stony terrain whose pronounced slope requires manual work. Jacques derives a streamlined but tonic wine, elegantly tactile

Pouilly-Fuissé Sur la Roche 2015

For some strange reason, the dossier to redefine the hierarchy of the *climats* of Pouilly-Fuissé seems to exclude from promotion to Premier Cru some of the highest vineyards, from which in recent years have come some of the best wines of the *appellation*. The vineyard is at 400 meters, but the energy, contrasts and gustative persistence are in effect those of a Premier Cru.

SAUMAIZE-MICHELIN

VERGISSON

51, Impasse du Puits, Le Martelet - Tel. +33 (0) 3 85 358405
saumaize-michelin@wanadoo.fr | www.saumaize-michelin.com

9.2 hectares

Roger Saumaize is today one of the deans of the Mâconnais. If you plan to visit his home and cellars at Vergisson, we recommend allowing plenty of time. Proud of his country roots, Roger is in fact a passionate, generous and extremely competent storyteller, who likes to consider wine in a broad perspective, without skimping on details. With his wife Christine and son Vivien, he runs a *domaine* of about nine hectares of scrupulously maintained vineyards, converted to biodynamics since 2006, but without certification. From some of the finest *climats* of Pouilly-Fuissé of the Vergisson area, Roger produces classic-style whites, creamy and elegant, focused on balanced maturity, the result of expertise in *bâtonnage* and refinements in the cellar.

Pouilly-Fuissé Pentacrine 2015

Carrying the name of a small starfish fossil, this is an assemblage of several *terroirs* of Vergisson, united by the calcareous matrices *à gryphées* (in sheets), the white allies consistency and elegance.

Pouilly-Fuissé Le Haut des Crays 2015

The vineyard is close to 400 meters high and is therefore likely to remain outside the file of Premier Cru. To judge by the purity and depth of Roger's version, that would be a colossal error.

Pouilly-Fuissé "Clos" Sur la Roche 2015

More than a hectare and a half *en monopole*, with ninety-year-old vines covering a third of the parcel planted on bedrock for a white that is svelte and brisk on the palate, though the freshness, tension and mineral persistence are those of a marathoner.

Pouilly-Fuissé Les Courtelongs 2015

The northern exposure and red ferrous soils account for the unusual complexity of a white that can equal in class many a Premier Cru of the Côte d'Or, but at half the price.

Domaine de THALIE

BRAY

La Moutonnerie - Tel. +33 (0) 3 6 15 076565
domainedethalie@gmail.com | www.domainedethalie.com

5 hectares

If you're willing to venture off the beaten wine track and make your way to Bray, you may be surprised to discover a couple of wineries in decidedly original settings. Besides La Vigne Mouton of Sébastien and Delphine Boisseau, the destination of note is the Domaine de Thalie of Peter Gierszewski. After running a wine shop in nearby Cluny, Peter chose to become a *vigneron* in a rather atypical context—atypical for the landscape, resembling the pastures of the nearby Charolais; atypical for the exposure of the vineyards, almost entirely facing west on soils on the same slopes with different geological matrices, ranging from granite in the lower part to the blue marls of the median strip to the calcareous clay soils of the highest exposures (reserved for Pinot Noir) all, needless to say, out of the ordinary. Peter's winery has about five hectares of vineyards, mostly replanted in 2010 and managed with biodynamic preparations. Following phases of the moon in vineyards and cellars he produces fresh and light wines offered at very competitive prices.

Bourgogne Pinot Noir Balancine 2016

The parcel has mainly calcareous soils, source of an agile and juicy red that Peter vinifies with 50% whole clusters for three weeks of maceration.

Mâcon-Bray Rouge Les Pierres Levées 2016

The soils are bluish marls, which enhance the spicy profile (juniper) of a smooth and savory Gamay that would make a convivial companion at the table.

Mâcon-Bray Blanc Atout Vent 2016

"*Atout Vent*" refers to the beneficial winds of the vineyard of the *lieu-dit* Les Creux Robin, planted on calcareous *foie de veau* soils. The wine from young vines was vinified in stainless steel tanks, rendering a white focused on fruity flavors with pleasant hints of nectarine.

Philippe VALETTE

CHAINTRÉ

227, Rue des Buissonnats - Tel. +33 (0) 3 85 356297

Separating himself from the winery of his father Gérard, Philippe Valette progressively carved out a *domaine* of his own with vineyards distributed between the Chaintré district and other Mâconnais *appellations* and managed in a curious sharing relationship with his brother Baptiste. Chemicals have been banned in the vineyards since 1992 and vinifications have long been conducted without added sulfites, even for decanting. The work of Philippe, flanked by his wife Cécile, has thus been radicalized in a direction that we might hastily describe as inspired by an "oxidative style." Defying local customs and preconceptions, he has focused on very long refinements for the whites, which are bottled at irregular intervals, case by case, after long stays on the lees. The wines have gained in energy and expressive personality in a way that should be appreciated especially by fans of natural whites. If savory and digestible, they are sometimes confusing in typology and style, though their originality preludes a surprising capacity for evolution in the bottle.

Mâcon-Chaintré Vieilles Vignes 2015

The commune of Chaintré has some of the hottest vineyard sites in the region, yet even in such a precocious vintage, Philippe's white retains a dynamic free-rein pace.

Viré-Clessé 2015

The scents of yellow flowers and propolis evoke a bright aromatic array. A high percentage of clay in the soils is at the origin of a creamy texture, tasty internal density and a captivating final.

Pouilly-Vinzelles 2014

This white is reactive and savory, renouncing the centrality of the fruit to express a more subtle and penetrating flavor, innervated by somewhat salty iodate nuances.

La VIGNE MOUTON

BRAY

La Cour des Bois - Tel. +33 (0) 3 85 500602
sebastien-delphine@orange.fr

6.5 hectares

Sébastien Boisseau and his wife Delphine run a *domaine* nestled into the pastoral countryside at Bray at the northwestern edge of the Mâconnais. Bray, a village of 120 souls, seems light years away from the glamour of the wine buffs' Burgundy, but, as we've said about other lost paradises, getting there is well worth the trip. The vineyard is mainly a single unit of more than six hectares on soils that are poor in organic substance but laden with calcareous stones rich in iron. Some parcels are very old, including one which was planted in 1900 with ungrafted vines of a strain of Chardonnay. Though vineyards were converted to organic in 2000, then to biodynamic in 2011, the *domaine* only began to bottle wines in 2012 after leaving the local cooperative. Today the guiding philosophy seems to be to keep it slow, both in pressing and fermentation, conducted in stainless steel tanks at low temperature and protracted for about nine months, sometimes until July. The *domaine* offers easygoing *vins d'auteur* (including reds) at honest prices, despite climatic adversities that have decimated production in recent years.

Mâcon-Bray Blanc Mouton Blanc 2016

The parcel, situated on a very steep slope (30% incline) renders a taut and slender white of bracing flavor.

Mâcon-Bray Rouge Ratatouille 2016

The blend of Gamay and Pinot Noir with 20% white grapes (including Aligoté) blossoms into a light red of inviting freshness.

Mâcon-Bray Rouge Descente Dangereuse 2016

The "dangerous descent" indicated on the label refers not only to the steepness of the vineyard but also to the perils of falling under the spell of a red from Gamay of such insidious fluidity that it risks drowning you with pleasure.

TOURISM IN BURGUNDY

TIPS FROM THE VIGNERONS

We asked producers of Burgundy to tell us about some of their favorite places in the region, local places that are truly dear to their hearts. The *vignerons* responded with descriptions, anecdotes and observations that were brief yet detailed and deeply affectionate. We present their choices here as a series of travel tips, often out of the ordinary and, in some cases, unique.

What emerges are intimate points of view that allow us to "taste the landscape" of Burgundy often away from the standard wine itineraries. These notes indicate possible excursions by foot, by bicycle, and even by car into the various villages as a reminder that Burgundy is home to many artisans, not all of them winemakers. Below is a brief selection of their suggestions, which we gathered and faithfully translated to retain the sensitivity and "vision" of each.

ANNE-LAURE KRIKKE

Domaine Jean-Marc BROCARD

Préhy – Chablis

I love walking through the Préhy vineyards in spring, when the vegetation sprouts and nature awakens. Every day the landscape becomes greener and the grapes on the vines begin to form. The most beautiful view? The church of Préhy at sunset, immersed in the heart of the vineyards, with the vaulted amphitheater of the Grand Cru of Chablis in the background.

SOPHIE et MATTHIEU WOILLEZ

Domaine La CROIX MONTJOIE

Tharoiseau – Vézelay

We were seduced by Vézelay, a hidden gem in the woods of the Morvan park. Only a hundred hectares of vineyard furrowed by numerous paths and isolated from the rest of wine-growing Burgundy. The medieval village is perched high, with its magnificent basilica dominating the so-called "eternal hill." Inside the church, light plays a fundamental role and merges with architecture: towards the summer solstice a sort of "path of light" is created, which breaks through the darkness of the church's entrance until it intensely illuminates the central nave. This vision is truly unforgettable.

ALICE et OLIVIER DE MOOR

Domaine Alice et Olivier de MOOR

Courgis – Chablis

The most evocative landscape of our area is located on the D62 road between Courgis and Chitry. There the road descends and, at the end of a hairpin bend, suddenly opens to a splendid view of the entire verdant valley, animated by small hills teeming with vineyards, cherry trees, cultivated fields and small woods scattered here and there. The valley itself is alive and it is lovely to experience a piece of the landscape where there is still an intimate relationship between man and nature. In our opinion there are three particular things you shouldn't miss: the village of Chitry with its fortified church and its small leaning tower; the area a little beyond the medieval village of Noyers-sur-Sereil, a real pearl; and finally, the quiet valley of the Serein river, an ideal place for cycling.

SYLVIE ESMONIN

Domaine Sylvie ESMONIN

Gevrey-Chambertin

I am the daughter, niece and great-granddaughter of *vignerons*. My family has always worked in the vineyard and I took over from my folks after studying engineering. I advise you absolutely to not miss a trip to the foot of Côte Saint-Jacques (toward the Combe de Lavaux) which for me is the most charming part of Gevrey-Chambertin. The vines butt up against the rock wall and the agricultural landscape surrounding them is dotted with fruit trees at the edges. The landscape suggests a feeling of quiet industriousness: there are the small houses called *cabottes*, which often hide a well inside them. You will also find *merguets*, piles of stones that have been removed from the vineyards as the land has been worked, and were collected around the edges of the vines.

LAURENT FOURNIER

Domaine Jean FOURNIER

Marsannay-la-Côte

Behind the Hautes Côtes, half an hour from Marsannay, a pleasant route unfolds from the village of La Bussière-sur-Ouche. Here, in the old Cistercian abbey of the twelfth century, there is both a refined restaurant and a more popular bistro. Continuing on the D33B road, you can digest your meal while you enjoy a walk around Lake Panthier, a place infiltrated by a wonderful light. Not far away you will find the Château de Commarin. To those who want to stay in the environs of Marsannay, I recommend lunch at the restaurant Les Gourmets, a visit to the wine press of the Dukes of Burgundy and a walk through the vineyards of Chenôve, with their curious contrast between vineyards and Dijon's city outskirts, that seem to intertwine. Next to our *domaine*, you can take a look at the Colombier's circular tower (unfortunately it cannot be visited), which survived the destruction of the ancient monastery built there in the thirteenth century. For dinner you can choose between the traditional cuisine of the Auberge du Clos du Roy, in the historical center of Chenôve, or the more modern cooking of Le Clos du Roy restaurant in the new district of the village.

NICOLAS ROSSIGNOL

Domaine ROSSIGNOL-TRAPET

Gevrey-Chambertin

I am passionate about mountain-biking, and our vineyards and our woods are fantastic for those who love cycling. Those who want to explore the territory of Gevrey-Chambertin cannot miss a 30-kilometer circuit (which can be shortened to 8 or 12) that rises gently above the vineyards of the Grand Cru to take you to the top of the Hautes Côtes de Nuits. Passing through the meadows and then through the woods, you will discover the surprising diversity of vegetation and landscapes. After the vineyards, you reach the limestone plateau to continue through the numerous *combes*, the valleys covered with moss and boxwood, passing under dense vegetation. In any season this corner of the landscape offers scenery that is absolutely charming. In winter with a white coat of snow and in the spring with thousands of colored flowers, from the blue of the forget-me-nots to the white of the lilies of the valley. In summer redolent of the sweetness of the undergrowth; in autumn punctuated by the crunch of dry leaves.

ALEXANDRINE ROY

Domaine Marc Roy

Gevrey-Chambertin

Burgundy is a magical land shaped by the hands of man, a mosaic of shadings with all those variations of green in spring and gold and purple in autumn. It is probably one of the most beautiful viticultural landscapes in the world, with its succession of small villages overlooking the Rue des Grands Crus. Among the things I love is the fog on autumn mornings when it enshrouds the vines trailing small drops of water that make the leaves sparkle. I love the scent of the vine flowers and the colors at dawn, when the sun rises and Mont Blanc appears in the background. I love the small village of Bouilland, the beautiful walks on the Hautes Côtes and in the Ouche Valley.

GILBERT HAMMEL

Domaine des VAROILLES

Gevrey-Chambertin

Burgundy is rich in history, famous for its great wines and its gastronomic specialties, singular in the quiet beauty of its landscapes—hills, plains, vineyards and streams. When the harvest is over and the wine is resting in the cellars, winter arrives with its gray fogs, snow and its rigor. The smell of vine shoots burning after pruning hovers in the air. This is the time to find yourself in front of a fireplace, sheltered by the thick stone walls of a *vigneron*'s home, sharing a bottle of an old Gevrey-Chambertin or reading a poem by Lamartine, just passing time.

CYPRIEN ARLAUD

Domaine ARLAUD

Morey-Saint-Danis

We produce wine in Morey-Saint-Denis created by love for our land that mixes all our values: our desire to share, the pleasure of the dining table, our desire to encourage respect for nature. If you want an alternative walk to the classic routes in the vineyards, I suggest you go up in the hills above Morey-Saint-Denis, and follow (by foot) the route of the ancient railway that connected Morey to Gevrey. Passing through the old tunnel, and over Clos de la Roche and Latricière-Chambertin, you will arrive in Gevrey. The path is about two kilometers, alternating through the woods and offering views of the vineyards from an unusual and original perspective.

CHANTAL REMY

Domaine Chantal REMY

Morey-Saint-Denis

I was born in Gevrey-Chambertin, but my *domaine* is based in Morey-Saint-Denis, a village with a particular history. We inhabitants are called "*les loups de Morey*", because of an obscure legend lost over the centuries that tells how the "wolves of Morey" devoured the sheep of Saint-Philibert, a tiny village near Gevrey. This story is remembered today in the emblem of our village, two wolves running.

This is an image often found on the crests of Morey producers and we, too, are pleased to have the wolves on our labels! I propose a nice walk on the path that runs along the vineyards of Morey, looking out onto our five Grand Cru, of which we are so proud. This route allows you to admire the gorgeous landscape, which extends toward the Saône plain and reaches the Jura. Take the little stony path from Place du Monument and don't forget to supply your backpack with a good piece of bread and cheese from the Abbaye de Citeaux and a nice bottle of Clos de La Roche, maybe from 1998? Allow yourself time to stop on a stone wall and savor your "snack" while admiring this magnificent view.

JEAN-LUC PÉPIN

Domaine Comte Georges de VOGÜÉ

Chambolle-Musigny

I love a really unique landscape. This is what you'll find on the walk up through the village of Pernand-Vergelesses to the Oratoire Notre Dame de Bonne Espérance, where there is a chapel with the statue of the Virgin as well as an area equipped for scenic picnics. From there the view toward the south, over Pernand-Vergelesses and its vineyards, is truly splendid.

ETIENNE GRIVOT

Domaine Jean GRIVOT

Vosne-Romanée

Not far from our *domaine*, Château du Clos de Vougeot is one of my favorite places. It is right in the middle of the vineyard, an icon for us, and a magnetic place full of history. When you are lucky enough to have a sunny, crisp autumn, the vineyards of the Côte d'Or offer yellows, oranges and marvelous reds that, blending in with the color of the trees, make for a superb show. I would also include my favorite restaurants in the Côte d'Or. In Nuits, La Gentilhommière, a hotel-restaurant that manages to smartly modernize the local cuisine and further south in Levernois (not far from Beaune) the Hostellerie de Levernois, on the river's edge. This Relais & Chateaux has a distinctly luxurious ambience, but also includes a *bistro*, perfect for a quick lunch.

ANNE GROS

Domaine Anne GROS

Vosne-Romanée

The soul of Burgundy does not always seduce at first impact, because its diversity cannot be savored in one gulp, nor can it be understood in one glance. It is a land of water, stones and wine, but understanding its many facets requires time. It is a land of transit, of hurried tourists, of compulsive purchases, but if your eyes and heart can find time to pause, you will always be rewarded. You may find yourself wrapped in an almost monastically austere shadow, uncovering a certain taste for sobriety, for discretion, in which deep and very human vibrations resound. The people who live here often reflect the character of the region: at first they are somewhat reserved, but they soon become welcoming and warm. This is a coveted land, rich and fertile with woods, expanses of meadows, vineyard slopes, steep valleys, streams and canals. Each landscape helps to create the mosaic of Burgundy's colors and flavors. For me, the most beautiful way to make this interlude your own is to walk the extraordinary path dedicated to the memory of Félix Batier, which connects Nuits-Saint-Georges to Dijon through the valleys. It is a sporty hiking route that can be divided into stages and offers magnificent sensory perspective cutting through the smells of boxwood, earth, juniper, pine and herbs. Unfortunately, it is a hike that I have not done for many years, although I think about it often.

ALICE RION

Domaine Armelle et Bernard RION

Vosne-Romanée

I was born "*dans les raisins*", among the grape bunches, and I always wanted to become a *vigneronne*, like my father. A walk that I love, incomparable in the Côte d'Or on foot or by bike, is that between Chambolle-Musigny and the Château du Clos Vougeot, also called Chemin de Musigny. The stone walls, the forest, the Grand and Premier Cru, the view of the cliffs above Chambolle and the northern facade of the Château allow you to imbue yourself with the feeling of our vineyards. On those rare clear days you are even able to see Mont Blanc in the distance. Attention, however, as this phenomenon perfectly coincides with an incoming rain, to arrive within a couple of days!

ARMELLE RION

Domaine Armelle et Bernard RION

Vosne-Romanée

In terms of our land and the emotions it can induce, one of the most beautiful walks in the Côte de Nuits starts from the church square of Chambolle. This is a circular path that climbs along the Route de Vergy, a small path above the vineyards from which you can admire a beautiful view of Chambolle-Musigny and our Maison Toscane. When you reach the bend in the road, turn left onto the path marked for the ancient route to Santiago de Compostela. Passing over Chambolle-Musigny and skirting the vineyards of the Grand Cru Musigny, you can look down on the Château du Clos de Vougeot, a magnificent view of the castle and the vineyards of Vougeot and Vosne-Romanée. The road descends and, turning left again, you return in the direction of Chambolle, passing the narrow road that runs along the upper part of the Clos de Vougeot, with a view of the mill and the mouth of the Vouge. The path then continues over the vineyard of Les Amoureuses and finally provides a vision of Morey-Saint-Denis and Gevrey-Chambertin in the distance, as well as a glimpse Dijon. When you reach the crossroads, turn left onto the D122 and continue past the cemetery and Henry IV's famous linden tree, and return to your starting point in the Chambolle church square. Entering the church from the side door, you can admire some monumental frescoes of the sixteenth century: they are very beautiful and represent the *combe* of Chambolle and images of the Virgin. This walk, done casually and with time to take some photos, can be accomplished in about an hour. It offers an original angle of observation both on the vineyards and on the work of the *vignerons*.

PASCALE CHICOTOT

Domaine Georges CHICOTOT

Nuits-Saint-Georges

My family and I have lived in Nuits-Saint-Georges for generations, working the vines and producing wines with artisanal passion. As Nuits is already well known to enthusiasts, I therefore invite you to climb into the Hautes Côtes de Nuits, perhaps using Nuits as a starting point and experiencing the pleasure of encountering the villages you find along the way. At any time of the year landscapes are beautiful, and when you arrive in Arcenant it is imperative to stop for Jean-Baptiste Joannet and his beautiful cassis.

CLAIRE NAUDIN

Domaine Claire NAUDIN

Magny-lès-Villers Hautes Côtes

I was born in Beaune and raised in Magny-lès-Villers, but even though I have traveled a lot and lived in very different places, from Lyon to Toulouse, from Montpellier to Australia, it is only in this little corner of the Hautes Côtes that I really feel at home. To understand the Hautes Côtes you have to go through them slowly, exploring the roads that connect the various villages. One example is the route between Magny-lès-Villers and Pernand-Vergelesses: it covers a short distance, but its views are astounding. Alternatively, you can also take the road from Magny-lès-Villers to Echevronne, a small and delightful village, which is worth a stop!

JEAN-CHARLES LE BAULT DE LA MORINIÈRE

Domaine BONNEAU DU MARTRAY

Pernand-Vergelesses

Our *domaine* has the privilege of cultivating all the vineyards on the hill of Corton, inside the *climat* Charlemagne, in the place where Charlemagne owned his vineyards over twelve centuries ago. The *domaine* is located in the center of the ancient village of Pernand-Vergelesses, five kilometers to the north of Beaune. La *butte de Corton*, our hill capped by a forest, is one of the most fascinating places in the Côte and deserves to be explored. The best viewpoints can be discovered along the road from Beaune to Pernand (D18). Many hikers walk the half-way trail called *chemin en Charlamagne*, which allows you to make a complete tour of the hill. When you can see Mont Blanc from the southeastern slope (this usually happens at the height of Aloxe-Corton) the show is unforgettable. An alternative way to experience this area's imposing beauty follows the road that descends from Villers-La-Faye to Pernand-Vergelesses (D115C). If, on the other hand, you are looking for a vantage point from which to admire the landscape from above, you have to ascend all the way to the lookout at the top of Frétille. The path to get there on foot begins at the church of Pernand-Vergelesses, which also deserves a stop, and continues along the rue de Frétille. At the top, where there is a chapel dedicated to the Virgin, the panorama is remarkable.

JULIETTE CHENU

Domaine Louis CHENU et Filles

Savigny-lès-Beaune

There are two places that I particularly love, both a little outside the town of Savigny-lès-Beaune. The first place I love because it regenerates me. You need to leave the village behind and follow a beautiful, verdant valley, which some call "little Switzerland," for about ten kilometers toward Bouilland. Arriving in Bouilland, take right toward the church and drive up until you reach a clearing that opens to a small footpath that will take you to the top of the so-called "cliffs of Bouilland," where you can enjoy a magnificent view. My second favorite place is the castle of Changey, a mysterious place, lost in time and little-known. You reach it starting from Pernand-Vergelesses in the direction of Echevronne-Changey. However, you cannot enter, and you will have to settle for admiring it from the street.

DAVID CROIX

Domaine des CROIX

Beaune

I am originally from Tours and my parents still live in Montlouis-sur-Loire. It is in the Loire that I began to be interested in wine, after which I moved to Dijon in 2001 and studied enology at the university. Since then I have not left Burgundy. There are countless places to discover in the Côte de Beaune, but I would recommend that you take a nice walk inside Beaune itself, following an itinerary along the old ramparts of the city. From the ramparts you can walk down the Rue du Château and turn left at the bastion of Saint-Jean. From here, following the walls and the ramparts, the city reveals itself in a different light.

ALEXANDRE BRAULT

Domaine Alex GAMBAL

Beaune

I'm originally from Touraine, but I married an Italian and I go crazy for Italian wines, especially those from Piedmont. It's a short way between Touraine and Turin, and following my passion I found myself organizing a twinning between

Meursault and Monforte d'Alba! Unlike the Langhe landscape, the Côte d'Or is more linear and you can fully appreciate it just admiring it from above. I suggest going to Saint-Romain and from there to Nantoux, allowing yourself some detours into the Hautes Côtes, according to the moment's inspiration. In fact, it is only from the top of the cliffs that you can capture the interwoven landscape of the Côte d'Or in its perfect articulation of vineyards, fields, woods and plains.

PHILIPPE PACALET

Domaine Philippe PACALET

Beaune

I grew up in the wine world and very early I felt the need to satisfy a double thirst—to know and to taste. I let myself be guided by intuition with the aim of promoting local wines. I would say that my work is based on ancestral practices, improved here and there by a little science, with minimal interventions. It is the expression of mixed and cross-bred knowledge, made of awareness, intuition and love. Every time the sunlight caresses the yellowed vines of autumn, a very intense emotion returns for me. It is a vision of the Côte tinted with gold, so beautiful and fleeting. I suggest you take it all in from the sky in a hot air balloon, with *Air Escargot*: for me it was an unforgettable experience.

FRÉDÉRICK et FRANCK BUISSON

Domaine Henri & Gilles BUISSON

Saint-Romain

In Saint-Romain there is a hidden, almost secret place, accessible only by foot. Twenty minutes from the center of the village you reach Mont Marsan, and from there you find an astounding panorama opens up, over the majestic cliffs, on the houses of the village, the ruins of the Castle and of course, the vineyards of Saint-Romain! (N 46°59'37.9 - E 4°42'36.3)

ERIC DE SUREMAIN

Château de Monthelie

Monthelie

Above all, Monthelie is a nice countryside to wander around, to immerse yourself in its atmosphere, to inhale its aromas, to imagine its history. The twelfth century church and the Castle, built by my ancestors in 1746, testify to the immense history of this village, always marked by the rhythm of work in the vineyards. Among the different perspectives that allow you to explore it, I suggest arriving from Auxey-Duresses. Take the time to explore.

AUBERT LEFAS

Domaine LEJEUNE

Pommard

A part of my heart, there is no doubt about it, beats for all the beautiful and ancient houses of the village of Pommard. All of its historical buildings, built mostly between the fifteenth and the eighteenth century, are a remarkable testimony to the work of man and his link with this place for over 600 years. The producers of Pommard are proud of making a living by working this land and the fruits of its vineyards. Without a great *terroir*, even the best *vigneron* would find his work resulting in simply an agricultural product, pleasant but without character. It is only through the alliance between a man and the working of his land that great wines are made. A visit to our cellar, whose first foundation dates back to the eighteenth century, is proof that our traditions are still alive today, and you will find well-deserved refreshment after a promenade in the vineyards of Pommard.

ALEXANDRE VAUDOISEY

Domaine VAUDOISEY-CREUSEFOND

Pommard

I was born in 1988 and I have always lived in Pommard. I soon became passionate about becoming a winemaker, and from 2011, after studying in Beaune, I took over the management of my family's *domaine*. Here in Côte d'Or there are places that you must absolutely see, such as the splendid building of the Hospices de

Beaune, built in the mid-fifteenth century. Other itineraries are more obscure, as in the case of the Sentier des Cabottes in Auxey-Duresses: a walking path that starts from the church square follows along the path to some thirty late-medieval *cabottes*, which were built with stones and served as shelter for shepherds and for the *vignerons*.

DOMINIQUE LAFON

Domaine des Comtes LAFON

Meursault

I love the city of Beaune and the cycling routes that run toward Santenay or ascend in the direction of the village of Bouilland. I love to have a drink in the city center, at the *Bout du Monde*, and then have dinner right in front, at the *Caves Madeleine*. I love to walk the square of Meursault, feel its suspended atmosphere, its empty spaces, before a cheerful dinner at the nearby *Chevreuil* restaurant. I love coming back from the Mâconnais after a beautiful lunch at *Les Terrasses* restaurant in Tournus.

NICOLAS MESTRE

Domaine MICHELOT

Meursault

Here the seasons are marked by colors and views that change from month to month. Winters are cold, sometimes unforgiving; summers, hot and dry. But this is what the vineyard needs to complete its vegetative cycle. These changes of season can be best grasped along the Rue des Grands Cru by bike, the landscape changing during every season! And to avoid the usual routes just go up the hill of Meursault, where you find the statue of Saint-Christophe, and admire the view of the village and the entire Côte, from Beaune to Santenay.

Be careful not to miss an opportunity for a visit to Beaune's Saturday morning market, with its inebriating scents and flavors: cheeses, flowers, chickens, honey, truffles, vegetables, salami ... a real carousel for the taste buds! And of course you cannot leave without drinking a glass of Meursault in one of the *bistrots* overlooking the squares of Beaune: most likely you will meet a *vigneron*!

JEAN-MARC ROULOT

Domaine ROULOT

Meursault

I am a *vigneron* and I am an actor. I did theater studies and since 1989 I started to make wine in the family *domaine*, while continuing my second job in acting. I feel like a citizen of the world, but also a man of my town: I am very attached to my Meursault. Here the walk that I love to do is the path that starts from the hill, at the height of the Saint-Christophe hollow: it winds through the woods passing under the houses of Blagny and from here climbs up the cliff until you see from above the village of Saint-Aubin. The return to Meursault is a passage through the vineyards, first those of Blagny, then Perrières, Genevrières, Bouchères ... For me it remains one of the most rewarding walks you can make among the vineyards.

JEAN MICHEL CHARTRON

Domaine Jean CHARTRON

Puligny-Montrachet

My sister Anne-Laure and I are the children and grandchildren of *vignerons*—our family has been involved in this profession for five generations! As a child we tagged along after our grandfather Jean-Georges in the vineyards and in the cellar, and every Sunday we opened a special bottle, THE bottle ... In our youth, we had a special place we would go, and to which we still return to this day. It's a wooded area full of trails near Gamay which passes over Chassagne-Montrachet and the village of Saint-Aubin, and overlooks the vineyards. Do not miss this extraordinary view! (N 46.95442° - E 4.73221°)

LAURENCE GAGNARD

Domaine FONTAINE-GAGNARD

Chassagne-Montrachet

More than a tourist itinerary, I want to share a moment of the year that is particularly close to my heart: it is the morning snack, the ritual of *casse-croûtes*, we share among the rows of vines on the day when we harvest our most panoramic vineyard, La Romanée. From there, high up among the vineyards of Chassagne, the view spills out below us, over the farm in Morgeot, further out toward the hill of Bouzeron, and as far as the eye can see towards the Saône plain.

ARNAUD MITANCHEY

Domaine Saint Marc

Paris l'hôpital – Hautes Côtes de Beaune

I started working in my family's *domaine* in 2012, driven by my love for the land and by the teachings of my father. My village, Paris l'Hôpital, is home to only 250 souls and is located under the Montagne des Trois-Croix. It is crossed by the Voie Verte, a path of about fifteen kilometers over the hills, between villages and countryside: from Santenay it leads to the medieval village of Nolay, retracing the trail of the old railway that connected Côte-d'Or and Saône-et-Loire.

FABIO MONTRASI

CHÂTEAU des RONTETS

Fuissé - Mâconnais

One of the various positive features of the Mâconnais is its proximity to the west with the gentle hills that distinguish the Charolais region. Here, vineyards give way to pastures and little woods and the breeding of cows and goats. For a short break from the almost hegemonic presence of the vineyard, walk less than four kilometers from the Roche de Solutré and you will reach a small village on the ridge: La Grange du Bois. In addition to offering a fantastic view of the calcareous formations of the two bluffs, recently promoted as one of the 41 *Grands Sites de France* (*rochedesolutre.com*), this tiny village, located about 500 meters above sea level, hosts the remains of a Romanesque chapel of the thirteenth century, and even more importantly, a great cheese producer. The farm Les Ptis Biloounes has about sixty goats and six cows, with a production that follows the natural rhythms of the animals left to freely graze (*www.ptis-biloounes.com*). This is a stop we recommend to friends, as well as to the enthusiasts who come to visit us, as it is essential to understand the different aspects of this territory and to taste some of its most typical and interesting products.

"NOT TO MISS"

THE CITY OF BEAUNE

It is not difficult to imagine the city of Beaune as a pastry, one of those eaten at tea time, or rather, like a soft and colorful *macaron*. Beaune is just so: round, enclosed by the ancient walls, tidy, aristocratic and lively. Its central streets are vital and buzzing between the continuous passage of tourists and the glitter of the windows of patisserie, wine bars and numerous art galleries and antique shops. Defined as a *Ville d'Art et d'Histoire* (a term used by the Ministry of Culture to describe and protect cities of particular value for their art and history), Beaune links its aristocratic history to the Dukes of Burgundy who, from the fourteenth century, chose it as their residence. Beaune is also a temerarious city that suffered a five-week siege by French troops when they refused to submit to King Louis XI in 1477. Beaune has numerous portals that interrupt the continuity of the walls around the ancient center of the town. There are two main historical entrances, the *Porte Saint-Nicolas* to the north and *Porte Marie de Bourgogne* to the south-east. Both retain the charm of their triumphal entrances. A pleasant ride around the city follows the *Remparts* and runs along the well-preserved walls with their bastions built in the fifteenth century.

Beaune offers tourists numerous treasures to discover, starting with the *Hôtel-Dieu-Les Hospices de Beaune* that Chancellor Nicolas Rolin founded in 1443. The architectural symbol of the city with its roofs decorated by multicolored majolica tiles attests to the magnificence of the Flemish-Burgundian style. The *Hôtel-Dieu* was built by Jehan Wiscrere to welcome and aid the poor and the sick. Inside, a tour takes you down the old halls, through the kitchen, the chapel, the Great Hall of the Poor and showcases more than 5,000 artifacts including carpets, tapestries, furniture, sculptures and tools for everyday use in the old hospital. Among the gems, the marvelous polyptych of the Last Judgment by Roger van der Weyden stands out, a masterpiece of Flemish art created between 1445 and 1448.

Another building not to be missed is the *Hôtel des Ducs de Bourgogne*, now the *Musée du Vin de Bourgogne*. This residence of the Dukes of Burgundy, built between the fourteenth and sixteenth centuries, holds a collection of everything that revolves around winemaking in Burgundy, the wines and the producers, from antiquity to today. On display are various instruments and tools, antique furnishings and the wonderful tapestries from the town of Aubusson and those created by Jean Lurçat and Michel Tourlière. The collection includes detailed geological charts and interesting historical documents that shed light on business relationships and the historical prices of *cuvées* coming from the various lieux-dits. Close to the museum is the *collegiate basilica of Notre-Dame de Beaune*, an example of the Burgundian Romanesque style onto which successive interventions have been grafted, in the Gothic period and then in the nineteenth century by the architect Viollet Le Duc.

Heading north from the center toward *Porte Saint-Nicolas* you come to the small *Musée Marey* dedicated to the physiologist Etienne Jules Marey, inventor of the chronograph, who was born in Beaune in 1830. The museum traces the passage from photography to cinema through documents, models and films. Moving from the central *Place Carnot* toward the southeast we cross the charming *Passage Saint-Hélène*, half-hidden on the side of the square that leads to *Rue Poterne* and the *Museum of Fine Arts* attached to the *Porte Marie de Bourgogne*. The museum presents a variety of works between the fifteenth and nineteenth centuries.

As a final destination, we suggest the *Moutarderie Fallot*, a historical mustard factory that welcomes you with an interactive and sensorial tour that allows visitors to discover through pictures, videos, experiments and tastings this exceptional local product, a key ingredient in many Burgundian recipes.

ATHENAEUM

BEAUNE

5, Rue de l'Hôtel-Dieu - Tel. +33 (0) 3 80 250830
www.athenaeum.com

Founded in 1989 in the heart of the city opposite the *Hôtel-Dieu*, the *Athenaeum* is no doubt one of the largest bookshops anywhere specializing in the world of wine, a unique place and essential point of reference for wine enthusiasts.

The center of the shop is dedicated to a remarkable wine library with an astounding array of titles: novels, travel books, comics, essays, precious historical tomes, trade magazines and every other wine-related literature imaginable, from vineyard maps to DVDs. Another section is devoted to tasting items and wine service accessories.

Next to this universe of wine paraphernalia is the area dedicated to gastronomy, with numerous books signed by important chefs as well as more general titles on both local and international cuisine.

For some years now the Athenaeum has also operated a wine bar with a wide selection built around the best of Burgundy. More than a specialized bookstore, the Athenaeum is a temple to wine culture, a fantastic place in which to spend hours searching and browsing and losing all notion of time.

FROMAGERIE ALAIN HESS

Beaune - 7, Place Carnot - Tel. +33 (0) 3 80 247351
www.fromageriealainhess.com

Entering from the elegant Place Carnot, this delightful boutique of cheeses and specialty foods will greet you with a great amount of odors that for some might be unbearable but is certain to intoxicate fans of *fromage*. Masters of cheese for three generations, the Hess family produces Délice de Pommard, Cîteaux, Ami du Chambertin and du Chèvre, Époisses (the most typical Burgundian cheese) just to give a few examples. But the offerings go well beyond the region, with specialties from all over France taking in an immense range of cheeses from milk of cows, sheep and goats. And not only. Many other delicacies await gourmets: from *foie gras* to chocolate, from tea to coffee. Prices are in line with those of top-quality products.

MARCHÉ HEBDOMADAIRE

BEAUNE

Place de la Halle - Sabato 6.00 h - 12.30 h

If you are in the Côte d'Or for the weekend, do not miss this market, a feast for the eyes, and of course for the palate. Each Saturday morning this lively event takes place in the elegant city center, at the foot of the Hotel-Dieu, inside and outside the Halles (the covered part of the market where, at the end of November, Hospices de Beaune wine auction event takes place). If you're not distracted by the many other items on offer, you might be able to concentrate on local gastronomy. People arrive early and wander among the stalls, armed with traditional woven baskets. Farmers offer fruit and vegetables from their gardens, the place is stuffed with *baguettes* and stalls full of *charcuterie*, cheeses and all food specialties of the region, including the famous *poulets de Bresse*, feathery incarnation of the French flag.

All this in a riot of colors and flavors that make the market a place of authentic Burgundian folklore, a miniature version of its older brother in Dijon (also worth a visit). The atmosphere evokes that of the nineteenth-century Parisian market, Les Halles, candidly described in *Le Ventre de Paris* by Émile Zola. If that book were a painting, it would be one of the most beautiful still-life's ever.

LES HAUTES CÔTES

The Hautes Côtes, where vineyards thin out and hills are splashed with green fields, hills, meadows and woods in the upper half of the Côte d'Or. Viticulture is augmented with all manners of agriculture, breeding, and cheese production. Nuits-Saint-Georges is a good starting point for excursions through the Hautes Côtes de Nuits. Stop in the village of Arcenant to taste the fruit liqueurs of Gilles Joannet (both his cassis and blackberry versions are delicious). Climb to Echevronne, in the area that separates the two Hautes Côtes and enjoy the scenery. Check out the small, hidden village of Bouilland, bisected by the river Rhoin and surmounted by rock walls where enthusiasts practice free-climbing. From Pommard or Meursault you'd reach the Hautes Côtes de Beaune starting from the village of Saint-Romain, one of the oldest in the region, surrounded by high clliffs that dominate the entire valley. There are also walks here: woods, hills, cliffs, villages and trails, in particular the charming *Sentier des Roches* that starts from Saint-Romain, crosses Orches, Évelle, Baubigny and arrives at La Rochepot, where the fairytale towers of the Château built on the peak stand out from the rock of the *Roche-Nolay*. The castle can also be reached starting from Saint-Aubin, an enchanting sight when it appears after a climb over a few curving hills. Passing Saint-Aubin you arrive in Nolay, with its famous covered market, a perfectly preserved medieval jewel in the heart of this small town, imposing in its architecture complete with red stone roofs that blend with the thatched-roof houses in an atmosphere of the Middle Ages.

RESTAURANTS

AU FIL DU ZINC

CHABLIS

18, Rue des Moulins | Tel. +33 (0) 3 86 339639

www.au-fil-du-zinc.restaurant-chablis.fr

Open for lunch and dinner, closed Tuesday and Wednesday.

Japanese chef Ryo Nagahama honed his skills through important Parisian experiences at the starred kitchens of Joël Robuchon (l'Atélier) and Yannick Alléno (Le Meurice). Today you can taste his cooking from the kitchen of this cozy restaurant in the heart of Chablis, already known as a wine-bar (Le Laroche) and now redesigned as a *néo-bistrot* by manager Fabien Espana, who also smartly revised Le Soufflot in Irancy. The menu is seasonally updated, with ingredients selected in large part from local suppliers (such as the unforgettable lamb from Ferme de Clavisy, in Noyers-sur-Serein). The wine list is also focused on local *domaines*, and even though you will find Chablis' most famous labels (Dauvissat and Droin, for example), there is also space for the more natural, organic producers of the moment (Pattes Loup, De Moor), as well as a careful selection of less-well-known wineries from obscure local *appellations* such as Irancy and Epineuil.

Several tasting menus from € 32 to € 60

CHEZ BRUNO

DIJON

80, Rue Jean-Jacques Rousseau | Tel. +33 (0) 3 80 661233
Open only in the evening. Closed Sunday and Monday.

Bruno Crouzat's wine bar has been attending to the most cultivated palates of the city of Dijon for years. The two big blackboards of this friendly *bar à vins* (and *à jambons*) include an almost exaggerated number of available wines, but this is only the tip of the iceberg. In the cellar you will find everything else, and more. Excellent options also abound in the *charcuterie* department, filled by suppliers such as Maison Conquet of Laguiole. The *coup de grâce* is dealt by the cheeses, such as the Saint-Marcellin of Mère Richard, whose name is enough to make your triglycerides go wild.

LA RÔTISSERIE DU CHAMBERTIN BISTROT LUCIEN

GEVREY-CHAMBERTIN

6, Rue du Chambertin | Tel. +33 (0) 3 80 343320
www.rotisserie-chambertin.com
Closed Sunday evening and Monday.

Gevrey has needed a spot like this, and it's no coincidence that the Bistrot Lucien has established itself in only a few years as a "must stop" on the itineraries of many wine tourists on the road in the Côte de Nuits. Chef Thomas Collomb and his wife Lucie (owners also of the starred restaurant La Maison des Cariatides, in Dijon) renovated this historical restaurant, now contemporary: welcoming, spacious and spread over several rooms. In the kitchen the focus is on traditional bistro recipes, such as the tender beef cheeks (*daube de joue de boeuf en cocotte*), revisited with a lighter hand and accessible prices, especially in the evening during the traditional menu (*entrée + plat + dessert* at 28 euros). The wine list is a well-articulated offering of the most famous Grand Cru (always welcome), as well as a range of more affordable options.

Menu from € 23 to € 48

LA JEANNETTE

GEVREY-CHAMBERTIN

1, Rue du Gaizot | Tel. +33 (0) 3 80 334195

Open from 10am to 7pm. Closed on Wednesday and Sunday afternoons.

Eccentric, original, curious—entering the little restaurant of Carine Veysset is a trip back to the sixties and seventies, between vinyl and anisette bottles, vintage posters and souvenirs, formica furniture and turntables that play the music our generation was weaned upon. The gastronomic offering is neither broad nor elaborate, but has character: the inevitable escargots and *jambon persillé*, a single dish of the day (the *boeuf bourguignon* is often delicious), pancakes and sweet *crêpes*. You will also find a discreet selection of teas and coffees, which satisfy even our most uncompromising Italian standards. If you're willing to opt for sentiment over gourmet ambitions, you cannot leave Gevrey without having set foot in Jeannette.

AUBERGE DU COTEAU

VILLARS-FONTAINE

Route de Côte de Nuits | Tel. + 33 (0) 3 80 611050

Open for lunch and dinner. Closed Monday and Tuesday.

To reach the Auberge du Côteau you leave the usual vineyard routes and climb from Nuits-Saint-Georges into the woods of the Hautes Côtes de Nuits to Villars-Fontaine. The Auberge is the destination of many local habitués and *vignerons*, with a country atmosphere that is genuine, noisy and lively. An imposing brazier dominates the main hall, where the scent and the heat of the fire further warm the environment. The cuisine is traditional and a bit rustic; the inn's specialty is grilled meats (the *côte de veau Charolaise* is particularly succulent). At lunchtime, the menu of the day is around 15 euros, and in general the prices are more than fair, also because of the abundant portions—keep this in mind when you order. We found the wine list to be a bit too "pared down." It's a pity not to be able to match some of these meat dishes with tastier bottles.

Menu from € 22 to € 29

LA FERME DE LA RUCHOTTE

BLIGNY-SUR-OUCHE

La Ruchottes | Tel. +33 (0) 3 80 200479

http://laruchotte.blogspot.it/

Open only for lunch, Tuesday, Friday, Saturday and Sunday. Indispensible to book.

If you wish to have lunch at an authentic Burgundian farm, there is only one option: the Ferme Auberge de la Ruchotte, in the village of Bligny-sur-Ouche, in the Hautes Côtes de Beaune, a fifteen-minute drive from Beaune. Frédéric Ménager, one of France's *haute cuisine chefs*, will be there to welcome you. He has clearly found his calling in Bligny-Sur-Ouche, where he brings substance and authenticity to the menu. The high quality of raw ingredients (all strictly organic and local) is enhanced with flavors of yesteryear: one dish particularly, the roasted guinea-fowl with *chanterelles*, was as simple as it was tasty. Lunch is shared with other guests at a huge oak table. The selection of cheeses is remarkable. The wine list, obviously of "natural" inspiration, is the fruit of much thoughtful research--and it's fun.

Menu around € 50

BISSOH

BEAUNE

1, Rue Faubourg St. Jacques | Tel. +33 (0) 3 80 249950

To suggest a Japanese restaurant in the heart of Burgundy might appear extravagant, however this ray of sunlight a few steps from Beaune's main *boulevard* is reputed to be the best in the region and is of certain quality. The cuisine is interpreted rigorously by chef Mikihiko Sawahat, turning out exemplary dishes thanks to a scrupulous selection of raw ingredients (sushi and sashimi of considerable quality). Pinot Noir, a faithful ally of his preparations, finds ample space on the wine list, with a wide and even surprising selection of labels, very focused on the smaller *domaines* of the Côte d'Or. For three years Bissoh has doubled its efforts by opening a second small space (42 Rue Maufoux, tel +33 (0) 3 80 240102) in which the dishes are even more traditionally Japanese.

Tasting menus between € 45 and € 75

LE BISTROT BOURGUIGNON

BEAUNE

8, Rue Monge (city center, pedestrian street) | Tel. +33 (0) 3 80 222324

Jean-Jacques Hegner, a photographer by profession, opened his photo equipment shop in Rue Monge in the mid-1970s. Infected by the festivities of the *Vente des Vins des Hospices*, he began offering wine and cheese samples at the counter. This experiment proved successful and soon became an unmissable stop, so much so that around 1985, the place was transformed into a real bistro with wine service by the glass. This was a gamble in a time when serving Puligny or Corton so casually would have sounded like sacrilege. Jean-Jacques unfortunately passed away in 2016, but the tradition continues thanks to his wife Agnès, who had always shared this adventure with her husband. The atmosphere is welcoming and eclectic, the vintage furnishings blend with design, art and walls full of history. At the Bistrot Bourguignon the kitchen offers a few tasty dishes, which incorporate the best of Burgundian tradition: the inevitable *oeufs en meurette*, *escargots*, *boeuf bourguignon*. The wine list is middling, but with a satisfying choice of wines by the glass.

Menu for € 15

LA BUISSONNIÈRE

BEAUNE

34, Rue Maufoux | Tel. +33 (0) 9 50 732175

Closed Saturday and Sunday.

We were advised to try this restaurant by two different Beaune *vignerons*, and we figured it was worth a shot. The restaurant is dominated by a long counter, furnished in vintage style. The open kitchen guarantees transparency and adds personality to the room, which the owners Sébastien and Charlotte (she is in the kitchen) have made a stylish, friendly place. The kitchen's offerings are colored by simple yet delicious dishes. While waiting for the main courses, we really enjoyed the breaded frog legs, and the veal sweetbreads with vegetable *tempura* were truly special. The selection of wines is in line with the type of restaurant, but for an establishment in Beaune does seem to lack a bit of passion, with several less expensive options from the Hautes Côtes, the Mâconnais and Beaujolais Average cost between € 25 and € 40.

CAVES MADELEINE

BEAUNE

8, Rue du Faubourg Madeleine | Tel. +33 (0) 3 80 229330

Closed on Wednesdays and Sundays.

The handing over from the old owner Laurent "Lolo" Brelin to the chef Martial Blanchon did not compromise all the good reasons we had for returning to this small and lively *bistro*. The furniture is still the same: a few small tables and a large communal table. You will find yourself in front of a seasonal soup or a plate of crunchy baked pork, elbow to elbow with other Burgundy-addicts, perfectly unknown to you until a moment before but immediately brought together by your common passion, and open to sharing. The menu of the day is indicated on a large blackboard at the back of the room and the dishes change seasonally, according to the availability of certain meats and vegetables purchased from local producers. The unique selection of wines is well visible on the shelves, offered at fair prices, far from the homogenous offerings of other local spots. If you are looking for an intimate and private place this is not the right choice, but if you prefer to make friends with strangers over a good bottle of wine, then Caves Madeleine is definitely for you.

LE COMPTOIR DES TONTONS

BEAUNE

22, Rue du Faubourg Madeleine | Tel. +33 (0) 3 80 241964

www.lecomptoirdestontons.com

Open only for dinner; closed Sunday and Monday.

A short walk from the center of Beaune is a small restaurant that will never disappoint. Le Comptoir des Tontons is fresh and essential, and even though the reception might appear a bit abrupt, you can rest assured of the substance and quality of the kitchen. This kitchen is the kingdom of Pépita, a generous matron with the inevitable scarf knotted in her hair and colorfully-framed glasses. She has the *physique du rôle* of a housewife, but the savvy ideas of a well-directed hostess: she uses only organic products from local farms and seasonal vegetables. Her delicious recipes, tasty and firmly rooted in the local area, demonstrate an incredible dedication to seeking out truly authentic ingredients.

The wine list is consistent with the menu, proposing a brilliant selection of wines from organic and biodynamic farms, with the studied boldness to place unknown *vignerons* alongside prestigious standards.

LA DILETTANTE

BEAUNE

11, Rue du Faubourg Bretonniere | Tel. +33 (0) 380 214859

Closed on Wednesdays and Sundays.

For those who frequent Beaune with a certain regularity, La Dilettante's Laurent "Lolo" Brelin is definitely a reference point, a sort of promoter of those yet-unknown *vignerons*. He has created a kind of "launching ramp" to fame and opportunity for new artisans to be discovered. For years he successfully managed Les Caves Madeleine, a bistro that helped shape his particular personality, with a clear desire to break the somewhat staid patterns of local restaurants. With La Dilettante he changed his mind and moved instead toward a concept of *bar à vin gourmet*: delicious terrines made in house, a remarkable selection of superb cheeses and cured meats. However Lolo's strength continues to be his incredibly researched wine list, bursting with his urgency to explore the margins of the two Côtes. For years this has been a place to talent-scout for the next great natural wines from smaller *domaines* outside of the mainstream. La Dilettante: amateur perhaps in name, but not in fact.

LOISEAU DES VIGNES

BEAUNE

31, Rue Maufoux | Tel. +33 (0) 3 80 241206

www.loiseau-des-vignes.com

Closed Sunday and Monday.

The restaurant was opened in 2007 a few steps from the Hotel Dieu by Dominique, widow of Bernard, and in only a few years assimilated itself among the classic establishments for high regional cuisine. The reassuring *boiserie* of the furnishings and the attention to detail play on measured but captivating color combinations, light years away from current minimalist trends in this jewel of a place.

A temperature-controlled wall-cellar cleverly displays about seventy bottles, all served by the glass, safe in their efficient conservation system. In how many other locales of this level is it possible to taste by the glass, without fainting, a white wine from Dominique Lafon or Jean-Marc Roulot or a red from Armand Rousseau or Cécile Tremblay? This repertoire of the great wines of the two *côtes* presides over a refined cuisine, with a meticulous precision in the execution (couscous with *Boeuf de Charolles*) and in exciting innovations (Saint-Jacques with pistachios and potato carbonara). The great classics are reinterpreted with a masterful awareness, such as in the *foie gras confit* or the egg with black truffle. In addition to a magnificent selection of wines by the glass, the wine cellar is absolutely up to the par with the rest of the place, designed with a sense of culture and uncommon means and without encyclopedic ambitions.

Menu Découverte at € 59
Menu Dégustation at € 75
Menu Saveurs at € 119
At lunch, two dishes € 23

LES PÔPIETTES

BEAUNE

10, Rue d'Alsace | Tel. +33 (0) 3 80 219181
www.les-popiettes.com
Open for lunch and dinner. Closed Tuesday and Wednesday.

An informal place a few steps from Place Carnot: it's called Pôpiettes but if you want you can also say *polpette*, since the kitchen, headed by Giada Scarton, speaks Italian. Originally from Turin, she studied anthropology, discovered her passion for food and spent years globetrotting through the kitchens of several restaurants in Australia, New Zealand and France. Her menu is simple but well executed, characterized by a lightness of aromas and flavors, clearly of Mediterranean inspiration. Her Sunday buffet brunch (€ 22) is tasty and convenient. Not the most extensive wine selection, but there are plenty of interesting bottles, with honest mark-ups.

Menu from € 17 to € 32

LA TABLE DU SQUARE

BEAUNE

26, Boulevard Maréchal Foch | Tel. +33 (0) 6 82146050

Closed Sunday and Monday.

Until a few years ago this locale was a staple of Beaune's nightlife loved more for its cool atmosphere as a stylish *bar à vin* than for the quality of its food and wine. Now it has been reimagined as a bistro driven by its kitchen. Romain Escoffier, the Table du Square's brilliant creator, has in fact decided to move from behind the bar to behind the stove, where he crafts a menu without frills, honest and sincere in its dependency on quality, seasonal products. He offers a few dishes that frequently alternate and spotlight strong and genuine flavors (slow-cooked shoulder of lamb, or the black pork ribs of Bigorre, to name a few). The wine list remains a point of pride, centered on classic Burgundy but always inclusive of the most interesting novelties (Mâconnais and Beaujolais included).

For two courses, around € 35

AUPRÈS DU CLOCHER

POMMARD

1, Rue de Nackenheim | Tel. +33 (0) 3 80 222179

www.aupresduclocher.com

Open for lunch and dinner. Closed Tuesday and Wednesday.

An old *maison vigneronne*, overlooking the tree-lined square of the church of Pommard, houses Jean-Christophe Moutet's restaurant. The elevated environment and rather condensed space (with only about thirty seats) is bright and free of affectation, animated by a spontaneous rhythm which is punctuated by the tolling of the bell tower a few meters away that inspires its name. Jean-Christophe has an all-Burgundian focus and opened his restaurant with years of experience as the "second" to Éric Pras from Lameloise at Chagny, always in pursuit of absolute excellence. Even without any particular media clamor, which moreover Moutet in his taciturn way seems to instinctively shy away from, the restaurant of the bell tower has quickly become a well-loved address throughout the entire region, supported by the widespread respect of a large, knowing clientele.

The cooking is decisive in its flavors, more "belly" than brain, and therefore little concerned with entertaining the customer with the usual artifices. Here structure is very present, and does not like to hide itself, a little like the wines of Pommard. We have eaten here often and we continue to return with the same enthusiasm, even if Jean-Christophe is not likely to fuss or make small talk. Instead we are guided by the polar star of the most delicious dishes, like the roasted pigeon with onion compote, or the not-to-miss "cappuccino e cornetto" of *Époisses au pain d'epices*. The wine list focuses on the Côte de Beaune: and if the whites are well-represented (a full page is dedicated to Coche-Dury and it is not unusual to find rare bottlings from Arnaud Ente here), the red *appellations* remain Pommard and Volnay above all, extensively and deeply researched. Art lovers might like to know that occasionally small personal exhibitions of local artists grace the walls of the restaurant. Just before going to press, we learned that since 2019 late spring Jean-Christophe will move his restaurant to a new location in Meursault, rue Charles Giraud, just in front to Jean-Marc Roulot's winery. Good luck and see you soon in Meursault.

Menu from € 32

L'AGASTACHE

VOLNAY

1, Rue de la Cave | Tel. +33 (0) 3 80 211230
http://lagastache-restaurant.com
Open for lunch and dinner. Closing: Sunday and Monday.

In Volnay's ancient bakery, Caroline Carlevato and Nunzio Iacono have recently carved out a local spot, which we found to be a breath of fresh air in the soporific panorama of the restaurants between Volnay and Meursault. Its name recalls a perennial plant with scented leaves, and the restaurant's dishes also follow the cycle of the seasons with flair and lightness. However, they also offer more serious plates, such as the duck breast in cassis sauce or the succulent *Aubrac* fillet with a Pinot Noir reduction. Nunzio derives perhaps from his Sicilian origins in Modica a particular empathy towards meat-based cuisine and garden produce. Seasonal fare is clearly one of his main inspirations, as evidenced by both the origin of the vegetables (from the best local suppliers, such as La Ferme de la Ruchotte, and Les loups' bio) as well as from his own gardens. A bit of Sicilian pride is felt at dessert, with citrus and chocolate often playing the protagonists.

The wine selections are a tribute to the Côte de Beaune, with the artisans of Volnay rightly taking center stage. We are also impressed and convinced by the decision to leave permanent space for a thoughtful selection of basic Bourgogne wines, as well as the Côte Chalonnaise.

A single menu for lunch at € 23, for dinner menus for € 39 and € 45

MAISON LAMELOISE

CHAGNY

36, Place d'Arme | Tel. +33 (0) 3 85 876565
www.lameloise.fr
Open for lunch and dinner. Closed Tuesday and Wednesday.

After their first three Michelin stars were accepted and maintained from 1979 to 2004, followed by two years of purgatory in 2005 and 2006 without the third star, only to conquer it again with honors in 2007, Lameloise has continued its full three-star status to this today. For what it's worth, the prestige indicated by the Michelen Guide does certify how Lameloise unquestionably belongs to the *elite* of French cuisine. Rigor and creativity, taste and aesthetics are composed here in a delicate balance. Chef Éric Pras, well-known for his intransigence, continues to refine and redesign the menu to enhance every single nuance of flavor, and to transmit and protect a sense of beauty, purged of excesses and never an end in itself. *Coquilles Saint-Jacques* steamed with a vintage port and truffle butter reduction, scampi tartare flavored with celery and cream of green apple and mustard, *Bresse* chicken in double preparation, fillet of pigeon glazed with almond cream and Mirabelle plums. Then timeless variations on chocolate-fondant, cream, and pralines nothing short of heavenly. Simply beautiful and delicious dishes leave superlatives in the drawer we would be tempted to always keep open. The formality of the ambience does not prevent you from feeling the welcoming warmth and the service, needless to say, is exceptional, with an attention that neglects no detail. The wine list is a library that collects the best (and not always necessarily the best known) of contemporary Burgundy. Lameloise is a dream. Seeing is believing.

Menu du déjeuner € 82
Menu de l'instant € 145
Menu dégustation from € 195 to € 215

AUX TERRASSES

TOURNUS

18, Avenue du 23 Janvier | Tel. +33 (0) 3 85 51 01 74
www.aux-terrasses.com
Closed Sunday and Monday.

Jean-Michel Carrette's personal journey is rooted in his passion for eating, but the turning point of his professional career came suddenly, on a January morning fifteen years ago. At the time Jean-Michel was running Troisgros in Roanne, but a phone call came, announcing the death of his father, and changed his life. Called back to his native Tournus, he found himself one day at the head of the 25-person brigade that runs the family restaurant, and where, under his father's guidance, a first Michelin star was already obtained. Among his first partners there was Amandine, his future wife, as well as Pascal and Victor, at his side even today. After the initial shock, Jean-Michel took very little time to adjust to his new "home" and was soon able to redirect the style of the cuisine more toward a farm-to-table concept. This is still the guiding concept in his work: you might find the *bioriginaux* beans of Jérôme Gaudillère, the lamb of Ferme de Clavisy, the citrus fruit of Michel Bachès. You will also find dishes with bright flavors, solid presence, juicy textures, composed in a talented way, so as to enhance even the least noble of ingredients. For example, the freshwater zander with black radicchio, shitaké mushrooms and mint, as well as the calf diaphragm with porcini foam, spinach and chickweed leaves. The wine list is the result of continuous research, with an ever more explicit preference toward those artisan-inspired *vins vivants*. From Lyon to Dijon, lists this extensive and intelligent are hard to match.

Menu between € 40 and € 95

L'O DES VIGNES

FUISSÉ

Rue du Bourg | Tel. +33 (0) 385 383340
www.lodesvignes.fr
Closed Tuesday and Wednesday.

Chef Sébastien Chambru's journey began long before he arrived in 2014 at Fuissé. He moved from Japan to Switzerland, from Lyon—where he worked for none other than the late Paul Bocuse—to the French Riviera, at the starred Moulin de

Mougins. The cuisine he developed in Fuissé sums up his the previous experiences in a fresh and inventive style, in which his loud and creative technique does not overwhelm, but rather enhances, the raw ingredients. It is not easy to understand Chambru's true inspiration. There is undoubtedly a playful side to his food, a basic irony that defies and defrauds conventions, proposing combinations of unexplored flavor, as in the *Ôdace* menu, which programs his impulse to dare. But on closer inspection, this is only the outer layer, because it seems that there is no common denominator that unites his compositions. The dishes live on contrasts, like that between water and wine which is recalled (and eluded) in the name of the place. Chambru is an authentic enthusiast of wine, and in fact his list misses none of the best labels from the Mâconnais, and his selection of *domaines* of the Côte d'Or is impeccably updated. Digressions from the local program will reveal some new bottles, proposed at fancy prices, especially in Beaujolais and Côte du Rhone. In January 2018 l'O des Vignes received its first Michelin star. That this should happen on the eve of the promotion of a valuable batch of vineyards in Pouilly-Fuissé to Premier Cru, seems good news all around in food and wine for the entire Mâconnais.

Menus from € 27 to € 70

LA TABLE DE CHAINTRÉ

CHAINTRÉ

72, Place du Luminiaire | Tel. +33 (0) 385 329095

www.latabledechaintre.com

Closed Sunday evening, Monday and Tuesday.

Sébastien and Floriane Grospellier, he in the kitchen and she in the dining room, illuminate a restaurant to which we gladly return. Set in an elegant and well-kept country house, La Table de Chaintré offers both solid and refined dishes, with a rich articulation of flavors. There is only one tasting menu for 60 euros. Among our favorites we recall the spinach and *girolles* salad, the *marbré de canard* with Malmort asparagus, and the scampi sautéed with morelles. Special attention is paid to fish, in deference to white-oriented nature of this cross-section of the Mâconnais, which the wine list smartly interprets (Viré-Clessé of Philippe Valette, Pouilly-Fuissé of Château des Rontets).

All prices reported are indicative and are intended to exclude beverages.

CARTOGRAPHY

LA BOURGOGNE ET SES CINQ RÉGIONS VITICOLES

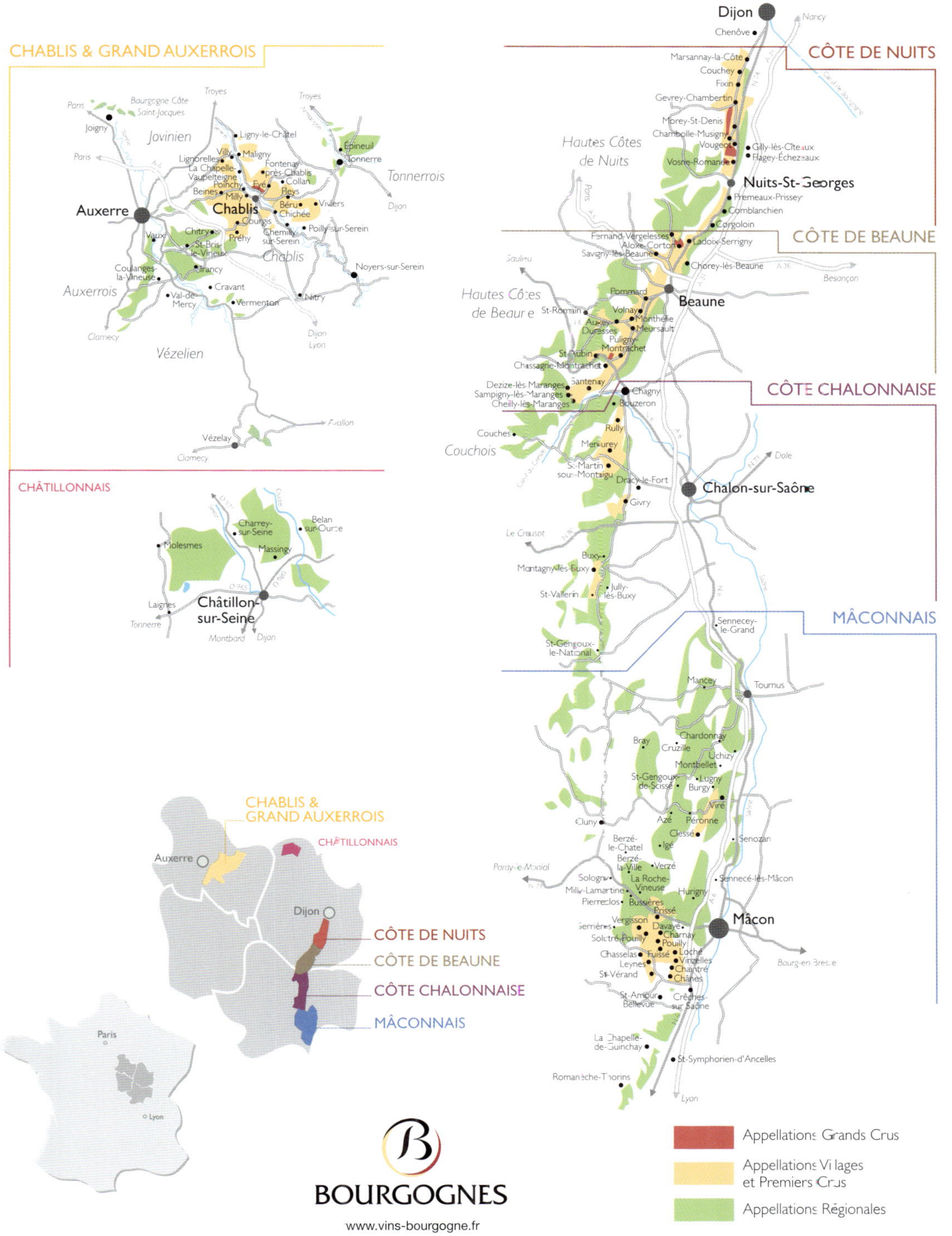

BOURGOGNES

www.vins-bourgogne.fr

CHABLIS

et les vignobles du nord de la Bourgogne

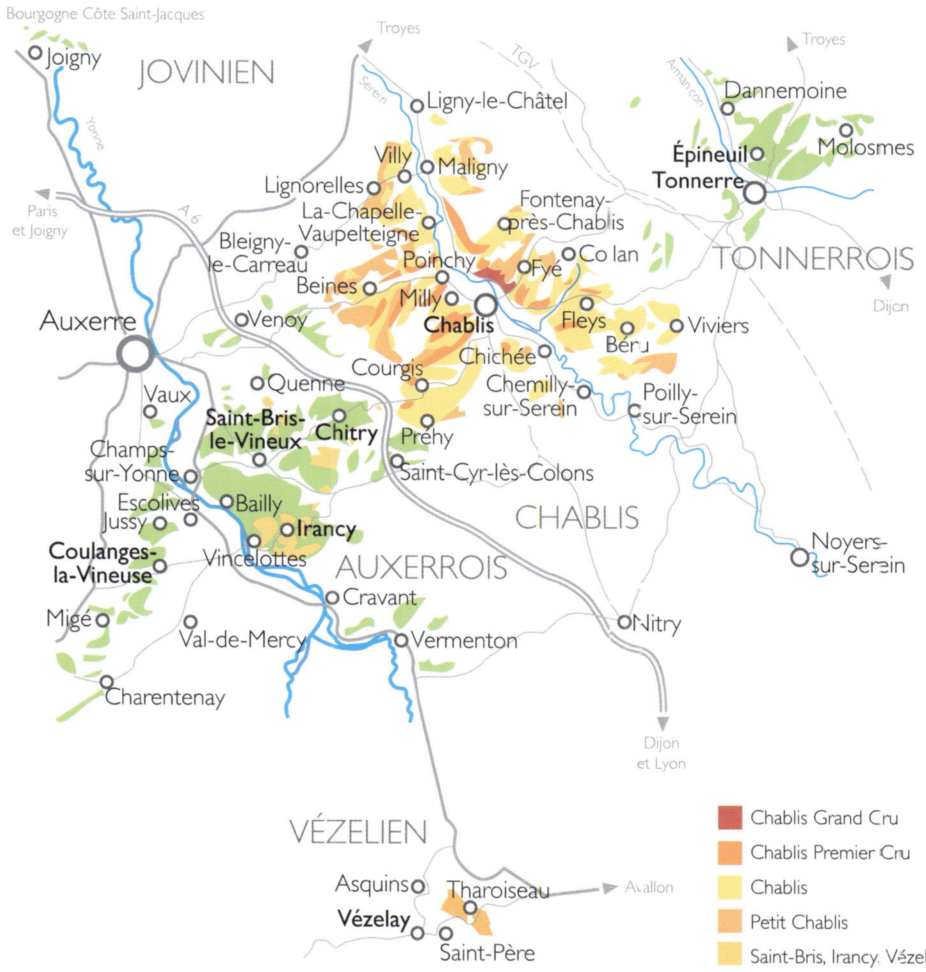

Chablis Grand Cru
Chablis Premier Cru
Chablis
Petit Chablis
Saint-Bris, Irancy, Vézelay
Bourgogne aligoté
Bourgogne Chitry
Bourgogne (blanc et rouge)
Bourgogne Côte Saint-Jacques
Bourgogne Côtes d'Auxerre
Bourgogne Coulanges-la-Vineuse
Bourgogne Épineuil
Bourgogne Passe-tout-grains
Bourgogne Tonnerre
Coteaux Bourguignons
Crémant de Bourgogne

BOURGOGNES

www.vins-bourgogne.fr

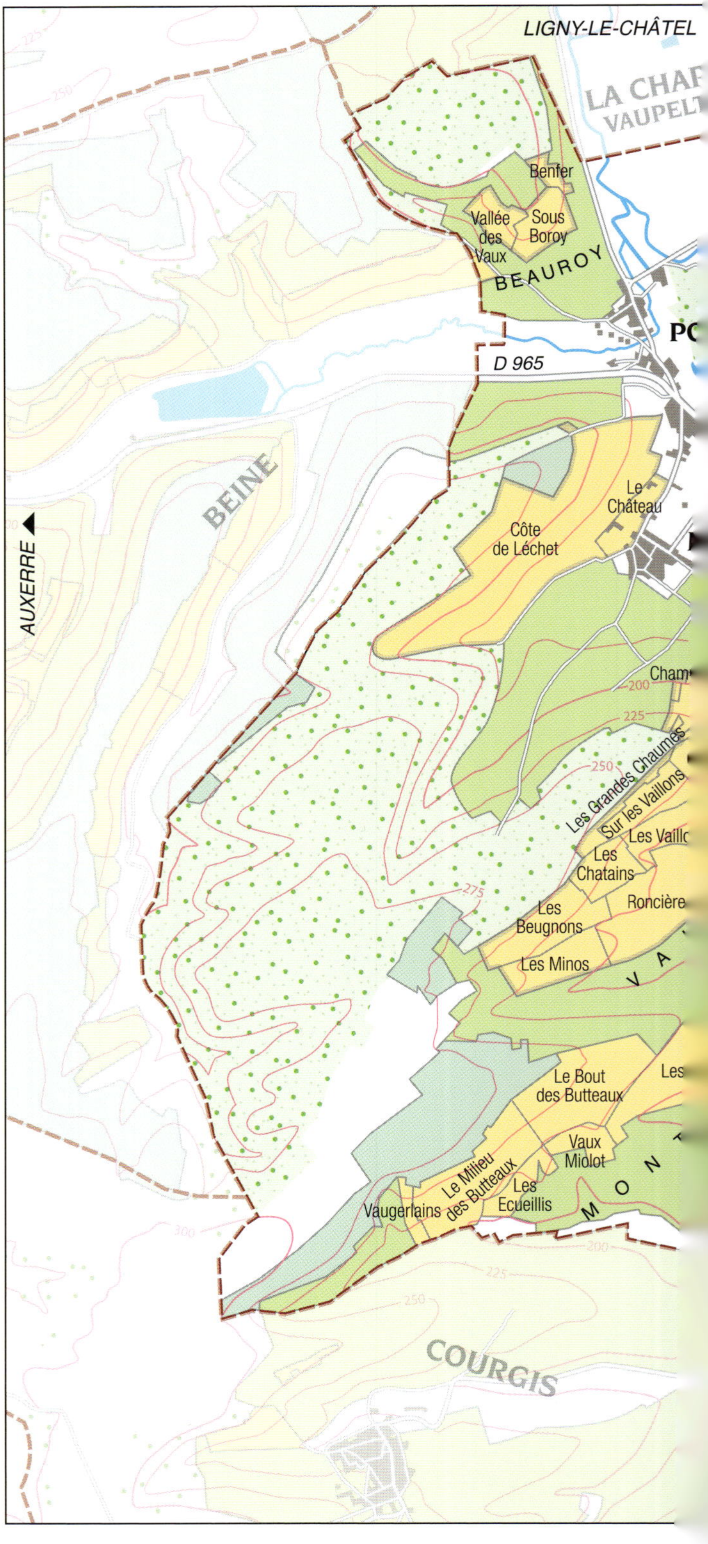

LIGNY-LE-CHÂTEL
LA CHAP
VAUPELT
Benfer
Vallée des Vaux
Sous Boroy
BEAUROY
PO
D 965
BEINE
AUXERRE
Le Château
Côte de Léchet
Cham
Les Grandes Chaumes
Sur les Vaillons
Les Vaillo
Les Chatains
Roncière
Les Beugnons
Les Minos
V A
Le Bout des Butteaux
Les
Vaux Miolot
Le Milieu des Butteaux
Les Ecueillis
Vaugerlains
M O N T
COURGIS

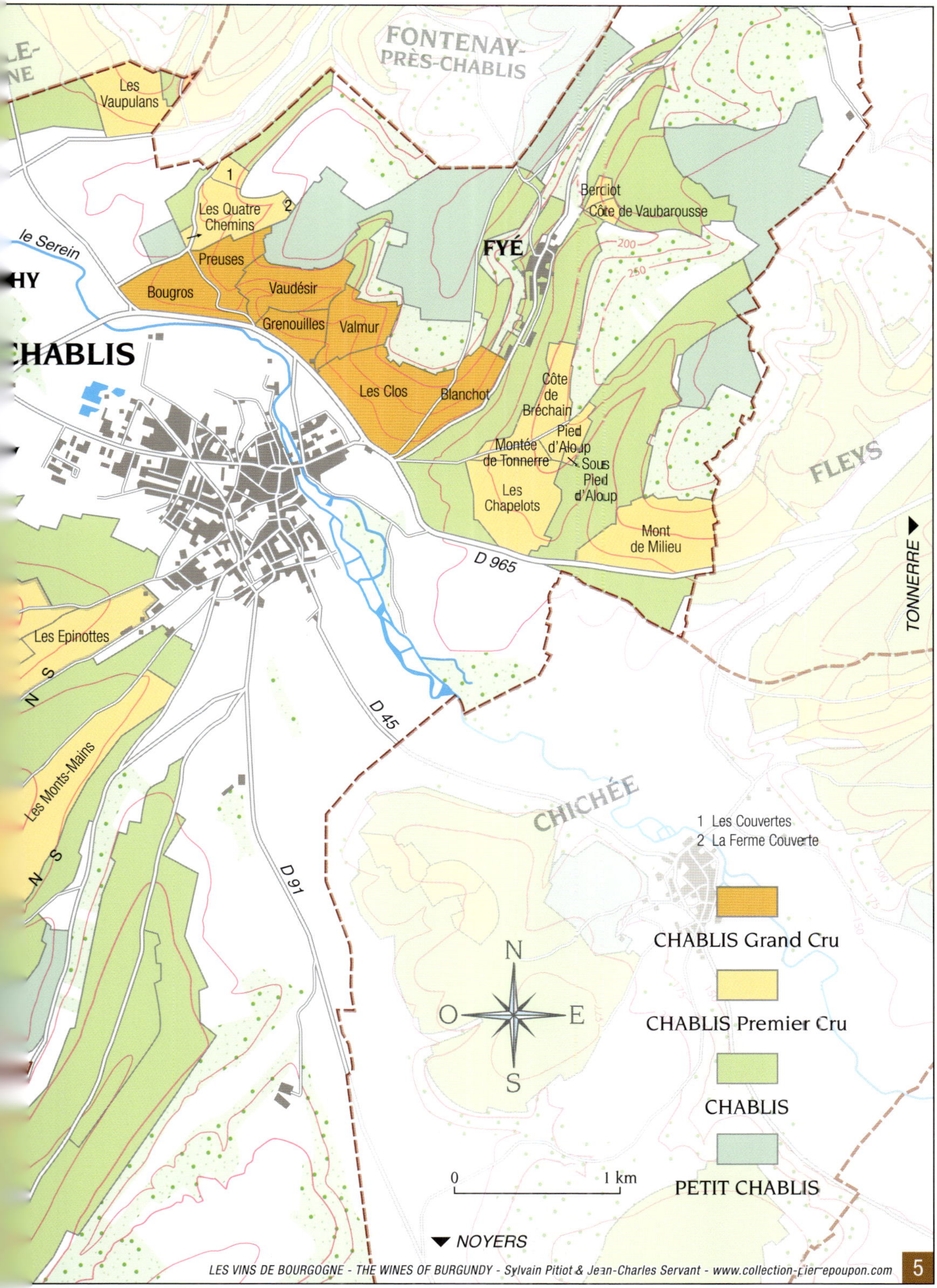

FONTENAY-PRÈS-CHABLIS
Les Vaupulans
1
2
Les Quatre Chemins
le Serein
Preuses
Bougros
Vaudésir
Grenouilles
Valmur
CHABLIS
Les Clos
Blanchot
FYÉ
Berciot
Côte de Vaubarousse
200
250
Côte de Bréchain
Pied d'Aloup
Montée de Tonnerre
Sous Pied d'Aloup
Les Chapelots
Mont de Milieu
FLEYS
TONNERRE
D 965
Les Epinottes
D 45
Les Monts-Mains
D 91
CHICHÉE
1 Les Couvertes
2 La Ferme Couverte
CHABLIS Grand Cru
CHABLIS Premier Cru
CHABLIS
PETIT CHABLIS
N
O
E
S
0
1 km
NOYERS

CÔTE DE NUITS

et Hautes Côtes de Nuits

BOURGOGNES

www.vins-bourgogne.fr

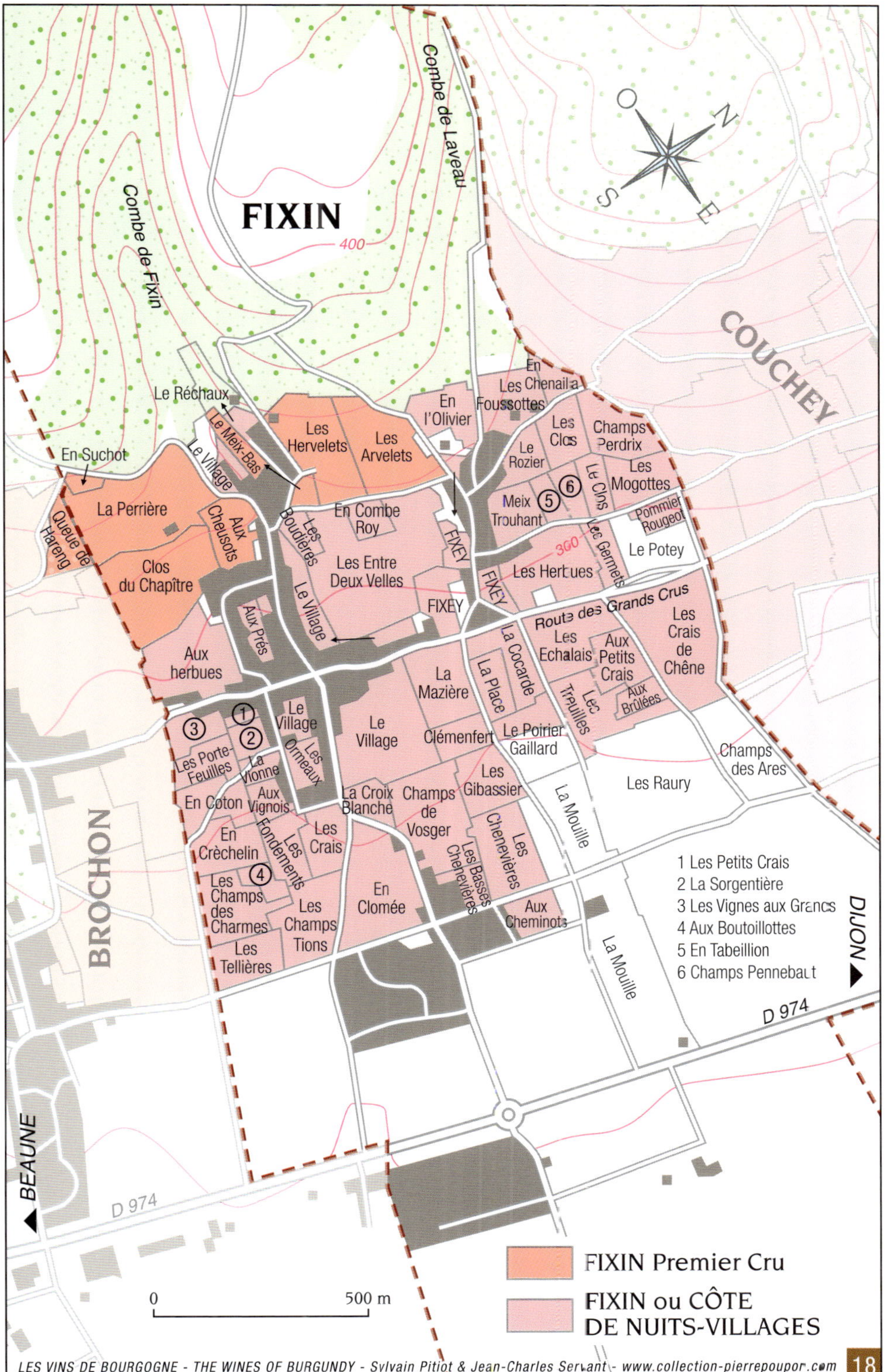
FIXIN
COUCHEY
BROCHON
Combe de Laveau
Combe de Fixin
400
300
Le Réchaux
En Suchot
Le Meix-Bas
Le Village
Les Hervelets
Les Arvelets
En l'Olivier
En Chenailla
Les Foussottes
Les Clos
Champs Perdrix
Le Rozier
Les Mogottes
Le Clos
Meix Trouhant
Pommier Rougeot
Les Germets
Le Potey
La Perrière
Queue de Hareng
Aux Cheusots
Clos du Chapître
Les Boudières
En Combe Roy
Les Entre Deux Velles
FIXEY
Les Herbues
Route des Grands Crus
Les Crais de Chêne
Aux Prés
Le Village
Aux herbues
Les Echalais
Aux Petits Crais
La Cocarde
La Place
La Mazière
Les Trouilles
Aux Brûlées
Le Village
Les Ormeaux
Clémenfert
Le Poirier Gaillard
Champs des Ares
Les Raury
Les Porte-Feuilles
La Vionne
Aux Vignois
En Coton
La Croix Blanche
Champs de Vosger
Les Gibassier
Les Chenevières
Les Basses Chenevières
La Mouille
En Crèchelin
Les Fondements
Les Crais
Les Champs des Charmes
Les Champs Tions
En Clomée
Aux Cheminots
Les Tellières
1 Les Petits Crais
2 La Sorgentière
3 Les Vignes aux Grands
4 Aux Boutoillottes
5 En Tabeillion
6 Champs Pennebaut
DIJON
BEAUNE
D 974
0
500 m
FIXIN Premier Cru
FIXIN ou CÔTE DE NUITS-VILLAGES

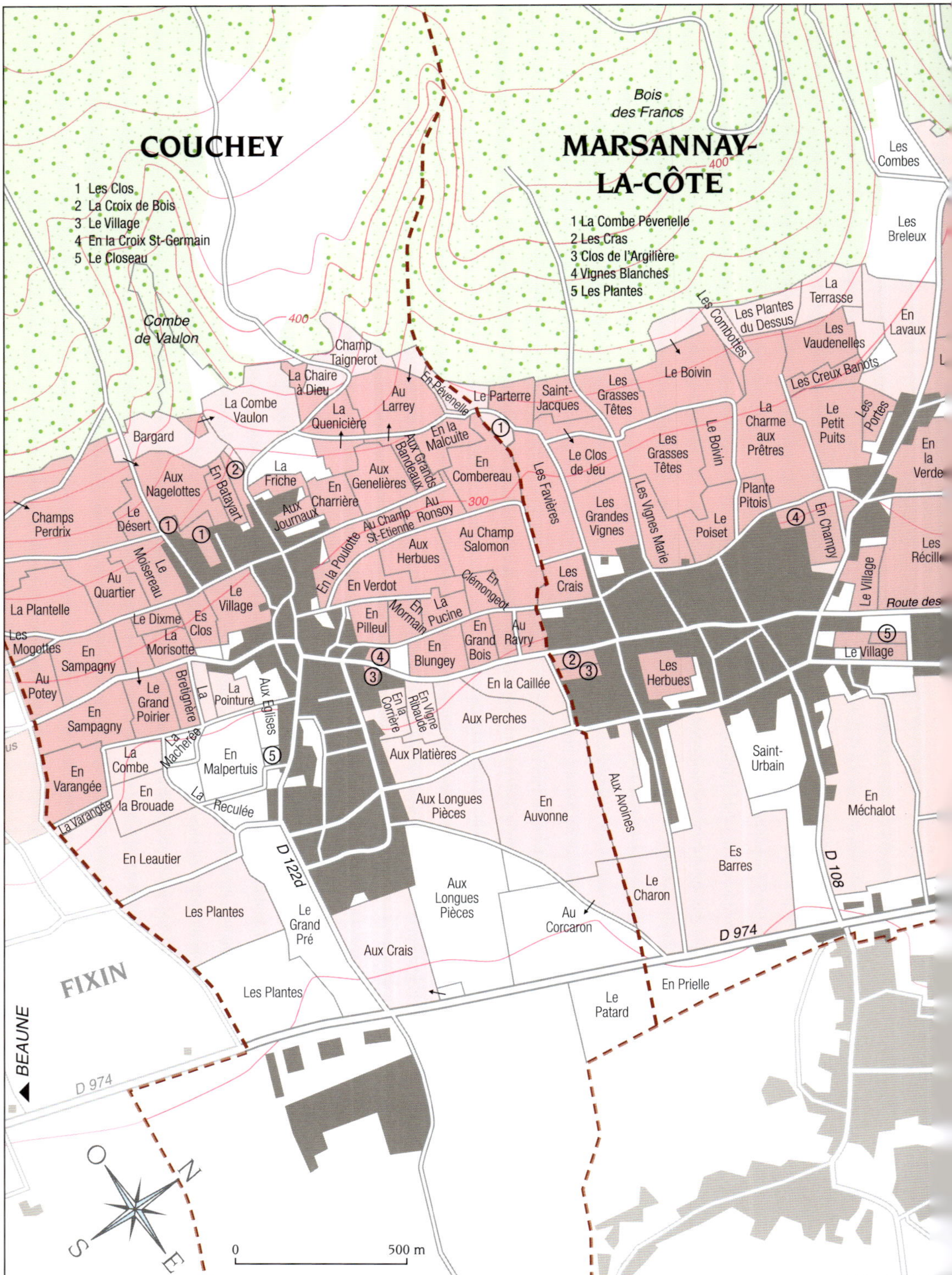
COUCHEY
1 Les Clos
2 La Croix de Bois
3 Le Village
4 En la Croix St-Germain
5 Le Closeau
MARSANNAY-LA-CÔTE
1 La Combe Pévenelle
2 Les Cras
3 Clos de l'Argilière
4 Vignes Blanches
5 Les Plantes
Bois des Francs
400
Combe de Vaulon
Les Combes
Les Breleux
La Terrasse
Les Combottes
Les Plantes du Dessus
En Lavaux
Les Vaudenelles
Les Creux Banots
Le Boivin
Champ Taignerot
La Chaire à Dieu
La Combe Vaulon
Au Larrey
En Pévenelle
Le Parterre
Saint-Jacques
Les Grasses Têtes
La Charme aux Prêtres
Le Petit Puits
Les Portes
En la Verde
Bargard
La Quenicière
En la Malcuite
Le Clos de Jeu
Les Grasses Têtes
Le Boivin
Aux Nagelottes
En Batayart
La Friche
Aux Genelières
Aux Grands Bandeaux
En Combereau
Les Favières
Plante Pitois
En Champy
Champs Perdrix
Le Désert
En Charrière
Aux Journaux
Au Ronsoy
300
Au Champ St-Etienne
Au Champ Salomon
Les Grandes Vignes
Les Vignes Marie
Le Poiset
Les Récille
Le Moisereau
Au Quartier
En la Poulotte
Aux Herbues
Clémongeot
Les Crais
Le Village
En Verdot
La Plantelle
Le Village
Le Dixme
Es Clos
En Pilleul
En Mormain
La Pucine
Route des
Les Mogottes
La Morisotte
En Grand Bois
Au Ravry
En Sampagny
En Blungey
Le Village
Les Herbues
Au Potey
Le Grand Poirier
La Bretignère
La Pointure
Aux Eglises
En la Corrière
En Vigne Ribaude
En la Caillée
En Sampagny
Aux Perches
La Combe
La Macherée
En Malpertuis
Aux Platières
Saint-Urbain
En Varangée
En la Brouade
La Reculée
Aux Longues Pièces
En Auvonne
Aux Avoines
En Méchalot
La Varangée
En Leautier
D 122d
Es Barres
D 108
Aux Longues Pièces
Le Charon
Les Plantes
Le Grand Pré
Au Corcaron
D 974
Aux Crais
FIXIN
Les Plantes
En Prielle
Le Patard
BEAUNE
D 974
O N S E
0 500 m

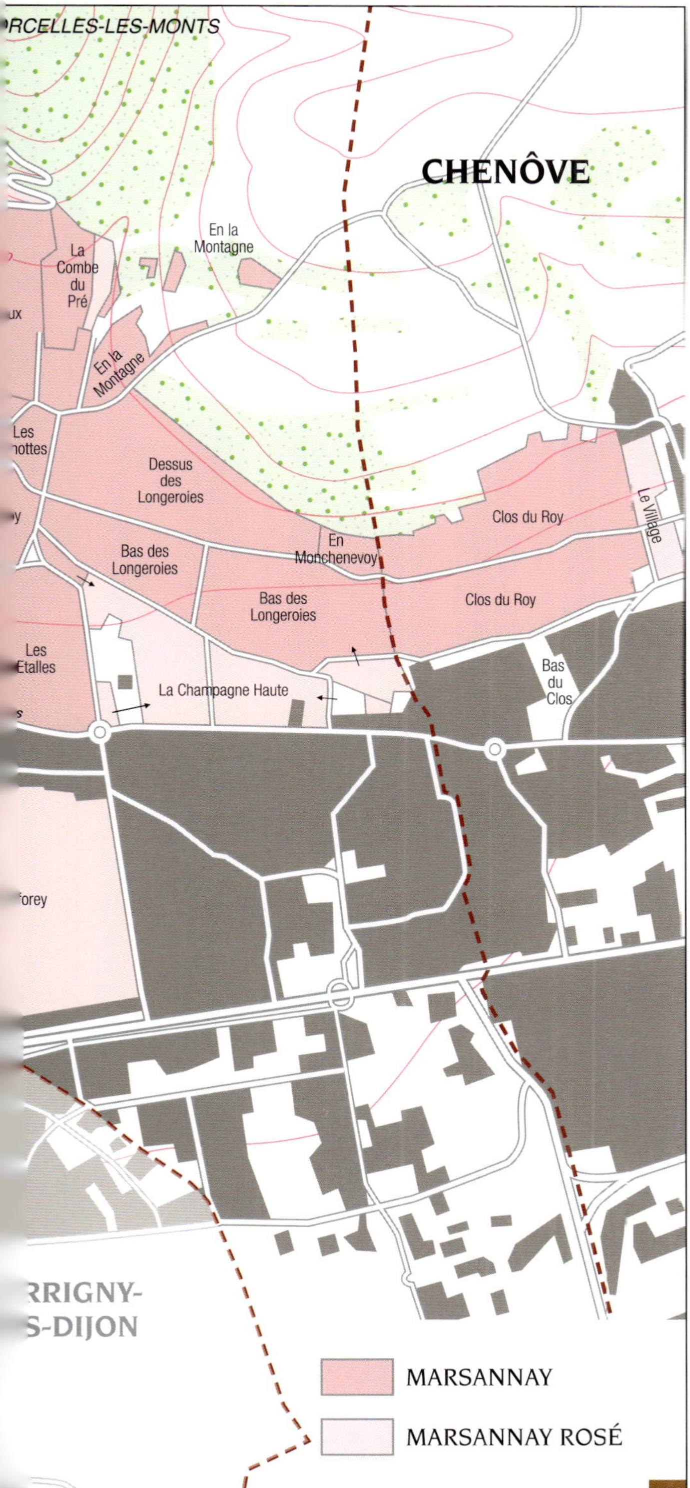
RCELLES-LES-MONTS
CHENÔVE
En la Montagne
La Combe du Pré
ux
En la Montagne
Les
ottes
Dessus des Longeroies
y
Clos du Roy
Le Village
En Monchenevoy
Bas des Longeroies
Bas des Longeroies
Clos du Roy
Les Etalles
Bas du Clos
La Champagne Haute
s
forey
RRIGNY-
S-DIJON
MARSANNAY
MARSANNAY ROSÉ

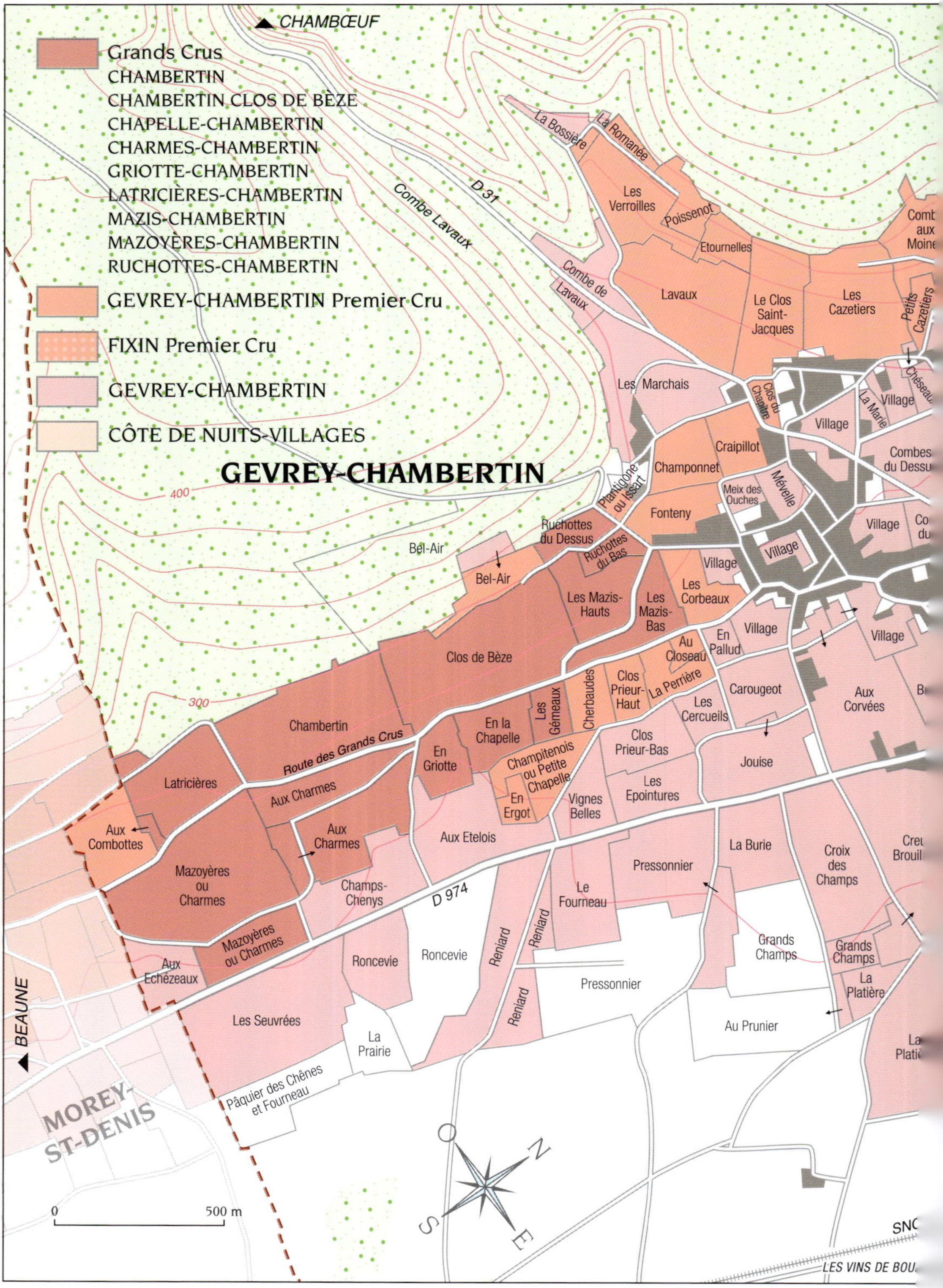

CHAMBŒUF
Grands Crus
CHAMBERTIN
CHAMBERTIN CLOS DE BÈZE
CHAPELLE-CHAMBERTIN
CHARMES-CHAMBERTIN
GRIOTTE-CHAMBERTIN
LATRICIÈRES-CHAMBERTIN
MAZIS-CHAMBERTIN
MAZOYÈRES-CHAMBERTIN
RUCHOTTES-CHAMBERTIN
GEVREY-CHAMBERTIN Premier Cru
FIXIN Premier Cru
GEVREY-CHAMBERTIN
CÔTE DE NUITS-VILLAGES
GEVREY-CHAMBERTIN
La Bossière
La Romanée
Les Verroilles
Poissenot
Etournelles
Combe Lavaux
D 31
Combe de Lavaux
Lavaux
Le Clos Saint-Jacques
Les Cazetiers
Petits Cazetiers
Les Marchais
Clos du Chapitre
La Marie
Village
Craipillot
Champonnet
Plantigone ou Issart
Meix des Ouches
Mévelle
Fonteny
Combes du Dessus
Ruchottes du Dessus
Ruchottes du Bas
Bel-Air
Les Mazis-Hauts
Les Mazis-Bas
Les Corbeaux
En Pallud
Au Closeau
Clos de Bèze
Clos Prieur-Haut
La Perrière
Cherbaudes
Les Gémeaux
En la Chapelle
Carougeot
Les Cercueils
Aux Corvées
Chambertin
Route des Grands Crus
En Griotte
Champitenois ou Petite Chapelle
Clos Prieur-Bas
Jouise
Latricières
Aux Charmes
En Ergot
Vignes Belles
Les Epointures
Aux Combottes
Aux Etelois
La Burie
Croix des Champs
Mazoyères ou Charmes
Pressonnier
Le Fourneau
Champs-Chenys
D 974
Reniard
Grands Champs
Roncevie
Aux Echézeaux
Les Seuvrées
La Prairie
Au Prunier
La Platière
BEAUNE
MOREY-ST-DENIS
Pâquier des Chênes et Fourneau
0
500 m
O
N
S
E
400
300
LES VINS DE BOU

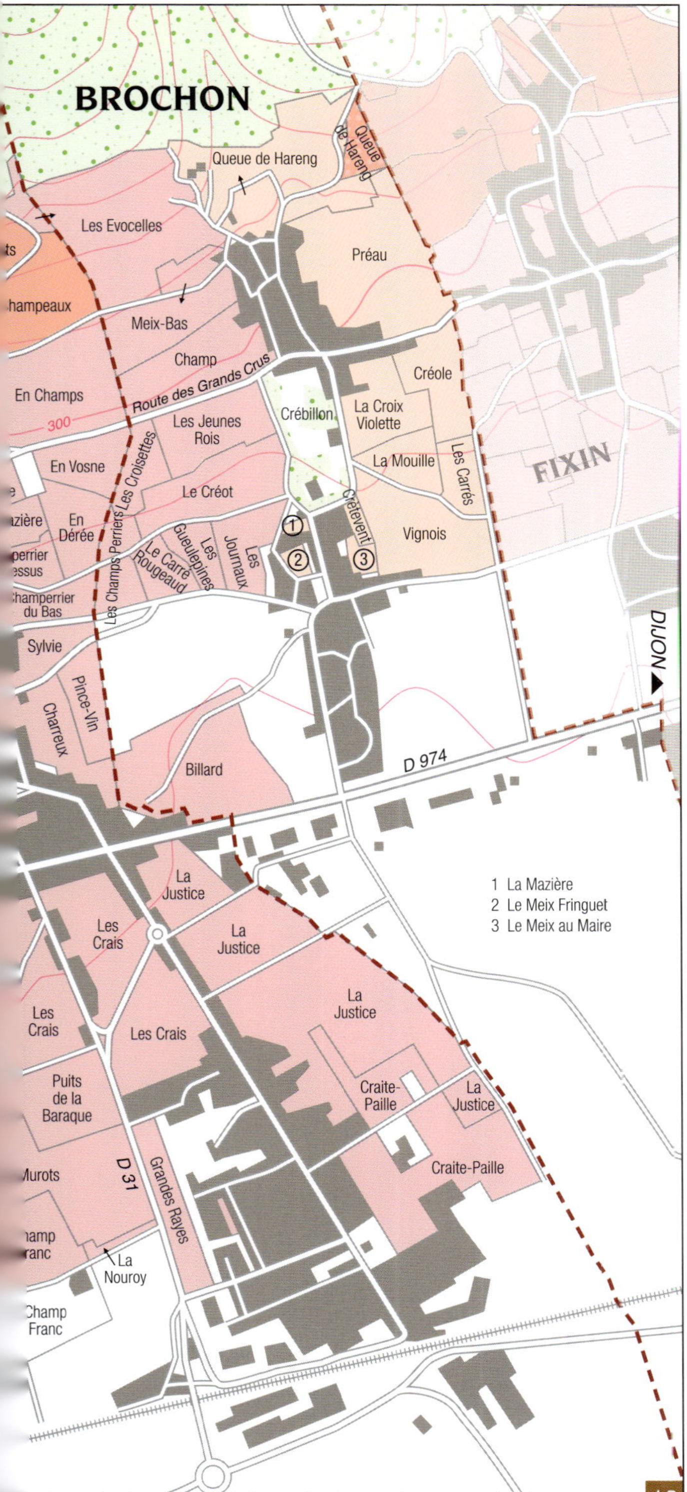
BROCHON
Queue de Hareng
Queue de Hareng
Les Evocelles
Préau
hampeaux
Meix-Bas
Champ
Route des Grands Crus
Créole
En Champs
Crébillon
La Croix Violette
300
Les Jeunes Rois
Les Croisettes
En Vosne
La Mouille
Les Carrés
FIXIN
Le Créot
Crêtevent
En Dérée
Vignois
Les Champs Perriers
Le Carré Rougeaud
Les Gueulepines
Les Journaux
1
2
3
hamperrier du Bas
DIJON
Sylvie
Pince-Vin
Charreux
D 974
Billard
La Justice
Les Crais
La Justice
1 La Mazière
2 Le Meix Fringuet
3 Le Meix au Maire
La Justice
Les Crais
Les Crais
Puits de la Baraque
Craite-Paille
La Justice
Craite-Paille
D 31
Grandes Rayes
La Nouroy
Champ Franc

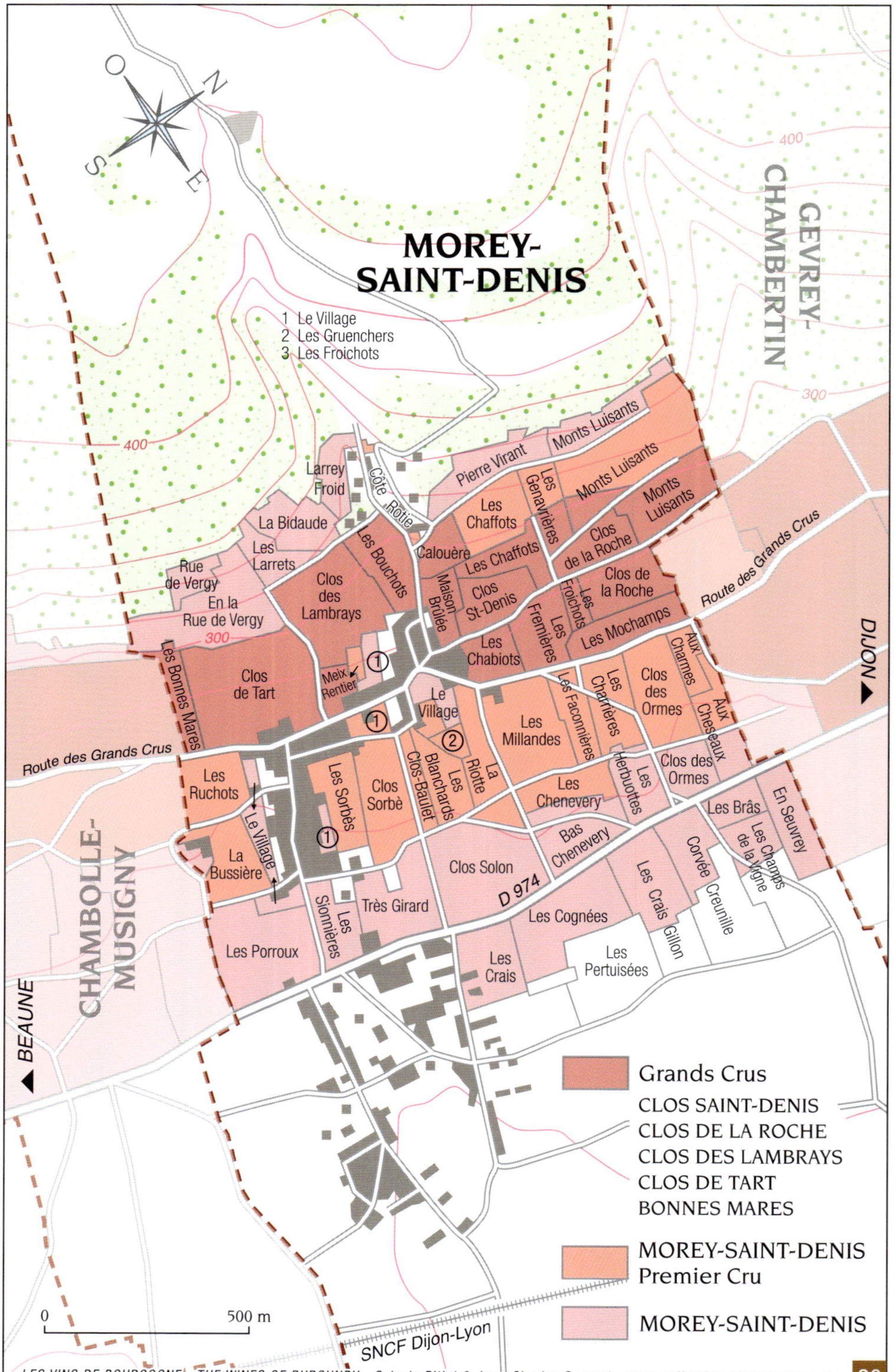
MOREY-SAINT-DENIS
GEVREY-CHAMBERTIN
CHAMBOLLE-MUSIGNY
1 Le Village
2 Les Gruenchers
3 Les Froichots
Monts Luisants
Pierre Virant
Larrey Froid
Côte Rotie
Les Genavrières
Les Chaffots
La Bidaude
Les Larrets
Les Bouchots
Calouère
Clos de la Roche
Rue de Vergy
En la Rue de Vergy
Clos des Lambrays
Maison Brûlée
Clos St-Denis
Les Froichots
Les Fremières
Les Mochamps
Route des Grands Crus
Dijon
Les Bonnes Mares
Clos de Tart
Meix Rentier
Les Chabiots
Aux Charmes
Le Village
Les Millandes
Les Faconnières
Les Charrières
Clos des Ormes
Aux Cheseaux
Les Ruchots
Les Sorbès
Clos Sorbè
Clos-Baulet
Les Blanchards
La Riotte
Les Chenevery
Les Herbuottes
Clos des Ormes
Les Brâs
En Seuvrey
La Bussière
Bas Chenevery
Clos Solon
Corvée Creunille
Les Champs de la Vigne
Très Girard
Les Sionnières
D 974
Les Cognées
Les Crais Gillon
Les Porroux
Les Crais
Les Pertuisées
Beaune
400
300
Grands Crus
CLOS SAINT-DENIS
CLOS DE LA ROCHE
CLOS DES LAMBRAYS
CLOS DE TART
BONNES MARES
MOREY-SAINT-DENIS Premier Cru
MOREY-SAINT-DENIS
0
500 m
SNCF Dijon-Lyon

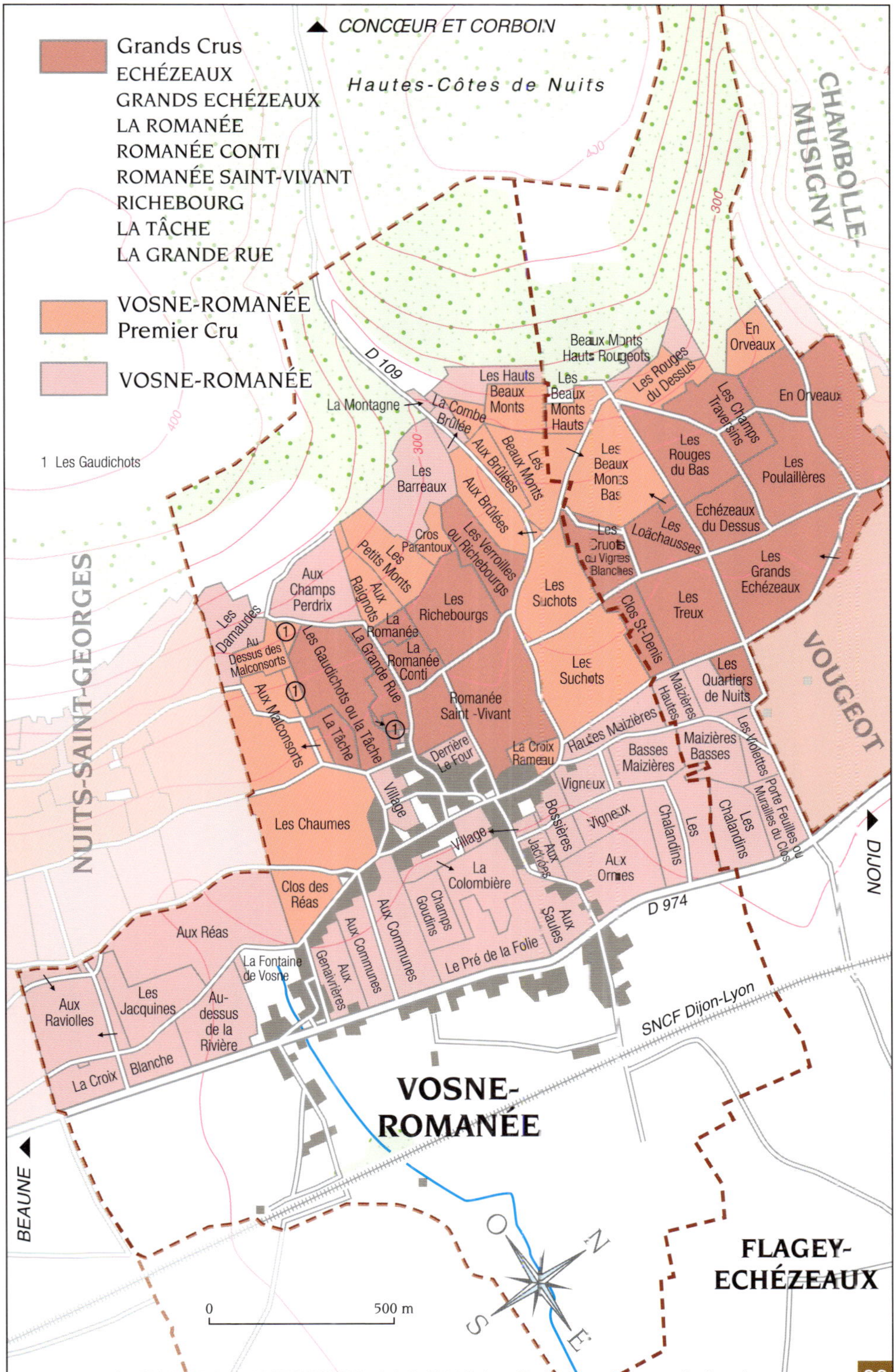

Grands Crus
ECHÉZEAUX
GRANDS ECHÉZEAUX
LA ROMANÉE
ROMANÉE CONTI
ROMANÉE SAINT-VIVANT
RICHEBOURG
LA TÂCHE
LA GRANDE RUE
VOSNE-ROMANÉE Premier Cru
VOSNE-ROMANÉE
1 Les Gaudichots
CONCŒUR ET CORBOIN
Hautes-Côtes de Nuits
CHAMBOLLE-MUSIGNY
VOUGEOT
NUITS-SAINT-GEORGES
DIJON
BEAUNE
D 109
D 974
SNCF Dijon-Lyon
VOSNE-ROMANÉE
FLAGEY-ECHÉZEAUX
0
500 m
300
400
En Orveaux
Beaux Monts Hauts Rougeots
Les Rouges du Dessus
Les Hauts Beaux Monts
Les Beaux Monts Hauts
La Montagne
La Combe Brûlée
Les Champs Traversins
Aux Brûlées
Les Beaux Monts
Les Beaux Monts Bas
Les Rouges du Bas
Les Poulaillères
Les Barreaux
Echézeaux du Dessus
Cros Parantoux
Les Verroilles ou Richebourgs
Les Cruots ou Vignes Blanches
Les Loâchausses
Les Grands Echézeaux
Aux Champs Perdrix
Les Petits Monts
Aux Raignots
Les Richebourgs
Les Suchots
Les Treux
Clos St-Denis
Les Damaudes
Au Dessus des Malconsorts
La Romanée
Les Gaudichots ou la Tâche
La Grande Rue
La Romanée Conti
Maizières Hautes
Les Quartiers de Nuits
Aux Malconsorts
Romanée Saint -Vivant
La Tâche
Derrière Le Four
La Croix Rameau
Hautes Maizières
Basses Maizières
Maizières Basses
Les Violettes
Village
Vigneux
Les Chaumes
Bossières
Chalandins
Les Chalandins
Porte Feuilles ou Murailles du Clos
Aux Jachées
Aux Ormes
La Colombière
Clos des Réas
Champs Goudins
Aux Communes
Aux Saules
Aux Réas
Aux Genaivrières
Le Pré de la Folie
La Fontaine de Vosne
Aux Raviolles
Les Jacquines
Au-dessus de la Rivière
La Croix
Blanche
O
N
S
E

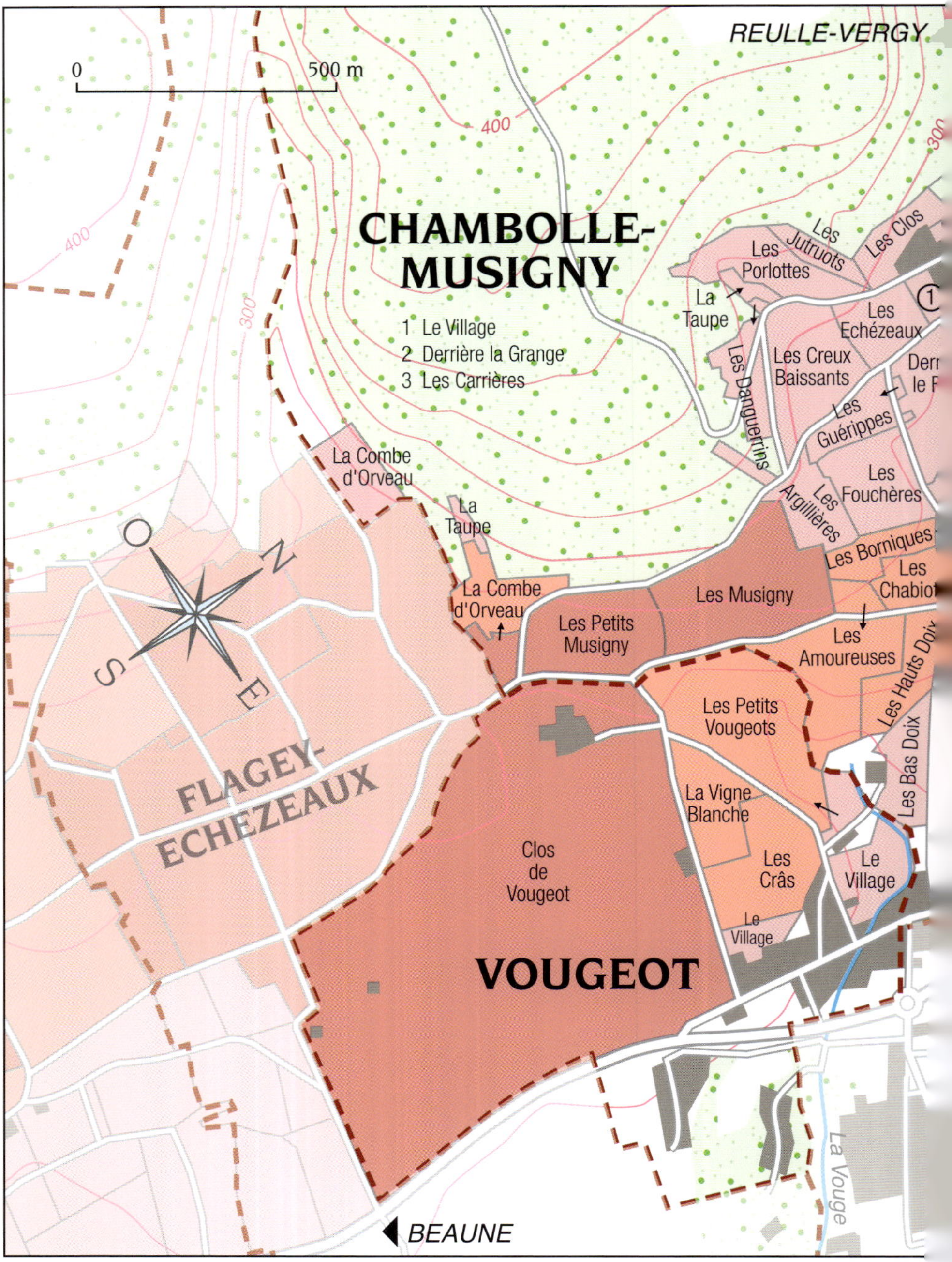

REULLE-VERGY
0
500 m
400
300
CHAMBOLLE-MUSIGNY
1 Le Village
2 Derrière la Grange
3 Les Carrières
Les Jutruots
Les Clos
Les Porlottes
La Taupe
Les Echézeaux
Les Danguerrins
Les Creux Baissants
Les Guérippes
La Combe d'Orveau
Les Fouchères
Les Argillières
La Taupe
Les Borniques
Les Chabiot
La Combe d'Orveau
Les Musigny
Les Petits Musigny
Les Amoureuses
Les Hauts Doix
Les Petits Vougeots
Les Bas Doix
FLAGEY-ECHEZEAUX
La Vigne Blanche
Clos de Vougeot
Les Crâs
Le Village
Le Village
VOUGEOT
La Vouge
BEAUNE
O
N
S
E

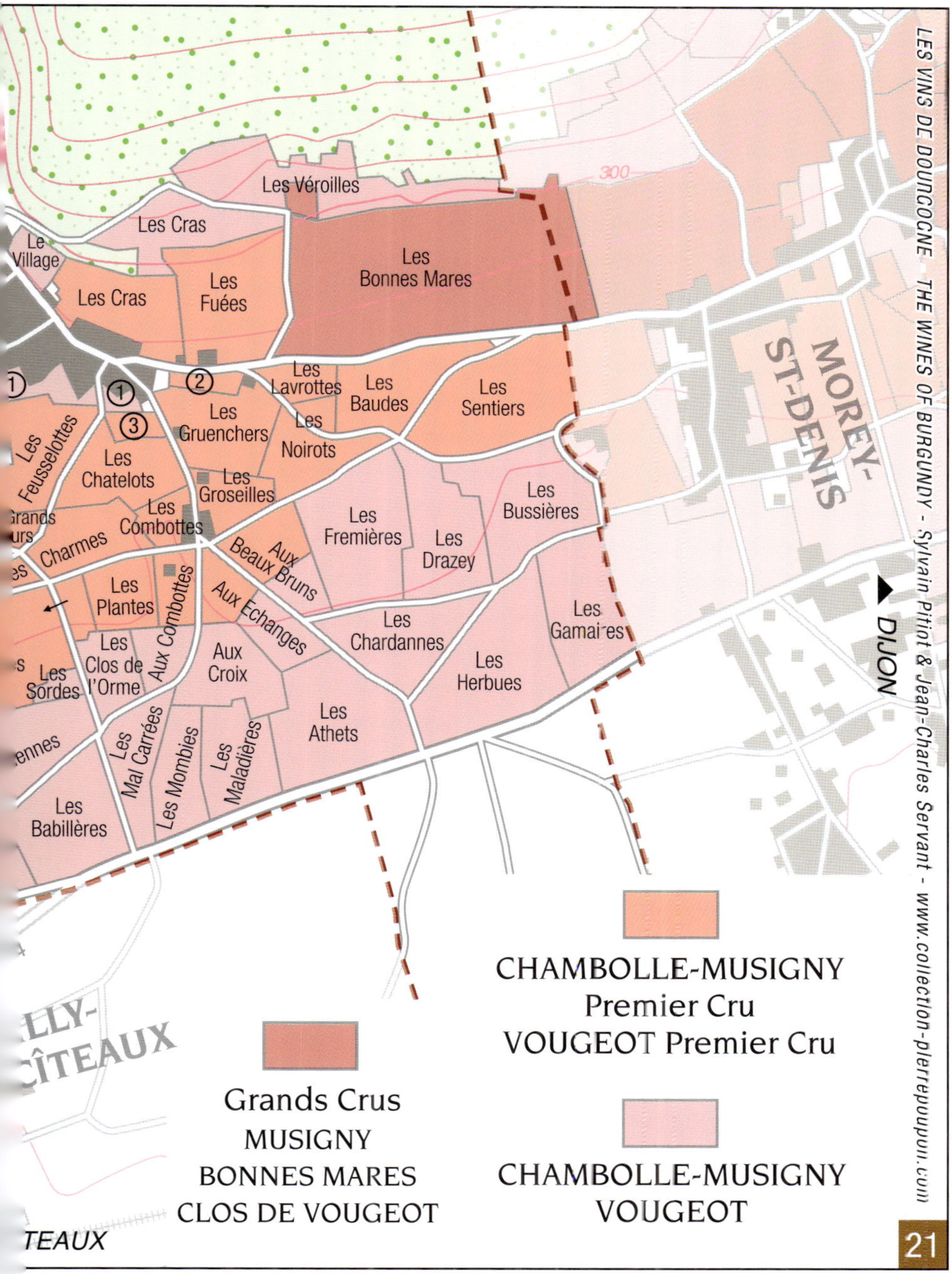

Les Véroilles
Les Cras
Le Village
Les Cras
Les Fuées
Les Bonnes Mares
300
Les Lavrottes
Les Baudes
Les Sentiers
Les Gruenchers
Les Noirots
Les Feusselottes
Les Chatelots
Les Groseilles
Les Combottes
Charmes
Les Fremières
Les Drazey
Les Bussières
Aux Beaux Bruns
Les Plantes
Aux Combottes
Aux Echanges
Les Chardannes
Les Gamaires
Les Clos de l'Orme
Aux Croix
Les Herbues
Les Sordes
Les Athets
Les Mal Carrées
Les Mombies
Les Maladières
Les Babillères
MOREY-ST-DENIS
DIJON
CÎTEAUX
TEAUX
Grands Crus
MUSIGNY
BONNES MARES
CLOS DE VOUGEOT
CHAMBOLLE-MUSIGNY Premier Cru
VOUGEOT Premier Cru
CHAMBOLLE-MUSIGNY
VOUGEOT
LES VINS DE BOURGOGNE - THE WINES OF BURGUNDY - Sylvain Pitiot & Jean-Charles Servant - www.collection-pierrepoupon.com
21

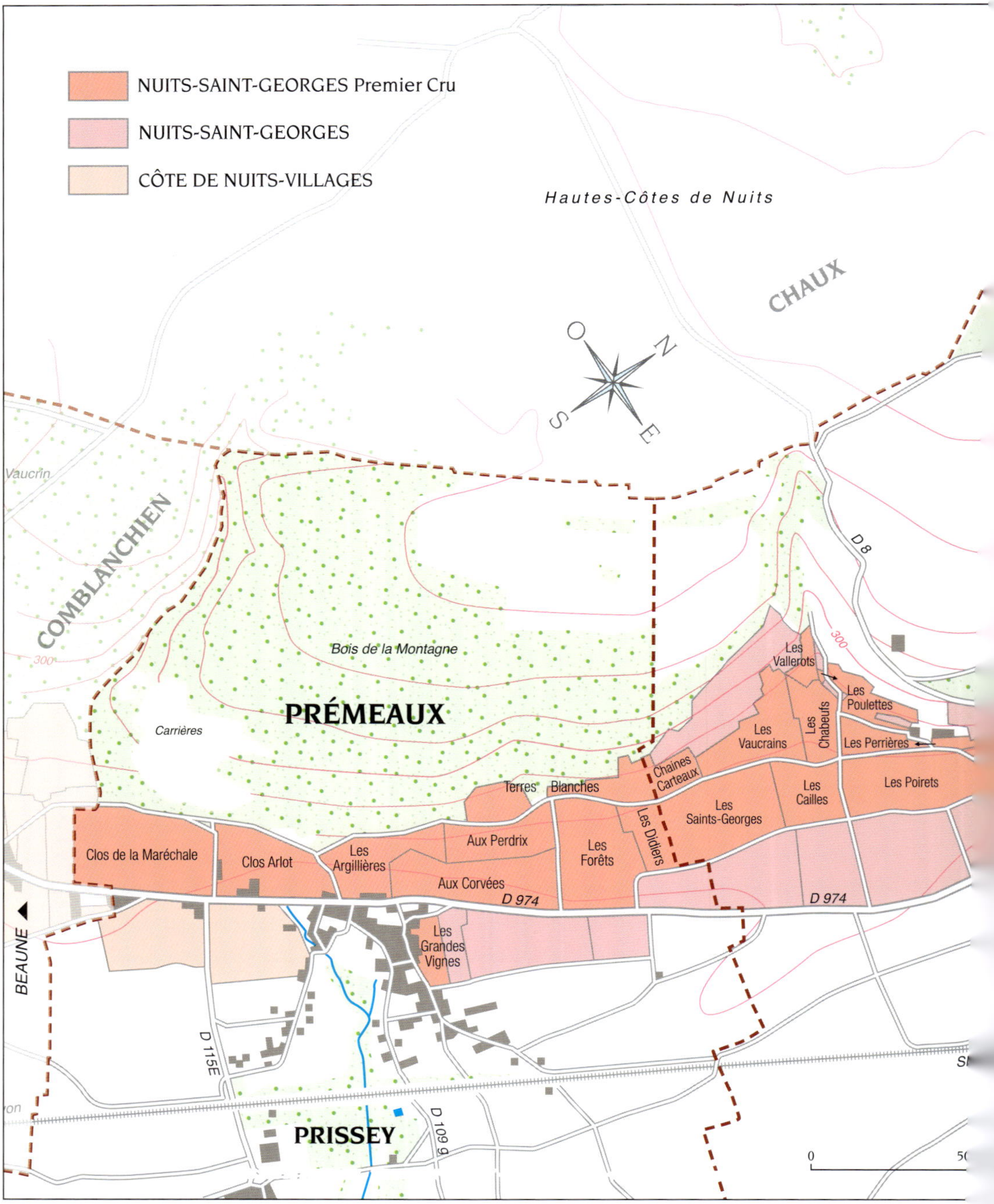
NUITS-SAINT-GEORGES Premier Cru
NUITS-SAINT-GEORGES
CÔTE DE NUITS-VILLAGES
Hautes-Côtes de Nuits
CHAUX
O
N
S
E
Vaucrin
COMBLANCHIEN
D 8
300
Bois de la Montagne
PRÉMEAUX
Carrières
Les Vallerots
Les Poulettes
Les Chabeufs
Les Vaucrains
Les Perrières
Chaines Carteaux
Terres Blanches
Les Poirets
Les Cailles
Les Saints-Georges
Les Didiers
Aux Perdrix
Les Forêts
Clos de la Maréchale
Clos Arlot
Les Argillières
Aux Corvées
D 974
BEAUNE
Les Grandes Vignes
D 115E
D 109 g
PRISSEY
0

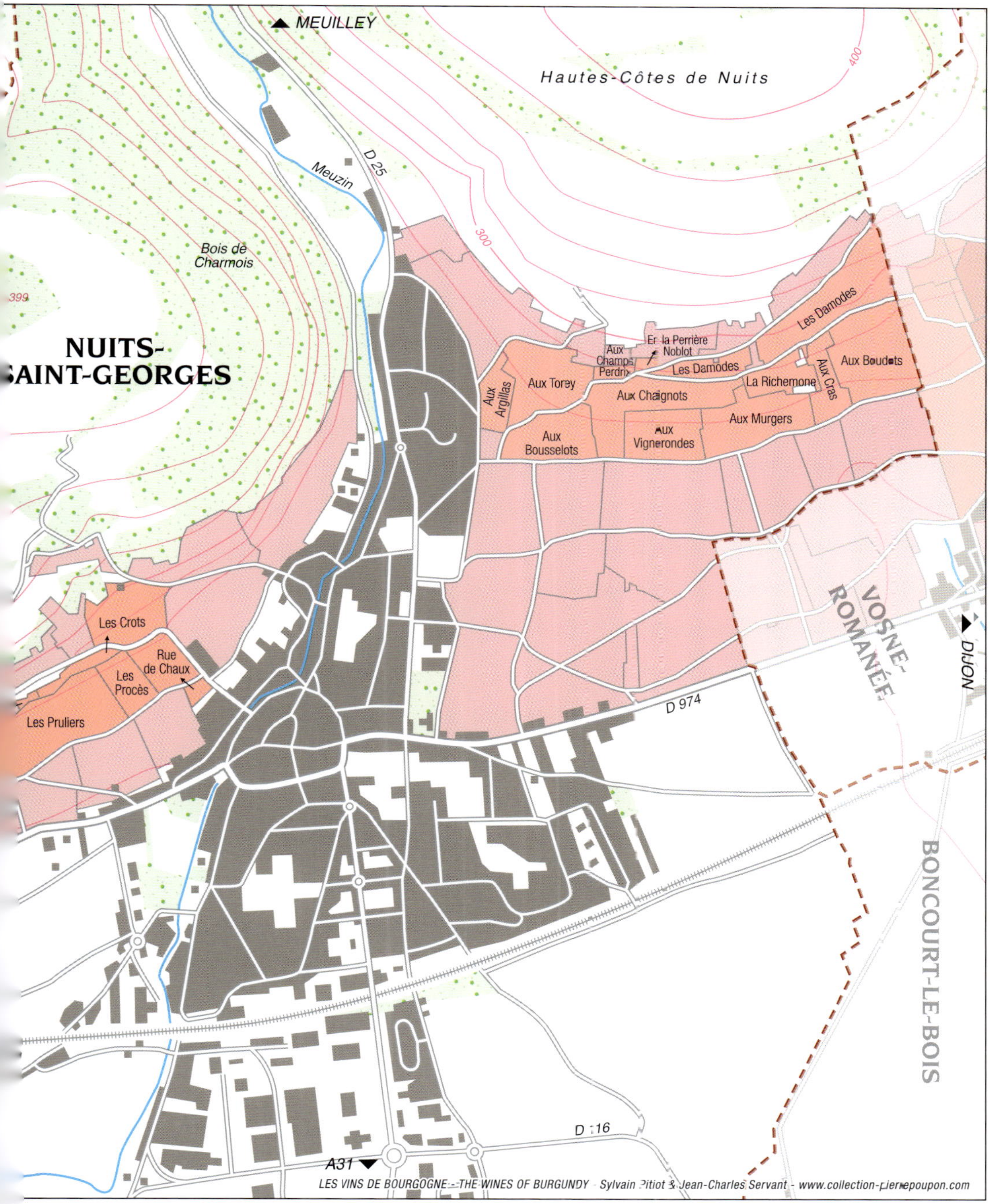
MEUILLEY
Hautes-Côtes de Nuits
400
300
399
Meuzin
D 25
Bois de Charmois
NUITS-SAINT-GEORGES
Les Damodes
Er la Perrière Noblot
Aux Champs Perdrix
Aux Torey
Aux Argillas
Les Damodes
La Richemone
Aux Cras
Aux Boudots
Aux Chaignots
Aux Murgers
Aux Bousselots
Aux Vignerondes
Les Crots
Rue de Chaux
Les Procès
Les Pruliers
D 974
VOSNE-ROMANÉE
DIJON
BONCOURT-LE-BOIS
A31
LES VINS DE BOURGOGNE - THE WINES OF BURGUNDY - Sylvain Pitiot & Jean-Charles Servant - www.collection-pierrepoupon.com

CÔTE DE BEAUNE

et Hautes Côtes de Beaune

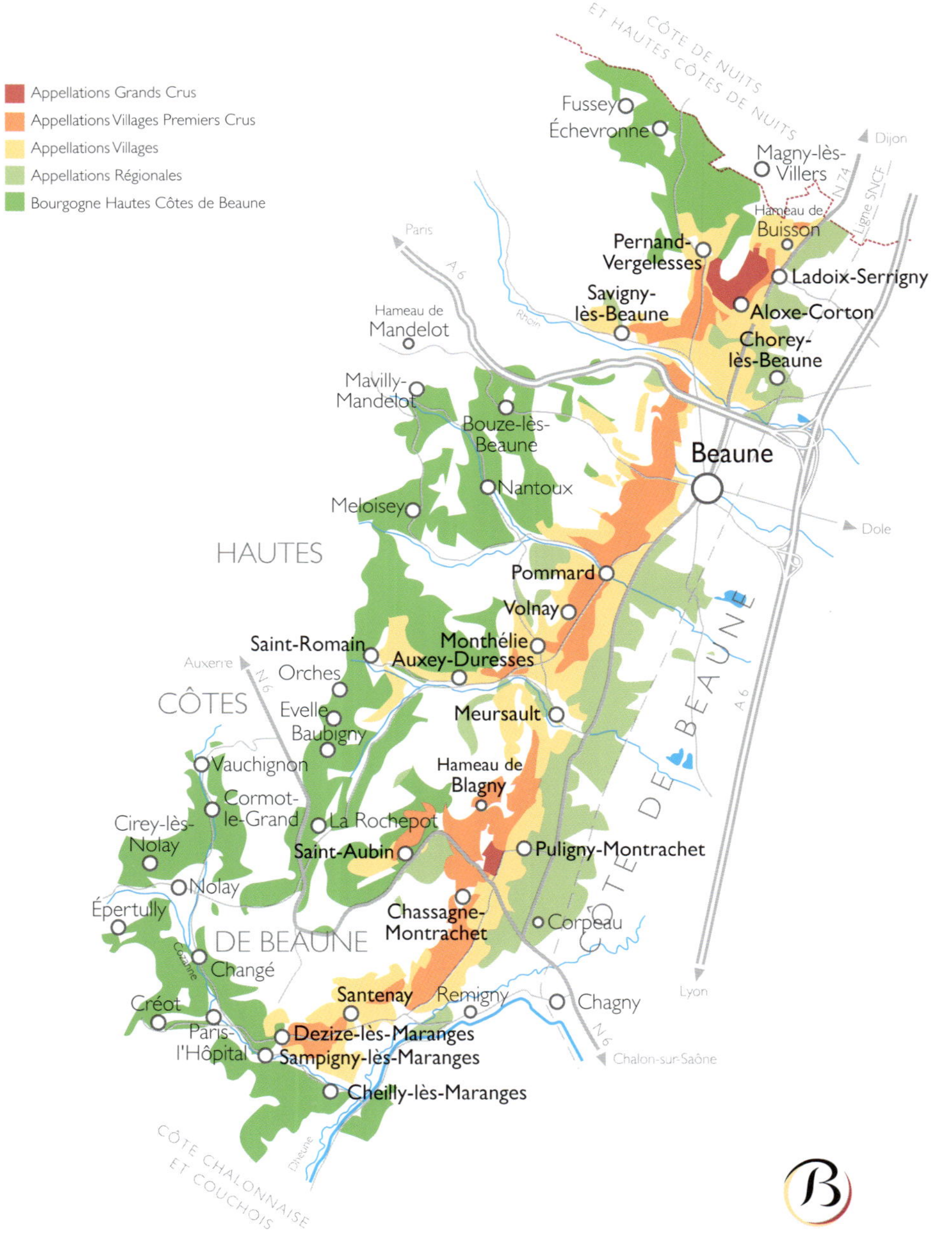

BOURGOGNES

www.vins-bourgogne.fr

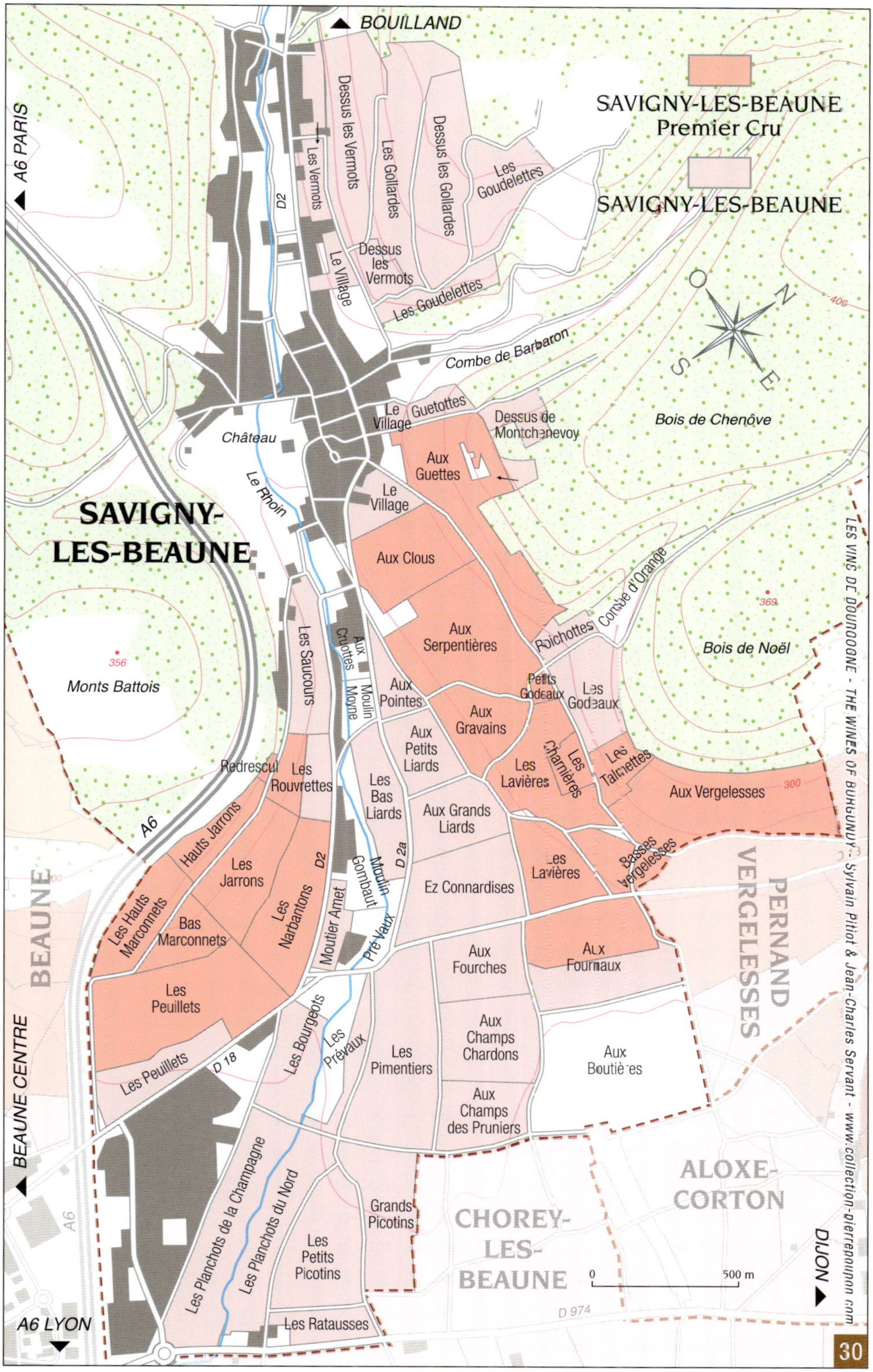
BOUILLAND
A6 PARIS
SAVIGNY-LES-BEAUNE Premier Cru
SAVIGNY-LES-BEAUNE
Dessus les Vermots
Les Vermots
Les Gollardes
Dessus les Gollardes
Les Goudelettes
Dessus les Vermots
Le Village
Les Goudelettes
Combe de Barbaron
Le Village
Guetottes
Dessus de Montchenevoy
Bois de Chenôve
Château
Aux Guettes
Le Rhoin
Le Village
SAVIGNY-LES-BEAUNE
Aux Clous
Combe d'Orange
Aux Serpentières
Poichottes
Bois de Noël
Monts Battois
Les Saucours
Aux Cruottes
Moulin Moyne
Aux Pointes
Petits Godeaux
Les Godeaux
Aux Gravains
Aux Petits Liards
Les Charnières
Les Talmettes
Redrescul
Les Rouvrettes
Les Bas Liards
Les Lavières
Aux Vergelesses
A6
Hauts Jarrons
Aux Grands Liards
Les Jarrons
D2
D 2a
Les Lavières
Basses Vergelesses
BEAUNE
Les Hauts Marconnets
Bas Marconnets
Les Narbantons
Moutier Amet
Moulin Gombaut
Ez Connardises
PERNAND VERGELESSES
Pré Vaux
Aux Fourches
Aux Fournaux
Les Peuillets
Les Bourgeots
Les Prévaux
Les Pimentiers
Aux Champs Chardons
Aux Boutières
Les Peuillets
D 18
Aux Champs des Pruniers
BEAUNE CENTRE
Les Planchots de la Champagne
Les Planchots du Nord
Grands Picotins
ALOXE-CORTON
A6
Les Petits Picotins
CHOREY-LES-BEAUNE
0
500 m
DIJON
D 974
A6 LYON
Les Ratausses
LES VINS DE BOURGOGNE - THE WINES OF BURGUNDY - Sylvain Pitiot & Jean-Charles Servant - www.collection-pierrepoupon.com
30

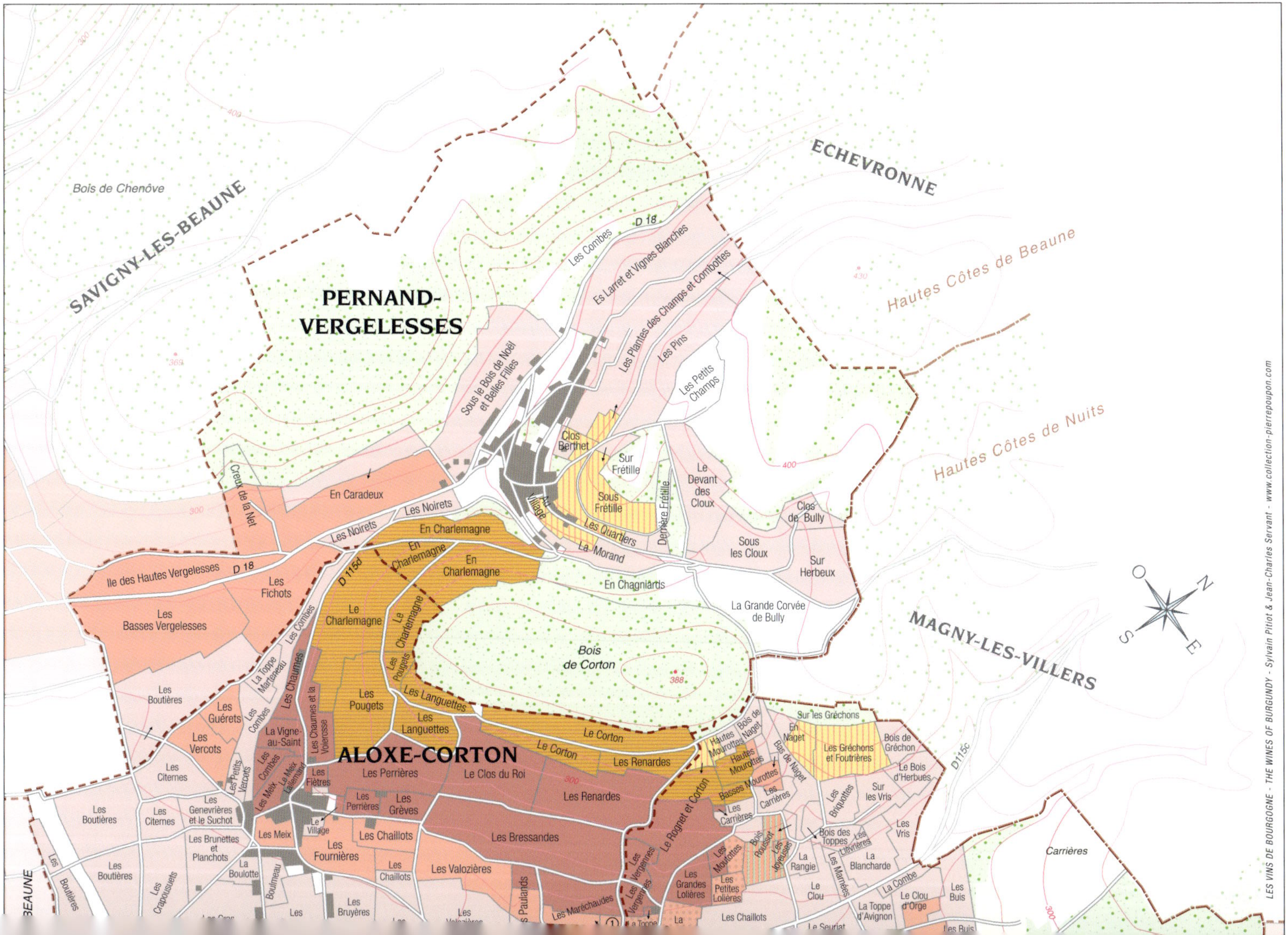
PERNAND-VERGELESSES
ALOXE-CORTON
SAVIGNY-LES-BEAUNE
ECHEVRONNE
MAGNY-LES-VILLERS
BEAUNE
Hautes Côtes de Beaune
Hautes Côtes de Nuits
Bois de Chenôve
Bois de Corton
Carrières
D 18
D 115d
D115c
En Caradeux
Creux de la Net
Les Noirets
Ile des Hautes Vergelesses
Les Fichots
Les Basses Vergelesses
Sous le Bois de Noël et Belles Filles
Les Combes
Es Larret et Vignes Blanches
Les Plantes des Champs et Combottes
Les Pins
Les Petits Champs
Clos Berthet
Sur Frétille
Sous Frétille
Dernière Frétille
Au Village
Les Quartiers
La Morand
Le Devant des Cloux
Sous les Cloux
Clos de Bully
Sur Herbeux
La Grande Corvée de Bully
En Chagniards
En Charlemagne
Le Charlemagne
Les Pougets
Les Languettes
Le Corton
Les Renardes
Les Perrières
Le Clos du Roi
Les Bressandes
Le Rognet et Corton
Les Chaumes
Les Chaumes et la Voierosse
La Vigne-au-Saint
Les Fiètres
Les Grèves
Les Chaillots
Les Fournières
Les Valozières
Les Paulands
Les Maréchaudes
Les Vergennes
Les Meix
Le Village
Les Boutières
Les Citernes
Les Guérets
Les Vercots
Les Petits Vercots
La Toppe Marteneau
Les Genevrières et le Suchot
Les Brunettes et Planchots
La Boulotte
Boulmeau
Les Crapousuets
Les Bruyères
Sur les Gréchons
Les Gréchons et Foutrières
Bois de Gréchon
Le Bois d'Herbues
En Naget
Bas de Naget
Bois de Naget
Hautes Mourottes
Basses Mourottes
Les Carrières
Les Moutottes
Bois Roussot
Les Joyeuses
Les Grandes Lolières
Les Petites Lolières
Les Chaillots
Les Brigottes
Sur les Vris
Les Vris
Bois des Toppes
Les Lièvrières
Les Marnées
La Rangie
La Blancharde
Le Clou
La Combe
Le Clou d'Orge
La Toppe d'Avignon
Les Buis
Le Seuriat
La Toppe
300
400
388
369
430
O
N
E
S
LES VINS DE BOURGOGNE - THE WINES OF BURGUNDY - Sylvain Pitiot & Jean-Charles Servant - www.collection-pierrepoupon.com

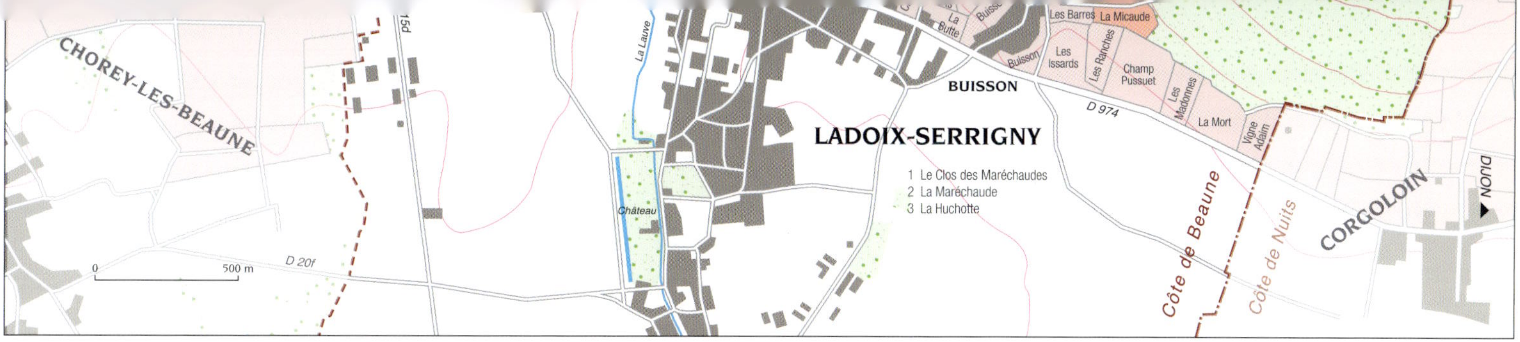

ALOXE-CORTON

Grands Crus
- CORTON
- CORTON (*rouge*) ou CORTON CHARLEMAGNE (*blanc*)
- ALOXE-CORTON Premier Cru
- ALOXE-CORTON

PERNAND-VERGELESSES

Grands Crus
- CORTON (*rouge*) ou CORTON CHARLEMAGNE (*blanc*)
- PERNAND-VERGELESSES Premier Cru
- PERNAND-VERGELESSES Premier Cru (*blanc*) ou PERNAND-VERGELESSES (*rouge*)
- PERNAND-VERGELESSES

LADOIX-SERRIGNY

Grands Crus
- CORTON
- CORTON (*rouge*) ou CORTON CHARLEMAGNE (*blanc*)
- LADOIX Premier Cru
- ALOXE-CORTON Premier Cru
- LADOIX Premier Cru (*blanc*) ou Ladoix (*rouge*)
- LADOIX Premier Cru (*rouge*) ou Ladoix (*blanc*)
- LADOIX

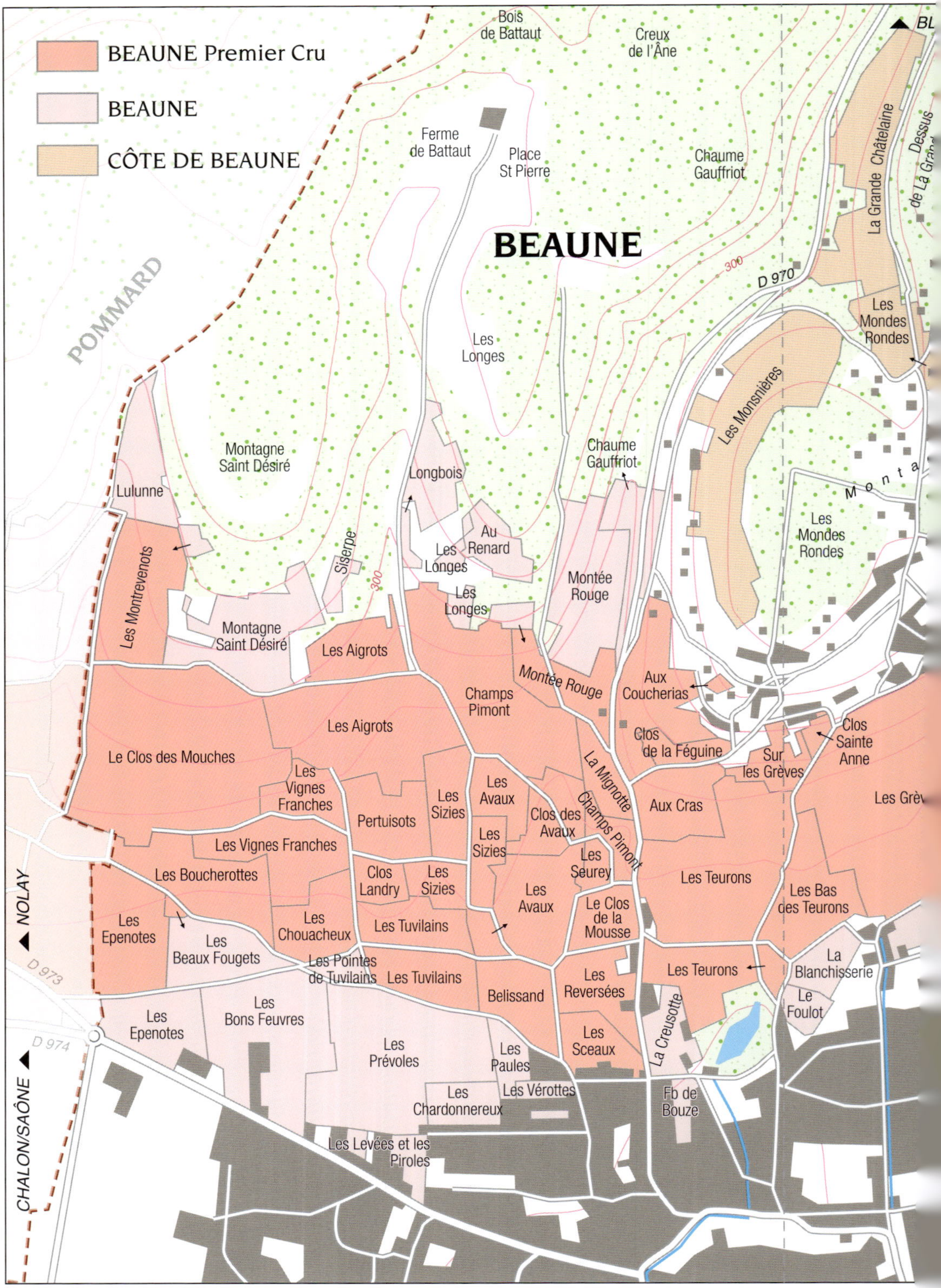

BEAUNE Premier Cru
BEAUNE
CÔTE DE BEAUNE
BEAUNE
POMMARD
Bois de Battaut
Creux de l'Âne
Ferme de Battaut
Place St Pierre
Chaume Gauffriot
La Grande Châtelaine
Dessus de La Grand
D 970
300
Les Longes
Les Mondes Rondes
Les Monsnières
Montagne Saint Désiré
Longbois
Chaume Gauffriot
Lulunne
Au Renard
Siserpe
Les Longes
Les Montrevenots
Montée Rouge
Les Longes
Montagne Saint Désiré
Les Aigrots
Montée Rouge
Champs Pimont
Aux Coucherias
Les Aigrots
Clos de la Féguine
Clos Sainte Anne
Le Clos des Mouches
Les Vignes Franches
La Mignotte
Sur les Grèves
Les Avaux
Les Sizies
Aux Cras
Pertuisots
Clos des Avaux
Champs Pimont
Les Grèv
Les Vignes Franches
Les Sizies
Les Seurey
Les Boucherottes
Clos Landry
Les Sizies
Les Avaux
Les Teurons
Les Bas des Teurons
NOLAY
Les Epenotes
Les Chouacheux
Les Tuvilains
Le Clos de la Mousse
Les Beaux Fougets
Les Pointes de Tuvilains
Les Tuvilains
Belissand
Les Reversées
Les Teurons
La Blanchisserie
D 973
Le Foulot
Les Epenotes
Les Bons Feuvres
Les Sceaux
La Creusotte
D 974
Les Prévoles
Les Paules
Les Vérottes
CHALON/SAÔNE
Les Chardonnereux
Fb de Bouze
Les Levées et les Piroles
Monta
BL

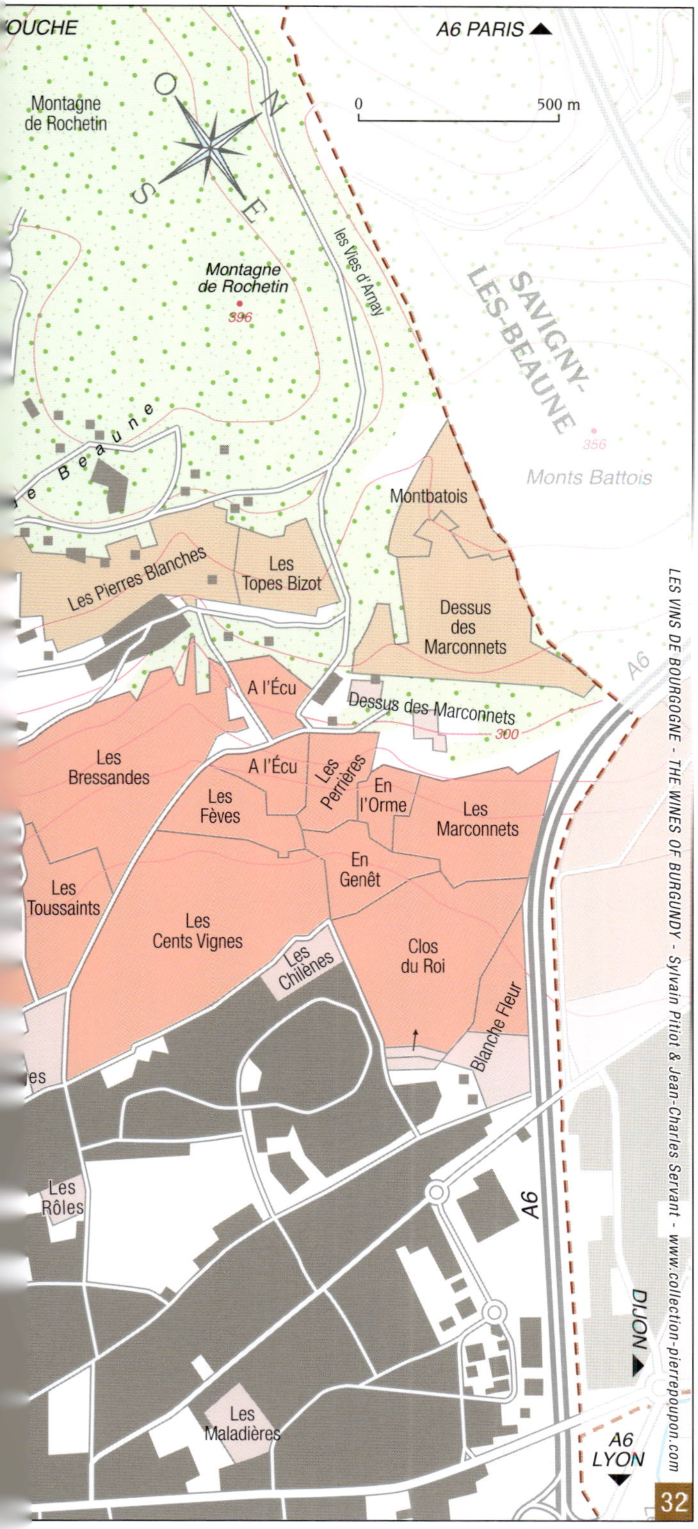

LES VINS DE BOURGOGNE - THE WINES OF BURGUNDY - Sylvain Pitiot & Jean-Charles Servant - www.collection-pierrepoupon.com

32

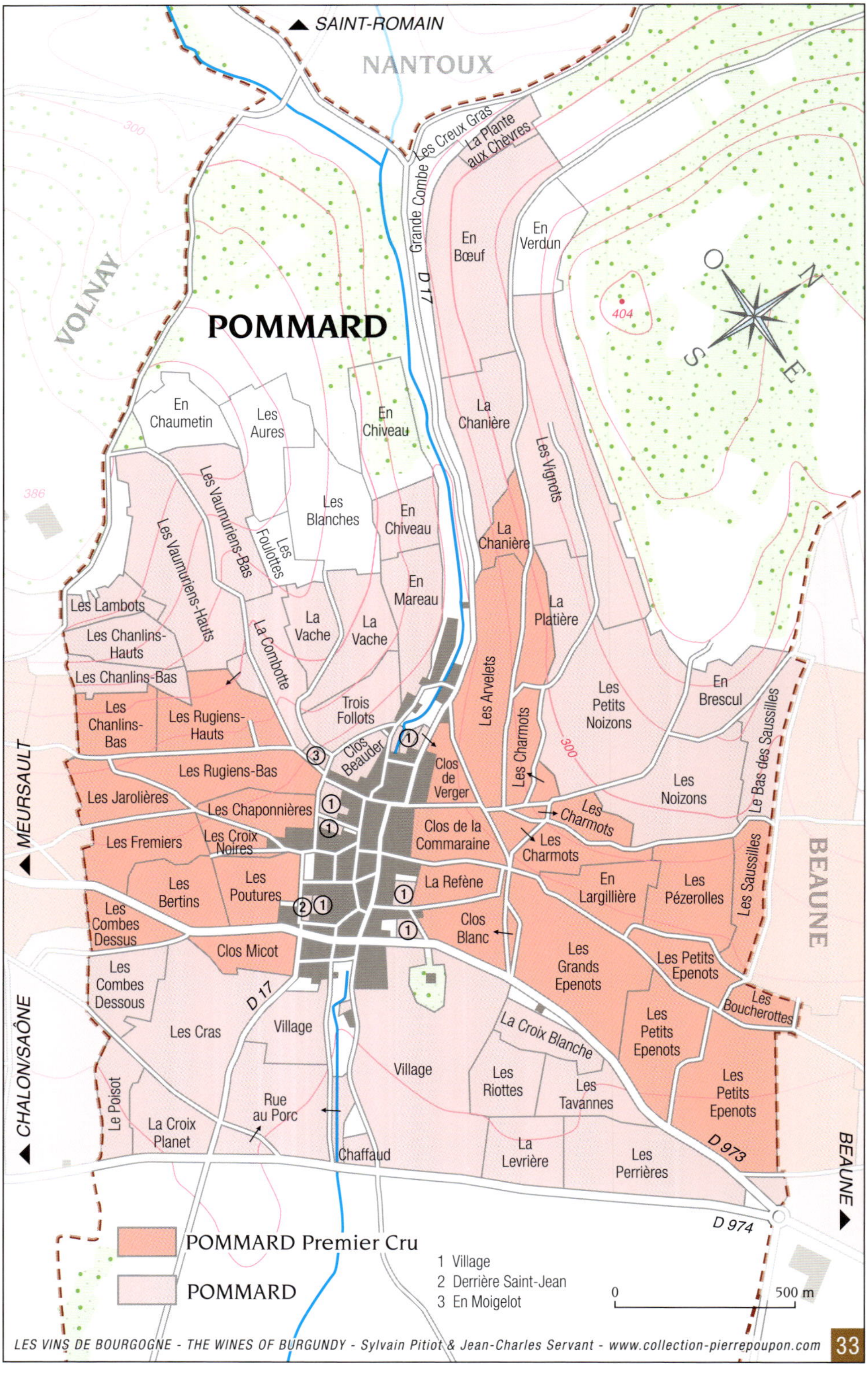
SAINT-ROMAIN
NANTOUX
VOLNAY
POMMARD
MEURSAULT
CHALON/SAÔNE
BEAUNE
BEAUNE
O N S E
404
386
300
300
Les Creux Gras
La Plante aux Chèvres
Grande Combe
D 17
En Bœuf
En Verdun
En Chaumetin
Les Aures
En Chiveau
La Chanière
Les Vignots
Les Blanches
En Chiveau
La Chanière
Les Vaumuriens-Bas
Les Vaumuriens-Hauts
Les Foulottes
Les Lambots
Les Chanlins-Hauts
Les Chanlins-Bas
La Vache
La Vache
En Mareau
La Platière
La Combotte
Les Arvelets
Trois Follots
Les Petits Noizons
En Brescul
Les Chanlins-Bas
Les Rugiens-Hauts
Clos Beauder
Clos de Verger
Les Charmots
Les Bas des Saussilles
Les Rugiens-Bas
Les Noizons
Les Jarolières
Les Chaponnières
Les Charmots
Les Croix Noires
Clos de la Commaraine
Les Charmots
Les Fremiers
La Refène
En Largillière
Les Pézerolles
Les Saussilles
Les Bertins
Les Poutures
Les Combes Dessus
Clos Blanc
Clos Micot
Les Grands Epenots
Les Petits Epenots
Les Combes Dessous
Les Boucherottes
D 17
Les Cras
Village
La Croix Blanche
Les Petits Epenots
Village
Les Riottes
Les Tavannes
Les Petits Epenots
Le Poisot
La Croix Planet
Rue au Porc
Chaffaud
La Levrière
Les Perrières
D 973
D 974
POMMARD Premier Cru
POMMARD
1 Village
2 Derrière Saint-Jean
3 En Moigelot
0
500 m

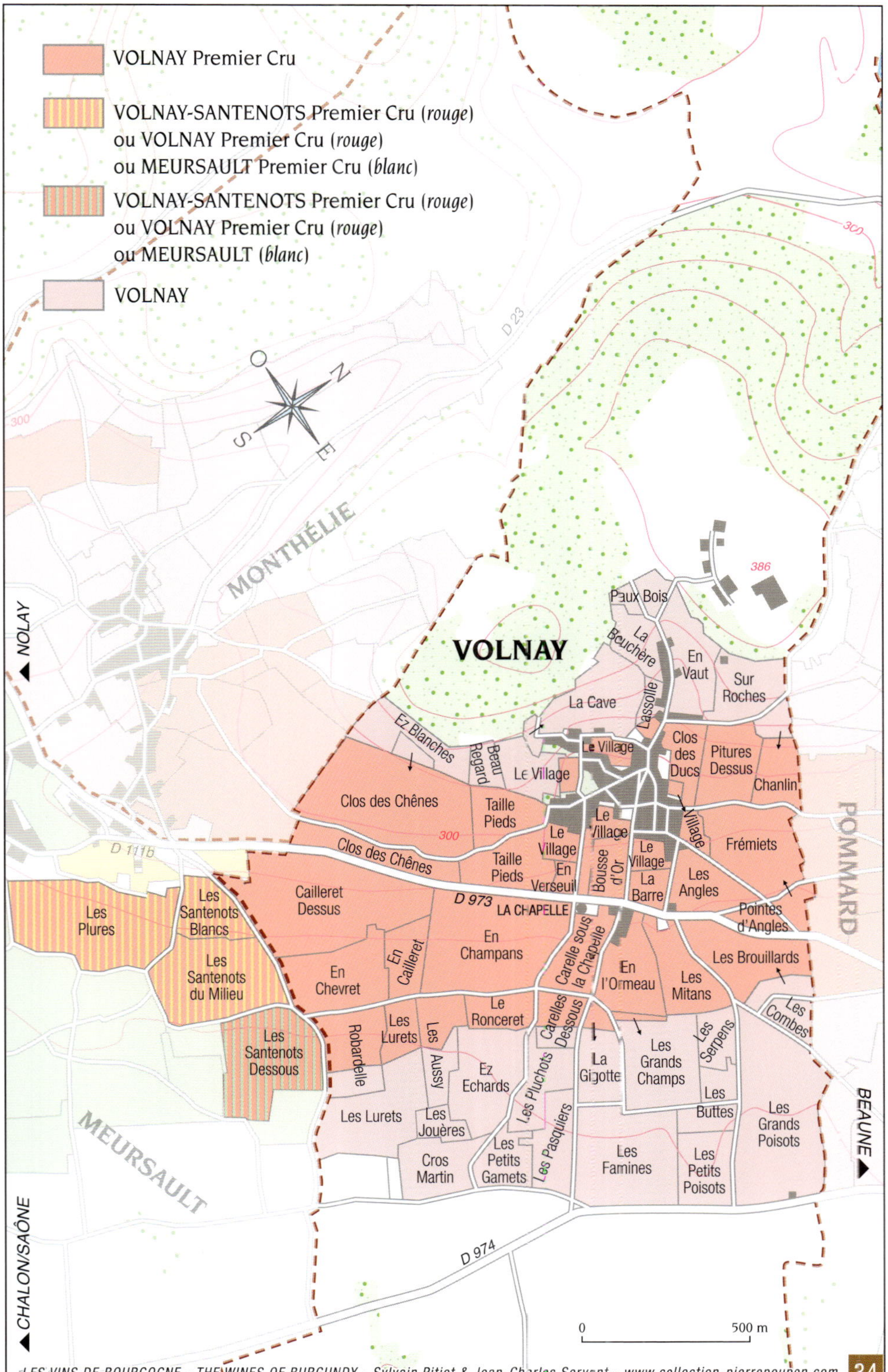
VOLNAY Premier Cru
VOLNAY-SANTENOTS Premier Cru (rouge) ou VOLNAY Premier Cru (rouge) ou MEURSAULT Premier Cru (blanc)
VOLNAY-SANTENOTS Premier Cru (rouge) ou VOLNAY Premier Cru (rouge) ou MEURSAULT (blanc)
VOLNAY
VOLNAY
MONTHÉLIE
POMMARD
MEURSAULT
NOLAY
CHALON/SAÔNE
BEAUNE
D 23
D 111b
D 973
D 974
LA CHAPELLE
Paux Bois
La Bouchère
En Vaut
Sur Roches
La Cave
Lassolle
Ez Blanches
Beau Regard
Le Village
Clos des Ducs
Pitures Dessus
Chanlin
Clos des Chênes
Taille Pieds
Frémiets
Les Angles
La Barre
Bousse d'Or
En Verseuil
Pointes d'Angles
Cailleret Dessus
En Champans
En Cailleret
En Chevret
Carelle sous la Chapelle
En l'Ormeau
Les Mitans
Les Brouillards
Les Combes
Les Plures
Les Santenots Blancs
Les Santenots du Milieu
Les Santenots Dessous
Robardelle
Les Lurets
Les Aussy
Le Ronceret
Carelles Dessous
La Gigotte
Les Grands Champs
Les Serpens
Ez Echards
Les Pluchots
Les Buttes
Les Grands Poisots
Les Jouères
Les Pasquiers
Les Petits Gamets
Cros Martin
Les Famines
Les Petits Poisots
0
500 m

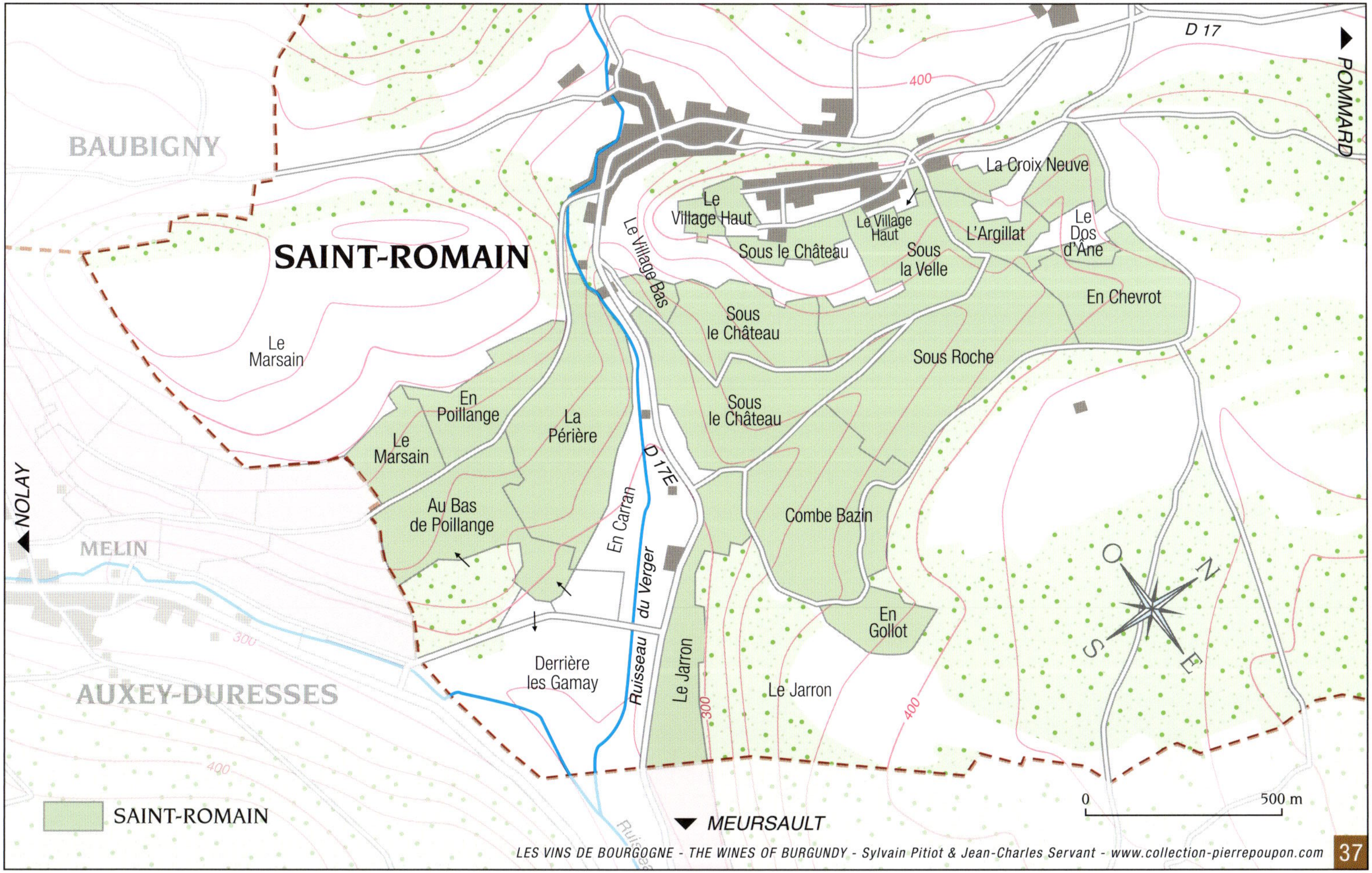
POMMARD
D 17
NOLAY
MEURSAULT
BAUBIGNY
SAINT-ROMAIN
MELIN
AUXEY-DURESSES
La Croix Neuve
Le Village Haut
Le Village Haut
Sous le Château
L'Argillat
Le Dos d'Âne
Sous la Velle
En Chevrot
Le Village Bas
Sous le Château
Sous le Château
Sous Roche
Le Marsain
En Poillange
Le Marsain
La Périère
Au Bas de Poillange
En Carran
D 17E
Ruisseau du Verger
Combe Bazin
En Gollot
Derrière les Gamay
Le Jarron
Le Jarron
400
300
O
N
E
S
0
500 m
SAINT-ROMAIN
LES VINS DE BOURGOGNE - THE WINES OF BURGUNDY - Sylvain Pitiot & Jean-Charles Servant - www.collection-pierrepoupon.com
37

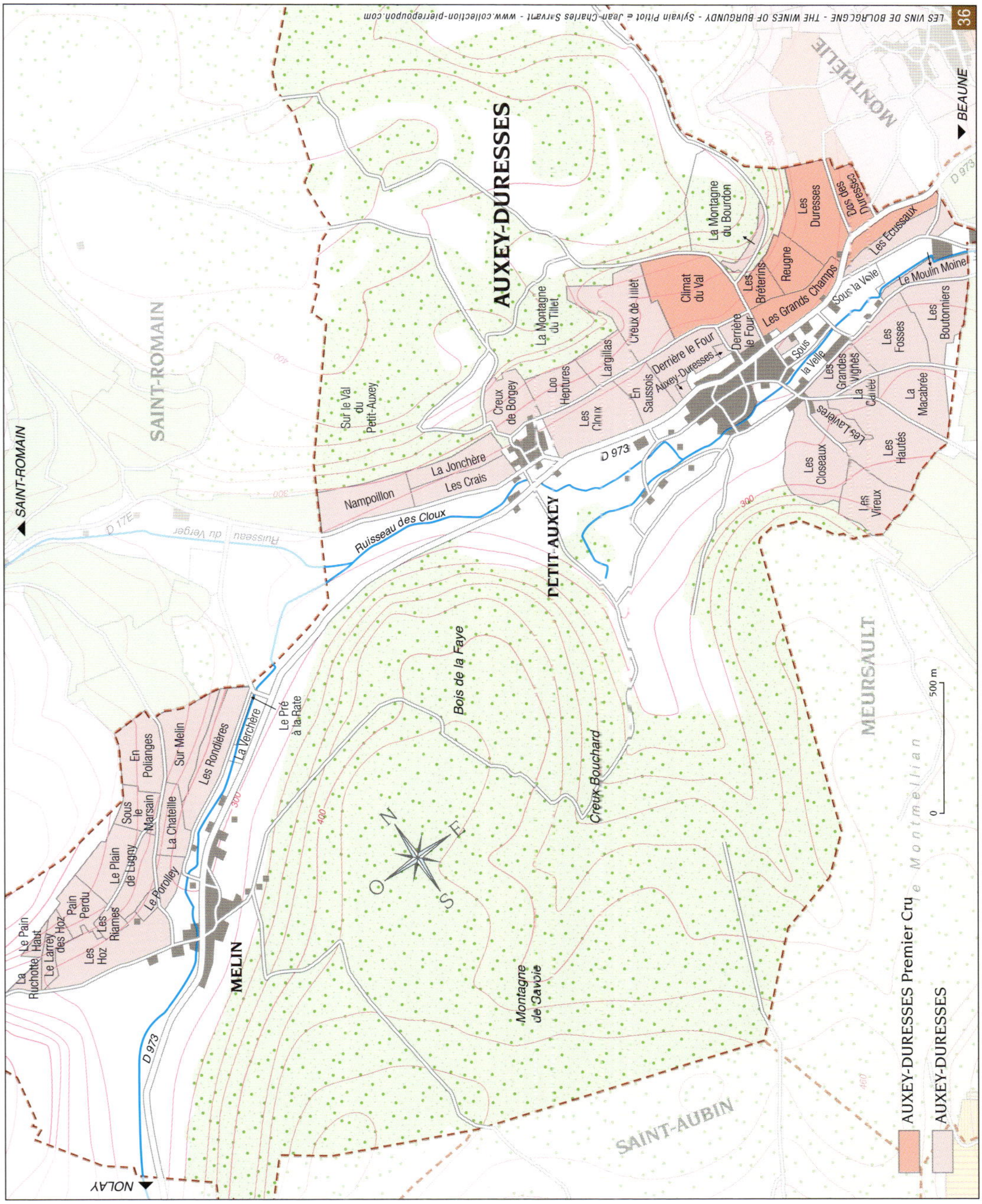
36
LES VINS DE BOURGOGNE - THE WINES OF BURGUNDY - Sylvain Pitiot & Jean-Charles Servant - www.collection-pierrepoupon.com
AUXEY-DURESSES
MONTHELIE
SAINT-ROMAIN
MEURSAULT
SAINT-AUBIN
PETIT-AUXEY
MELIN
BEAUNE
SAINT-ROMAIN
NOLAY
D 973
D 17E
Ruisseau des Cloux
Ruisseau du Verger
Bois de la Faye
Creux Bouchard
Montagne de Savoie
Le Montmellian
Sur le Val du Petit-Auxey
La Montagne du Tillet
La Montagne du Bourdon
Nampoillon
La Jonchère
Les Crais
Creux de Borgey
Les Heptures
Les Cloux
Largillas
En Saussois
Creux de Tillet
Climat du Val
Derrière le Four
Auxey-Duresses
Les Bréterins
Reugne
Les Duresses
Bas des Duresses
Les Grands Champs
Les Ecussaux
Sous la Velle
Le Moulin Moine
Les Boutonniers
Les Fosses
Les Grandes Vignes
La Macabrée
La Canée
Les Lavières
Les Closeaux
Les Hautés
Les Vireux
Le Pré à la Rate
La Verchère
Les Rondières
Sur Melin
En Polianges
Sous le Marsain
La Chatelle
Le Plain de Lugny
Le Poroley
Pain Perdu
Les Riames
Les Hoz
Le Larrey des Hoz
Le Pain Haut
La Ruchotte
0
500 m
AUXEY-DURESSES Premier Cru
AUXEY-DURESSES

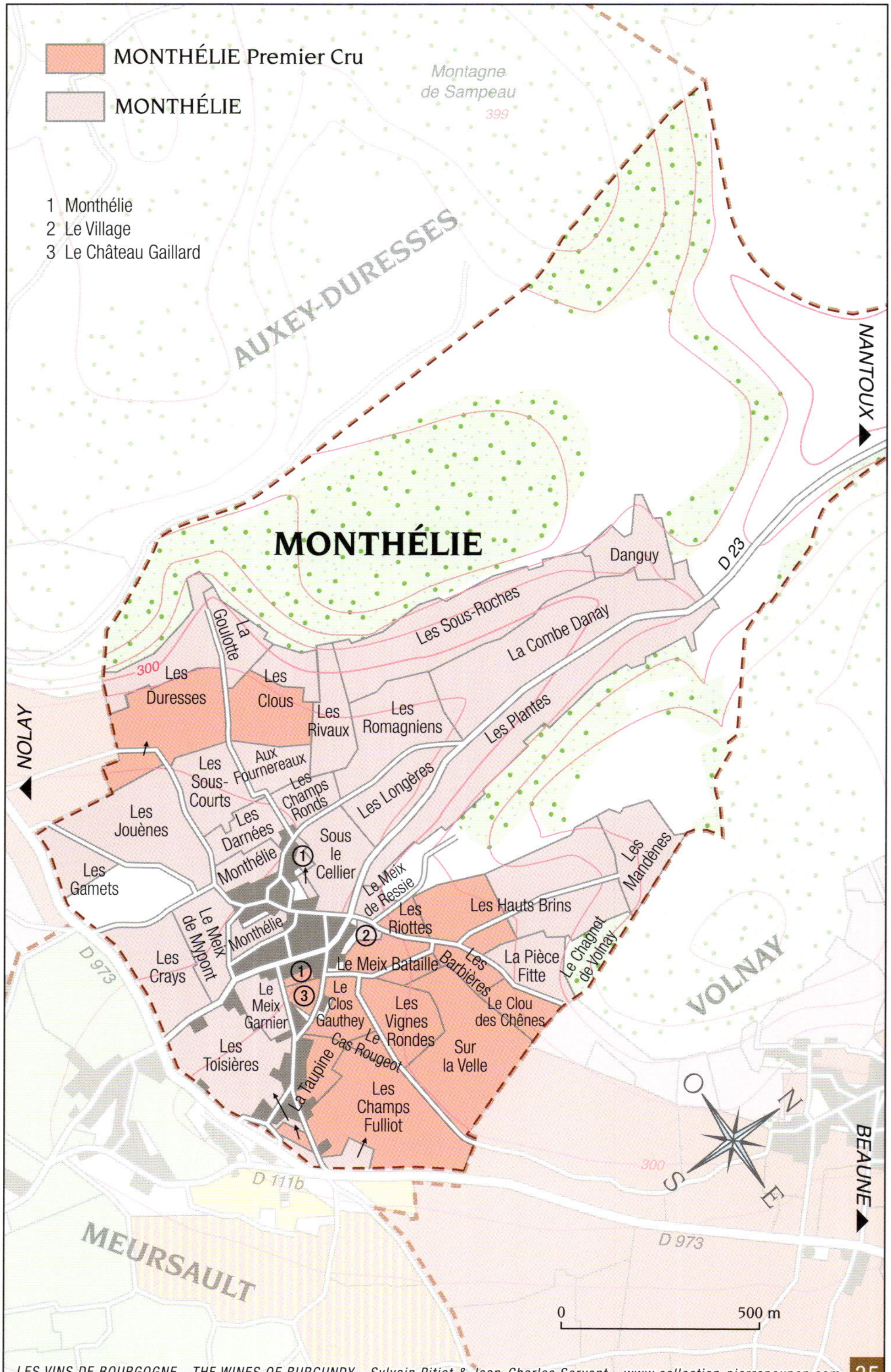
MONTHÉLIE Premier Cru
MONTHÉLIE
1 Monthélie
2 Le Village
3 Le Château Gaillard
Montagne de Sampeau
399
AUXEY-DURESSES
NANTOUX
MONTHÉLIE
Danguy
D 23
Les Sous-Roches
La Combe Danay
La Goulotte
300
Les Duresses
Les Clous
Les Rivaux
Les Romagniens
Les Plantes
NOLAY
Les Sous-Courts
Aux Fournereaux
Les Champs Ronds
Les Longères
Les Jouènes
Les Darnées
Sous le Cellier
Monthélie
Les Mandènes
Les Gamets
Le Meix de Ressie
Les Hauts Brins
Les Riottes
Le Meix de Mypont
Monthélie
Les Crays
D 973
Le Meix Bataille
Les Barbières
La Pièce Fitte
Le Chagnot de Volnay
VOLNAY
Le Meix Garnier
Le Clos Gauthey
Les Vignes Rondes
Le Clou des Chênes
Les Toisières
Le Cas Rougeot
Sur la Velle
La Taupine
Les Champs Fulliot
O
N
S
E
300
BEAUNE
D 111b
D 973
MEURSAULT
0
500 m

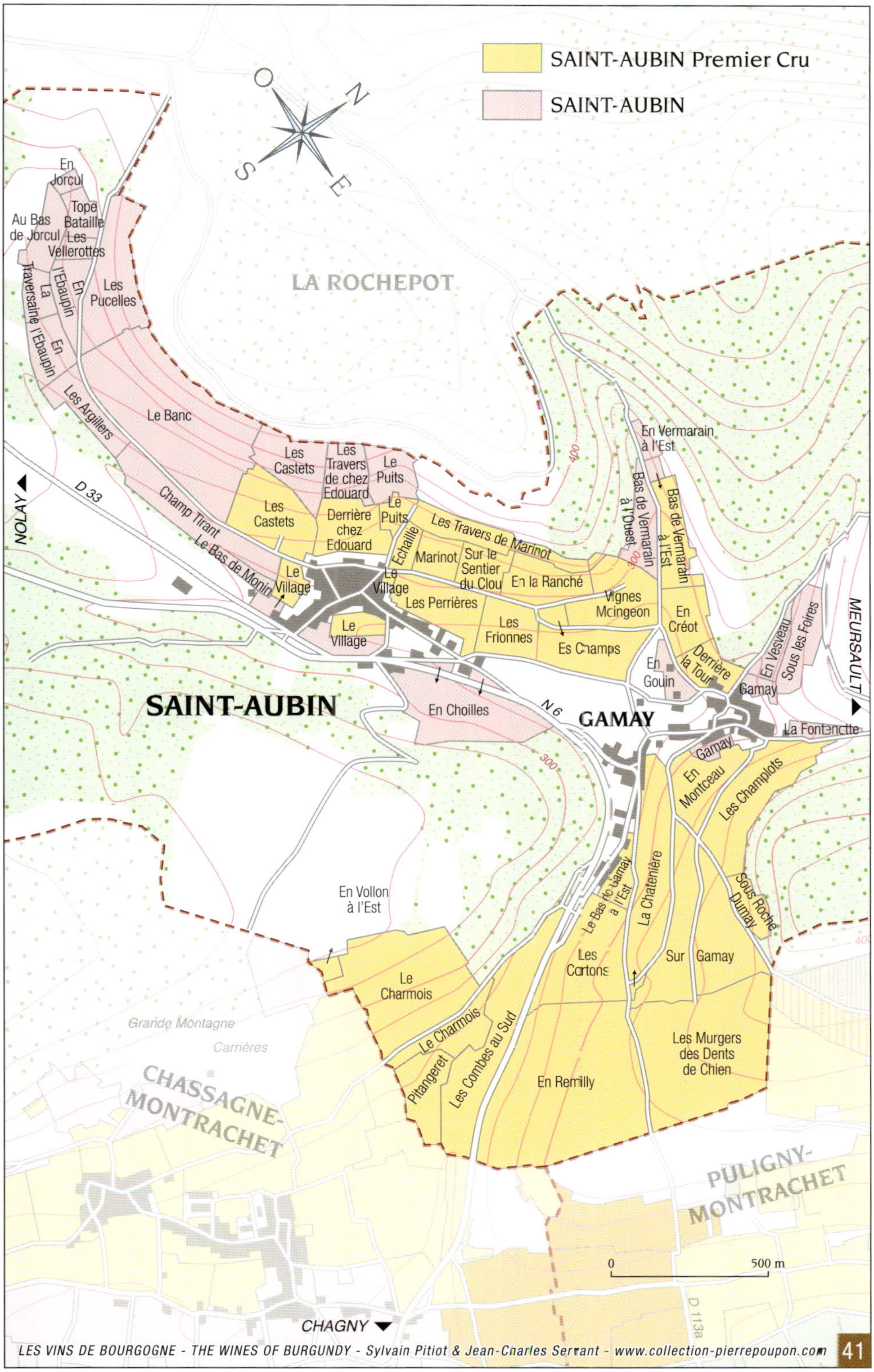
SAINT-AUBIN Premier Cru
SAINT-AUBIN
LA ROCHEPOT
SAINT-AUBIN
GAMAY
CHASSAGNE-MONTRACHET
PULIGNY-MONTRACHET
NOLAY
MEURSAULT
CHAGNY
D 33
N 6
D 113a
En Jorcul
Au Bas de Jorcul
Tope Bataille
Les Vellerottes
La Traversaine
En l'Ebaupin
En l'Ebaupin
Les Pucelles
Les Argillers
Le Banc
Les Castets
Les Travers de chez Edouard
Le Puits
Les Castets
Derrière chez Edouard
Le Puits
Echaille
Les Travers de Marinot
Marinot
Sur le Sentier du Clou
En la Ranché
Champ Tirant
Le Bas de Monin
Le Village
Le Village
Le Village
Les Perrières
Les Frionnes
Es Champs
Vignes Moingeon
En Vermarain à l'Est
Bas de Vermarain à l'Ouest
Bas de Vermarain à l'Est
En Créot
En Gouin
Derrière la Tour
Gamay
En Vesveau
Sous les Foires
La Fontenotte
En Choilles
Gamay
En Montceau
Les Champlots
Sous Roche Dumay
Le Bas de Gamay à l'Est
La Chatenière
En Vollon à l'Est
Les Cortons
Sur Gamay
Le Charmois
Le Charmois
Pitangeret
Les Combes au Sud
En Remilly
Les Murgers des Dents de Chien
Grande Montagne
Carrières
0
500 m
300
400

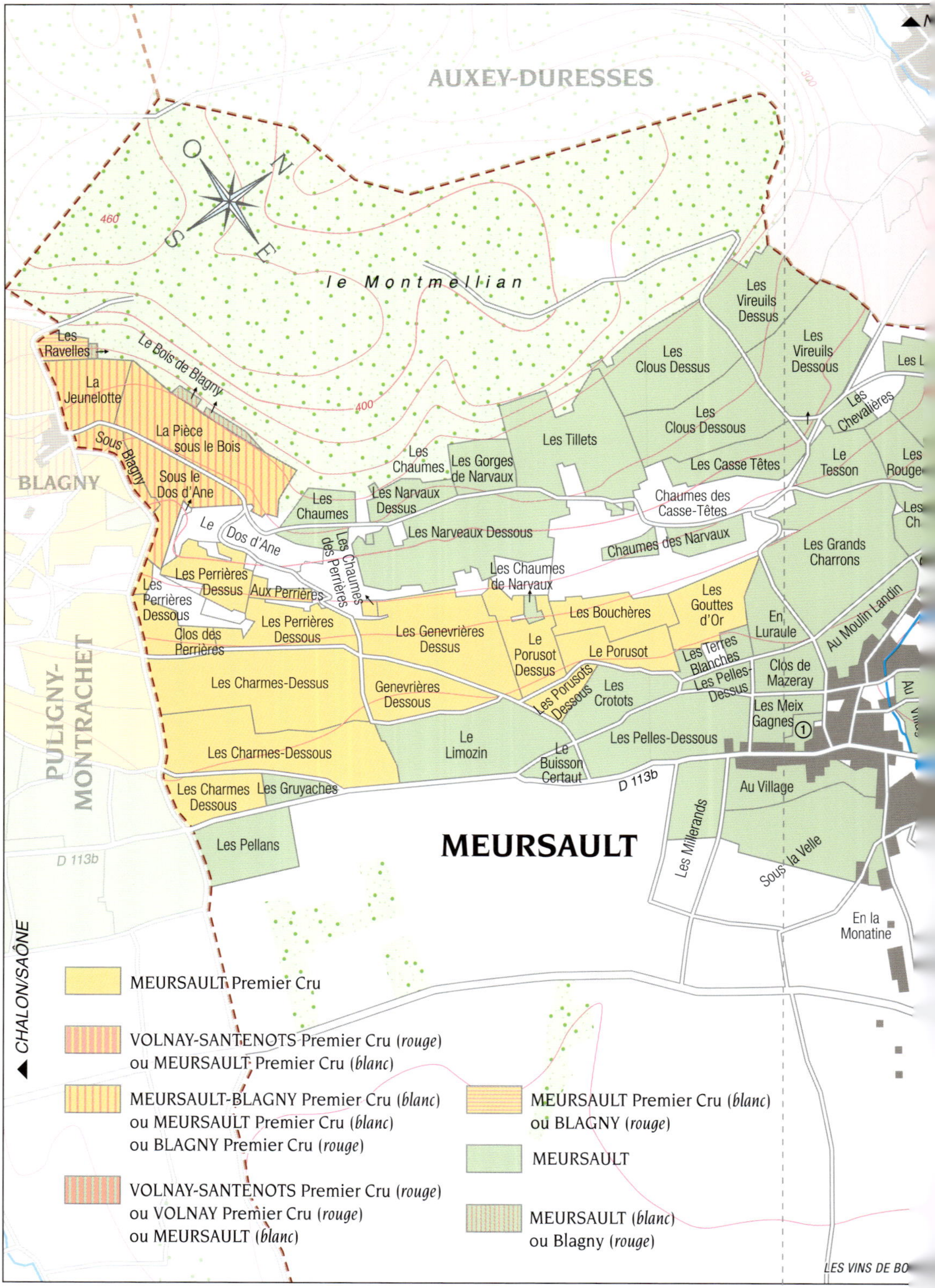

AUXEY-DURESSES
le Montmellian
O
N
S
E
460
400
300
Les Ravelles
Le Bois de Blagny
La Jeunelotte
La Pièce sous le Bois
Sous Blagny
Sous le Dos d'Ane
BLAGNY
Le Dos d'Ane
Les Chaumes des Perrières
Les Chaumes
Les Narvaux Dessus
Les Gorges de Narvaux
Les Narveaux Dessous
Les Tillets
Les Clous Dessus
Les Clous Dessous
Les Vireuils Dessus
Les Vireuils Dessous
Les Chevalières
Les Casse Têtes
Chaumes des Casse-Têtes
Chaumes des Narvaux
Les Chaumes de Narvaux
Le Tesson
Les Grands Charrons
Les Perrières Dessus
Aux Perrières
Les Perrières Dessous
Clos des Perrières
Les Genevrières Dessus
Les Bouchères
Les Gouttes d'Or
En Luraule
Au Moulin Landin
Le Porusot Dessus
Le Porusot
Les Terres Blanches
Clos de Mazeray
Les Pelles-Dessus
Les Charmes-Dessus
Genevrières Dessous
Les Porusots Dessous
Les Crotots
Les Meix Gagnes
Les Charmes-Dessous
Le Limozin
Le Buisson Certaut
Les Pelles-Dessous
Les Charmes Dessous
Les Gruyaches
D 113b
Au Village
Les Pellans
MEURSAULT
Les Millerands
Sous la Velle
En la Monatine
PULIGNY-MONTRACHET
CHALON/SAÔNE
MEURSAULT Premier Cru
VOLNAY-SANTENOTS Premier Cru (rouge) ou MEURSAULT Premier Cru (blanc)
MEURSAULT-BLAGNY Premier Cru (blanc) ou MEURSAULT Premier Cru (blanc) ou BLAGNY Premier Cru (rouge)
VOLNAY-SANTENOTS Premier Cru (rouge) ou VOLNAY Premier Cru (rouge) ou MEURSAULT (blanc)
MEURSAULT Premier Cru (blanc) ou BLAGNY (rouge)
MEURSAULT
MEURSAULT (blanc) ou Blagny (rouge)

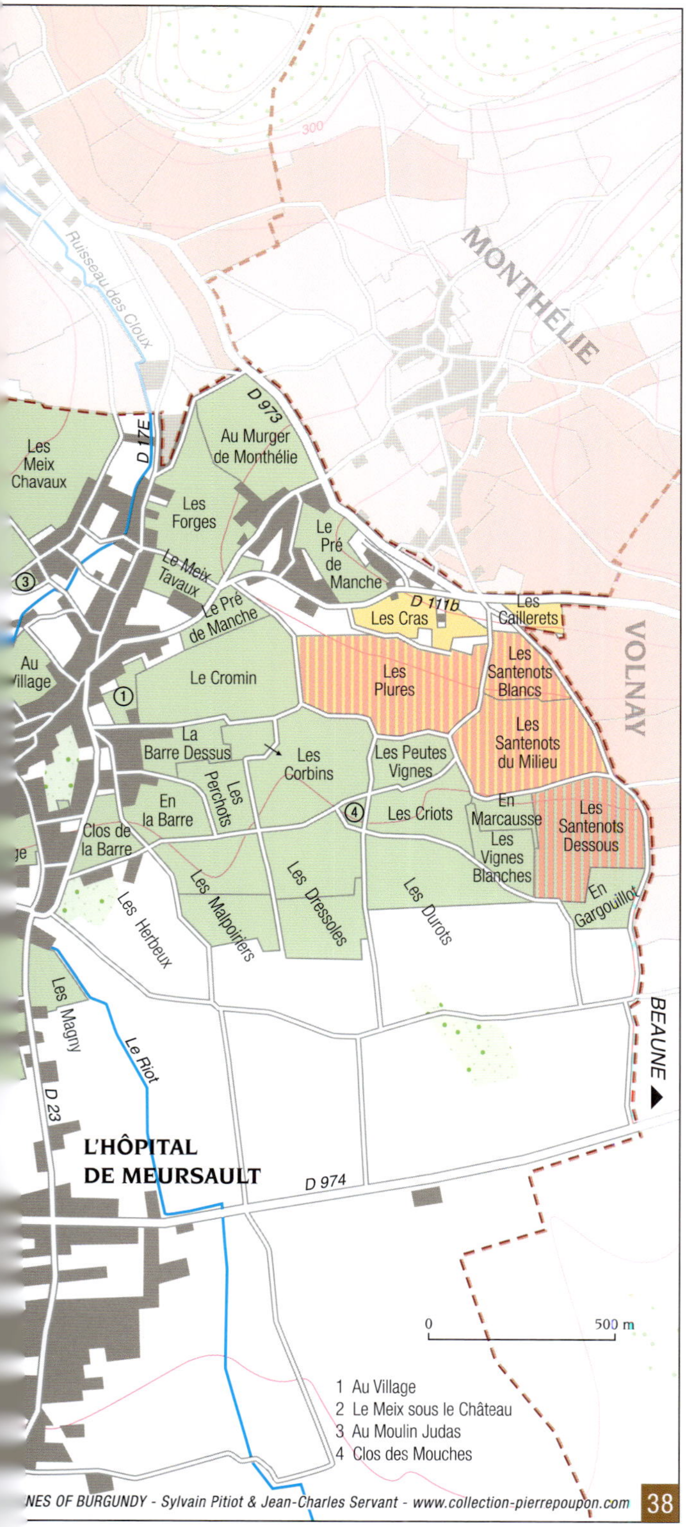
MONTHÉLIE
300
Ruisseau des Cloux
D 973
D 17E
Les Meix Chavaux
Au Murger de Monthélie
Les Forges
Le Pré de Manche
Le Meix Tavaux
Le Pré de Manche
D 111b
Les Cras
Les Caillerets
VOLNAY
Au Village
Le Cromin
Les Plures
Les Santenots Blancs
Les Santenots du Milieu
La Barre Dessus
Les Corbins
Les Peutes Vignes
Les Perchots
En la Barre
Les Criots
En Marcausse
Les Santenots Dessous
Clos de la Barre
Les Vignes Blanches
En Gargouillot
Les Herbeux
Les Malpoiriers
Les Dressoles
Les Durots
Les Magny
Le Riot
BEAUNE
D 23
L'HÔPITAL DE MEURSAULT
D 974
0
500 m
1 Au Village
2 Le Meix sous le Château
3 Au Moulin Judas
4 Clos des Mouches

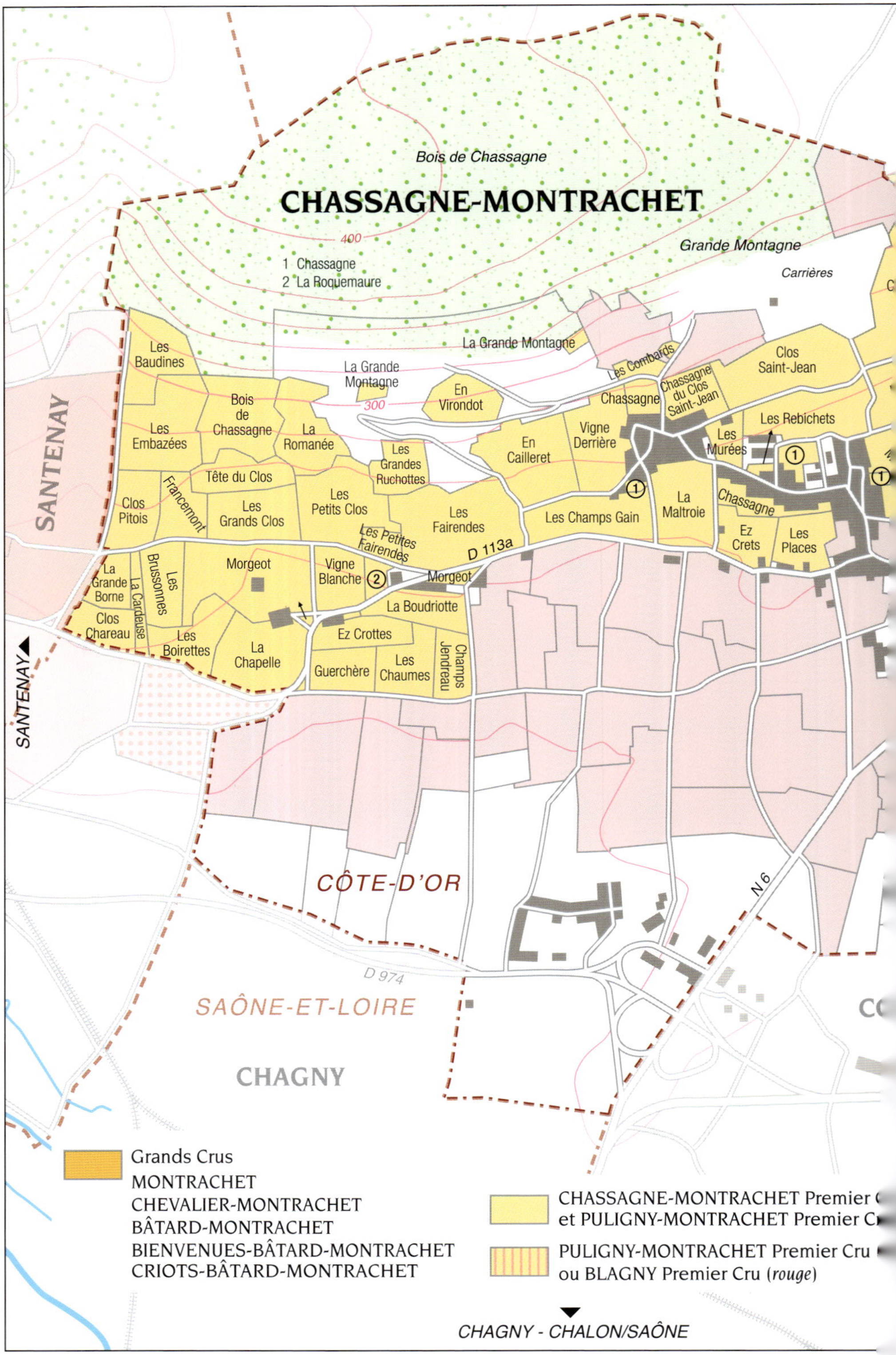

CHASSAGNE-MONTRACHET
Bois de Chassagne
Grande Montagne
Carrières
400
300
1 Chassagne
2 La Roquemaure
La Grande Montagne
Les Combards
Clos Saint-Jean
Les Baudines
La Grande Montagne
En Virondot
Chassagne
Chassagne du Clos Saint-Jean
Bois de Chassagne
Les Embazées
La Romanée
Vigne Derrière
En Cailleret
Les Rebichets
Les Murées
Les Grandes Ruchottes
Tête du Clos
Clos Pitois
Francemont
Les Grands Clos
Les Petits Clos
Les Fairendes
Les Champs Gain
La Maltroie
Chassagne
Ez Crets
Les Places
Les Petites Fairendes
D 113a
SANTENAY
La Grande Borne
Les Brussonnes
Morgeot
Vigne Blanche
Morgeot
La Cardeuse
La Boudriotte
Clos Chareau
Les Boirettes
La Chapelle
Ez Crottes
Guerchère
Les Chaumes
Champs Jendreau
SANTENAY
CÔTE-D'OR
N 6
D 974
SAÔNE-ET-LOIRE
CHAGNY
Grands Crus
MONTRACHET
CHEVALIER-MONTRACHET
BÂTARD-MONTRACHET
BIENVENUES-BÂTARD-MONTRACHET
CRIOTS-BÂTARD-MONTRACHET
CHASSAGNE-MONTRACHET Premier
et PULIGNY-MONTRACHET Premier
PULIGNY-MONTRACHET Premier Cru
ou BLAGNY Premier Cru (rouge)
CHAGNY - CHALON/SAÔNE

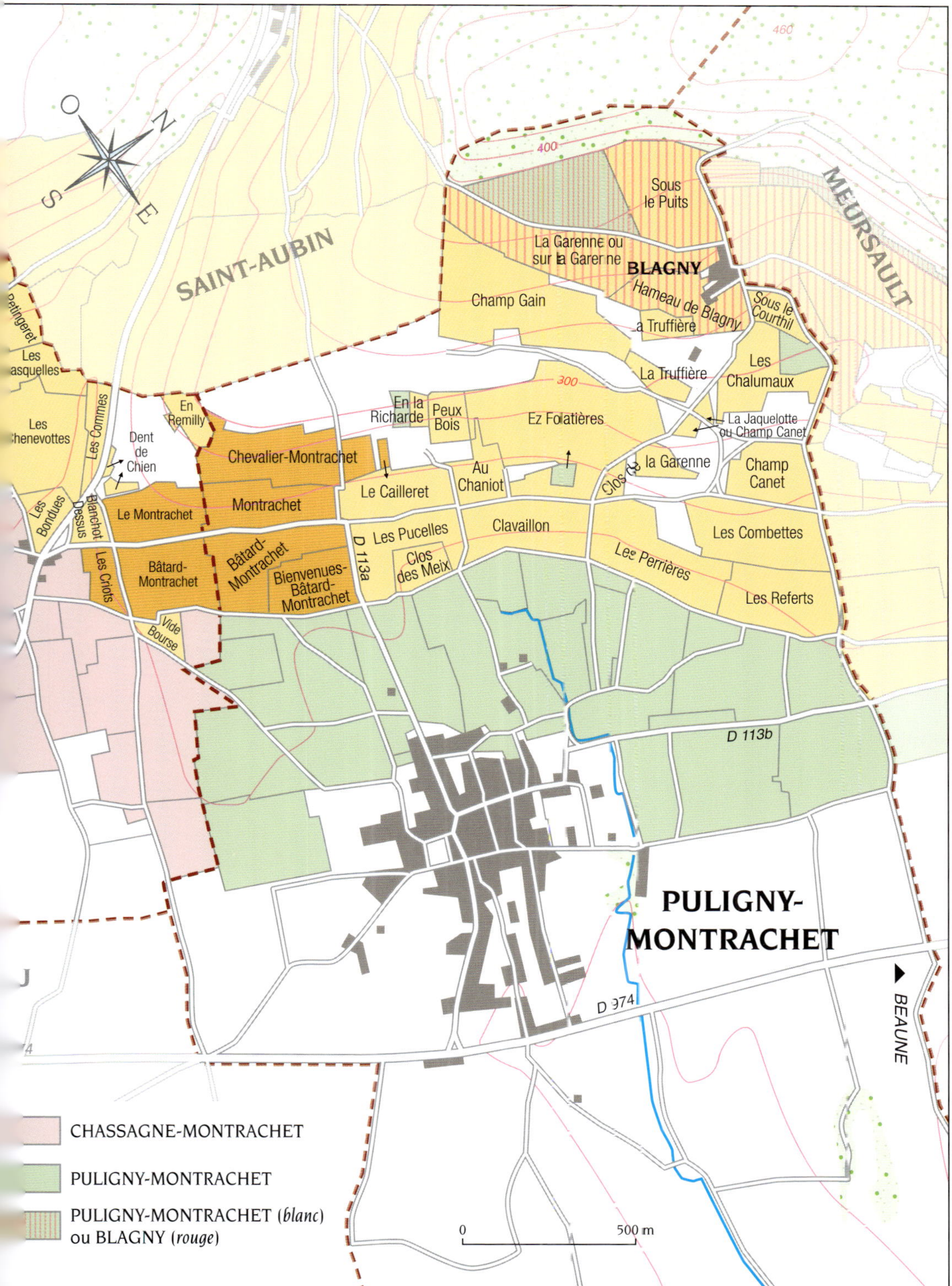

N
E
S
O
460
400
300
SAINT-AUBIN
MEURSAULT
Sous le Puits
La Garenne ou sur la Garenne
BLAGNY
Hameau de Blagny
Champ Gain
a Truffière
Sous le Courthil
Les Chalumaux
La Truffière
Petingeret
Les Masquelles
Les Chenevottes
Les Commes
En Remilly
Dent de Chien
En la Richarde
Peux Bois
Ez Folatières
La Jaquelotte ou Champ Canet
Chevalier-Montrachet
Au Chaniot
Le Cailleret
Clos de la Garenne
Champ Canet
Les Bondues
Blanchot Dessus
Le Montrachet
Montrachet
Les Pucelles
Clavaillon
Les Combettes
Les Criots
Bâtard-Montrachet
Bâtard-Montrachet
Bienvenues-Bâtard-Montrachet
D 113a
Clos des Meix
Les Perrières
Les Referts
Vide Bourse
D 113b
PULIGNY-MONTRACHET
D 974
BEAUNE
CHASSAGNE-MONTRACHET
PULIGNY-MONTRACHET
PULIGNY-MONTRACHET (*blanc*) ou BLAGNY (*rouge*)
0
500 m

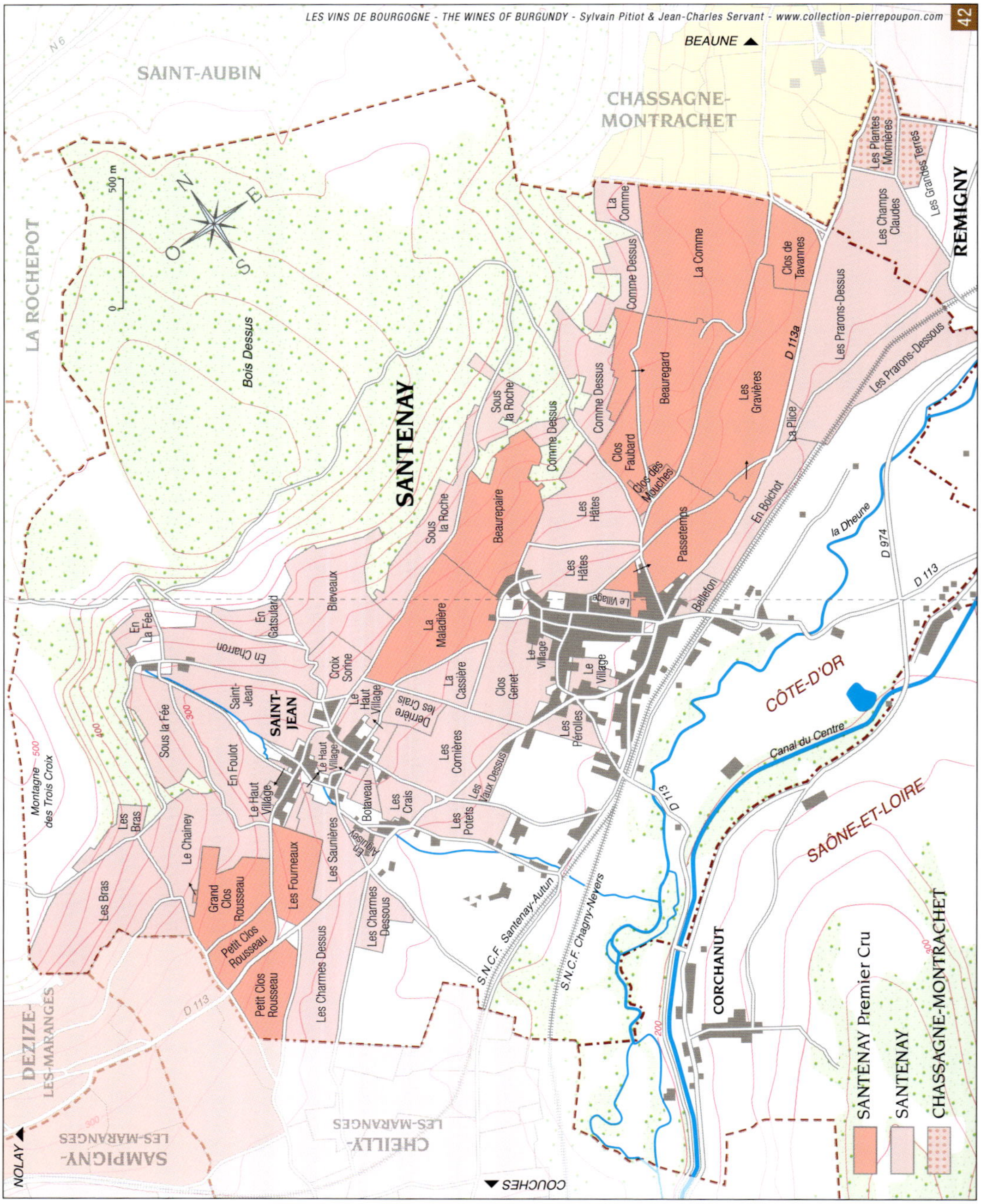

LES VINS DE BOURGOGNE - THE WINES OF BURGUNDY - Sylvain Pitiot & Jean-Charles Servant - www.collection-pierrepoupon.com
42
BEAUNE
NOLAY
COUCHES
SAINT-AUBIN
CHASSAGNE-MONTRACHET
LA ROCHEPOT
REMIGNY
SANTENAY
SAINT-JEAN
DEZIZE-LES-MARANGES
SAMPIGNY-LES-MARANGES
CHEILLY-LES-MARANGES
CORCHANUT
CÔTE-D'OR
SAÔNE-ET-LOIRE
Bois Dessus
Montagne des Trois Croix
500 m
La Comme
Comme Dessus
Clos de Tavannes
Beauregard
Les Gravières
Clos Faubard
Clos des Mouches
Sous la Roche
Comme Dessus
Beaurepaire
Les Hâtes
Passetemps
En Boichot
La Plice
Les Prarons-Dessus
Les Prarons-Dessous
Les Champs Claudes
Les Plantes Momières
Les Grandes Terres
Bievaux
En Gatsulard
En La Fée
En Charron
Croix Sorine
La Maladière
La Cassière
Clos Genet
Le Village
Beaufeton
Saint-Jean
Sous la Fée
En Foulot
Le Haut Village
Derrière les Crais
Les Cornières
Les Pérolles
Les Vaux Dessus
Les Crais
Botaveau
Les Potets
Les Bras
Le Chainey
Grand Clos Rousseau
Petit Clos Rousseau
Les Fourneaux
Les Saunières
Les Charmes Dessous
Les Charmes Dessus
En Aiguisey
S.N.C.F. Santenay-Autun
S.N.C.F. Chagny-Nevers
Canal du Centre
la Dheune
D 113
D 113a
D 974
N 6
SANTENAY Premier Cru
SANTENAY
CHASSAGNE-MONTRACHET

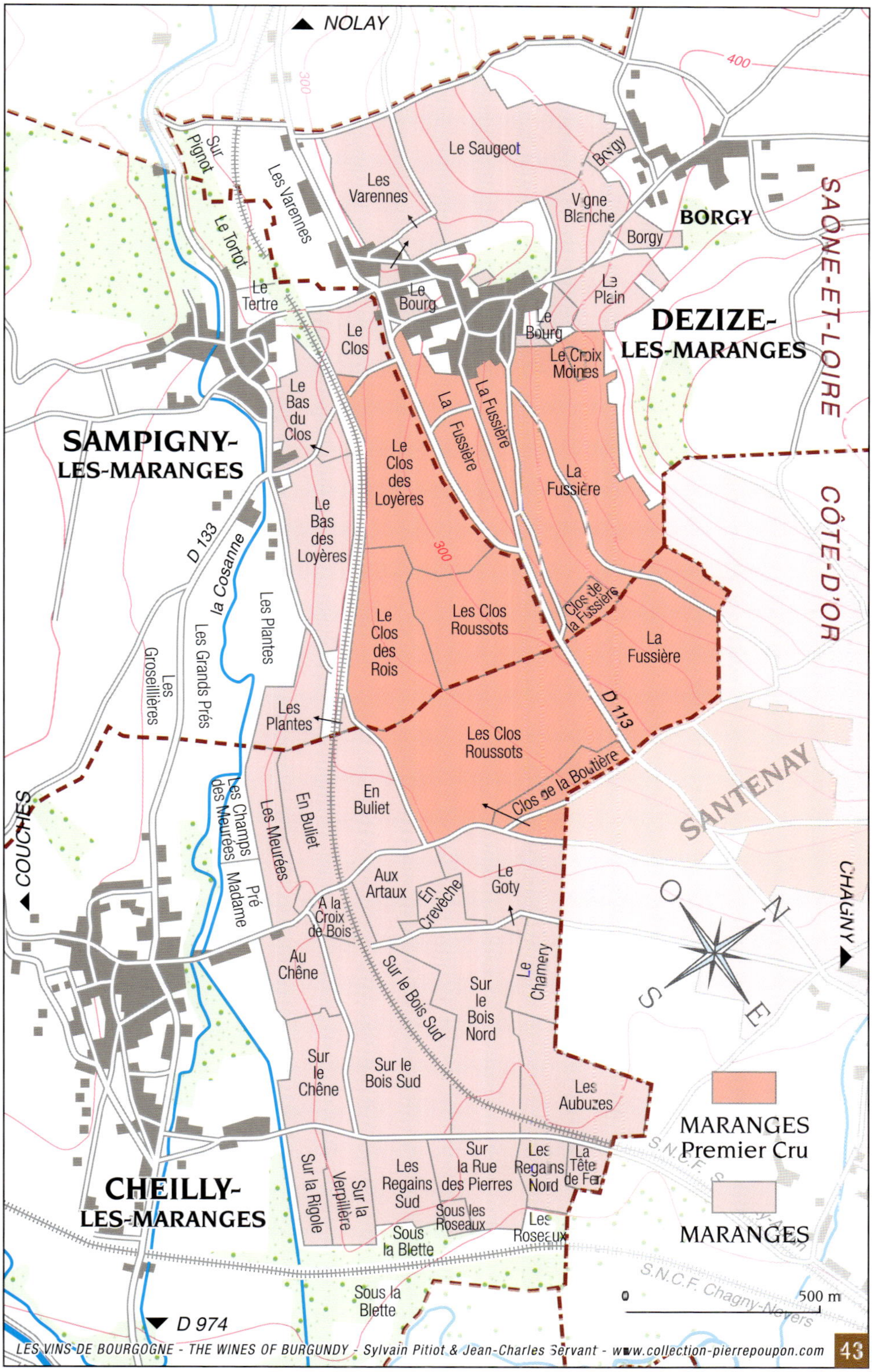
NOLAY
Sur Pignot
Le Tortot
Les Varennes
Les Varennes
Le Saugeot
Borgy
Vigne Blanche
Borgy
BORGY
SAÔNE-ET-LOIRE
Le Tertre
Le Bourg
Le Bourg
Le Plain
DEZIZE-
LES-MARANGES
Le Clos
Le Croix Moines
Le Bas du Clos
SAMPIGNY-
LES-MARANGES
La Fussière
La Fussière
Le Clos des Loyères
La Fussière
CÔTE-D'OR
Le Bas des Loyères
D 133
la Cosanne
Les Plantes
Les Grands Prés
Les Groseillières
Clos de la Fussière
Les Clos Roussots
Le Clos des Rois
La Fussière
D 113
Les Plantes
Les Clos Roussots
SANTENAY
COUCHES
Les Champs des Meurées
Les Meurées
En Buliet
En Buliet
Clos de la Boutière
Pré Madame
Aux Artaux
En Crevèche
Le Goty
CHAGNY
A la Croix de Bois
Au Chêne
Sur le Bois Sud
Sur le Bois Nord
Le Chamery
O
N
S
E
Sur le Chêne
Sur le Bois Sud
Les Aubuzes
MARANGES Premier Cru
MARANGES
Sur la Rigole
Sur la Verpillière
Les Regains Sud
Sur la Rue des Pierres
Les Regains Nord
La Tête de Fer
S.N.C.F.
CHEILLY-
LES-MARANGES
Sous les Roseaux
Les Roseaux
Sous la Blette
Sous la Blette
S.N.C.F. Chagny-Nevers
0
500 m
D 974
300
400

CÔTE CHALONNAISE

et Côtes du Couchois

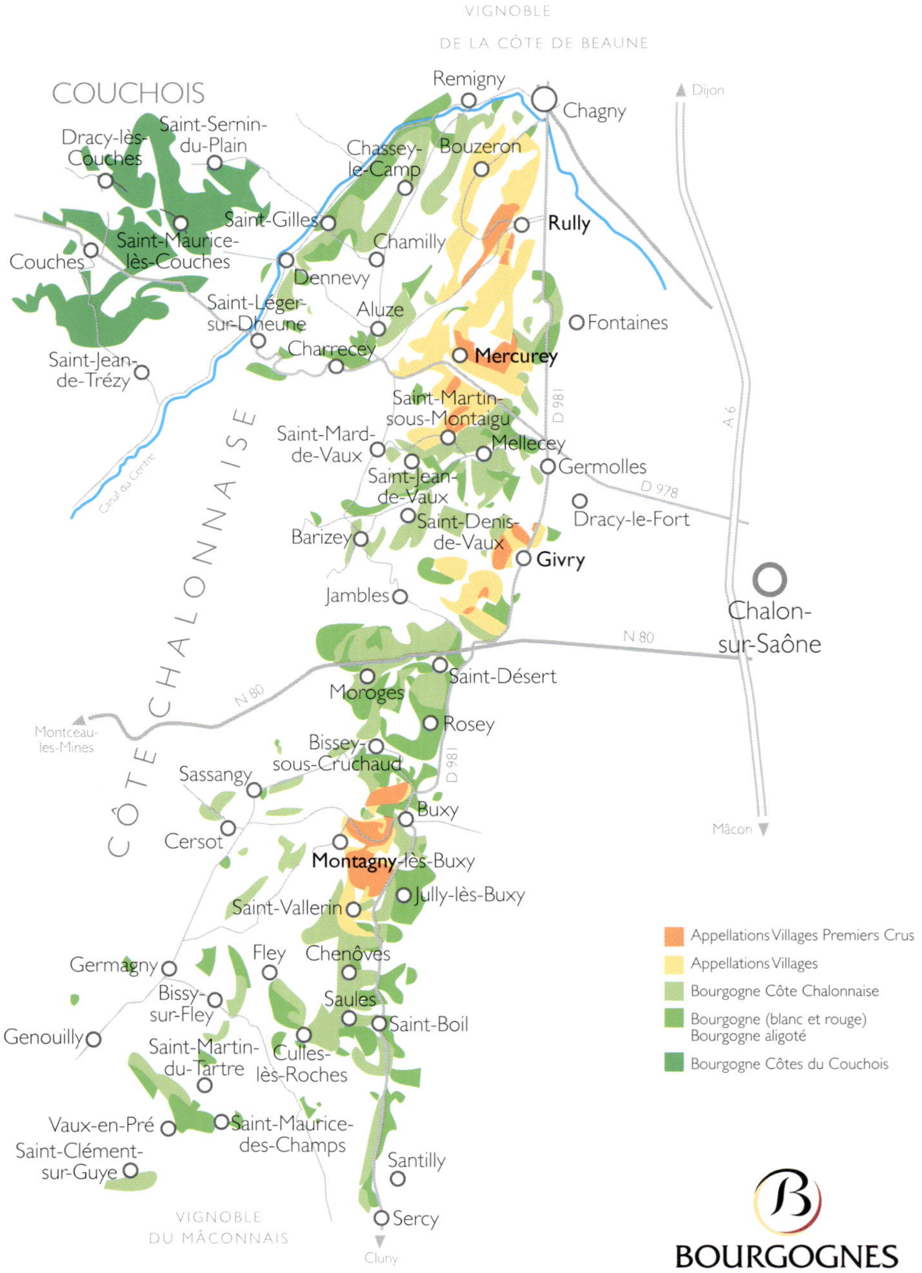

BOURGOGNES

www.vins-bourgogne.fr

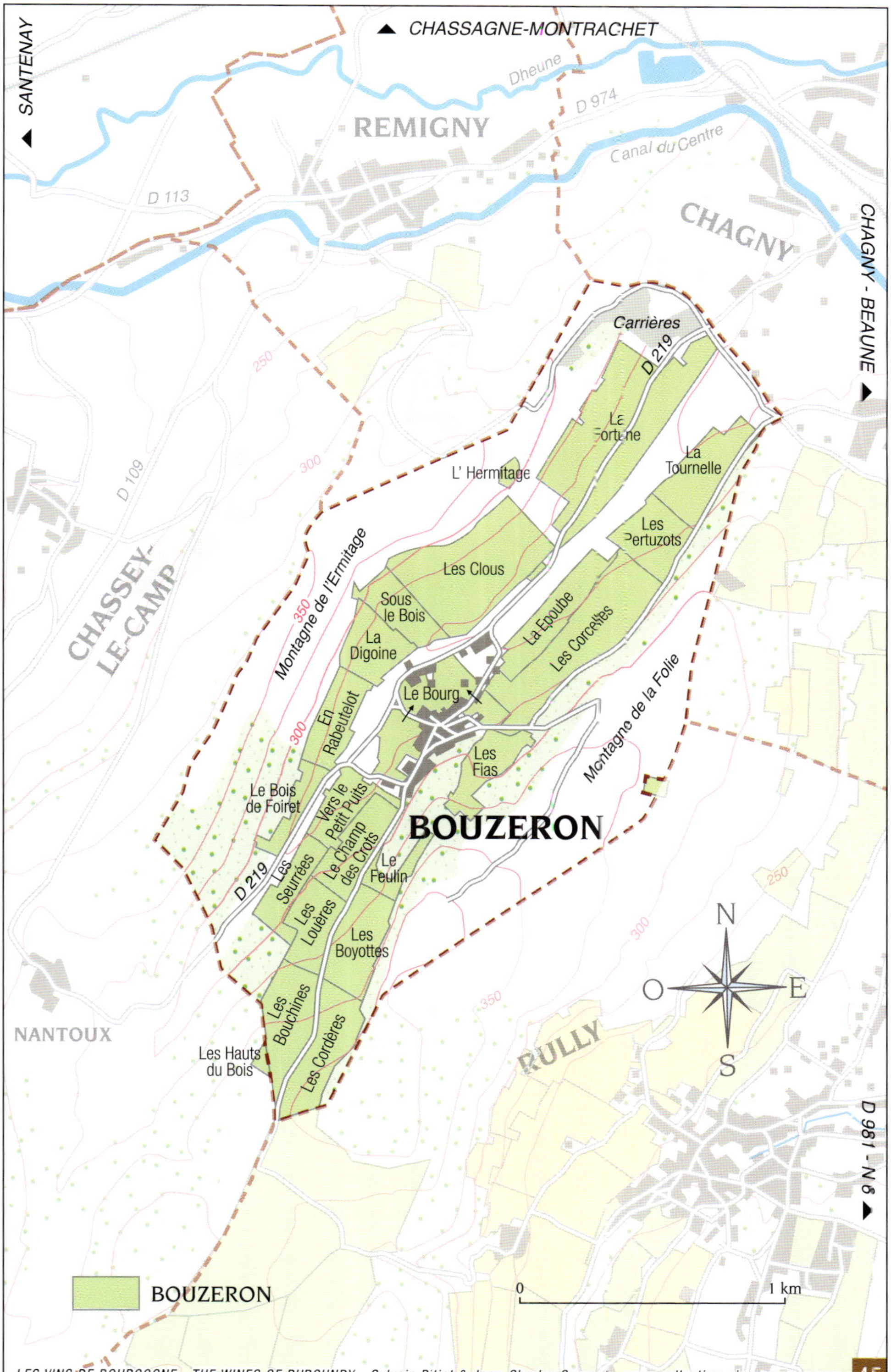
SANTENAY
CHASSAGNE-MONTRACHET
Dheune
D 974
REMIGNY
Canal du Centre
D 113
CHAGNY
CHAGNY - BEAUNE
Carrières
D 219
La Fortune
La Tournelle
L' Hermitage
Les Pertuzots
D 109
Montagne de l'Ermitage
Les Clous
CHASSEY-LE-CAMP
Sous le Bois
La Digoine
La Epoube
Les Corcelles
Le Bourg
En Rabeutelot
Montagne de la Folie
Les Fias
Le Bois de Foiret
Vers le Petit Puits
BOUZERON
Les Seurrées
Le Champ des Crots
Le Feulin
Les Louères
Les Boyottes
N
O
E
S
Les Bouchines
NANTOUX
RULLY
Les Hauts du Bois
Les Cordères
D 981 - N 6
250
300
350
BOUZERON
0
1 km

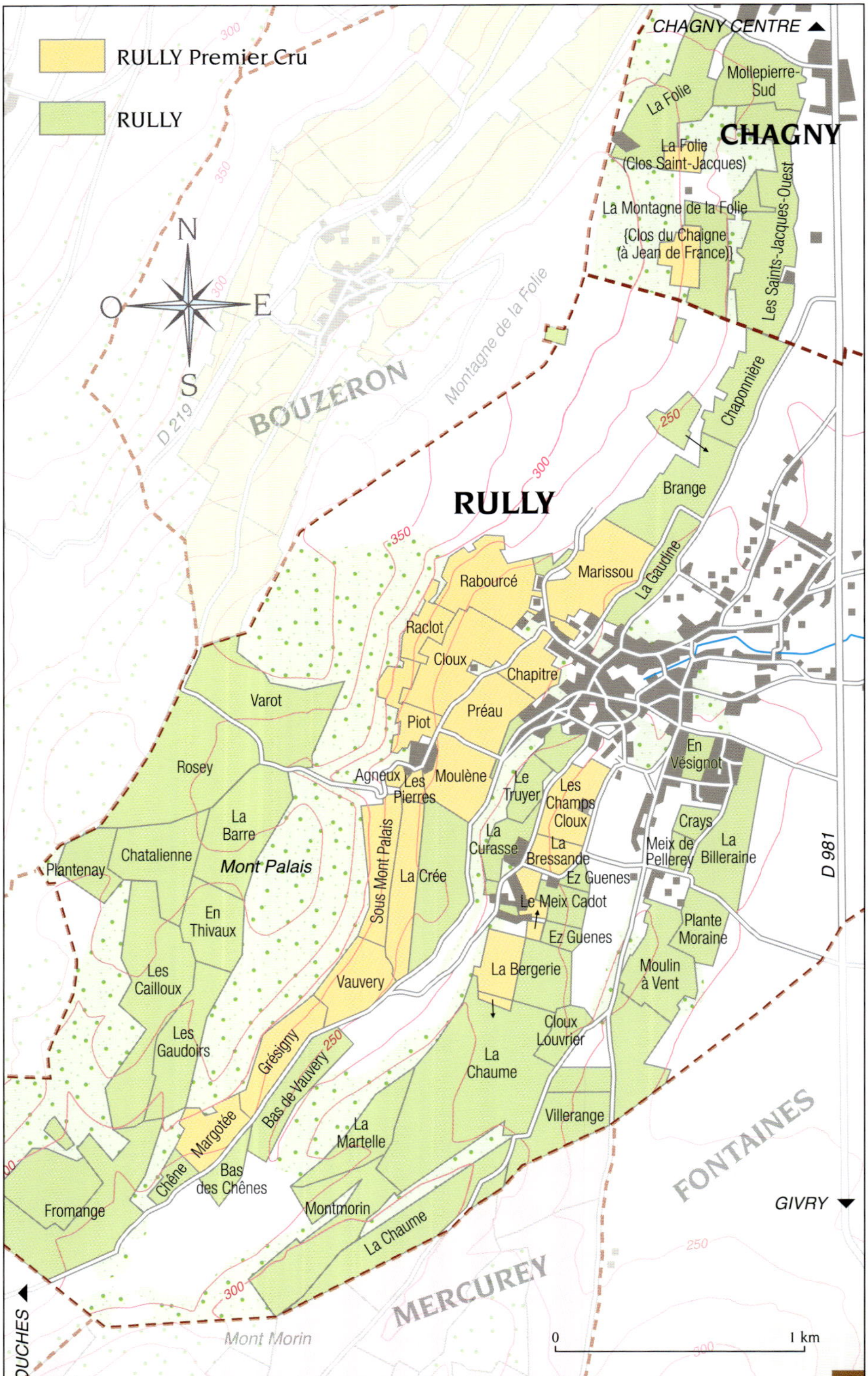
RULLY Premier Cru
RULLY
CHAGNY CENTRE
CHAGNY
Mollepierre-Sud
La Folie
La Folie (Clos Saint-Jacques)
La Montagne de la Folie
{Clos du Chaigne (à Jean de France)}
Les Saints-Jacques-Ouest
BOUZERON
Montagne de la Folie
D 219
Chaponnière
Brange
RULLY
Marissou
La Gaudine
Rabourcé
Raclot
Cloux
Chapitre
Préau
Piot
Varot
Rosey
Agneux
Les Pierres
Moulène
Le Truyer
Les Champs Cloux
En Vesignot
La Barre
Chatalienne
Mont Palais
Plantenay
Sous Mont Palais
La Crée
La Curasse
La Bressande
Ez Guenes
Crays
Meix de Pellerey
La Billeraine
D 981
Le Meix Cadot
Ez Guenes
Plante Moraine
En Thivaux
Les Cailloux
Vauvery
La Bergerie
Moulin à Vent
Les Gaudoirs
Grésigny
Bas de Vauvery
Cloux Louvrier
La Chaume
Villerange
Margotée
Chêne
Bas des Chênes
La Martelle
Fromange
Montmorin
La Chaume
FONTAINES
GIVRY
MERCUREY
Mont Morin
COUCHES
0
1 km

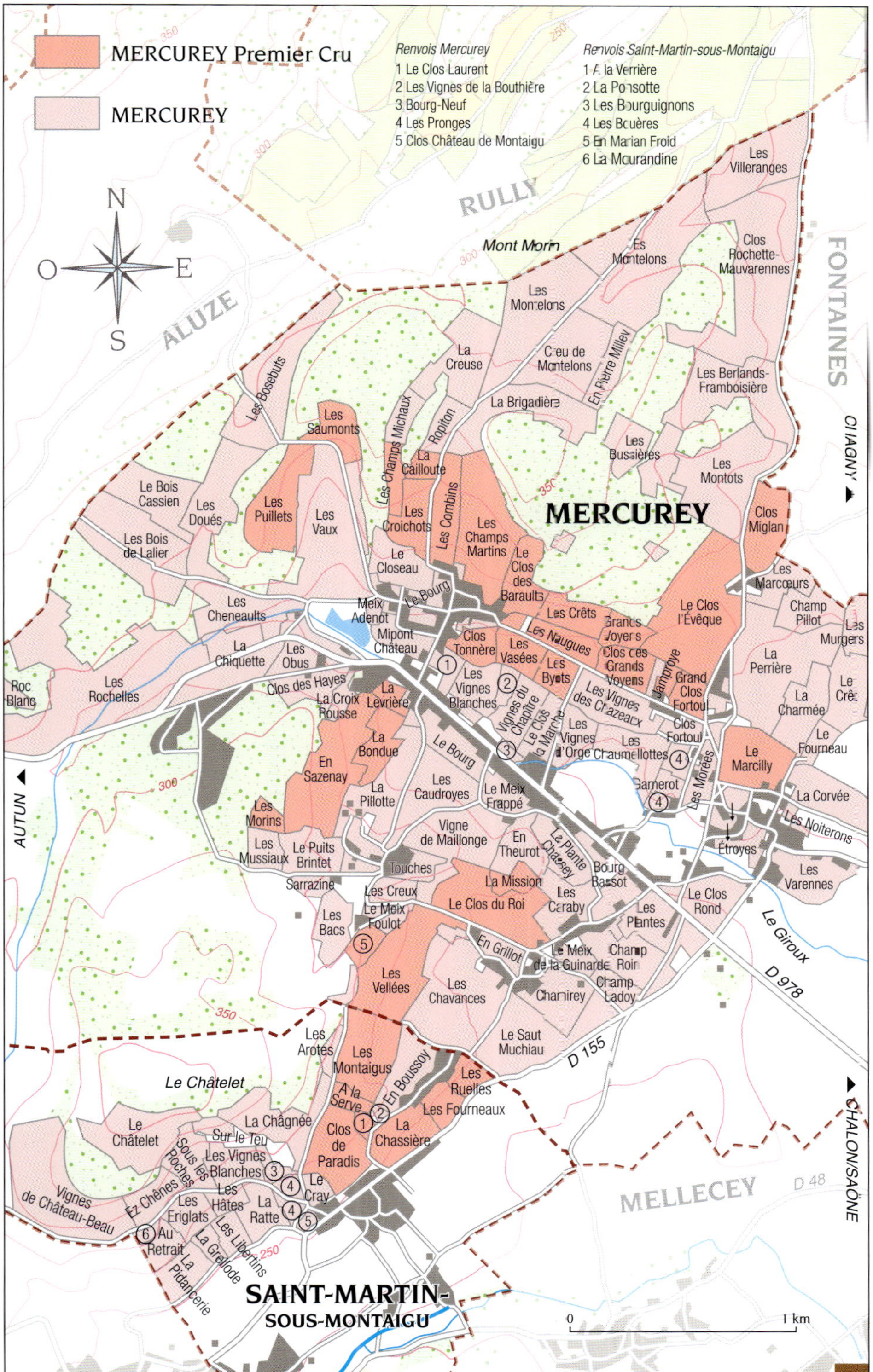
MERCUREY Premier Cru
MERCUREY
Renvois Mercurey
1 Le Clos Laurent
2 Les Vignes de la Bouthière
3 Bourg-Neuf
4 Les Pronges
5 Clos Château de Montaigu
Renvois Saint-Martin-sous-Montaigu
1 A la Verrière
2 La Ponsotte
3 Les Bourguignons
4 Les Bouères
5 En Marian Froid
6 La Mourandine
N
O
E
S
RULLY
ALUZE
FONTAINES
Mont Morin
CIAGNY
MERCUREY
AUTUN
CHALON/SAÔNE
MELLECEY
SAINT-MARTIN-
SOUS-MONTAIGU
Les Villeranges
Es Montelons
Clos Rochette-Mauvarennes
Les Montelons
La Creuse
Creu de Montelons
En Pierre Milley
Les Berlands-Framboisière
Les Bosebuts
La Brigadière
Les Saumonts
Les Champs Michaux
Ropiton
Les Bussières
Les Montots
La Cailloute
Le Bois Cassien
Les Doués
Les Puillets
Les Vaux
Les Croichots
Les Combins
Les Champs Martins
Clos Miglan
Les Bois de Lalier
Le Closeau
Le Clos des Barault
Les Marcœurs
Les Cheneaults
Meix Adenot
Le Bourg
Les Crêts
Grands Voyens
Le Clos l'Évêque
Champ Pillot
Les Murgers
Mipont Château
Clos Tonnère
Les Vasées
Les Naugues
Clos des Grands Voyens
La Chiquette
Les Obus
Jamproye
La Perrière
Roc Blanc
Les Rochelles
Clos des Hayes
Les Vignes Blanches
Les Byots
Les Vignes des Chazeaux
Grand Clos Fortoul
Le Crêt
La Croix Rousse
La Levrière
Vignes du Chapitre
Le Clos la Marche
La Charmée
La Bondue
Le Bourg
Les Vignes d'Orge
Clos Fortoul
Le Fourneau
En Sazenay
Les Chaumellottes
Les Morées
Le Marcilly
300
Les Caudroyes
Le Meix Frappé
Garnerot
La Corvée
Les Morins
La Pillotte
Les Noiterons
Vigne de Maillonge
En Theurot
La Plante Chassey
Étroyes
Les Mussiaux
Le Puits Brintet
Touches
Bourg Bassot
Les Varennes
Sarrazine
La Mission
Les Creux
Les Caraby
Le Clos Rond
Les Bacs
Le Meix Foulot
Le Clos du Roi
Les Plantes
Le Giroux
En Grillot
Le Meix de la Guinarde
Champ Roin
D 978
Les Vellées
Les Chavances
Champ Ladoy
Chamirey
350
Les Arotes
Les Montaigus
Le Saut Muchiau
D 155
Le Châtelet
En Boussoy
Les Ruelles
A la Serve
Les Fourneaux
La Chassière
La Chagnée
Clos de Paradis
Le Châtelet
Sur le Teu
Sous les Roches
Les Vignes Blanches
Le Cray
D 48
Vignes de Château-Beau
Ez Chênes
Les Hâtes
Les Eriglats
La Ratte
Au Retrait
La Grelode
Les Libertins
La Pidancerie
250
0
1 km

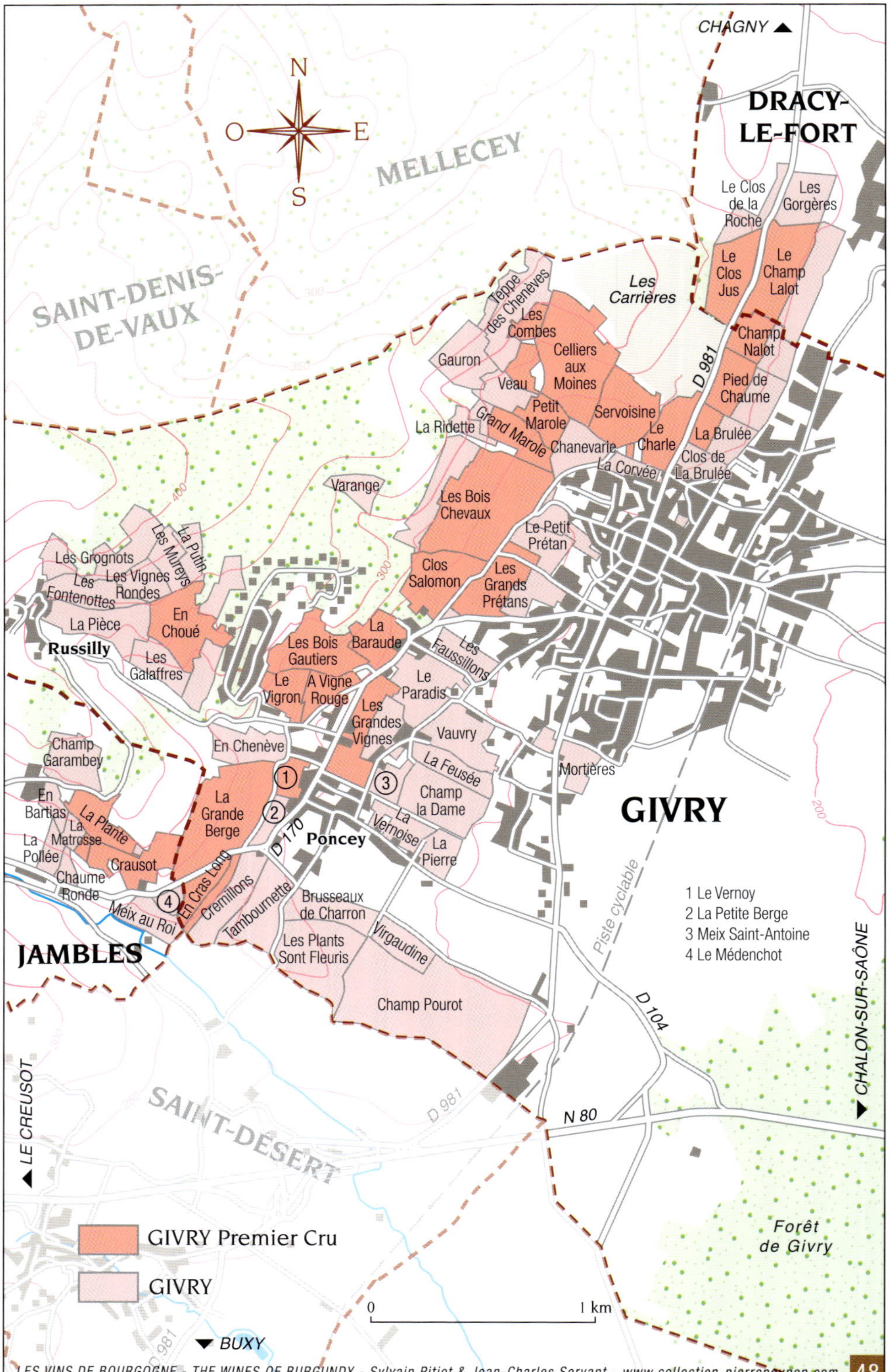
CHAGNY
DRACY-LE-FORT
MELLECEY
SAINT-DENIS-DE-VAUX
N
O
E
S
Le Clos de la Roche
Les Gorgères
Le Clos Jus
Le Champ Lalot
Les Carrières
Teppe des Chenèves
Les Combes
Celliers aux Moines
Gauron
Veau
Petit Marole
Servoisine
Champ Nalot
Pied de Chaume
La Ridette
Grand Marole
Chanevarie
Le Charle
La Brulée
Clos de La Brulée
La Corvée
Varange
Les Bois Chevaux
Le Petit Prétan
Les Grognots
Les Murey
La Putin
Les Vignes Rondes
Les Fontenottes
Clos Salomon
Les Grands Prétans
La Pièce
En Choué
Russilly
Les Galaffres
Les Bois Gautiers
La Baraude
Les Faussillons
Le Vigron
A Vigne Rouge
Le Paradis
Les Grandes Vignes
Vauvry
En Chenève
Champ Garambey
La Feusée
Mortières
En Bartias
La Plante
La Matrosse
La Pollée
La Grande Berge
Champ la Dame
La Vernoise
La Pierre
Poncey
D 170
GIVRY
Crausot
Chaume Ronde
En Cras Long
Cremillons
Tambournette
Brusseaux de Charron
Meix au Roi
JAMBLES
Les Plants Sont Fleuris
Virgaudine
Champ Pourot
Piste cyclable
D 981
1 Le Vernoy
2 La Petite Berge
3 Meix Saint-Antoine
4 Le Médenchot
D 104
CHALON-SUR-SAÔNE
LE CREUSOT
SAINT-DESERT
N 80
Forêt de Givry
GIVRY Premier Cru
GIVRY
0
1 km
BUXY

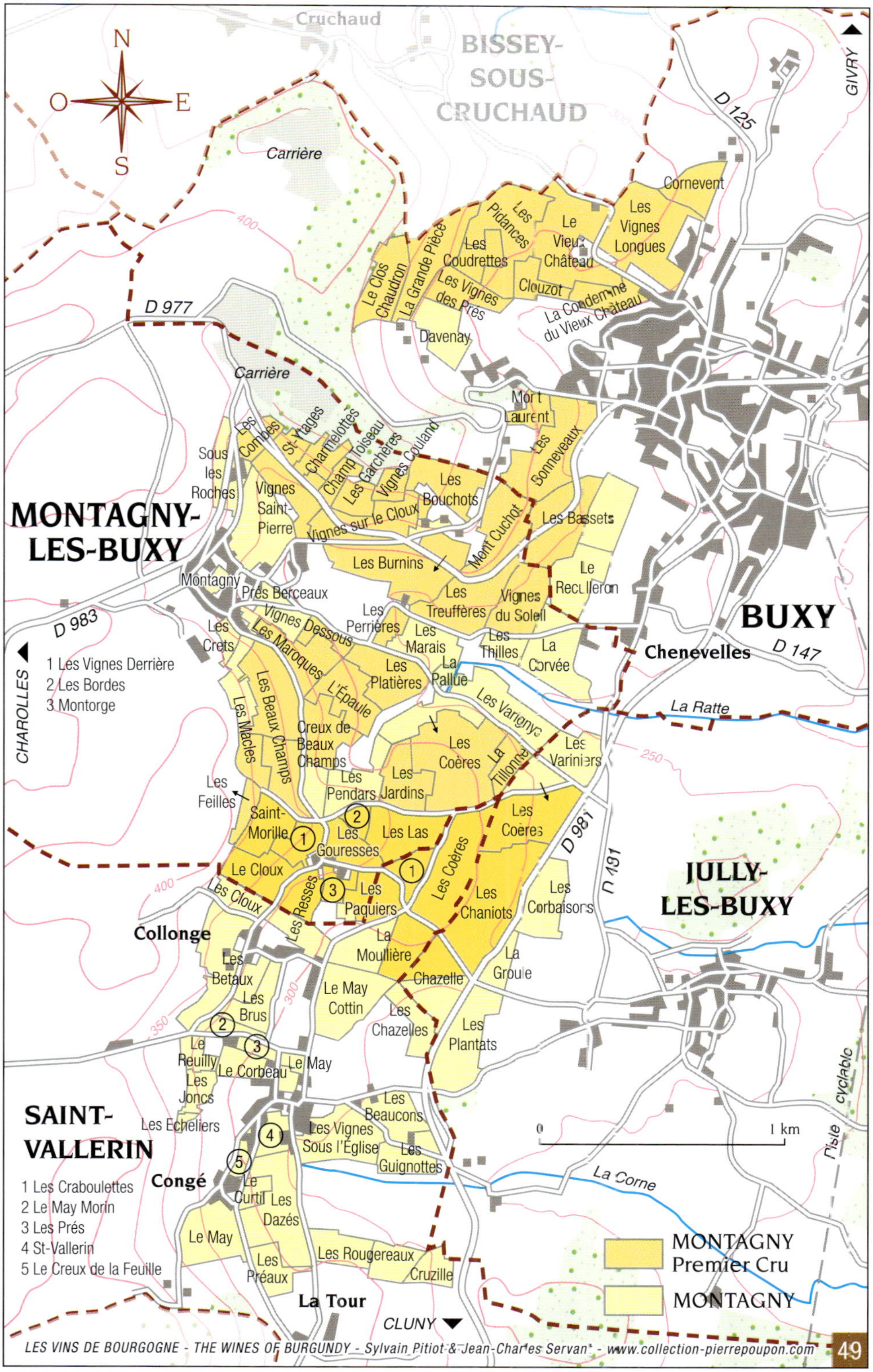
N
O
E
S
Cruchaud
BISSEY-SOUS-CRUCHAUD
GIVRY
D 125
Carrière
Cornevent
Les Vignes Longues
Les Pidances
Le Vieux Château
Les Coudrettes
Le Clos Chaudron
La Grande Pièce
Les Vignes des Prés
Clouzot
La Condemine du Vieux Château
Davenay
D 977
Carrière
Mont Laurent
Les Sonneveaux
Les Combes
St-Ytages
Charmelottes
Champ Toiseau
Les Garchères
Vignes Couland
Les Bouchots
Sous les Roches
Vignes Saint-Pierre
Vignes sur le Cloux
Mont Cuchot
Les Bassets
MONTAGNY-LES-BUXY
Les Burnins
Le Reculleron
Montagny
Prés Berceaux
Les Truffères
Vignes du Soleil
D 983
Les Perrières
BUXY
Les Crets
Vignes Dessous
Les Maroques
Les Marais
Les Thilles
La Corvée
Chenevelles
D 147
CHAROLLES
1 Les Vignes Derrière
2 Les Bordes
3 Montorge
Les Platières
La Pallue
Les Beaux Champs
Les Macles
L'Épaule
Les Varignys
La Ratte
Creux de Beaux Champs
Les Coères
La Tillonne
Les Varinières
Les Feilles
Les Pendars
Les Jardins
Saint-Morille
Les Gouresses
Les Las
Les Coères
D 981
D 981
Le Cloux
Les Coères
Les Chaniots
Les Corbaisons
JULLY-LES-BUXY
Les Cloux
Les Resses
Les Paquiers
Collonge
La Moullière
Chazelle
La Groule
Les Betaux
Les Brus
Le May Cottin
Les Chazelles
Les Plantats
Le Reuilly
Le Corbeau
Le May
Les Joncs
Les Beaucons
SAINT-VALLERIN
Les Echeliers
Les Vignes Sous l'Église
Les Guignottes
0
1 km
Piste cyclable
La Corne
Congé
1 Les Craboulettes
2 Le May Morin
3 Les Prés
4 St-Vallerin
5 Le Creux de la Feuille
Le Curtil
Les Dazés
Le May
Les Préaux
Les Rougereaux
Cruzille
La Tour
CLUNY
MONTAGNY Premier Cru
MONTAGNY
LES VINS DE BOURGOGNE - THE WINES OF BURGUNDY - Sylvain Pitiot & Jean-Charles Servant - www.collection-pierrepoupon.com
49

MÂCONNAIS

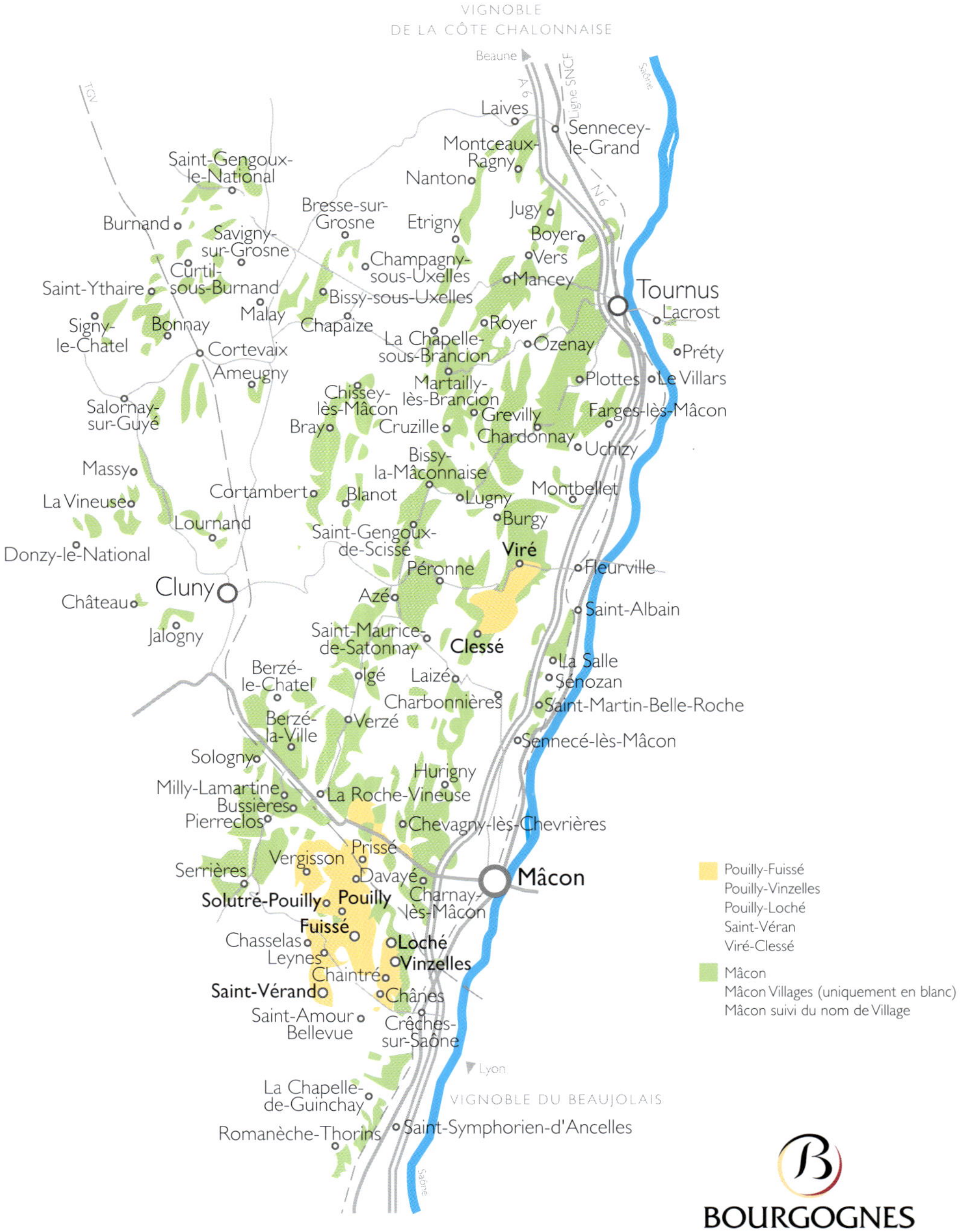

BOURGOGNES

www.vins-bourgogne.fr

PIERRECLOS
BUSSIÈRES
PIERRECLOS
SERRIÈRES
PRISSÉ
PRISSÉ
DAVAYÉ
N
O
E
S
300
400
350
550
500
450
400
En Tillier
La Toule
D 177
En Chatenay
Au Métertière
les Terres du Perret
Bois Dayer
Combe Poncet
La Côte
Roche de Vergisson
Petite Croix
En Carmentrant
Les Croux
VERGISSON
Aux Vignes Dessus
Les Crays
Sur la Roche
Le Sabotier
LE REPOSTÈRE
Le Nambret
En Ouche
La Maréchaude
En Ronchevat
En France
La Truche
La Folle
Aux Charmes
Le Moulin
Le Champ Rocher
Le Grand Pré
Vignes de la L'Eau
Bois du Molard
Les Courtelongs
Les Plasses
La Vigne des Verchères
la Denante
La Gorge au Loup
En Buland
La Mouille
En Rontenoux
Roche de Solutré
SOLUTRÉ-POUILLY
1 Vergisson
2 Le Martelet
3 Le Repostère
4 Vers la Croix
POUILLY-FUISSÉ
0
1 km
LEYNES
54

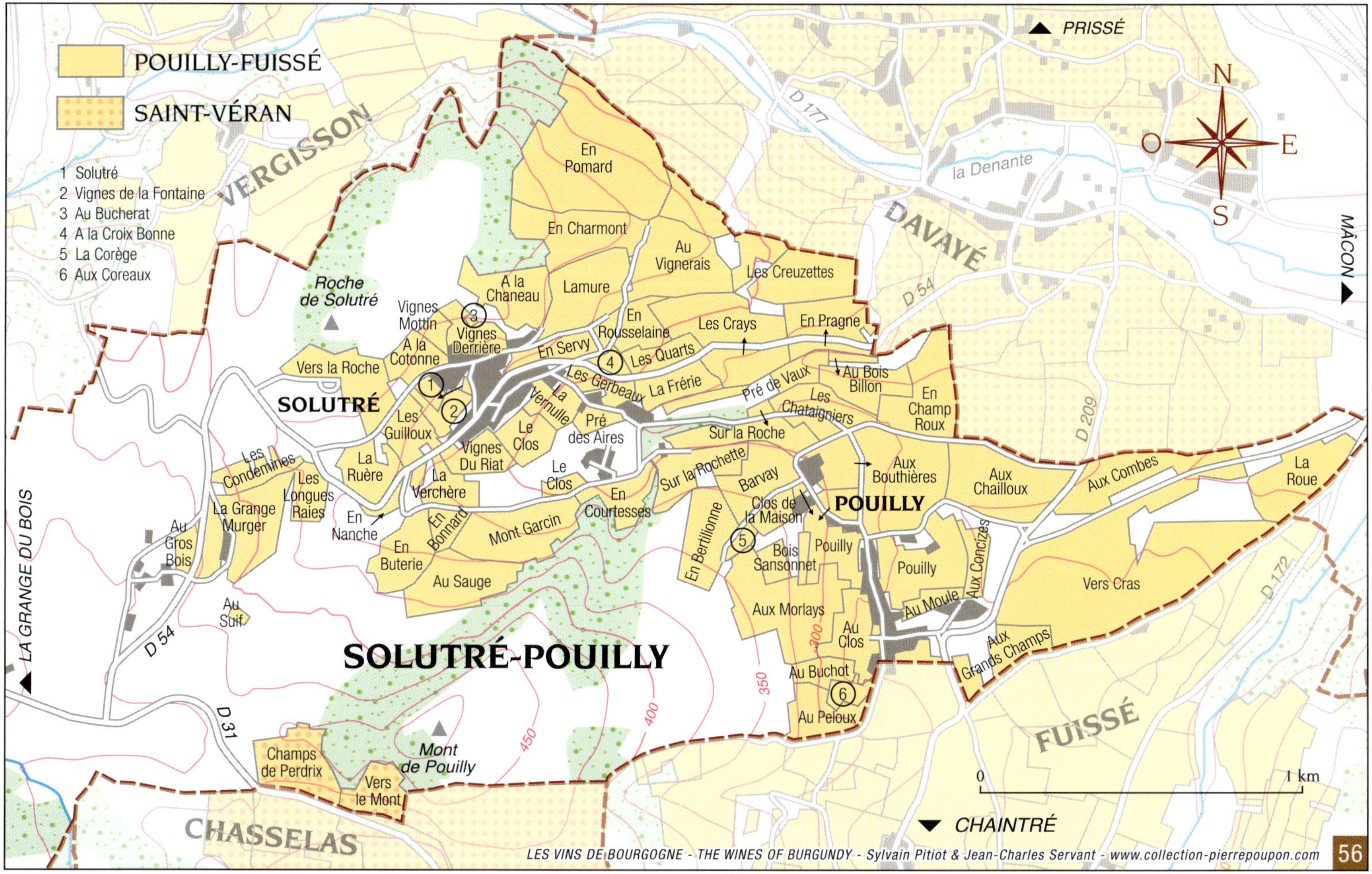

POUILLY-FUISSÉ
SAINT-VÉRAN
1 Solutré
2 Vignes de la Fontaine
3 Au Bucherat
4 A la Croix Bonne
5 La Corège
6 Aux Coreaux
PRISSÉ
MÂCON
CHAINTRÉ
LA GRANGE DU BOIS
VERGISSON
DAVAYÉ
FUISSÉ
CHASSELAS
SOLUTRÉ-POUILLY
SOLUTRÉ
POUILLY
Roche de Solutré
Mont de Pouilly
la Denante
D 177
D 54
D 209
D 172
D 31
En Pomard
En Charmont
Au Vignerais
Les Creuzettes
Lamure
A la Chaneau
Vignes Mottin
Vignes Derrière
A la Cotonne
Vers la Roche
En Rousselaine
Les Crays
En Pragne
En Servy
Les Quarts
Les Gerbeaux
La Frérie
Pré de Vaux
Au Bois Billon
En Champ Roux
Les Chataigniers
La Vernulle
Pré des Aires
Les Guilloux
Le Clos
Vignes Du Riat
La Ruère
La Verchère
Les Condemines
Les Longues Raies
La Grange Murger
Au Gros Bois
Au Suif
En Nanche
En Bonnard
En Buterie
Mont Garcin
Au Sauge
En Courtesses
Sur la Roche
Sur la Rochette
Barvay
Clos de la Maison
En Bertillionne
Bois Sansonnet
Pouilly
Aux Morlays
Au Clos
Au Buchot
Au Peloux
Aux Bouthières
Aux Chailloux
Aux Combes
La Roue
Vers Cras
Au Moule
Aux Concizes
Aux Grands Champs
Champs de Perdrix
Vers le Mont
300
350
400
450
0
1 km
LES VINS DE BOURGOGNE - THE WINES OF BURGUNDY - Sylvain Pitiot & Jean-Charles Servant - www.collection-pierrepoupon.com
56

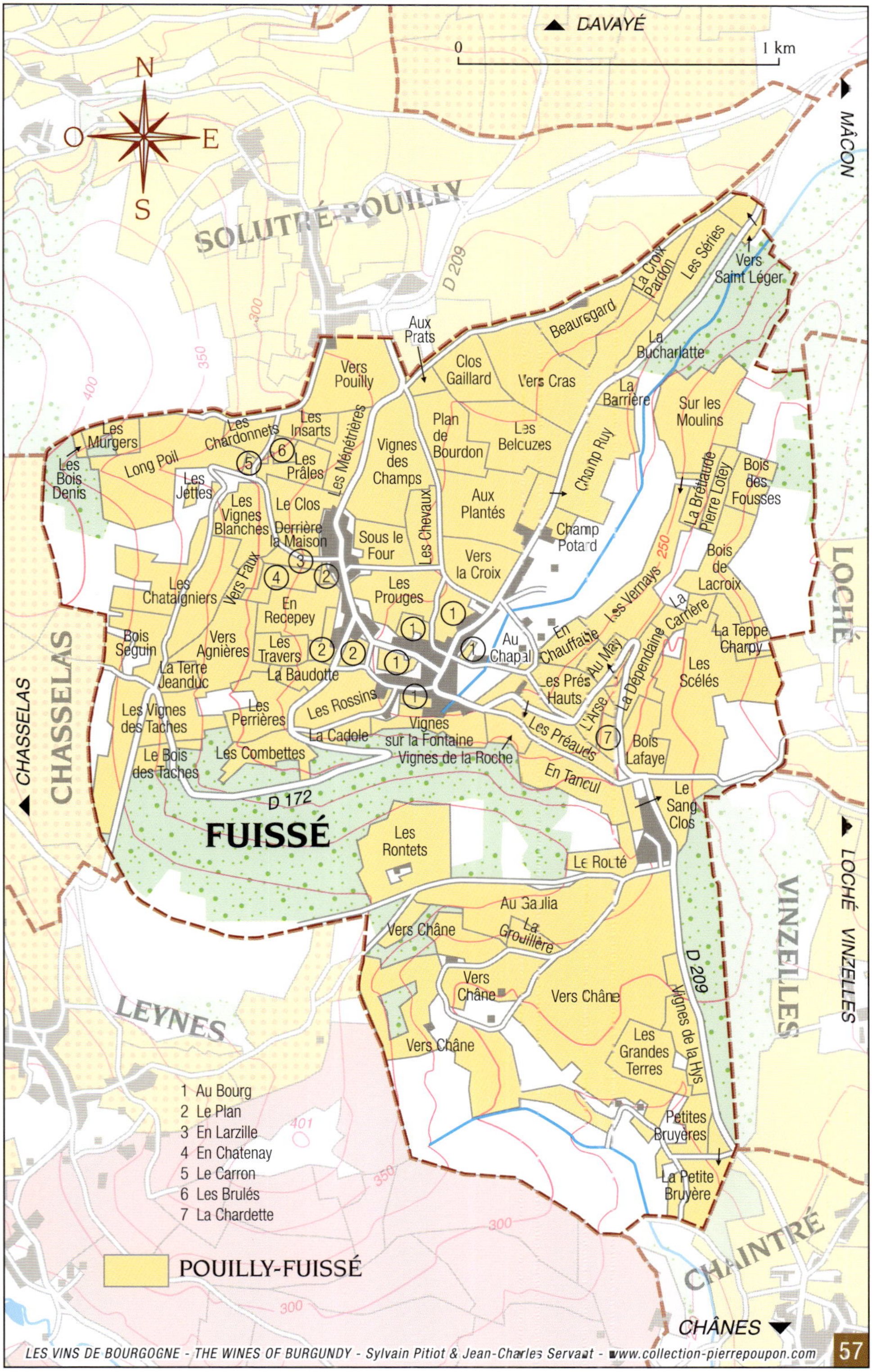
DAVAYÉ
MÂCON
SOLUTRÉ-POUILLY
LOCHÉ
CHASSELAS
LOCHÉ VINZELLES
VINZELLES
LEYNES
CHAINTRÉ
CHÂNES
FUISSÉ
D 209
D 172
Aux Prats
Clos Gaillard
Vers Cras
Beauregard
La Croix Pardon
Les Séries
Vers Saint Léger
La Bucharlatte
La Barrière
Sur les Moulins
Vers Pouilly
Les Insarts
Les Chardonnets
Les Murgers
Les Bois Denis
Long Poil
Les Jettes
Les Prâles
Les Ménétrières
Vignes des Champs
Plan de Bourdon
Les Belcuzes
Champ Ruy
La Brétaude
Pierre Lotey
Bois des Fousses
Les Vignes Blanches
Le Clos
Derrière la Maison
Sous le Four
Les Chevaux
Aux Plantés
Champ Potard
Vers la Croix
Bois de Lacroix
Les Chataigniers
Vers Faux
En Recepey
Les Prouges
Les Vernays
La Carrière
La Dépendance
La Teppe Charpy
Bois Seguin
Vers Agnières
Les Travers
La Baudotte
Au Chapal
En Chauffaille
Au May
Les Prés Hauts
Les Scélés
La Terre Jeanduc
Les Vignes des Taches
Les Perrières
Les Rossins
La Cadole
Vignes sur la Fontaine
Vignes de la Roche
Les Préauds
L'Arse
Bois Lafaye
Le Bois des Taches
Les Combettes
En Tancul
Le Sang Clos
Les Rontets
Le Routé
Au Gaulia
La Grouillère
Vers Chêne
Vers Chêne
Vers Chêne
Vers Chêne
Vignes de la Hys
Les Grandes Terres
Petites Bruyères
La Petite Bruyère
1 Au Bourg
2 Le Plan
3 En Larzille
4 En Chatenay
5 Le Carron
6 Les Brulés
7 La Chardette
POUILLY-FUISSÉ
0
1 km
N
S
E
O
57

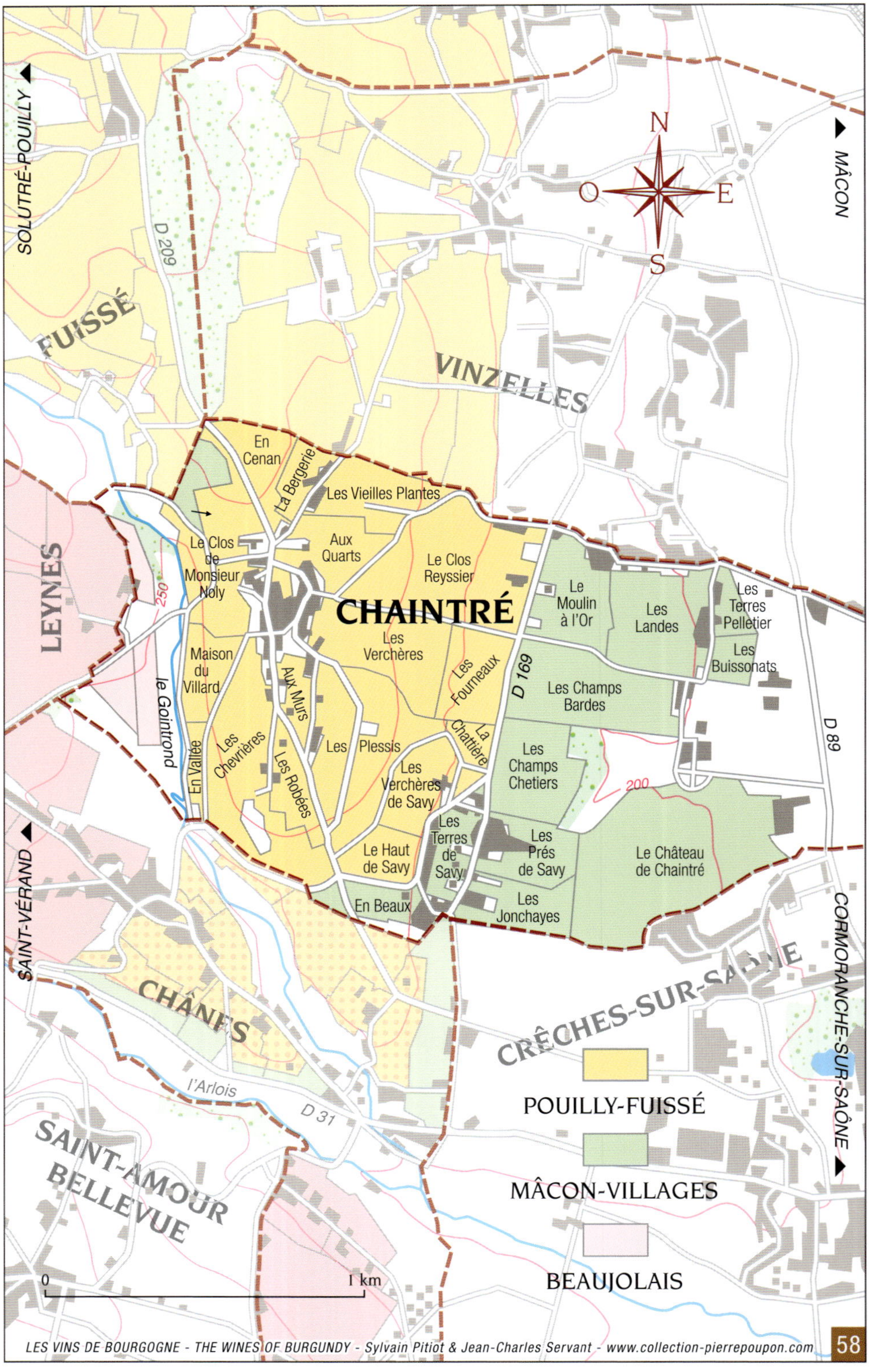
SOLUTRÉ-POUILLY
MÂCON
N
O
E
S
D 209
FUISSÉ
VINZELLES
LEYNES
En Cenan
La Bergerie
Les Vieilles Plantes
Le Clos de Monsieur Noly
Aux Quarts
Le Clos Reyssier
CHAINTRÉ
250
Le Moulin à l'Or
Les Landes
Les Terres Pelletier
Les Buissonats
Maison du Villard
Les Verchères
Les Fourneaux
D 169
Les Champs Bardes
D 89
le Gointrond
Aux Murs
La Chattière
En Vallée
Les Chevrières
Les Robées
Les Plessis
Les Verchères de Savy
Les Champs Chetiers
200
Les Terres de Savy
Le Haut de Savy
Les Prés de Savy
Le Château de Chaintré
En Beaux
Les Jonchayes
SAINT-VÉRAND
CORMORANCHE-SUR-SAÔNE
CRÊCHES-SUR-SAÔNE
CHÂNES
l'Arlois
D 31
SAINT-AMOUR BELLEVUE
POUILLY-FUISSÉ
MÂCON-VILLAGES
BEAUJOLAIS
0
1 km

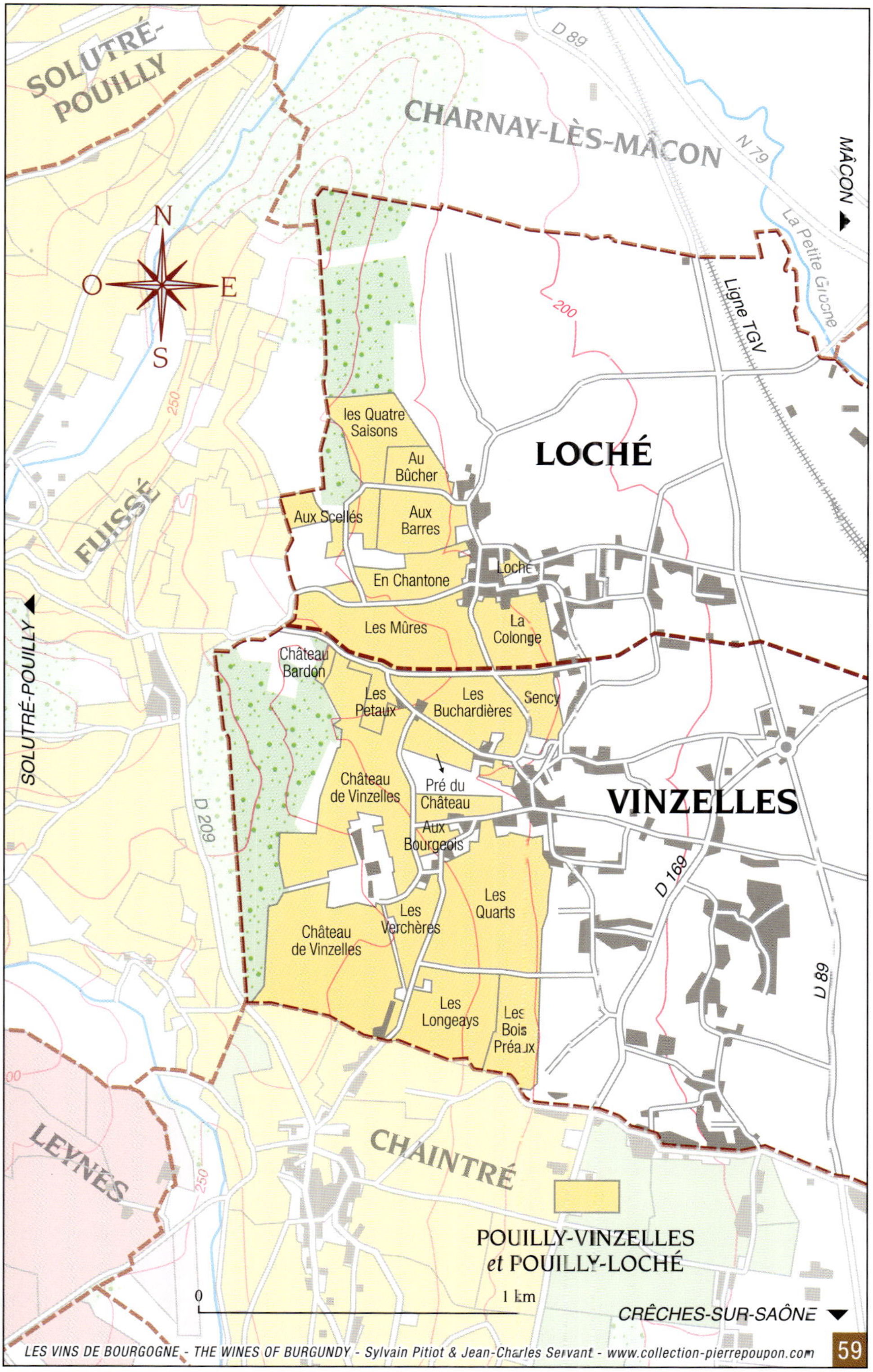
SOLUTRÉ-POUILLY
CHARNAY-LÈS-MÂCON
D 89
N 79
MÂCON
La Petite Grosne
Ligne TGV
200
250
N
O
E
S
LOCHÉ
FUISSÉ
les Quatre Saisons
Au Bûcher
Aux Scellés
Aux Barres
En Chantone
Loché
Les Mûres
La Colonge
SOLUTRÉ-POUILLY
Château Bardon
Les Petaux
Les Buchardières
Sency
Château de Vinzelles
Pré du Château
VINZELLES
D 209
Aux Bourgeois
D 169
Les Quarts
Les Verchères
Château de Vinzelles
D 89
Les Longeays
Les Bois Préaux
LEYNES
CHAINTRÉ
POUILLY-VINZELLES
et POUILLY-LOCHÉ
0
1 km
CRÊCHES-SUR-SAÔNE

B.V.I.B.

Bureau Interprofessionnel des Vins de Bourgogne

The *Bureau Interprofessionnel des Vins de Bourgogne* is a professional body that brings together *vignerons* and *négociants*. Burgundy is a mosaic composed of 29,000 hectares of vineyards (average production, in the 2012 to 2016 harvests, was 183 million bottles) which represents just 0.4% of world wine production.
No other French wine region is able to express and realize in equal measure the concept of *terroir*, which here reaches its paroxysm with *climats* and *lieux-dits*, the result of 2,000 years of history.
The role of B.I.V.B. is to represent and defend the interests of the wines of Burgundy and all the subjects that are part of the production chain, *négociants* and *vignerons* in the forefront, defining a common policy in the field of research, communications and economic studies.
Consumer education and information are at the center of its mission. The official website of the B.I.V.B. provides comprehensive and detailed information on the 84 appellations of Burgundy, offers suggestions for organizing visits by presenting the many events taking place in the region. It also provides a list of the wineries that have signed the "*De vignes en caves*" welcome card.
Then there is the *École des Vins*, where high-level training courses are organized and targeted to different types of participants, including small groups of tourists and enthusiasts who wish to approach the wines of Burgundy through a rigorous method.

www.vins-bourgogne.fr

BIBLIOGRAPHY

Aa.Vv., *Le Rouge & le Blanc - La seconda antologia*, Possibilia, 2012

Aa.Vv., *Mappatura statistica dei vigneti che producono i grandi vini di Borgogna*, Possibilia, 2012 (1861)

Aa.Vv., *Vini e percorsi di Borgogna*, Artevino, 2007

Aa.Vv., *Vins de Bourgogne*, Éditions SIC, 2010

Jean-François Bazin, *Histoire du vin de Bourgogne*, Gisserot, 2002

Dominique Bruillot – *Jacky Rigaux, Le code du permis de Bourgogne. Comprendre les vins de Bourgogne en 100 questions*, Bourgogne Magazine numéro special, 2017

Henri Cannard, *Meursault et ses vignobles*, Édition Cannard, 2000

Henri Cannard, *Morey-Saint-Denis et ses vignobles*, Édition Cannard, 2008

Henri Cannard, *Pommard et ses vignobles*, Édition Cannard, 2005

Armando Castagno, *Borgogna. Le vigne della Côte d'Or*, Paolo Bartolomeo Buongiorno, 2017

Sébastien Chambru – Jean-Patrick Menard, *20 déjeuners autour du vin. Rencontres viticoles & gustatives en Bourgogne*, Bamboo, 2016

Émile Chapulliot (curator), *Nuits-Saint-Georges, nos vignes & notre terroir*, Les Pistoleros, 2016

Clive Coates, *The Wines of Burgundy*, University of California Press, 2008

Claude Courtépée, *Description générale et particulière du Duché de Bourgogne*, Frantin, 1778

Camillo Favaro – Giampaolo Gravina, *Vini e terre di Borgogna*, Artevino, 2012

Jean-Luc Fernandez, *La critique vinicole en France*, L'Harmattan, 2004

Benoît France, *Grand Atlas des vignobles de France*, Solar, 2008

Charles Frankel, *Terre de vignes*, Seuil, 2011

Marie-Helène Landrieu-Lussigny, *Les lieux-dits dans le vignoble bourguignon*, Éditions Jeanne Laffitte, 1983

Guillaume Laroche – Frédéric Henry – Harry Annoni, *Entre les vignes. Conversations libres avec des vigneronnes & vignerons de Bourgogne*, Édition Reverse, 2016

Jules Lavalle, *Histoire et statistique de la vigne et des grands vins de la Côte d'Or*, Delarue, 1855

Paul Lukacs, *Inventing Wine*, Norton, 2012

Patrick E. McGovern, *Ancient Wine: The Search for the Origins of Viniculture*, Princeton, 2003

François Morel, Borgogna, *Côte d'Or – Il territorio, i vignaioli, i vini*, Possibilia, 2017

Denis Morelot, *Statistique de la vigne dans le département de la Côte d'Or*, Lagier 1831

Jasper Morris, *Inside Burgundy*, Berry Bros. & Rude Press, 2010

Bill Nanson, *The Finest Wines of Burgundy*, Aurum Press, 2012

Remington Norman – Charles Taylor, *The Great Domaines of Burgundy*, Kyle Cathie, 2010

Didier Nourrisson, *Une histoire du vin*, Perrin, 2017

Sylvain Pitiot – Jean-Charles Servant, *Les vins de Bourgogne*, Collection Pierre Poupon, 2010

Jacky Rigaux, *Les temps de la vigne. Henri Jayer, vigneron en Bourgogne*, Éditions Terre en Vues, 2001

Jacky Rigaux, *Le réveil de la côte dijonnaise*, Éditions Terre en Vues, 2016

Jacky Rigaux, *Millésimes en Bourgogne 1846-2009*, Éditions Terre en Vues, 2009

Jacky Rigaux, *Grands Crus de Bourgogne*, Éditions Terre en Vues, 2007

Jacky Rigaux, *Le terroir & le vigneron*, Clémencey, Éditions Terre en Vues, 2006

Jacky Rigaux, *Ode aux grands vins de Bourgogne*, Éditions de l'Armançon, 1997

Tim Unwin, *Wine and the Vine: An Historical Geography of Viticulture and the Wine Trade*, Routledge, 2005

John Varriano, *Wine. A cultural History*, Reaktion Books, 2010

Philip Whalen, *Vins, vignes & gastronomie bourguignonne selon Gaston Roupnel*, Terre en vues, 2007

James E. Wilson, *Terroir. The Role of Geology, Climate and Culture in the Making of French Wines*, University of California Press, 1998

INDEX OF PRODUCERS

A

B

C

D

E

F

G

H

J

L

M

N

O

P

R

S

T

V

ACKNOWLEDGMENTS

A special thank you goes to:

Joanie Bonfiglio: smiling travel companion.
Cécile Mathiaud: Breton transferred to Burgundy who has put up with us for years.
Fabio Montrasi: philanthropic inventor.

Among the many friends and the vignerons who in some way or other gave us a hand, thanks to:

Gaia Anderson, Hervè Bianchi, Jean-Baptiste e Sylvie Bouzereau, Fabio Cagnetti, Armando Castagno, Isabelle e Christian Clerget, Yves Confuron, Gianni Fabrizio, Claire Gazeau, Eve Gueydon, Erika Mantovan, Giancarlo Marino, Barbara Meroni, Claire Naudin, Fabio Rango, Armelle e Bernard Rion, Fabio Rizzari.

Thanks also to:

Athenaeum bookshop of Beaune, Buongiornovino, Bureau Interprofessionnel des Vins de Bourgogne (B.I.V.B.), DeGustate, Rosenthal Wine Merchant, Sagna, TDC, Teatro del Vino, Unicorno.

We're almost certain that we've forgotten someone who is a friend or a voice that has been rooting for us: Thanks !

Camillo Favaro

Giampaolo Gravina

ISBN 978-88-942465-1-3

First edition in Italian published in February 2018
First edition in English published in November 2018
by Arti Grafiche Meroni - Lissone (MB) - Italy

www.artevinostudio.it / www.fil-rouge.it